COLONY TO NATI

Cover illustration
Jomo Kenyatta being sworn in as Prime Minister before Governor, Malcolm MacDonald

Colony To Nation

BRITISH ADMINISTRATORS IN KENYA 1940–1963

Edited by
JOHN JOHNSON

THE ERSKINE PRESS
2002

First published in 2002 by
The Erskine Press, The Old Bakery, Banham, Norfolk

© John Johnson, 2002

ISBN 1 85297 074 X

British Library Cataloguing in Publication Data
A catalogue record of this book is available
from the British Library

Printed in England

*To the Members of
the Kenya Administration Club
and their Families*

Contents

Editor's Note	ix
The Provincial Administration	xi
1. To Africa: First Impressions	1
2. The Administrator's Day	31
3. Central Government	68
4. The District Boma	103
5. Development Work	131
6. Safari	150
7. Nomads and Borders	175
8. The Mau Mau Emergency	193
9. Preparing for Independence	217
10. Uhuru and After	245
A Rap on the Wrist	268
Valedictory	270
Conclusion	272
The Administrators	274
Chronology	287
Glossary 1	288
Glossary 2	290
Bibliography	293
Index	295

List of Illustrations

Plates   *Between pages 150 and 151*

1. Porters on foot safari, Turkana District
2. DC's house, Thika
3. Tax collection, Turkana District
4. Dam construction for drinking water, Turkana District
5. Fort and boma, Wajir
6. DC inspecting dubas, Wajir
7. Harambee: DC's lorry in sand lugga, NFD
8. Luo fish market, Lake Victoria
9. Queen Mother with Sir Evelyn Baring and Coast officials, Mombasa
10. Queen Mother and Maasai moran, Narok
11. Fortified village, Embu District
12. Captured Mau Mau fighter and Tribal Policeman
13. Senior Chief Njiri Karanja, Fort Hall District
14. Land consolidation: measuring with elders, Kiambu District
15. Governor, Sir Patrick Renison greeting Chiefs, Kiambu District
16. Jomo Kenyatta visiting settlement scheme, Escarpment Forest
17. DC Isaac Okwirry and family

MAP

Kenya 1960: Provincial and District Boundaries   *pages 300/301*

Editor's Note

JOHN JOHNSON

This book is about people – African, Arab, Asian and British – who administered the Colony and Protectorate of Kenya from 1930 to Independence in 1963, and the Kenyan people with whom they worked. The writers are all British; their words and style are their own. The youngest of them are in their sixties. Hence the need to record their experiences. They are now part of history, the history of Britain's personal engagement with Africa. These reminiscences will add to the growing archive on the colonial era.

What motivated young men in the United Kingdom to seek a career in Africa? The lure was complex: a long tradition of serving the Empire overseas, the promise of early responsibility and the challenge of bringing about economic and social progress. Perhaps too, it was the appeal of a life in the open spaces of a continent as opposed to a crowded island. Many came to Kenya after wartime and national service, having enjoyed working in Africa.

Most preferred to work in the African districts. Their life alternated between the district centre (the *boma*) and safari to the outlying areas. The jobs were attractively varied from court work to constructing dams. Few were humdrum. People and relationships were the key. Nothing useful could be achieved without the cooperation of the local community. Languages, culture, patterns of living, local geography had to be mastered. Many officers took their turn at doing a stint in central government, in ministries, in the Secretariat, in Government House and in agencies. Some found a liking for policy work and stable city life and stayed there. There were other jobs in the cities of Nairobi and Mombasa in municipal administration.

On the whole, the life of an administrator was orderly and full of interest. But the war in East Africa in 1940 and the threat to the country brought change and upheaval. This was followed within ten years by the stirrings of unrest. The Mau Mau rebellion was a challenge to law and order which had to be countered. In the short term this meant the imprisonment of leaders and the detention of many others. The settled pattern of work in Nairobi and the central highlands was disrupted. Personnel and resources were increased. Closer administration brought a spread of smaller divisional centres. More money was available for development, particularly under the Swynnerton plan, for agriculture and livestock farming.

At the same time the pace of constitutional change quickened. The development of local government institutions had been given a priority. Wider democracy led to clamour for rapid progress towards Independence. Political parties jockeyed for power. There were few senior Kenyan officers in the administration and a programme of Africanisation was pushed forward fast. Early retirement for European officers was encouraged and most of them had left by the time of Independence in 1963. A few chose to remain, usually in central government, in specialised work and in a training role. The outbreak of Somali irredentism however, led to the retention of some in the northern frontier areas. The short era of British administration came to an end. These men had gone out to Kenya with eager anticipation first as colonial servants and from 1954 as overseas civil servants. They left acknowledging that it was time for African officers to take over their jobs, and wishing them well.

In editing the book I owe gratitude to the contributors, and especially to those members of the Kenya Administration Club who responded to my requests for coverage of particular issues and incidents. I also thank all those who generously gave help: Vee Bellers (née Williams), Dick Cashmore, David Evans, Peter Fullerton, Terry Gavaghan, Chris Minter, Merrin Molesworth, Michael Philip and his daughter Caroline MacDonald, Hugh Walker, John Williams, and my wife Jean.

The Provincial Administration
FRANK LOYD

The hierarchy in 1960 was:

Minister
|
Chief Commissioner
|
Provincial Commissioners (PCs)
|
District Commissioners (DCs)
|
District Officers (DOs)
|
District Assistants.(DAs)

A key role in office management was played by the Executive Staff, many of them from Goa in India.

1
To Africa: First Impressions

The Old Days in Kenya	Desmond O'Hagan
A Wartime Introduction	Tom Watts
A Different Way into the Service	W. H. (Tommy) Thompson
Justice and Big Game	David Shirreff
Liverpool to Lake Victoria	Patrick Crichton
Starting from Scratch	George Hampson
First Post	Peter Johnson
Learning about the Maasai	Hugh Walker
Back to Kenya	David Lambert
From KAR to Administration	Chris Minter
Bright White Sunlight	Alan Liddle
The Lure of Dust	Robin Williamson

Introduction

Africa was the magnet. Many administrative cadets cherished visions of distant horizons, lonely outposts and interesting people. It would be different from life on a crowded island: a job for active young men.

Many came straight from university followed by a one-year course in Swahili, development economics, law, social anthropology and colonial history. Others came from the armed services. Until the 1950s they usually travelled by ship to Mombasa with a group of like-minded young graduates. The sense of anticipation was palpable. The Indian Ocean coast and the line of rail to Nairobi and beyond fulfilled the vision of Africa.

What would this job be like? For the early arrivals, Desmond O'Hagan in 1931 and Tom Watts ten years later, it was what they expected: safari, *boma* duties and a wide range of responsibilities. Peter Johnson who followed in 1951 wondered why he was paid to live and work in such an exciting place. Later recruits often had experience of Africa, notably from national service with colonial troops. They were drawn back not only by the country but also by the comradeship of Africans.

The Old Days in Kenya

DESMOND O'HAGAN

I was one of twelve District Officer Cadets, aged twenty-two, appointed to Kenya in 1931. Now only I am still alive*. Dick Turnbull, a good friend, was highly intelligent and able. He spent most of his early years in the Northern Province, known in those days as the NFD or in the Secretariat, and later was the last Governor of Tanganyika before Independence. Sir Philip Mitchell minuted on one occasion in red ink 'When Mr Turnbull drafts a despatch, would senior officers kindly put their comments on the side and not alter the draft'. There will be many recollections written by others after 1945, so I will confine mine mainly to my early service.

Many of us sailed on the British India Line ship *Modasa*. I had a pleasant cruise with a two-berth cabin to myself. I remember particularly the heat of the Red Sea, air-conditioning on passenger ships being unknown in those days, the Gully Gully Man at Port Said and the splendid shop Simon Artz where we bought *Raha Lakoum* (Turkish Delight). The few young women on board were going out to get married so we had to rely mainly on deck tennis for recreation.

I was appointed to Kisii, the Southern District of Nyanza Province. The Provincial Commissioner was Harold Montgomery, the elder brother of Field Marshal Montgomery of Alamein, and probably the best PC under whom I served. My salary at this time was thirty pounds a month and this was enough to enable me to employ a cook and a house servant. Sometimes a detainee helped in the garden. Much of my time was spent on safari collecting poll or hut tax from all able-bodied men and the richer widows, exempting many for one reason or another. Failure to pay poll tax resulted in a sentence of one month's detention, a less severe punishment than a jail sentence with hard labour. The detainees were well fed and were put to various duties in the *boma* and were not always supervised. To many this was a far better option than paying an annual tax of ten shillings. In the unlikely event that a detainee should run away, he was liable to receive a jail sentence when recaptured. I also heard appeals from the Native Tribunals, with the help of clan elders. Nearly all cases involved the return of bride price after a married woman deserted her husband, often for good reason. When on safari I used a hired lorry to take me to the first location and when

---

* Desmond O'Hagan died in December 2001.

it was time to move on, the chief supplied porters whom I paid, to carry my safari equipment to the next location. After my first safari I bought a second hand bicycle which enabled me to ride out along the footpaths ahead of the porters. I would leave it when I reached a hill and walk. The bicycle would be pushed up the hill for me by a Tribal Policeman. The only thefts in those days involved cattle or women.

I remember many hours spent turning every able-bodied man, woman and child out to beat locust hoppers and to drive them into trenches where they could then be buried. In those years before the war, large swarms of locusts invaded Kenya nearly every year. They ate every crop growing and decimated grazing land. They also settled on coffee trees in the Kiambu District breaking the branches and causing immense damage. The Desert Locust Control has done a splendid job and locusts are now seldom seen in Kenya.

The safaris among the Luo near Lake Victoria were a trial because it was impossible to avoid mosquitoes and they nearly always resulted in a bout of malaria. Malaria in those days was not regarded as a serious disease and was cured by taking twenty grains of quinine a day for one week, followed by ten grains a day for two weeks. One was usually back in the office within three or four days. The danger of black water fever from frequent bouts of malaria was realised. The Government was too poor at that time, and so were we, to provide a safari mosquito net for the dining table. Such nets later became a regular issue.

I was on safari in the Lambwe Valley supervising the clearing of bush so as to recover land inflicted with tsetse fly. On one day a baby elephant aged about two months was brought to my tent. His mother had been shot by the Game Department when driving elephant from the area. He became a dear friend and would not leave me at any time. He refused to sleep in my spare room, which consisted of a mud hut with a thatched roof, door and window, so he shared my bedroom. If I went out to dinner he came with me almost treading on my heels. He insisted on being allowed into my host's sitting room and dining room. He always got his way by making and continuing a very loud screech. In the daytime he went to the office with me and made no trouble while I held court and interviews. When I went on safari I left him with the nursing sister whom he had learned to like and to accept. I spent all my spare money buying milk for him; he was never satisfied and always wanted more. Other officers helped me to buy milk. Alas, he died after nine months while I was away on safari. A real loss for me.

Towards the end of 1931, the Governor, Sir Joseph Byrne, announced that the economy of Kenya was in a perilous state and nothing but a miracle could save the situation. He imposed a cut of ten percent on the salaries of all government officers and also on himself. Coffee prices had fallen to disastrously low levels. The miracle happened. Gold was found in the

Kakamega District and many impoverished coffee farmers travelled to Kakamega to pan for gold and to stake claims. American gold companies paid large sums for many of these claims. Sadly only a few of the mines were successful and most came to an end after about ten years; by then they had helped to tide Kenya over a difficult time until the economy fortunately improved in 1934.

At the end of 1932 I was transferred to Kakamega where the District Commissioner was Colonel Brooke-Anderson who had lost a leg in the Great War. I shared a house with another District Officer who had come out with me, Paul Osborne. The custom was for one of us to be on safari and the other in the *boma* office. I remember at one time Colonel Anderson had the daughter of an old friend to stay with him called Anne Pease. She was about twenty and very attractive. When her departure time drew near Paul and I tossed up as to who was to do the safari during the last days of her visit. Paul won and I sadly went on safari. Once again I was struck down with malaria with a temperature of a hundred and four. I had to come back to Kakamega on my camp bed in the back of a lorry. Paul had to take my place and I had Anne to nurse me back to health for her last ten days in Kenya. The DC had a tiresome habit of arriving at our house at six a.m. on six mornings a week expecting Paul and me to accompany him around the *boma* to see the prisoners and detainees at work. He would then return to his workshop at seven a.m. to repair the government mowing machines. I remember in those days he played a good game of tennis in spite of his false leg.

Before 1950 wives were not allowed to accompany their husbands to the Northern Province, known in those day as the Northern Frontier District, although it covered nearly one third of Kenya with six separate districts. As I did not marry until I was thirty-one I spent many years in the NFD as DC Isiolo, Garissa and Wajir. I used to spend ten days every few months on camel safari travelling between water holes or wells where the various tribes could be found. The custom was for the local chief to order the senior families to provide working camels for the safaris for which we duly paid a fee. The camel bell used to be rung at one a.m. for camp to be struck and the loading of camels. We would set off an hour later in the cool, walking about sixteen miles until nine or nine-thirty a.m. On one occasion I was camped near the Kinna River in Isiolo District when, a few minutes before we were due to depart, two hippos charged through the camp returning to the river. Away went most of the camels returning to their owners with most of my food and equipment which was never recovered. On another occasion I was camped in the shade near the river at Merti. One night elephants came through the camp creating havoc in the pitch darkness and down came my tent. We were all frightened but fortunately no serious damage was done to us or to the tents. One of my main duties in the Isiolo District was to ensure that no Somalis came west of the Somali Line imposed by Sir Harold Kittermaster in 1920. This ran from Moyale in the north to Habaswein and then down the Tana River. It was generally felt that Kenya would be invaded by impoverished Somalis from the north, if this rule was not strictly observed.

The average rainfall in Wajir was around four inches a year but in 1942 over seven inches fell in one night. Wells and water holes were few and far between and were invaluable as they allowed tribesmen to graze their cattle, sheep and goats over a ten-mile radius and their camels over a much wider area. To avoid trouble, each well was allocated to a single tribe. If there was a dispute between tribes over ownership there was no option but to sit at the well until the elders of the tribes concerned decided on the rights. An arbitrary decision by the DC would never have worked. If we found a tribe trespassing when we arrived at a well, a heavy fine was imposed. However, the Government had created an NFD Trust Fund into which all such fines were paid, to be used for the benefit of NFD tribesmen only, such as the deepening or creation of new wells. It is of interest that a single DO could maintain order in a large district of many thousands of square miles with about twenty Kenya Police and a similar number of Tribal Police.

I was posted to Mombasa as Provincial Commissioner of the Coast Province in September 1952. I had not been in office two months when there was a general strike by the eleven thousand, mainly Luo, port workers. They became troublesome as a great deal of beer had been consumed. A delegation of port employers, led by Hugh Robinson, head of Smith, Mackenzie and the British India Line, called on me. They complained that it was only three months since the previous strike, when the employers had reluctantly agreed to a thirty percent increase in wages in return for a firm promise that there would be no further strikes for at least two years. I was asked to have the strike called off at once as it was causing serious damage to the economy and there were many ships in the port waiting to be unloaded. I telephoned Tom Mboya, the General Secretary of the Kenya Trade Unions and explained the position. He came down by train from Nairobi that night. I showed him the signed contract stating the agreement quite clearly. Tom said he would do his best but could make no promise. Meanwhile the District Commissioner and the Police were doing an excellent job maintaining law and order in very difficult circumstances. We were also greatly helped by Edward Rodwell, the Editor and Manager of the Mombasa Times. At the end of two anxious days, Tom returned to say he could achieve a settlement but it would be necessary for the employers to make some small contribution so that the union leaders did not lose too much face. I pointed out it was the leaders who had called the strike. Tom agreed but said it was the only way of ending the strike quickly. I telephoned Hugh Robinson to come and see me, a settlement was agreed and the strike was over, but not before a considerable loss had been suffered. Fortunately the two-year agreement was now respected. I had known Tom for many years; he was born on Rusinga Island in Lake Victoria in the Kisii District. He was well educated, extremely able and a wise trade union leader. It was a sad loss to Kenya when he was murdered.

A Wartime Introduction

TOM WATTS

Early In 1941 those of us who had been called to the Colonial Office in November 1940 were brought together in the Colonial Office for a pep talk by the Secretary of State, Lord Moyne and were told where we were going. I received commiserations from some on being posted to Kenya 'with all those settlers'. Some posted to the Far East were delighted. I wonder what happened to them!

Liverpool had suffered a week of heavy bombing in April 1941 and there were ships lying partially sunk in the Mersey Channel. Our convoy was looked after by a bevy of American four funnel destroyers. We ran into a pack of submarines and after four days were told to scatter. It is an odd detached experience to feel and hear the thud of a torpedo hitting a ship in convoy and to see it drop astern as the convoy ploughed slowly on its way.

It was a long, lonely haul out into the Atlantic down towards South America and then across to Cape Town which we reached after nearly four weeks. During this time the ship's officers knew of the loss of HMS Hood and the search for the Bismarck and its destruction. They had a worrying time. We were kept in the dark until after the final battle.

There were four administrative cadets, three for Kenya and one for Tanganyika on the ship and one young doctor. Most of the passengers including young children were for the naval base at Simonstown with quite a number of civilians for the farms, schools and industry of South Africa. We had short spells in Cape Town and in Durban and finally arrived in Mombasa in June 1941 after calling in at Dar-es-Salaam to drop off cargo and passengers, some of whom were returning from leave in the Union.

Mombasa was humid and uncomfortable for us and it was a relief to catch the evening train for Nairobi where the three of us were met the next morning by an assistant secretary in the Secretariat who took us to our hotel and told us of our postings. We were introduced to the Nairobi Club and shown the chairs in the lounge, which were reserved for VIPs such as the Chief

Justice and Chief Secretary. From there we were taken to sign the books of these potentates. During the next thirty-four years I never crossed their front doors again.

My brother was serving in the Uganda Administration and had been on leave in Nairobi. He had left for me a Chevrolet touring car, which he had had from our father on his retirement from Uganda in 1938. I collected the car at the Forces Auxiliary Nursing Yeomanry (FANY) mess in Nairobi.

We three cadets found ourselves posted to different districts. One went to Nyanza and the other two to Ukambani (Kamba country), one to Machakos and the other, myself, to Kitui. Our heavy baggage was to be sent up from Mombasa by the Government Coast Agent so we dispersed to our first districts only with light baggage which I had in the old Chev tourer together with a case of two four gallon containers of petrol. I had to follow the Garissa road for ninety miles and then turn right at Ndolo's Corner for the thirty miles leg to Kitui *boma*.

The Garissa road was still a busy military road with large convoys using it, generating thick dust. The road surface was badly corrugated by these military trucks most of which belonged to the South African army driven by Cape Coloureds who were adept at quenching their thirst by extracting the contents of ration beer and brandy without disturbing the bottle tops.

I was now rising twenty-one with a year at university and four months in the army but with no administrative training. I was assigned to a long service bachelor District Commissioner who was very much a loner. He looked after me for my first few days at Kitui until I had got together staff to man the very pleasant bungalow allotted to me. He then went on safari leaving me alone in the *boma* to cope as best I could in the office. I had been assigned an English speaking interpreter who had first learnt his English in the 1914–18 war with the Carrier Corps where he had become a store-man. His English was of the barrack room. He had then served with the KAR as a clerk. He was good-humoured and reasonably sober for a Kamba.

My service in Kitui was for only a few months but it gave me a permanent and great interest in tribal customary law and in soil conservation. From the start I found myself involved with the Native Tribunals as the local customary courts were then called and it was these courts that exercised original jurisdiction over enforcement of soil conservation regulations passed by the local Kamba council at the behest of the Government Agricultural Officers.

Many of these soil conservation rules were unpopular and needed to be enforced with forbearance. The local Agricultural Officer, known for his temper as Nzuki (the bee), finally caused the local Kamba women to revolt when he forbade them from burning any of their pigeon pea stalks and ordered them instead to pile them high into trash lines on the contour. The DC was away and I was in the office when the Tribal Police Sergeant warned me that hundreds of women were marching on the *boma*. I went out to meet them and was told that they wanted to get hold of Nzuki who had already received a warning and had locked himself in his office where he was to remain for two days guarded by the TPs. The women remained quite good humouredly in the *boma* for two nights. Kitui was ringed with fire as all the trash lines were burnt. After two days the ladies went home and Nzuki returned to his house. I think that as a result of this demonstration of resentment agricultural field staff were less inclined to harry the people over their soil conservation.

I spent my safari time in the southern, more arid areas of Ukambani where women often spent a day walking to a well, a night gradually filling two large gourds with water then a day staggering home with this heavy load on their backs. In later years, after the war, we were able to improve this water situation with dams and bore holes.

There was a widespread complaint about the damage caused to crops by baboon whose natural enemy was the leopard. The Game Warden was much concerned with the use of metal leg traps by the Kamba who were encouraged to trap leopard by Arab and Indian traders for their skins. We found many such traps when searching dukas out in bush markets.

There was little social activity. I met with the DC at the information department wireless in the evening to listen to the BBC News but apart from that I saw him only in the office if we were both in the *boma*. After three months I was transferred to Meru. The PC at Nyeri allowed me to travel via Nairobi in order to purchase a Hardy fishing rod. On his recommendation I stayed the night at the New Stanley Hotel and drove up to Meru the next day via Nanyuki with one of my servants. On arrival in Meru I found that he had cleared the hotel bedroom of all towels and bed linen!

A Different Way into the Service

W. H. (TOMMY) THOMPSON

At the end of the 1939–45 war, I was serving with the East African Artillery where I discovered I liked working with Africans and found myself intrigued by the many tribal backgrounds of the soldiers under my command. So much so that I decided to chance my arm and take my discharge in Kenya. The defining moment had come during an attachment to the DC Embu who, at that time, was Dennis Hall. Having the use of army transport I was able to get around the district, often in the company of Dennis Hall or his DO, and my eyes were opened. With only an Agricultural Officer,

TO AFRICA: FIRST IMPRESSIONS

Medical Officer and a Nursing Sister it was a matter of great wonderment as to how this man managed to run the equivalent of a county with very little power except that of quiet authority. I sat in at his courts, heard the DO deal with the daily *mashauri*, went on a pay safari, saw roads and bridges being built with not much more than imagination and patience, besides seeing so much more than we callow young army officers could ever have envisaged as the goings on in the home districts of our soldiers. I was enthralled. However I was not the possessor of a university degree and my background did not exactly provide what would be required for the storming of the heights I saw before me.

I stayed in the army until 1946 and found myself a job as Civil Reabsorption Officer employed by the Kenya government on a month-to-month basis. Little did I know it but I had fallen on my feet with a posting to Fort Hall where Wally Coutts was the DC, a wonderful man with a splendid command of the Kikuyu language and great knowledge of Kikuyu affairs. Neither of us knew what I was supposed to do. Most Kikuyu had already been demobilised and all I had was an extremely light load of ex-soldiers' problems. What I did have was a vehicle of sorts, which made it possible to get around the district. Because the *boma* transport in those days consisted of but one lorry, Coutts was delighted. Chiefs and headmen started asking me questions and giving questions to be taken back to District Headquarters. Coutts began to trust me, even with my army version of Swahili, and before long I was being given odd commissions such as simple pay safaris, checking on road works, popping into the dispensaries for the MO, and so on. When the job folded I applied for the newly created post of Community Development Officer – later entitled DO (CD). I was appointed back to Fort Hall where I carried on very much as before. Good administration on the ground was really what community development was about, providing a back up and publicity methods which had not hitherto been available.

In 1948 Wally and 'Bones' Coutts and their family departed for the West Indies and Frank Loyd arrived on the scene. I was beginning to become useful. All the time I was learning as much as I could about the Kikuyu, their history, beliefs, systems, conservatism and politics. Frank Loyd made me sit down and think and put down on paper what my job was about and how it could be put over at a time of increasingly nervous tension and unease. He made his district team work.

All the while the storm clouds were darkening. Kenyatta was large on the scene and, from our point of view, more and more threatening. Having been in the *boma* longer than the other officer, my knowledge was becoming useful. Without the space to develop this saga I have to jump to 1952 when my post was abolished at the behest of the white settler majority in the Legislature who had some points-scoring to do. The Chief Native

Commissioner sent for me and suggested I apply to join the Colonial Service, which I did. The result was an extremely hurtful and pompous letter from London saying it was not the policy of HM Government to recruit 'persons from overseas'. Being young and, I suppose, somewhat cocky, I let fly pointing out that I was UK born, white, had commanded His Majesty's troops and that the writer had been gratuitously rude. In no time at all I was back before the CNC for a London-ordered wigging. The interview was short, the CNC saying, 'I wish I could write a letter like that to the bloody Colonial Office'. He pressed me to try again. Frank Loyd must have given me a strong recommendation because, in due course, I appeared before the ten wise men. Later I learned that my exposition on the politics of the Kikuyu Independent Schools Association had won the day. I was appointed an Administrative Officer with the rank of DO dated back to 1947.

Justice and Big Game

DAVID SHIRREFF

My first posting was to Machakos. I arrived there in December 1945 straight from the army without doing any Devonshire course, but as I had served for nearly five years in 5 KAR, a Kenya battalion, at least I spoke Swahili fairly well.

George Brown was DC, the DO1 was John Thorp and DO2 was John Howard with whom I had served in 5 KAR until he was ordered back to the Administration in 1943.

The Kamba were a delightful, friendly people and the fact that about twenty thousand of them had served in the KAR helped. They were also extremely bibulous, and as junior DO, I was frequently called off the cricket ground or golf course on a Sunday morning to deal with a homicide resulting from a drunken weekend brawl.

The Kenya Police then had no jurisdiction in the reserve, so it meant collecting a vehicle and a few TPs, driving to the nearest point, then walking, possibly several miles, to the scene of the crime. One usually found that the chief had arrested the offender and had the witnesses ready, so the body was collected with the offender and driven back to the *boma*. The body was delivered to the mortuary for post-mortem examination and the offender to the cells. The witnesses were warned to attend for the committal proceedings.

These took place quite quickly, before the same junior DO sitting as a

Third Class Magistrate, who was thus Investigating Officer and Adjudicating Magistrate in the same case. Usually the offender was committed for trial before the Supreme Court in Nairobi, and in due course was sentenced either for murder or manslaughter. The penalty for murder was death, and an onerous duty then fell on the DC (not the junior DO) whether to advise the Governor to exercise his prerogative of mercy.

Another job I had at Machakos was connected with Makueni; an area of tsetse infested bush at the southern end of the district, which was being cleared for resettlement. I was sent down by the DC to do a census of the Kamba families living in Makueni. Camping in the area was J.A. Hunter; a poacher turned gamekeeper now working for the Game Department, whose job was to eliminate the rhino in Makueni in preparation for settlement. Hunter was alleged to have been forced to leave Scotland in about 1910 for putting the minister's daughter in the family way, and even now, though he was in his sixties and had a wife in Nairobi, there was always a nubile Kamba *ndito* (girl) in his tent, supplied by the local chief.

It is sad to record today, when there are fewer than five hundred black rhino in the whole of Kenya, that Hunter shot more than a thousand rhino in quite a small area, and a considerable number of elephant also. I must plead guilty to shooting one rhino with Hunter's Gibbs .500, and also one elephant on licence under his supervision. I sold the tusks for two hundred pounds and later, in Mombasa, bought two Persian rugs which lasted for many years.

John Thorp left to be DC Kapsabet where, amongst many good things, he encouraged the young Nandi to take up athletics, laying the foundation for future Olympic champions. Later, as Governor of the Seychelles, he was tragically drowned trying to rescue his son and a friend when they got into difficulties swimming.

Myles North succeeded Thorp as DO1, a keen ornithologist who at a time when few people were doing this was already recording African birdsong. It is said that when DC of an NFD district, he was awaiting the arrival of the Governor at the local airstrip when he spotted a rare bird on the edge of the airstrip and went off to study it. The DC was absent from the welcoming party when the Governor arrived!

Myles and John Howard were both keen climbers and used to practise on the Lukenya rocks. Once they were half way up a difficult climb when they were attacked by a swarm of bees and both badly stung. They were lucky to get down and survive.

Liverpool to Lake Victoria

PATRICK CRICHTON

The *Orbita* was not a young ship in 1939, when she was requisitioned and refitted as a troopship. I forget what line the ship belonged to, anyway, she knew South America well enough. After the war was over, she brought 'time-expired men' back from India and the Far East, and when that was done she was used briefly, to take civilians to East Africa; for that task she was still fitted as a troopship. In April 1947 an enlightened Government decreed that troopships need no longer be dry ships, and the *Orbita* was quick to take note for she was certainly not dry when she left Liverpool the following day.

Although I had been given a berth in the *Orbita*, my wife Barbara had not, she was to travel some three months later in the *Llandovery Castle*. So, with other young men destined for East Africa, I settled down to look for congenial companionship. Before long a small group congealed; there was Dr Pat Murphy and his wife, destined for the Catholic Mission Hospital in Kampala, Dr Donagh Hurley, also destined for a Mission Hospital, Dr Evans, bound for Tabora, Dr Olaf Mackenzie for the Seychelles, and me.

By the time we reached the Mediterranean we were more or less apprised of one another's alcoholic preferences, but still, as is only proper for staid middle class gentlemen, being careful not to be too familiar with one another. Indeed we were, from the outset and to the end of the voyage, always on our best behaviour.

Some time, during the passage of the Mediterranean we were joined by a funny little man who was destined for the diamond workings of Dodoma; his preference was for double gins without water 'It's adding the water that makes you drunk, you know!' We never saw him drunk, of course, but one evening when we were playing Tombola, he shouted 'House', jumped on the table, sang 'God Save the King', and collapsed. We carried him out and laid him reverently on the top of the No 9 hatch, where he still was the following morning. He disappeared about noon, and we never saw him again, although I was reliably informed that he was seen disembarking at Dar-es-Salaam.

Once in the Canal, the troop decks became intolerably hot. After dinner, therefore, we sat on the upper deck and told improbable stories about leprechauns and kelpies, and rugby footballers, and other mythical creatures who roam the hills and the bogs in the Celtic twilight. Later on we even brought our bedding up from below and slept on deck, rather to the annoyance of the bosun, since it interfered with morning washdown. By this time, we had also been joined by a beautiful blonde and her small boy, who had met and made friends with Mrs Murphy.

We passed Socotra and wondered whether it was really true that one of the lighthouse keepers had been eaten by the locals, and laughed at the RN Hydrographer's note – 'Soundings terminated here as the Midshipman has lost his last log line'.

We all rose early for the spectacular entry into Kilindini Harbour. There we split up, each looking for his own luggage and reception party. It was very hot in the godown and there was a measure of relief in boarding the train and then chugging through Mombasa to the town station. I don't remember too much about the evening meal; I was probably much too excited by the Garrett locomotive, and the spacious carriages; but I do remember my joy in tasting orange squash that actually tasted of oranges. Kenya really did its stuff the following morning, when a misguided rhino charged the engine. The engine was not seriously damaged, and the rhino trotted off disgruntedly, so I suppose it survived, if a little bent.

On arrival in Nairobi I was swept up by someone from the Secretariat. The following day he took me to be introduced to a small man in the Secretariat sitting behind an enormous desk. I could just see the braces and the simian face peering over. 'Keen on climbing mountains?' he asked. 'Yes Sir,' I said, 'but primarily on funicular railways'. The interview was short.

I boarded a train for Kisumu; no rhino on this trip, but I do recall the wonder of the train stopping at the *dak* bungalow at Londiani, for dinner and puffing into Kisumu just before dawn. Peter Gordon met me and took me home for breakfast; later on he introduced me to Charles Atkins and Peter Brothers (DSO and bar, DFC and bar) feet on the table, 'How are you old boy? Personally I'm bored stiff'. The 'phone rings, the feet swiftly leave the table, Peter is all alert, 'Quiet please, a client'.

The rains had been particularly heavy in 1947, and the Nyando road had yet to be rebuilt. When I was due to go to Kisii, the road had sunk into the black cotton soil of the Nyando plain, so those bound for Kisii took a boat to Kendu Bay, where one of the Administration lorries met us, driven by Arap Kipkoi. Since the lorry was enclosed, I opted to ride on the roof. Naive Patrick was astounded at the murram road – something he had not envisaged. It was an excellent introduction to the terrain as we crossed the plain to Oyugis, Paul Mboya's capital (Paul was very much the 'King' of the South Kavirondo Luo at this time). We drove on up the escarpment to Kisii country and the *boma* itself, where I was delivered into the hospitable care of Bobby Winser and his dog Brutus. I was briefly introduced to Arthur Lawrence, then DC before being taken up to unpack at Bobby's house.

At teatime Bobby came up from the office; we took tea and then at

Bobby's suggestion wandered off to the golf course. I think we were somewhere about the seventh green when a lovely voice cried, 'Good God, there's the man I slept with on board the boat'. It was, indeed, Kay Waterston, the lovely blonde from the *Orbita* and the very respectable wife of Bill Waterston the doctor, who had as a Scotsman's wife, very properly joined the Celtic fringe. But she might have phrased her astonishment a little more tactfully.

Starting From Scratch

GEORGE HAMPSON

While in East Africa Command at the end of the war I served for a time after VJ day in the Military Administration of the Reserved Area, Ethiopia, with responsibility for Dire Dawa and the Issa Somali. On leaving the Army I returned to Cambridge and completed the first post-war Devonshire Course for the Colonial Administrative service. I was then posted back to Kenya as a cadet in the Provincial Administration in February 1948. In the following sixteen and a half years I served as District Officer and District Commissioner in reserve and settled area districts, Assistant Secretary in the Ministry of Defence, Secretary of the Kenya Intelligence Committee and Provincial African Courts Officer.

I had sought and obtained formal permission to marry but approval for my wife to accompany me was withheld on the grounds that I was to be posted to a frontier station where wives were not then allowed. In the event I was posted to Meru. I therefore made arrangements for my wife to join me. She eventually sailed as I had done in the *Llangibby Castle* but by the time she arrived, I had left Meru and was living on safari in a remote frontier area!

Meru was an enviable posting with a pleasant *boma*. On the outward voyage I had met and got to know the DC who was returning from leave. The other two DOs had also recently been demobilised, an RAF Battle of Britain ace and the other a Gunner as I was. A spirit of camaraderie pervaded the whole district team. An open air squash court and a golf course constructed with the aid of the 'goat bag' over the years, together with good trout fishing and a friendly pub added to the delights of the station. I was soon sent on a foot safari and covered some hundred and eighty miles in the remote northern area of the district. It was a traditional safari with porters and, as well as the routine administrative tasks, I had to shoot a marauding buffalo. In about four months I covered much of the district on safari and began to learn something of the Meru people, their tribal organisation and the application of their traditional institutions, particularly the *Njuri Ncheke* (a council of elders) in furtherance of government policies. At the same time the ex-RAF DO flew his own light aircraft, which provided an invaluable additional resource in emergencies and for observation of movement and changes in areas which were not easy to reach.

I was then sent to take over a remote area between Isiolo and the Uaso Nyiro known as Mukogodo. It consisted of three hundred and fifty square miles of semi arid country and some extensive cedar forest in the east. The population was basically Maasai. They had been left behind when the Maasai as a whole were moved south to their present areas in 1911. It had never been effectively administered and was consequently seriously over grazed and a haven for criminal activities, intrigue and stock theft from the European ranches in the south. I was given finance and required to establish an Administrative Headquarters and bring the area under control using an 'iron hand in a velvet glove' in the words of the Provincial Commissioner. I had a tent to live in and eventually acquired another to serve as a District Office. With the assistance of a water engineer from the African Land Development Board, I sited two dams, one in the far north at Tura and a larger one at Dol Dol where there was a small collection of huts. The dams were successful and I decided to establish my headquarters at Dol Dol. There were no roads and mules were the only means of transport. My priorities were to build up a force of Tribal Police and make a significant reduction in the number of stock. This required careful handling as the people were basically Maasai and, therefore, entirely dependent upon their cattle. The largest group was pure Il Purko Maasai, the Il Mwesi had intermarried mainly with Meru and Kikuyu and the Mukogodo were a mixture of Maasai and the original Wanderobo. The establishment of the headquarters had therefore to take second place to gaining the co-operation of a majority of the population to enable a census to be conducted with a view to organising stock sales.

I met my wife in Mombasa and we stayed with the Chief Native Commissioner in Nairobi before she was introduced to my tent as our first home with no other European for fifty miles and no facilities. We shot for meat but otherwise lived from tins. There was no shortage of milk as we moved from manyatta to manyatta. For two months she helped with the counting of thousands of cattle throughout the area, travelling by mule. We had employed a Kikuyu cook who was to stay with us for sixteen years. I employed road gangs which made a passable road from the settled area border to Dol Dol and we acquired a small lorry which greatly facilitated our supply position. Game was abundant including lion and leopard. Leopard occasionally raided our food-store. On one occasion our lorry was charged by a rhino and only the quick reaction of the driver averted serious damage and injury.

Ngomas and inter clan sports combined with barazas and strict law enforcement gradually created the conditions in which stock sales could be organised. These, together with opportunities for direct employment on various construction works provided cash for the payment of taxes and facilitated payment of the fines which I imposed in the exercise of my third class magisterial powers in stock theft and other minor criminal cases. Other incentives to convert surplus stock into cash such as the attractions of an increasing range of goods brought into the area for sale by Somali and Indian traders also helped the sales. With good rains and opportunities to sell stock, the grazing improved and the better-fed cattle brought higher prices and were more valuable in bride price deals. These benefits were not lost on the people.

I also designed and built a house at Dol Dol and began the construction of Tribal Police lines using detainee labour under an open prison system. Cedar from the Anandongoro forest was used, the wood being dragged by teams of oxen for several miles. We eventually moved into the house with no furniture other than our camp equipment. Later we learned that the reflection from the *mabati* roof of this isolated house became a landmark and beacon for over flying aircraft. Today Dol Dol is a thriving township.

First Post

PETER JOHNSON

I went to Kwale in Coast Province in 1951. The Duruma, the inland tribe, were straight from Old Testament, whereas the coastal strip was a nicer version of the Caribbean. I simply could not understand why I was paid to live and 'work' in this exciting spot. Close to the *boma* is a sable antelope reserve. At that time sightings were rare and visitors minimal; now the Shimba Hills figure in every Kenya tourist guide.

Coastal safaris were particularly fascinating: lions roaring at the quaintly named township of Lungalunga on the Tanganyika border and exotic fish on view at the port of Vanga in the mangrove swamps, a location gently administered by the sultan of Zanzibar's nominee, the Mudir. Well-kept graves of our predecessors at Vanga reminded me how much we owed to the discoverers of Paludrin and Mepacrine. It was also fascinating to run across Major Wavell's grave (brother of the Viceroy) enclosed by expensive wrought iron railings in the middle of nowhere in the Kwale bush. He was killed by the Germans in 1917. The big challenge on these safaris was to think of something original to write in the visitor's books at every dispensary and school on the route! On the Coastal run it was difficult to resist a pause at the well-known watering hole of Jadini hotel, the Le Poer Trench stronghold, and a favourite holiday resort for the upcountry settler.

Early in the tour there was a sad experience. On the morning of February 6th 1952, together with all other DOs in the Province, I was at a rehearsal in Kilindini docks Mombasa for the arrival later of Princess Elizabeth. Suddenly over a loudspeaker came the statement that the King had died and the Princess was leaving Treetops in Nyeri and flying straight home to London. A great wave of sorrow and disappointment swept over us all.

For such a peaceful and sleepy district it was surprising, suddenly to witness my first 'flying picket'. This took the form of Digo women persuaded by the politicians to camp outside DC's office to protest at the appointment of a new chief. The women manned a twenty-four hour shift, which lasted for several days. Jomo Kenyatta had visited the area shortly before and had obviously signalled the need for provocative demonstration. At that stage there was nothing in the textbook to tell a DO (in the absence of the DC on local leave) how to cope, so a few experiments were tried – not with much success I have to admit. It seemed somewhat comical during this incident to have to step one's way carefully over prone female bodies and screaming *totos* sprawled on the veranda, in order to reach the office. Once there, I caught sight of the honours board carrying the names of all previous DCs Kwale on a wooden plaque behind the desk. I am sure that none of them would have permitted such untidiness during their reigns.

When the time for local leave came round – I must say there was precious little excuse for 'leave' in these conditions. I was persuaded by Geoff Mackley, stationed at Machakos, that DO Cadets were expected to show a spirit of adventure by climbing, or rather scrambling up, Mount Kenya. This we did under the guidance of that delightful eccentric Raymond Hook. We set off from Naro Moro complete with guides and mules. It was fun but a weird experience, the muleteers were sulky and sullen in daylight yet came to life with what seemed to be passionate hymn singing in the evenings. Little did we realise that we were witnessing Mau Mau celebrations.

Looking back over that very happy first year one thing particularly sticks in the memory: being told by a bunch of elders on the Coast that they preferred the German administration to the British because the Germans were consistent bullies, not like the British who were so unpredictable.

I salute the very happy memory of DC Pat Hughes who gave me my first taste of Africa.

Learning About the Maasai

HUGH WALKER

In 1952 I was doing my National Service in a long since disbanded colonial battalion, the Somaliland Scouts, formerly the Somaliland Camel Corps. During that time I was studying the Somali language and as a result I was asked if I would like to be considered for the Somaliland Administration. As I had no clear idea of what I wanted to do after my National Service, the offer was a godsend. I was sent on a one year postgraduate Colonial Service 'Devonshire' course at Oxford. However, in October 1952, the Mau Mau Emergency was declared in Kenya and I was switched to go there instead. We had to learn Swahili, which was much easier than Somali.

My first posting, however, was to a district only partly affected by the Mau Mau – Maasailand. Like many others before me, I soon got 'Maasai'itis' ie. the conviction that their way of life was almost perfect and should be interfered with as little as possible. Had one actually had to live it, one might soon have changed one's mind. I spent much of my time in Narok District mobilising almost naked Maasai warriors (*moran*) to hunt down Mau Mau gangs in the forests on the Mau escarpment, up to ten thousand feet above sea level. Although they relished official sanction to use their spears again, the *moran* were most undisciplined and largely ineffective. They were too easily distracted by sleeping with the girls, eating meat and looking to steal Dorobo honey. After one long and abortive hunt for a Mau Mau gang in the huge area, we returned to the war *manyatta* where all the girls came out to greet their warriors. I was apportioned one strapping lass. As she was covered almost all over in sheep fat mixed with red ochre I declined the honour. She also happened to be the wife of the Maasai butcher in Narok from whom I got my meat. She had no time to be offended as a rampant warrior leapt obligingly into the breach.

As a result of my daily contact with the *moran* I got a unique opportunity to learn some of their most difficult language. The night before I took the Maasai language exam I over imbibed at Hoppy's Inn at Karen in order to steady my nerves. On the way back to my hotel I crashed the Government land-rover in my charge. It was a complete write-off. Amazingly I was unscathed. Next morning during my exam I saw the mangled remains of the land-rover being driven past on the back of a lorry. I pointed them out to my missionary examiner and invoked the Almighty for my deliverance in the most unctuous Maasai I could muster. Consequently she awarded me a totally undeserved distinction. Within a week of the exam I was posted away to Fort Hall, a Kikuyu district, first as DO Kigumo and then Kandara. But the hot war had just about finished; the work was mainly mopping up the few surviving gangsters. I moved over to reconstruction which involved the consolidation of thousands of fragments of land holdings. But I was only there for fifteen months, and that was not long enough to learn Kikuyu.

Back to Kenya

DAVID LAMBERT

I first went to Kenya in 1954 as a platoon commander in the 3rd Battalion, Kings Africa Rifles. I so liked the country and the people that when my National Service was finished and I returned to England I was determined to find a job which would take me back. This determination was reinforced when I started work in my pre-service job in the City during a wet August and very soon I found myself at the Crown Agents in Millbank asking if they had any opportunities in Kenya for a fit twenty year old with fluent, if ungrammatical Swahili and a knowledge of small arms.

Which is how, seven weeks later I found myself landing in Nairobi as a District Assistant on a two-year contract with the Kenya government. There were five other newly recruited DAs on the flight including Paul Whitcher, another 3 KAR subaltern and a life-long friend.

We were taken from the airport to a safari outfitters where we all bought camp beds, canvas baths (never used) and the ubiquitous Tilley lamps. Then on to the Secretariat where, feeling very 'new-boyish', we lined up in an office, were welcomed and given details of our postings. For me it was Naivasha where I was to help to recruit and train a force of Farm Guards.

When I arrived in Naivasha, Noel Hardy had just taken over as DC, Peter Johnson was DO1 and there were several temporary DOs of whom one was based on the Kinangop and another at Gilgil. By that time the peak of the Mau Mau Emergency was over, however the work of the Administration in Naivasha was still dominated by security, and the Farm Guard force had been created to prevent terrorists from obtaining food and shelter from the African workers on the European farms. The idea was similar to that of the Home Guard in the Kikuyu Districts and the force was recruited and organised by the Administration with the Tribal Police acting as NCOs and doing most of the training. Unlike the Home Guard there was no indigenous population to draw on, so Farm Guards had to be recruited from outside the district, and many from Maasai Narok.

Almost as soon as I arrived I was given a dozen TPs, half a dozen tents and told to establish a new divisional centre on the west side of Lake Naivasha. Young and keen I set up camp in a superb tactical position on the side of a hill supposed to be on a terrorist route from the Mau escarpment to the lakeside farms. Tactical it might have been but convenient it was not. The nearest water being two miles and the site only approachable through numerous farm gates. Quickly I found equally good 'tactical' reasons to move into an empty house on Rocco's farm bordering the lake.

Having planted the flag my next task was a safari to the Mara to enlist new Farm Guards. There was no shortage of volunteers. On arriving in Naivasha Farm Guards were fitted out with a khaki jersey, a beret with the Kenya lion badge and issued with a single barrel shotgun.

Training was a makeshift affair lasting two weeks. It included drill, instruction in the use of their newly issued weapons and lectures on their duties with the warning that if they saw any particularly sleek cattle they were not to take off back to Maasailand with them. Given that the new recruits spoke little if any Swahili, these lectures were probably half understood as an invitation to help themselves! To liven things up I introduced some section attack training and to add realism 'borrowed' surplus thunder flashes from a nearby army unit. I still bear the scar where one went off prematurely.

Eburru is a hill to the north west of Lake Naivasha. It is an area of high geo-thermal activity, and in the fifties extensive drilling took place in an unsuccessful search for a source of thermal power. The lower slopes of Eburru hide hundreds of steam vents and in the early morning the steam condenses into a ground hugging mist giving the country a Brigadoon quality. On my first visit I saw hidden in the mist a building with a vaguely familiar shape. On closer inspection it had every appearance of a railway station – but the railway from Nairobi to Nakuru ran miles to the east. On enquiry, I learnt the buildings had indeed been a railway station; the story being that when the Uganda Railway was extended to Kisumu, Lord Delamere, the European settler, who owned this particular part of the Rift Valley had insisted, as a condition of the right of way, that the line should detour to his front door. The kink had long since been straightened out leaving the station abandoned.

On top of Eburru was a crater with meadows and the remains of a forest. It was farmed by two or three European families, including the Tatham Warters. I can remember on my first visit trying to persuade Digby Tatham Warter to accept a detachment of Farm Guards and holding forth on how he should improve the security of his labour lines. He was polite, changed the subject and sent me on my way after a good meal and some excellent whisky. Some time later I learned he had been at Arnhem. Years later in Cornelius Ryan's 'A Bridge Too Far' I read of his exploits with the 2nd

Parachute Battalion defending the north end of the Arnhem Bridge for five days. I still blush at the memory of myself at twenty advising him how to defend his farm.

From KAR to Administration

CHRIS MINTER

Like many others I first came to Kenya with the army, as a National Service officer in the King's African Rifles. Ten of us from 23 (Kenya) Battalion eventually joined the Administration, eight becoming DOs in Kenya and two in Tanganyika.

Early in the Emergency I met several DCs and DOs and I was impressed by their dedication, energy and optimism. One learned something of what they were trying to do but the emphasis was (and had to be), very much on building up the numbers and morale of the Tribal Police and Home Guard, training and leading them, and replacing chiefs and headmen who were murdered or were simply not up to the pressures of the time.

I was in Nyeri on the day Senior Chief Nderi was killed and in Fort Hall (now Muranga) when the mutilated bodies of a Headman and two TPs were recovered. I viewed them in the company of Jerome Kihori, a Kikuyu DO, who was himself killed later. When I moved to Kiambu, Chief Hinga (wounded a few days earlier) had just been murdered in hospital. Administration and Police were each blaming the other.

On the lighter, more cheerful side of life, I took tea with Harry Thuku, a distinguished nationalist of an earlier generation, and enjoyed the back-dated rum ration, which we received once we were in the forest and over a certain altitude. I cooked for myself when detached from my company, talked to the askaris, and began to take an interest in the future of the country. Contrary to much received opinion, a significant number were interested in politics or at least in economic and social issues.

In 1955 I returned to Kenya on a brief visit, crossing Africa by car and, after an accident, as a hitch hiker. That's another story, but it explains why the stay was brief. I was amazed at the progress made through closer administration and good teamwork, towards better agricultural practices, villagization, and land consolidation, at the same time that a small-scale civil war was being fought and won. So I applied to join the Colonial Service, specifically to become a District Officer in Kenya.

'You've got flat feet' said the Colonial office doctor as he examined me in London sometime in 1956. I made my excuses. 'Listen, young man, my brief is only to accept men who'll be capable of walking forty miles a day when they are forty years old' to which I had no reply. Perhaps the doctor would have agreed with the view (which I kept to myself) that the likelihood of still being a DO (or a DC or PC) in Kenya in 1973 already seemed remote.

I arrived back in Kenya in July 1957 and reached my first post, Kisii (by train and lorry) six days later. At some time there or perhaps in Nairobi I bought the camp bed, bath and basin which I must have used for about six hundred of my one thousand or so nights as a DO in the field. I had bush jackets and shorts made, also a pair of 'brothel creepers' (desert boots) and bought the rather absurd 'Bombay bowler' or solar topee that was also official dress, worn perhaps on a dozen occasions in five years and given to my cook in 1962.

I had also brought with me a shotgun, tennis and squash rackets, a portable radio and record player (both battery operated), a growing collection of jazz records and a few books, to be supplemented by magazine subscriptions to *The Economist* and *Paris Match*. Most useful of all, I had a book of my mother's recipes, written in her hand and limited to dishes and ingredients which were likely to be practical in the prevailing conditions. I also started a visitors' book (which now runs to four volumes). After a while I bought a barely roadworthy car which I abandoned in Nairobi when I moved from Kisii to Moyale where (as later in Pokot and Turkana) it would have been of no use. I always served in areas where one earned five or six days long (ie. UK) leave for every month in the field: I also earned about fifteen weeks local leave in five years, of which I suppose I was able to use about ten. I never lived in a house with electricity.

My first shock on my arrival in Kisii was to find that as a bachelor I had to share a house with two or three others. The district had been reinforced with additional administrators, agricultural and community development officers and police inspectors. This was rather a comedown from an officers' mess or a Cambridge college. There were compensations in the garden such as an endless supply of avocados; and in any case I was on safari most weeks. I was eventually moved to an empty mission-owned house fifteen miles from the *boma* but in the middle of what by then was my 'parish'.

Nyanza Province, containing about a third of the colony's population, was under-resourced in every way. The staff was increased but, as far as the Provincial Administration was concerned, not the provision of land-rovers and lorries or the funds for fuel. The 'Laws of Kenya' volumes had not been kept up to date with the numerous amendment slips needed, so I failed to pass the law exams at my first attempt: one had to pass all six of the three hour papers at one sitting, not all on the same day of course!

In South Nyanza district the Bantu Kisii occupied the highlands and the Nilotic Luo occupied the much larger low-lying areas around Lake Victoria.

Before *Uhuru* the district, by then with a population of one million, was split in two, the new *boma* being at Homa Bay. The two districts were still the fourth and fifth most populous in Kenya. One of my tasks was to set aside land for community projects, running into noisy opposition when I arrived at Homa Bay to mark out the square mile needed for the future district's *boma* and township. I was pelted with stones and had to make a few arrests, prosecuting the offenders before the DO1, the same evening. On another occasion, the DC noted that I had sailing experience and I was sent to Kisumu to collect and sail a large dhow, which had been bought by the African District Council, back to Homa Bay.

From the same file, presumably the CV I had submitted to the Colonial Office, the DC learned I had boxed at one time. I was taller, weightier and longer-armed than Nigel Marsh, Assistant Superintendent of Police, but he was the Kenya fly weight champion and he needed a sparring partner.

I found African Court work interesting. My 'mission house' was near Ogembo, a traditional Kisii site for hearing cases. The Elders' charges sometimes read strangely: 'Assault causing grievous bodily harm in that (accused) did hang (victim) by TASTES'. Questioning the court I was relieved to learn that it was not the victim's tongue which had been bound in a wire noose, but it must have been equally unpleasant for his testicles, and it was lucky for all parties that the consequences did not lead to an even more serious charge. Nor were the Elders' judgements always sound in law, eg. in a prosecution for illegal distilling, possession and sale of spirits: 'We, the Elders of Ogembo Court, have drunk the Nubian Gin (Exhibit 1) and it is clearly adulterated with water. Case dismissed'. In another case it was six of one and half a dozen of the other. The Court Process-Server swore he had delivered the summons to the accused, and the latter swore he had never been approached. Now he was in court both on the original charge and for ignoring a summons. A traditional but irregular course of action was decided upon. Nearby stood an ancient tree which, Kisii custom dictated, had to be embraced by anyone swearing a serious oath. The accused found no difficulty in this, but the Process-Server sweated profusely before taking the oath with the greatest reluctance. The Court adjourned for a week: it did not meet again for by then the Process-Server had died – of 'natural causes'.

I did not always agree with my first DC. A colleague and I were rebuked one Monday for 'leaving the district without permission' and 'failing to attend church' when we ought to have 'set a good example to other government servants': we had instead gone water-skiing with friends at Kericho.

I was also told that 'you should never discuss politics with Africans'. This criticism (via Special Branch) arose from an occasion when I found myself buying the Kenya Weekly News in the *duka* at the same time as the late

Robert Ouko (then a government clerk, later his country's Foreign Minister) was getting his copy, and we exchanged a few remarks. As for the strict colour bar in the Kisii Club (and not even in a settled area), I could only agree with the English wife of the Indian doctor who commented that there were one or two members she would only have into her home 'for a particularly nasty plumbing job'.

Early in 1959 I was puzzled to receive a letter from the Ministry of African Affairs, which had been sent to all DOs 'recruited in the last two or three years' enquiring whether 'there is a justification for the general statement that the information in regard to local conditions on recruitment is inadequate'.

Clearly (and I had this confirmed later) there had been complaints. I replied with 'an emphatic negative' subject to what I have already said about bachelor housing, but made the point that I had served in Kenya previously so knew something of what to expect.

I might have expressed things a little differently had I ever seen a Kenya Government publication, 'Life and Duties of an Administrative Officer in Kenya' (1958) which I first saw forty years later. This was largely fictional. It would be tedious to outline all the errors but it is the 'Suggested Reading' list which intrigues me today: nine books, only two of which were remotely connected with the life we led (Dick Hennings' admirable *African Morning* and Elspeth Huxley's *The Sorcerers Apprentice*). Three predated 1914 and two were from the 1920s and 30s. Nothing about land and agricultural questions, or Mau Mau, or constitutional and political change in Africa. Farson, Hailey, Leakey, and various Royal Commissions – let alone Kenyatta – might never have existed.

Bright White Sunlight

ALAN LIDDLE

In the early summer of 1957 at Cambridge there was much speculation about our first postings among those of us on the Overseas Services 'A' course. Of the Cadets destined for Kenya only Claude Heywood lacked personal experience of the Colony, so the bar chat in the Oversea Services Club in Petty Cury was reasonably well informed. Chris Minter, John Williams, and I had all served in a Kenya battalion of the King's African Rifles during the Mau Mau Emergency. Jeremy Lunn and Mike Fletcher had been largely brought up in Kenya, and Carr Newton had been a District Officer Kikuyu Guard in Central Province during the Emergency.

Between us we envisaged, and hoped for, a wide variety of districts for our first postings. Elgeyo Marakwet, Nandi and Kitui topped my personal list, probably because of past associations with my KAR askari. In addition, uniquely among the Cadets on the 1956/57 Course, I had a young bride who would be new to Kenya, to think of as well as myself. Fortunately however, she viewed Kenya with the same enthusiasm as I did, and had some idea of the self-reliance that might be necessary on many stations since she had spent her early years on her family's more or less remote sheep and cattle estancias in the Argentine and Uruguay.

When our postings arrived, mine came as a bit of an anti-climax: DO Kilifi, in the Coast Province. Not that I had anything against the Coast, indeed during my KAR service I had never visited its shores having preferred to take such short leaves as came my way up-country. It simply did not have the appeal for me of the hot and dry plains, or the cooler and wetter highlands, and their tribes. But there was an added interest in the Coast, that of the long established Arab population as well as the indigenous Africans, which exerted a pull of its own. Within twenty-four hours we were looking forward to a new life, new work, and Kilifi's apparent domestic attractions.

Our propeller driven aircraft, noisy, hot and bumpy over the North African Desert, was second best to the British India liners to Mombasa. But it was speedy, and we were keen to start our new life. The Nile and some seductive Kenya scenery on a bright East African morning were the best views on our flight and adequate compensation for our slight discomfort. On arrival at Eastleigh Airport we were met by the urbane figure of Christopher Denton, Assistant Secretary in the Ministry of African Affairs, which I thought a civilised touch and a reminder that we had joined a proper service. We were seen to the Norfolk Hotel, a charming, rural looking bit of old Kenya in Nairobi, where we spent a relaxing night in great comfort. After a day seeing Nairobi, lunching with old friends, and generally giving Sue her bearings, we caught the evening train for an overnight journey to Mombasa. The East African Railways ran in considerable style with wood panelled sleeping cabins, a splendid dining car, impeccable African servants, the whole pulled by steam locomotives through matchless scenery. In those days this included big herds of game on the Athi plains.

Our arrival the next morning at Mombasa struck us forcibly for the intensity of the bright white sunlight, the huge and highly scented frangipani shrubs down one side of the station, the heat and humidity, and the bustle and noise of the colourful crowds of Africans, Swahilis, Arabs, and Indians. The light, heat, smells and sights were a heady concoction.

At the end of the station platform stood the immaculate and, for a Giriama, surprisingly tall figure of Gideon the DC's driver in spotless white shirt and shorts, with a smart TP, both looking out for a fairly lost DO

Cadet and his wife. They took charge of our luggage, welcomed us – Gideon in good English, the TP in Swahili – and led us to OHMS 7762, the DC's shining new land-rover, with 'District Commissioner, Kilifi' painted in white on its green door. We went off into Mombasa's morning traffic apparently to find the grocer in those days most favoured by the Coast's Europeans. Alibhai Essa's turned out to be a treasure trove, and we were able to stock up with basics for our new home as well as surprisingly sophisticated provisions including a range of excellent South African wines, and an assortment of delicious looking exotica that would not have disgraced the food halls of Harrods. With the necessities for life stored in the land-rover we were ready to make for Kilifi some forty miles northwards up the coast from Mombasa. The first creek which we had to cross, a fairly narrow one coming in from the Indian Ocean, was Shimo la Tewa, in those days crossed on a chain ferry carrying vehicles and foot passengers. The flat, open, ferry worked its way across the creek, taking in and paying out a chain, with a chugging diesel engine for power. The road north, once Shimo la Tewa was behind us, was unpaved murram, thick in orange dust which soon covered everything, and we bumped through this, passing featureless low bush interspersed with big coconut plantations, and finally, as we approached Kilifi Creek, the vast sisal plantations at Vipingo. Kilifi Creek was an altogether grander and bigger affair than Shimo la Tewa. Here one looked right to the Indian Ocean, and left to a huge inland sea loch, with another flat, open, diesel powered ferry describing a wide seawards arc as the outgoing tide carried it sideways on its route towards our concrete landing stage. Cheerful crowds of Giriama women, bare breasted and wearing multi pleated skirts, boarded the ferry on foot with us, and, amid much banter with the ferry driver, we were on our way across. Up a short steep hill above the landing stage, at the top of which we turned right, and we were soon entering the *boma* with Gideon pointing out the Post Office, Police Station, African District Council Offices and Hall, and the District Administration offices in front of which we parked. These were brand new and sparkling white, built round a three sided, or hollow, square on which an attempt was being made to grow grass under a thick seaweed mulch. A broad, cool looking, verandah shaded the offices, which looked out over the creek to the back and over the square to the front. Planted along the blindingly white road from the Post Office to the new District Offices, were beautiful flamboyant trees with their flame red flowers reflected on the ground in a circle of fallen petals round each tree. An imaginative and unforgettable bit of planting. But over all this scene it was the heat and humidity of midday Kilifi as much as anything else that remain the outstanding first impression.

We had been told the DC was away on leave and that for our first few months we would be using his house as our home because our house was to undergo repairs and redecoration. 'You can have any colour you like, so long as it's brown, cream or green', as Pop Sykes, the delightful Yorkshire head of the PWD, told us later. For the moment however we had to report to the DO1, who was acting as DC, the genial and welcoming figure of Gerald Johnson-Hill. Gerry, previously a rubber planter in Malaya, and a Japanese prisoner of war taken on the Malaya/Siam border when his territorial unit the Kedah Volunteer Force, was overrun by vastly superior forces, made us feel both welcome and wanted. He was informally clad in well pressed and starched khaki drill shorts, a short sleeved white shirt, and long white stockings. The usual turn out, I gathered, for a coast DO. He looked in need of lunchtime refreshment, which he wasted no time in attending to as he shepherded us along for the short walk from the offices, through a grove of dark leafed cashew-nut trees and tall, waving, coconut palms, to the DO1's house. This turned out to be the oldest on the station, and was a charming bungalow built of coral blocks, plastered and painted white, and surrounded by a deep, cool, green-tiled verandah on which Pam Johnson-Hill stood to meet us. It overlooked a nine-hole golf course, dotted about with massive baobab trees into which earlier DCs had trained bougainvillaea of varied colours to spectacular effect. Beyond this foreground were Kilifi Creek, and to the left the reefs and the Indian Ocean. As we sat down on the verandah with an ice cold Coast lager at hand, we thought we had arrived in something approaching paradise.

Back in the DC's office, I was particularly interested to have my principal duties and responsibilities outlined to me. These were to be the Northern Division of the district with its four locations of Sokoke, Ganze, Bamba, and Vitengeni, and their chiefs, liaison with the Arab officials of the Coastal Strip such as the Kadhi and Mudir (Sharia Judge and Administrative Officer) at nearby Takaungu in its shady mango and coconut groves, the prison, a third class Magistrate's court, the Tribal Police, and the *boma* itself including its roads surfaced with coral rag from our own quarry, its airstrip to the North, and their orderly appearance and effective running. A good and varied portfolio for a DO Cadet embarking on his new career and one, so I was told, to be conducted with the maximum use of my own judgement and initiative, and the minimum of reference back to my senior officers. All this sounded promising, as more mundanely I was reminded that I had to pass language and law exams within two years as a prerequisite to being confirmed in my appointment as District Officer.

I was intrigued, that first evening, by the thought of the DC, Denis Hall, away with his wife and family on home leave. He enjoyed a reputation in the *boma* for being very much in command of his district while at the same time being a delegator, for thoroughness, and an eye for detail, and for not suffering fools for a minute. This formidable list was apparently illuminated by a considerable charm. Earlier in the evening while down by the creek I had been taken and shown *Safina*, the Administration sailing boat, up on chocks near the bathing place. She was a clinker built, quarter decked Coot class boat, apparently very much Denis Hall's personal toy. I had succumbed to her charms and, being keen on sailing, determined to sail her as soon as possible rather than await the DC's return. Though this would mean handing her over on his arrival from leave in one hundred and one percent good order, it seemed to be a risk worth taking. In other areas than the immaculate *Safina* I believed I had already seen the absent DC's hand not least in the layout and efficient order of the new District Offices, and now looked forward to meeting him a few months hence. In the meantime there would be work to get on with, starting soon after dawn the next morning at the prison's *tamaam* parade, to be followed by an inspection tour of the *boma* with the Station Headman and TP Sergeant. Not a bad life in prospect!

The Lure of Dust

ROBIN WILLIAMSON

From the gravel road that wound endlessly through the desiccated thorn bush towards the massive mountain block of Moroto my mind was jolted back to my childhood. The family photograph album that I had gazed through as a boy in Uganda filled the gap left by my father's untimely death in uniform in Abyssinia, and it suddenly replaced the baking, dust filled cab of Sirdar Mohamed's truck.

>PRIVATE BURIAL GROUND
>(Skull & Cross Bones)
>FOR
>RECKLESS DRIVERS
>AHEAD

I had been here many times before. In my childhood that ominous sign, its words and its symbol of death, had figured in the same landscape that now stretched out before me. And it does so again thirty seven years later, in a group of black and white pictures of Turkana's pulse-rousing wastes, its feathered, beaded and semi-naked inhabitants and, in contrast, the uniformed *askari* of the King's African Rifles. The photographs of goats being herded by a *shuka*-clad group of young men amongst thorn trees. The sandy expanse of the bed of a dry *lugga* with a riverine strip of tall acacia trees and the distinctive outline of Mount Pelekech in the background, were to be subjects of views often enjoyed by me in my five years in Turkana. The *boma* at Lokitaung, digging out lorries from muddy tracks and recently swollen riverbeds were to be familiar sights. The fort at Todenyang, however, was not to survive the passage of time quite as well, and the temporary buildings for the military, consisting of stone-walling, characteristic of field divisions in the British Isles, roughly roofed with palm leaves, were to be a thing of the past. Even so a dwelling built of *doum* palm trunks and thatch was to be my final residence in Turkana.

As the lorry slowed and negotiated ever tighter bends in its gear-grinding descent, the road sign's stern warning took on an alarming relevance. However, the precipitous nature of the Loiya escarpment lost its threatening aspect in the breathtaking views it offered of the central Turkana plain that marched eastwards into a distant haze of heat and dust, its aridity veined with the dark lines of vegetation nourished by seasonal watercourses. To the north the mountain mass of Murua Ngithigerr stood out invitingly from the surrounding land. Its mystery and allure, like so much else in Turkana, were to draw me to its luxuriant plateau of open glades and mist forest after a tortuous ascent with donkeys in the years to follow, as it had done others.

We reached the floor of the Rift Valley as the sun began to cast a shadow of the escarpment wall on the Loiya Tribal Police Post. Here there was a barrier across the road watched over by TPs dressed in blue mini *kikois* edged with red, wearing red *shuka* turbans and sandals and carrying .303 rifles. A large notice declared that Turkana District was a Closed District and that entry was only permitted to holders of permits issued by the District Commissioner. There was now a welcome delay as formalities were observed, news exchanged, small purchases delivered and supplies of chewing tobacco replenished.

One of the last three officers to be recruited by HMOCS for service in Kenya, I had finally arrived in my first and only district as District Officer. Following the Overseas Service Course in Oxford, I would share in the transitional steps to Independence in Kenya after the Lancaster House agreement. Five years were all that the change would allow me. Richard Luce and Robin Paul had been posted to Isiolo and Meru respectively.

A slow train journey took me from Nairobi to Kitale, and this brought back memories of journeys by rail from Uganda to Nakuru as a young schoolboy – smuts and steam. Two nights at the Kitale Hotel gave me time to engage a cook and equip myself with items for life in the Northern Province under the guidance of 'Windy' Wild, DC Kitale, whose experience at Marsabit served me well.

The final leg of the journey to Lodwar started in the bracingly cool hours of a Kitale morning filled with the characteristic scent of black wattle and eucalyptus. Sirdar Mohamed's instructions were to transport me with a load of famine relief maize, dried milk powder, dried meat and vitamin supplements to Turkana. We were accompanied by half a dozen passengers, including my newly acquired cook Francis Serebi, all perched on our load. From the fertile settler farmland of the highlands we entered West Pokot District through the Police post at Keringet. We then descended the first escarpment from Makutano to the lower regions at Kacheliba and wound our way through the thorn scrub to Amudat and on to the final descent to the lowland semi-desert, where we were now waiting.

The Loiya barrier was lifted and we were on our way again.

The late afternoon drive was along an open, graded, dusty road occasionally broken by strips of gravel and intersected by dry *lugga* beds, which the heavily laden lorry churned through in low gear, whining and juddering. These strips of sand, some narrow, some vast, would turn into raging torrents in the rains and claim the vehicles of reckless drivers. Rusting skeletons were visible from time to time. The expansive crossing at Lorugumu was especially treacherous. The roadside vegetation was predominantly low thorn bush with patches of grass supporting browsing camels, flappable donkeys, and scatterings of goats and sheep. Cattle were seen infrequently here, as the cattle camps were for the most part some distance from the main homesteads except when the grazing was particularly favourable. The *lugga* banks were graced with lines of large acacia trees, *doum* palms and patches of undergrowth. To our north Murua Ngithigerr, under a wreath of cloud, dominated the plain whilst ahead, to the east, a distant but distinct cone on the horizon appeared to be our target.

As we drew nearer, this harsh feature of dark red volcanic rock stood out in the evening light of the sun, setting behind us, to mark out Lodwar, District Headquarters of Turkana District. For much of the latter stages of the journey across the central plain the continuous tree line of the Turkwell River had become evident to our south. As we drove into Lodwar the groves of *doum* palms in and around the township indicated that Lodwar was set at the confluence of the two seasonal rivers, the Kawalathe and the Turkwell. The former rises in the dry hills to the north and west and the latter drains the Pokot escarpment to the west and south.

Our short drive through the township in a cloud of dust took us past the Tribal Police lines and the prison before we climbed a short hill up to the *boma*, the District Offices, stores, workshops, the radio beacon for international aircraft and housing for government staff and officers. All this was set upon a flat outcrop of volcanic rock that overlooked the township, the large airstrip to the north and the Turkwell River to the south.

We paused at the District Offices. The Union Jack was about to be lowered by the TP guard with customary ceremony at the day's end. I had arrived in time to enjoy Empire even if it was to be for a relatively short time.

We passed the stone-walled Guard compound for me to be delivered to my residence. My childhood imagination was marvellously stirred in the next moment when the whitewashed houses came into sight. These solid square structures were surrounded by square pillared verandas shaded with palm screens. Each flat roof was edged all round with a low latticed wall and had a mosquito gauzed sleeping cage in its middle. The roof was reached by an external brick staircase. My romantic imagination fed in childhood by PC Wren's 'Beau Geste' and 'Beau Sabreur' and a nature already drawn to the desert were excited.

For a while the thrill of the adventure that life as a District Officer offered overcame the idealistic intentions that had been fostered in me by Macmillan's 'wind of change' speech and by strong currents of thought in Oxford. I had come to help prepare a colony for self-government and Independence. It was not until after Independence that I reflected on how fortunate I had been as one of the last three to be engaged for this service to be able to share in some degree the colonial experience of the generations that had preceded me. There were names that took on the mantle of heroes but the most immediate inspiration was to be found just below the rocky outcrop that I was to live on for the duration of my administrative service. There, in a grove of *doum* palms just below the house, a rough stone mound starkly topped by a weathered wooden cross marked the grave of Capt. Eric von Otter, 1923. For me his service in Turkana and his death from blackwater fever whilst in service were a reminder of the spirit of earlier pioneers and induced a sense of reverence and challenge.

My host for my first few days in Lodwar was Michael Thompson, who was to move and take over Lokitaung Sub-District. As introductions were exchanged, my dust-covered cook and my luggage were removed from amongst the sacks of famine relief maize and boxes of dried meat powder and vitamins. Soon it would be time for romance to give way to the realities of what I had come to, setting up famine camps and administering relief in addition to other routines of administrative duty.

2

The Administrator's Day

Learning through Mistakes	Harold Williams
An Unexpected Duty	H. (Pat) de Warenne Waller
Apprenticeship in Kwale	Michael Wasilewski
Tax Collection	Michael Philip
Multiple Duties at Malindi	Oliver Knowles
A Posting to Mombasa	Michael Power
Urban Work	Gerald Pratt
The Joys of Nature	Eric Fox
A District Officer and the Law	Philip Jones
A Popular Judgement	Ted Alleyne
A Failure of Justice	Roger Horrell
Sport and Education	Eric Gordon
Athletics and the Administration	Michael Philip
A Young Man's Job	Peter Dempster
The Coloured Shirt	Peter Dempster
Politics in Fort Hall	David Nicoll Griffith

Introduction

District Officers rejoiced in the variety of the tasks they had to perform. There was always the prospect of the unexpected situation to deal with. The new DO, usually fresh from Britain, had to learn the ropes and at the same time study law and Swahili. He was at first heavily dependent on his support staff. Harold (Ngombe) Williams, who rose to be a Provincial Commissioner, records how easy it was to get things wrong. And Pat Waller recounts one of the dangers he had to face.

There had to be routine duties. Michael Wasilewski describes the range of work he was given in a rural district. Tax collection was a primary task and Michael Philip explains how the tribal chiefs did it. At Malindi on the coast Oliver Knowles was responsible for almost every job in the *boma*. But work in the urban areas was different. Michael Power and Gerald Pratt were DOs in Mombasa dealing with greater cultural and social diversity.

Virtually every DO was also a magistrate. Some enjoyed court work and became experienced at it. Others did it rarely and were often afflicted by doubt over judgements. Philip Jones became an expert on African Courts, the system of respected elders dispensing local justice. He, Eric Fox, Ted Alleyne and Roger Horrell illustrate court work from their own experience.

The administrators were men of all work. Sport, and especially athletics, had to be organised and this task usually fell to the DO. From the beginnings, which Eric Gordon describes, Kenya's athletic prowess flourished, as Michael Philip tells us.

It was the outdoor nature of administrative work in the districts which held so much appeal, particularly for the young DOs getting to grips with African issues, as Peter Dempster explains. Some of the seniors might be stuffy, but in a small and scattered service comradeship was warm. The politics of nationalism posed new challenges and David Nicoll Griffith records these in the Kikuyu heartland. Time was running out for one of the most interesting jobs young Britons could aspire to.

Learning Through Mistakes

HAROLD WILLIAMS

In the first year of my service, I was sent out to evict some Boran from Isiolo who were alleged to be poaching grazing in Meru district. When I located these Boran and moved them on, I allowed the chief and interpreter to persuade me that the wisest course of action would be to burn their village as they would return and continue poaching as soon as I had left. Having done so, although I knew it was wrong, the storm was not long in breaking. The Boran lost no time in making fantastic claims for many thousands of shillings, despite the fact that I was careful to make sure that the huts contained no goods. My two superiors were men of great practical experience who resolved the matter and kept it within the family. Nonetheless, it gave me a nasty jolt and it could have had serious repercussions. It taught me never to accept the advice of interpreters and their ilk against my own judgement.

An Unexpected Duty

H. (PAT) DE WARENNE WALLER

One quiet afternoon in Meru when both the District Commissioner, C.M. (Monkey) Johnston and Derek Holman, the District Officer, were away on safari I received a visit from Montou Iburi, a tall lean-boned headman whose parish bordered upon the Imenti Forest, from whom I received the following account.

A herd of elephant passing through his area four days previously on their seasonal migratory trek down from the slopes of Mount Kenya into the low country, had paused to feed in the maize fields which bordered the forest. Whereupon the villagers had sallied forth chanting and shouting, ringing bells and beating iron trays until the elephants taking fright returned into the forest. The following morning, whilst the main herd had moved on, one lone bull remained behind resting in the forest from whence he emerged that evening to make his way to the cluster of maize stores where the entire stocks of food for the winter months were kept. Ripping off a thatched roof from its walls he dipped in his trunk and ate his fill before departing back into the forest.

On the second night that the elephant returned the villagers were waiting and when it entered the compound of a man named Imwega he had flung a spear at it with such ferocity and judgement that the blade penetrated its belly. Imwega had then turned to run but with a scream of rage the elephant spun round and chasing him between the huts, caught him before he could reach safety. Whereupon, lifting him in its trunk as if he were a doll, it had battered him to death against a tree before returning to the forest wounded and in an evil mood. 'The family of Imwega have sworn revenge' said Montou Iburi 'for they have no doubt, and nor have I, that he will return, but with the head of the spear still embedded within him paining him greatly, I fear that more men will die before he himself is either killed or driven away. I therefore told my people that I would ask the District Officer to come and shoot him.'

Absolutely aghast at this bland statement, I managed not a word as he rose with a cheerful 'be sure to bring a heavy rifle' and took his departure. A piece of advice, which in the circumstances and with the knowledge that the armoury contained nothing heavier than a .303 rifle was no comfort.

That evening my interpreter Rintari and I bumped our way down to the village in my little Fordson van, purchased with a loan from Government, to be met by a large crowd assembled as Iburi put it 'to watch the District Officer overcome the elephant'. Personally I could not avoid the uneasy feeling that they might also perhaps be there to watch the delectable sight of the elephant overcoming the District Officer – but it was too late to worry about that.

Having conducted me to a point where a narrow but well-defined track led out of the forest into the maize fields, Iburi halted. 'Behold! his highway' he said in a hollow voice, 'stand here and you will observe him as he emerges from the forest and your bullets will slay him with certainty at such short range'. Refraining from mentioning that on this last small point I felt rather less certain than he, I took up my stand, heart beating wildly and cold shivers of anticipation running up the back of my neck, as the crowd returned to the village and I am left alone.

The evening suddenly became incredibly still; the small wind dropped, the bird-song ceased, and even the bright coloured butterflies seemed to have retired from the arena; a brooding silence settled over the forest edge like a shroud.

As the elephant came down the track it would present a side view and I decided that I would take my shot on the line between eye and ear-hole, one known by experts as 'the brain shot'. Lifting the rifle to my shoulder I aimed experimentally at a flower head but the barrel swayed like a leaf in the wind causing me to visualise my firing and missing, and the elephant plucking me up in its trunk to disdainfully tear me limb from limb rather as if it were plucking the feathers from a chicken.

Despite their enormous bulk elephants move remarkably quietly and I did not hear the old bull approach until he was within 20 yards of the edge of the forest when the sudden clatter of the spurfowl rising into the air focused my attention. The bushes grew thickly at this point and only his back was visible above them as he moved down the track towards me. Gripping the rifle more tightly I pushed forward the safety catch, hands shaking with excitement. Then the appalling thing happened! He changed course and instead of coming out down the track commenced to move along parallel to the edge of the forest towards my little Fordson van, whose windscreen was reflecting the low beams of the setting sun directly into his eyes infuriating and blinding him. Clearly his intentions were far from honourable, and I could almost hear the voice of the Accountant General intoning 'we are sorry about your car Waller. You do realise of course that you will have to continue paying the instalments even though it no longer exists; after all you could hardly expect the insurance to accept its destruction by an elephant as anything but an act of wilful sabotage.' Panic seized me and I began to run wildly through the edge of the maize determined to get to the van before the elephant, now moving steadily through the edge of the forest invisible except for the tall bristly hump of his back, could arrive and commit mayhem. I have never been a good runner but I covered that 400 yards like Seraphino Antao and the elephant was still a clear 50 yards away in the forest when, panting with exertion, I collapsed onto the front bumper and leaning my back against the radiator lifted the rifle to my shoulder where it rocked up and down with every breath like a boat on a rough sea.

Voices began to shout in the village; sweat ran down my forehead and into my eyes and the blood hammered in my temples and then with a crash of breaking branches the elephant erupted into view on the track ten yards ahead, ears fanned out at right-angles from its head, trunk curled upon its forehead, staring straight at me. The brain shot was impossible and I was finished! In despair I lifted the rifle when a shout rang out and there, not twenty yards away, was Montou Iburi waving his arms and jumping up and down his blanket flapping from his lean frame and his face contorted with passion as he screamed insults at the elephant and pelted it with clods of earth. The elephant swung sideways, paused, then with a squeal of rage surged towards him. I fired. The next few seconds were a confused maelstrom of noise and movement and then I remember looking down at the tip of the elephant's trunk lying twitching on the ground not two yards from Iburi's feet. I was violently and uncontrollably sick.

The next morning when I tried to thank Montou Iburi for saving my life he merely smiled and with that innate and graceful genius of the Meru for saving face replied 'It is of no account, we were but afraid that the elephant in his cunning might seek to escape'. Rintari added for my future guidance, 'The Meru deem it no disgrace for a man to vomit, it would have sufficed to turn the back rather than to have run all the way to the car in search of privacy'.

Apprenticeship in Kwale

MICHAEL WASILEWSKI

I applied for the Colonial Service, giving my preference as Kenya. That was partly because I had heard it was a wonderful country, but principally because the continuing Mau Mau Emergency had created a demand for more staff. At the final selection board one of the questions I was asked was whether I had read something of value: my reply, that of course I had, for instance Dickens and Thackeray, caused much amusement. What the questioner had meant was the recent novel about Mau Mau, 'Something of Value' by Robert Ruark. Nevertheless I passed.

THE ADMINISTRATOR'S DAY

In mid-September 1957 I flew out to Nairobi and, after reporting to the Ministry of African Affairs, caught the night train to Mombasa. My destination was Kwale, a small *boma* a few miles inland, on top of the Shimba range of hills, and so somewhat cooler and less humid than the coastal belt below. It was just within the zone of lush tropical vegetation; bush and scrub started a little way up-country from there. My District Commissioner was the Hon. Roger Mills, efficient and good-natured. Altogether, I could hardly have been more fortunate in my first posting.

The administrative system was akin to the French one of 'Prefects'. An administrative officer was the senior representative of government in a given area. The heads of other departments represented there reported along their own line of hierarchy but were also expected to liaise closely with the administrative officer whose task it was to co-ordinate government activities in the area and who was ultimately responsible for all that happened there. His own primary duties were law and order, and the overall development of his district.

As a District Officer, one had to turn one's hand to just about anything: contact with chiefs and headmen about problems in their localities, explaining government policies to their people, collecting tax and perhaps raising the necessary money by holding stock auctions, advice to the local African District Council and the native courts, supervising the new governmental building and the repair of minor roads and bridges, training of Tribal Police, ensuring that government staff were paid on time and – perhaps one of the most important and certainly the most time-consuming tasks – hearing the *shauris*, that is individual problems (that bore some similarities to the work of Citizens' Advice Bureaux back at home).

In a letter to my parents two months after coming to Kwale, I wrote that I had had a very full week. I had spent, with a DO from Mombasa, the whole of Tuesday 'walking the boundary'. A slightly changed one, between Kwale and Mombasa districts, so that the chiefs concerned knew exactly where it ran. As we had to demarcate every change accurately, we had only managed seven miles a day and needed another day to finish the task. The coconut milk I had drunk at lunchtime had slaked my thirst better than water or lemonade. On the Wednesday, I had been to Tsunza, a small peninsula jutting out into Mombasa harbour, to check progress on the digging of a new well and to encourage the villagers to improve the track to their village. On the Thursday, I again 'walked the boundary' but that time to establish on the ground what the magistrate's court decision had been in a land dispute. I had also started work, as a third class magistrate being empowered to hear only minor criminal offences, eg. cycling without lights at night. As I wrote the letter, the rain was pouring down; no doubt a good time to get down to study criminal and civil law, and Swahili grammar, subjects which had to be passed within two years in order to qualify for confirmation in the appointment as a District Officer.

Colonialism has, currently anyway, a bad name. The reaction to Hitler's master race theories partly accounts for that. Yes, the European had a privileged life in the colonies, and often did not deserve it. But the British system aimed to protect subject peoples, and to steer them towards maturity as we Westerners understand it. I doubt whether the average colonial servant was particularly idealistic in his approach. For most, certainly for myself, it was a matter of interesting work in generally agreeable conditions, but I think we were, with only rare exceptions, honest, fair and conscientious. By the time I arrived in Kenya, such legal discrimination as might once have existed had been almost entirely expunged. However, we administrative officers were perhaps too aloof to be wholly successful in understanding the people we ruled.

Tax Collection

MICHAEL PHILIP

A major duty of the Administration was the supervision of the collection of *kodi*, the tax payable by every adult, male, African. This tax funded the local African District Councils, which were responsible for primary education, dispensaries, road maintenance, sport and social welfare. Location chiefs kept registers of individuals liable for the tax and recorded payment or otherwise. The generality throughout Kenya was that locations were well behind target with their tax collection and District Officers had to help by organising *kodi* checks at markets and other gatherings and by jogging the chief into greater efforts.

An exception to this generality was the Suk, a pastoral tribe living in the north of Baringo District. In a perennial effort to be left alone by government, the chiefs of the Suk locations would have their *kodi* registers checked by the District Revenue Officer in January, asking to be given the total tax bill for that year. At the same time they would ask the DO to organise a stock sale. At the stock sale the chiefs would pay their locations' entire tax total. In this way they hoped to keep visitations by officialdom to the minimum. The Suk are a proud people, rich in cattle, asking little from government. A District Officer, who understood them, would receive the accolade 'the DO is quite a good man: a pity he isn't a Suk'. Just after the war, they were persuaded to allow a Catholic Father to open a mission. In ten years the Father had made not one convert. He had, however, built a school, which remained stubbornly empty. Eventually the DC suggested to the Suk chiefs that their people were being left behind in Kenya's progress by having no formally educated children. The chiefs agreed and promised that Form 1 would be filled. In order not to inconvenience their tribesmen the chiefs filled the school with their own offspring.

Multiple Duties at Malindi

OLIVER KNOWLES

My predecessor in Malindi, Mike Power, handed over to me as soon as possible. My wife June and I moved into the District Officer's flat which was above the office, in a stately old house which had been constructed at the turn of the century by the old British East Africa Company, the predecessor of the colonial government. No one had in fact bothered to change the district seal since the days of the Company and all my official reports were sealed with the Company seal.

The house was beautifully situated facing the beach. It was solidly built, with high ceilings and a high roof, which harboured a swarm of bats. Our rooms thus smelt permanently of bat droppings, and we received periodic complaints from the nearest hotels about the smell of bats when the wind blew in their direction. There was a wide first floor veranda where we lived for most of the day and ate all our meals, enjoying the cool sea breeze, since it was usually too hot to sit in comfort in the inside rooms. At the end of a day's work it was a great luxury to be able to go straight out on to the beach to swim and surf. The hour before sunset, when the setting sun cast shadows over the sea, was always the most pleasant hour of the day. It was also the time of the evening parade when a large part of the town's population took to the beach and promenaded up and down. This could lead to culture clashes, as stately old Arab gentlemen, even if they might cast appreciative glances towards the figures of scantily dressed lady tourists, felt it necessary to complain to the DO about such improprieties of dress.

North of the district office was a Muslim cemetery, and then began the hotels – first Lawfords, then Brady's Palm Beach (later to become the Blue Marlin), the Sinbad, and finally the Eden Roc. The latter was owned by an Irish Earl who disliked the British and was known locally as 'JC'. It had the best swimming pool in town, but this attraction was somewhat offset by his rather cavalier attitude towards the guests. The Sinbad had the best all-round reputation, though Lawfords provided the best food. The Palm Beach did not seem to do much business, and on the only occasion that I ventured to lodge an official visitor there, he found a mouse's nest in his bed. P. O'Hara Brady was better at propping up his bar than at running his hotel.

We spent an interesting, enjoyable, and very exhausting year in Malindi. At first, coming from Turkana, we found conditions so different as almost to make the transfer traumatic. In Turkana we had lived a 'Sanders of the River' existence in a strictly tribal and uncomplicated society. In Malindi we were plunged into a multi-racial society with a complex of development problems. Except for an Assistant Agricultural Officer and a Fisheries Officer, I was the sole white representative of his Imperial British Majesty. The legal status of the coast was a typically British compromise. I was called in Swahili the '*Balozi*' meaning 'consul'. I had as assistant a *Liwali*, who was paid by the Kenya Government, but could be regarded as the representative of the Sultan of Zanzibar, from whom the coastal strip, alias the Protectorate as opposed to the Colony of Kenya, was leased for a nominal sum, which appeared each year in the Treasury Vote. This legal fiction that the soil belonged to the Sultan and was only leased by the British Government was preserved by a tradition which laid down that only the Sultan's flag should fly from a flagpole in the ground, and the Union Jack should only fly from a flagpole attached to a building. The special status of Muslims was also ensured by the presence of an official *Kadhi* (Muslim judge) whose business was to administer *sharia* law in all family disputes between Muslims.

My status as the sole administrative representative of His Majesty meant that not only were there certain ceremonial and entertainment functions to be carried out, but I was also a Gilbertian Pooh Bah: District Officer, Magistrate, Ex-Officio Agent of the Public Trustee, Port Officer, Keeper of the Lighthouse, Receiver of Wrecks, Sub-District Accounting Officer, Officer in charge of the prison and the detention camp, Officer in charge of the Tribal Police, Receiver of stolen ivory, Town Clerk, Chief Sanitary Inspector, Keeper of Burial Grounds, and custodian generally of law and order and public decency (the latter was no sinecure in a tourist resort with a largely Muslim population). These several roles had to be filled at a time of post-war development and economic expansion. In the year we spent in Malindi a new hospital was sited and built, a piped water supply was laid down and installed throughout the township, the groundwork was laid for the introduction of a rating system, and several new bore holes and roads were completed. Never in my life have I been so busy. In the heat of the coast, the pressure of work, combined with the endemic malaria and dysentery from which we were not immune, exhausted both myself and June. Eventually, after June had suffered an attack of cerebral malaria, we were forced to ask for a transfer to a cooler and less demanding post. But we greatly enjoyed both the work and the people and made many friends among all communities, so that subsequent holiday visits to Malindi were always a great pleasure and an opportunity for reunions with old friends.

As HM's official representative the main social event was the King's Birthday. On this occasion I had to don my white uniform and solar topee and formally inspect the Tribal Police, after which inspection a cocktail party was given at government expense for the entertainment of local VIPs. The selection of guests for this occasion was a matter requiring considerable tact, particularly among the fifty or so white residents. It was only too easy to make a *faux pas*. We managed to make one by forgetting to arrange for the collection of the widow of a Provincial Commissioner who could not drive and had to be brought to the party.

As the magistrate I was naturally responsible for the maintenance of law and order, though Malindi was generally a law-abiding area. The duties could however be rather bizarre. On one occasion the normal somnolence of my courtroom was brightened by the Arab Police Inspector. He marched in two rather scantily dressed German women tourists on a charge of creating a disturbance. As the evidence unravelled it became apparent that the disturbance was primarily in the minds of the observers. But I was custodian of public decency and the *heshima* of the Inspector was at stake. I fined the two women five shillings each and suggested that they kept the receipts as souvenirs of their holiday.

A Posting to Mombasa

MICHAEL POWER

In mid 1950 I was posted to Mombasa. It had been settled by Arabs in the thirteenth century; visited by Vasco de Gama in 1498; taken over by the Portuguese until 1698 when the Arabs moved back; and remained largely Arab until the British took over in the latter part of Victoria's reign. The building of the Kenya and Uganda railway and the development of the deep water berths at Kilindini enhanced its importance. The Mombasa District consisted of the island, three miles long and two miles wide, and the adjoining districts connected by bridge, all in the coastal strip flying the Zanzibar flag. It was prosperous. There were about two thousand Europeans, thirty thousand Indians, Hindu and Muslim, fifteen thousand Arabs and Swahilis (mainly the latter) and around fifty thousand Africans of many tribes. Its prosperity derived from: import/export, shipping, banking, insurance, the livestock trade, tourism, and transport. It was also the Provincial capital, which enhanced its status. An elegant Government

House, occupied occasionally by the Governor, overlooked the harbour entrance.

It was a hierarchical, multi-racial, colonial society, tolerant and friendly. The small European community held the reins of government, its members holding all the top posts in administration, police, port, railway, customs, magistracy, prisons, and municipality. The managers of the leading commercial houses, Jardine Matheson, Bousteads, Mackinnon Mackenzie, Mitchell Cotts, Harrison, Guthries, and the banks, had large offices, staffed by Goan and Indian clerks, and lived in handsome houses on the ridge overlooking the golf course, and in view of the Union Castle, British India, Blue Funnel and Glen Line ships which passed to and fro into Kilindini. Apart from the Governor and Provincial Commissioner, whose residences commanded the best views, government officials lived modestly, but nonetheless quite well, in and around the environs of the old town of Mombasa. Their social life took place in their houses – sundowners and dinner parties, men sweating in black ties and tuxedos, women in long dresses – or in the exclusively European clubs like Mombasa Club, Sports Club, Yacht Club and Golf Club.

The Indian community owed its existence to the introduction of indentured labour in the early years of the century, to build the railway. Many Asians still served in the railway as station masters, train drivers, engineers, mechanics, guards, and clerks. By 1950 the Indian community was wealthy as a result of commerce and possession of land in and around the island, and virtually all the big shops in the town centre. Dr Rany was the leader of the community, Vice-Chairman of the Municipal Board, and their leading spokesman. He did much for race relations. Many of the Indians were Ismaili Muslims. They were visited in 1950 by the Aga Khan and his wife, Rita Hayworth. She was beautiful, but bored.

The Arab/Swahili community owned property and land in the district and were still the principal traders in livestock brought down from Lamu and Garissa. In 1950 Mombasa was an oriental more than an African town. The Old Town by the port on the north side of the island was Arab in character with its narrow streets, whitewashed houses, carved wooden doors, mosques, men wearing head cloths, women in veils, coffee houses with spicy food, and *dhows* sweeping in and out of Mombasa harbour, or anchored and being unloaded by the old Customs House. Another place which held on to its Arab character was *Mwembe Tayari* (mango tree – 'ready'). This was in the centre of the island, a flat dusty little plain flanked by mango trees. There, each day, was a noisy assembly of traders, porters, vendors, touts, vagabonds, camels, donkeys, cattle, sheep, goats, old buses, lorries, taxis, trishaws, beggars, pickpockets, and riffraff – the sort of riot of humans, animals and vehicles which could be found, and probably still is, in Cairo, Baghdad, or Damascus. It was at *Mwembe Tayari* that intrepid

Englishmen assembled their caravans of camels, porters, soldiers, and stores before venturing into the interior to discover the source of the Nile. Here Arab slavers formed up their expeditions and in due course, auctioned their human cargoes for shipment by *dhow* to the Persian Gulf.

Not much of Portugese influence remained except for a few houses in the old town and Fort Jesus, then the provincial prison, now a museum. Yet the Goan community, inheritors of Portuguese influence, played a key role in the life of Mombasa, indeed of Kenya. The De Souzas, Da Silvas, Fernandes, Lourencos, and the like, occupied key positions in the government secretariats all over the colony. Every DC's office relied on a Goan head clerk or cashier. The Secretariat in Nairobi would have ground to a halt without their quiet devotion, honesty and painstaking accuracy. The leading finance houses in Mombasa employed first and foremost, Goans, and failing them, Indians. The Goan community was staunchly Roman Catholic, filling their churches every Sunday.

The majority of people in Mombasa were Africans, numbering about fifty thousand: stevedores, porters and labourers in the ports of Mombasa and Kilindini, servants in hotels, clubs and private houses, clerks, railway workers, market traders, small shopkeepers, coffee sellers, taxi drivers, trishawmen, vagrants and loafers. The unskilled labour force of the municipality was African. Outside the island were thousands of squatters and farm labourers on land owned mainly by Arabs and Indians. Many of the single women in Mombasa were prostitutes, mainly from Tanganyika. Many tribes were represented: Giriama or Digo from the coast; Luo, huge men, mostly in the port; Taita, mostly domestic servants; Kikuyu, Kamba and Meru. Kamba, Nandi, Kipsigis and other Kalenjin tribesmen and some Luo filled the ranks of the police. Many of the Africans were single, temporary residents who returned to their tribal areas after accumulating wages and spending the evenings in brothels and beer halls. It was a decentralised community, lacking in cohesion. The trade unions in the port and municipality created some kind of unity, but the unions were poorly organised. In the hierarchical society of Mombasa in 1950 the Africans were at the bottom of the heap.

As DO Majengo my main responsibilities were with the Africans, but my duties were ill-defined. Whereas the DC Kilifi and his District Officers were responsible for all aspects of local administration, the DC Mombasa was a shadowy figure with more status than substance. The DC was a kindly, taciturn New Zealander called Gordon Skipper. His instructions to me were 'Your job is to take an interest in the Africans in Mombasa, and to let me know of any signs of trouble'. Thus briefed, I spent a couple of hours with my predecessor, Donald Hodge, at a wooden office opposite the Majengo market. Adjacent was the *Mudir*, a charming young Arab, called Al Amin bin Said. The chief headman was Ali bin Namaan, a genial Swahili, who in his earlier days ran a brothel. There were two other headmen, one a huge Luo, the other a Taita from Wundanyi. These three, a couple of clerks and two Tribal Policemen constituted my staff. On the mainland there were some unpaid elders (*wazee*).

About three in every four Africans in Mombasa were employed. Most of these were adequately housed and regularly paid. I saw little of them. My dusty, hot little office in Majengo was more concerned with the self-employed, unemployed, vagrants, itinerant vendors, homeless, '*malaya*' (prostitutes), brothel keepers, debtors, unscrupulous landlords, quarrelsome tenants, tax defaulters, petty criminals, the sick, maimed and halt, and the riffraff in search of a quick shilling. Africans in their reserves were used to having headmen, elders, chiefs and District Officers available to cope with problems or provide some kind of rough justice. No such point of reference was readily available in Mombasa except an employer, or the District Officer. The trade unions were only concerned with their employees of the municipality and port.

So the DO's office was a mixture between a Citizen's Advice Bureau and a sorter out of little problems. When only Africans were involved I relied largely on the headmen or the African Court. Disputes between Africans and non-Africans were more complicated, particularly those involving landlords and tenants. Sometimes the *Mudir* and I would lean on a local landlord; at times I would visit the doss houses where Africans lived, often in crowded unsanitary conditions. There were no laws protecting tenants, but a visit or a threat of a visit by the Health Inspector usually made a landlord more reasonable. There was a good deal of petty crime; offenders usually pleaded guilty and went off for a spell in the detention camp or paid a fine. GBH and murder or serious thefts were referred to the police. There were many vagrants and the standard practice was to repatriate them to their reserves, hoping (often vainly) that they would not come back. Much of the violent crime took place in the brothels or in the vicinity of the beer halls. However given the size of the floating African community, the number of different tribes represented, and the poor living conditions, Mombasa was a remarkably peaceful place. There were no riots, and few strikes.

I spent mornings at Majengo and most afternoons on the mainland. The main job there was to clean up the filthy little townships by getting the local Health Inspector to issue orders to rebuild or improve shop premises. I spent a month running a vaccination campaign following an outbreak of smallpox – queues of Africans waiting to be jabbed, some complaining that if the *sindano* (needle) did not hurt, then the *dawa* (medicine) was no good. North of Mombasa Island was Freretown, founded in Victorian times by Sir Bartle Frere, for emancipated slaves. It was a little township surrounded by a forest of coconut trees which were the main source of palm wine for the Mombasa beer halls, and the scene of much drunkenness and brawling. In its midst stood (no doubt still stands) a large church, built when the slaves were freed, where the Christian gospel was taught by missionaries. I was the President of the Freretown Local Native Council, and the vice Chairman was a delightful man called Jimmy Jeremiah, the grandson of an emancipated slave. We met quarterly, using our limited funds to maintain the church, Jimmy and his few fellow Christians worshipped regularly in their church while the *tembo* tappers nearby brewed their *pombe* and got drunk.

Urban Work

GERALD PRATT

I reported to my new post as DO2 Mombasa, where I was based at the divisional office of Majengo. The DO Majengo, the district's other and senior DO, David Nicoll Griffith, presided good-naturedly over a brand-new office opposite the municipal *tembo* (beer) hall in the noisy slums of Majengo (literally, I suppose, 'building site'). It was handy for keeping a neighbourly eye on the numerous layabouts who had, as usual, consumed too much of the fermented coconut-palm sap, but otherwise it had absolutely nothing to commend it as a place to work; located in the very centre of the Island, it was ugly, pokey, hot and noisy. The great compensation was one's colleagues. Here I met up with the Arab officials and this time, I was working alongside them in a team under David's direction. More agreeable or helpful colleagues than the *Mudirs*, Sheikhs Rashid Ali el Riyamy and Masoud Mohamed Mahashamy, I could not have wished for.

Apart from the Old Town Ward, the historic heart of the city, where the *Liwali* of Mombasa held sway, Mombasa district was divided among the three of us, so we were all doing the same job, assisted by an exceptionally able group of ward chiefs. There was no safari in this smallest of all districts, though its extremities, abutting onto Kilifi and Kwale districts, were wholly rural. But there was a good deal of tramping about the dusty roads and alleys of the wards, accompanied by their respective chiefs. In this urban environment the arrival of a DO meant little to all those preoccupied with their daily town lives. So one's only companion was usually the chief himself, ready to describe all the varied problems – a standpipe not functioning, a particularly bad instance of overcrowding, a Tribal Policeman not up to the mark and so on. Being men of initiative, they usually had the measure of these problems and most were a matter of liaising with the appropriate government departmental officer or with the Mombasa Municipality, sometimes invoking the good offices of its African Affairs Officer, then John Gardner. There was no court work: the *Kadhis* looked after the *Sharia* and the resident Magistrate dealt with the rest. Majengo was a division and lacked the independence of a sub-district. Tax collection and all money matters were handled directly from the DC's Office.

A few months after my arrival, we were all heavily involved in helping to organise and supervise, in the Mombasa division of the coast constituency, the first national elections for African members of the Legislative Council. This was something new to everyone and it was a complex and fascinating administrative task to get it all set up from scratch. In the event it went without any serious hitch. The *Liwali* of Mombasa, Sheikh Al-Amin bin Said El-Mandhry, we two DOs and Sheikh Rashid, the *Mudir*, were the Presiding Officers at the four polling stations. The electorate had the choice of a motor car, an elephant, a tree, a hawk or a cock, choosing the last, which was thus magically transformed into the Honourable Ronald Ngala, MLC, a Giriama school-master, who later became a political leader.

Thereafter life became more routine though never dull. The inner wards had all the expected problems of inner city slum housing. Railway Ward, which included the docks at Kilindini, gave rise to sporadic labour troubles, but Chief David Kavyu had a good grip on most of these before they spread outside the industrial confines. The major civil engineering project on the Coast at that time, the extension of the Kilindini Harbour quays to Kipevu, had necessitated the importation of a labour force of strong and willing workers. With the Emergency Regulations still very much in force, the only practical source of these was Nyanza Province at the other side of the Colony. At the end of the day's labour in the steamy heat of Port Reitz, hundreds of these strong young Luo, far from their families, returned to their quarters in Chief David's ward.

I was visiting, in his company, one afternoon, the shanty town of *dukas* and cafes at Shimanzi as the workers were returning to the Island. It happened to be pay day. Outside one sizeable mud hut a cheerful queue had formed. Chief David explained the purpose of these premises and somewhat hesitantly asked me if I'd like to see inside: I knew I was not being asked to inspect or sample their facilities – no Kenya chief would have expected a DO to do that. The inside was painfully spartan, severely functional; the first room was empty for our scrutiny, the others were not and we did not penetrate further. We left the paying guests to get on with that. I had enough sense not to cavil with vigorous Luo labourers having their well-earned two shillings' worth. That was all it cost and the queue moved forward rapidly. I suppose some aspect of that establishment may have been illegal, but the need for it was so demonstrable that neither the chief nor I saw good reason to rock the boat. Their need may not have been greater than mine, but this was a social service and I've little doubt that the new docks at Kipevu were completed all the sooner for it.

Kipevu was over the water, in the vast Changamwe Ward on the mainland. Here, another highly-competent Kamba, Chief Judah Wilson Paul, coped with the entirely new issues being presented by widespread industrial and communications projects and the construction of purpose-built municipal housing estates for the rapidly-growing immigrant community from up-country. It was all ideal for showing the Governor around on a visit to the district. With Chief Judah's intelligent help, we were able to plan a suitable tour for our superiors when they accompanied HE to this rapidly-developing ward. Such preoccupations would keep me busy in the long, hot afternoons; the mornings were devoted to far more paperwork than I had previously experienced and to long meetings with David Nicoll Griffith and Peter Derrick, the District Commissioner. Every meeting produced another crop of varied things to be seen to, so the next day's agenda was never brief. Royal and gubernatorial visits relieved any tendency to monotony. That tendency never had time to develop because, at the close of 1957, I was translated to the PC's Office. A kaleidoscope of tasks and a rich helping of ceremony were to bring my first tour to an end.

The Joys of Nature

ERIC FOX

In February 1953 I went to Taveta on the Tanganyika border, a lovely spot with a two-storey DO's house built by Italian POWs. I woke each morning to a magnificent view of Kilimanjaro, which I was later to climb. The VIP local resident was Col. Ewart Grogan, of 'Cape to Cairo' fame, who had built himself a splendid house over-looking Lake Jipe. With some trepidation I paid him a courtesy visit. He received me at noon wearing only his dressing gown and explained that he had just taken his monthly purgative and had to be ready to dash. Despite his age he was alert mentally and great fun to listen to. I don't think the Kenya Government and Administration met entirely, if at all, with his approval.

My DC, who was stationed at Voi, Myles North, was a delightful man. He came to visit in a small Austin A40, which was crammed full of recording equipment. He was an internationally known recorder of bird song. We did chat a little about administrative matters but spent most of our time in Taveta Forest listening to and recording bird song.

I had little experience of African Court work and in Taveta was completely flummoxed when hearing a hard appeal case. The *Kiama* (court) record clearly indicated that the appellant had more than proved his case as did the evidence I had heard. It was only when one of the leaders, the Chairman of the *Kiama* in the original hearing, referred to the respondent as his eldest son that the penny dropped. I upheld the appeal.

A District Officer and the Law

PHILIP JONES

Life can sometimes seem very perverse. I have always been attracted by the law and I studied very hard for the Kenya Administration law exam, with the hope of obtaining a distinction. I sat the exam in the DC's office at Kabarnet, together with the DC, a charming if sometimes unconventional officer, who was himself belatedly taking it too. We sat across his office table and his idea of invigilation appeared to be to grab each of my answers as soon as I had completed it – for him, a sort of self-service rather than self-invigilation. I am glad to say that we both passed, but neither with distinction. He went on to be knighted after leaving the service.

Shortly afterwards I was told that I had been selected for a Second Devonshire Course at Oxford and was asked what subject I wished to specialise in. On the advice of a colleague who had done it, I asked to specialise in law, with a view to taking the bar exam. My request was turned down so I opted for agriculture. On my return to Kenya I was posted as senior DO in North Nyanza, where my duties were almost entirely legal, with no interest in agriculture at all. I sat for one or two days a week in the magistrate's court at Kakamega and the remainder of my time was spent on safari supervising the eight African Divisional courts and two Appeal courts. I also acted as a further court of Appeal from the latter.

My next posting was as DC Maralal, a cattle district with no arable farming. The magisterial duties were light, consisting mainly of the occasional case of stock theft. From there I was posted to Central Government – where else but to the Ministry of Agriculture.

Having passed the law exam, I was gazetted as a first class magistrate with powers to sentence an offender to up to three years in prison, or a substantial fine (sentences over a year being subject to confirmation by a judge). One held court in the District Office or, as in Kakamega, in a special courthouse. In cases involving Africans, proceedings were conducted in Swahili, with an interpreter translating from Swahili into the local vernacular. Whilst speaking in Swahili, the magistrate had to keep a record of the proceedings in English in longhand. One needed, of course, to be fluent in Swahili.

I think that most administrative officers, in carrying out their magisterial duties, were more concerned with doing justice, rather than observing the letter of the law. Unfortunately this was not a view which was always shared by the learned Judges in Nairobi.

In a case at Kakamega a man was charged before me with stealing a quantity of blankets, or alternatively with receiving them knowing that they were stolen. The blankets had been found buried in his *shamba*. The accused produced an ingenious story that whilst on remand he had met another man who had asked him what he was charged with. When he told him, the other remand prisoner claimed that he himself had stolen the blankets and buried them in a spot which, quite by chance, turned out to be the accused's *shamba*. Needless to say, the other remand prisoner was not produced in court.

Now I had learned that when a person was found in possession of stolen property, there was a presumption in law that he was either the thief or had received the property knowing it to be stolen. I did not believe the accused's explanation for a moment, so it seemed an open and shut case. Unusually, the accused was represented by a clever Kisumu lawyer who argued volubly that there was no direct evidence that the accused had himself stolen the blankets. Eventually, partly to save time, I agreed to proceed on the charge of receiving only. With little more ado I convicted and sentenced the accused.

With the help of his lawyer the accused appealed against his conviction and a learned Judge in Nairobi allowed the Appeal. Apparently I had erred in dropping the theft charge and should have proceeded with both charges in order to convict. This did not appear to me to be justice, but I did at least have the satisfaction of knowing that the accused must have had to pay the lawyer a pretty fat fee.

Perhaps the most unusual case I had to deal with as a magistrate was when a man was brought before me charged with unnatural intercourse with a cow. The owner of the cow and three witnesses had evidently rehearsed their evidence well, each adding a little more artistic verisimilitude to the story. The accused was naturally distraught and claimed that the whole story was a fabrication. He said that he had actually been making love to the wife of the owner of the cow and when he heard people approaching, he had slipped out and hidden in the cattle *boma* where he had been discovered. Once again the accused's story had a definite ring of truth, but it was only his word against that of his four accusers. I therefore found myself in a quandary. However, I remembered that adultery was considered to be a serious offence under the local African law. I therefore convicted him, reminded him that even what he had admitted to was a serious offence, and gave him the rather lesser sentence than he would have received for adultery under African law and custom.

In the African courts one had much greater discretion to dispense justice without the judges breathing down one's neck. One travelled around the district with an interpreter and two African 'assessors' appointed to advise on African law and custom. The courthouses were built of mud and wattle with low side walls for the convenience of spectators. They were set out on the lines of an English court and the elders wore distinctive robes. However the majority of the Appeals I had to hear concerned disputes over land ownership. These had to be heard on the ground, sitting under a convenient tree if possible, often with a partisan audience seated around. Early on, when hearing a case about a disputed boundary, I naively held up the remains of a maize cob and asked the spectators which of the two parties had actually cultivated it. Of course half of them voted for one party and half for the other.

In nearly all cases both sides appeared to be genuinely convinced that they had right on their side and it was virtually impossible to reconcile their conflicting evidence in any way. Fortunately one had brief records of the proceedings in the lower courts to refer to and one did not often disturb the decision of the African Appeal court without good reason. Even so, one's decision was generally received with distress by the losing party and one sometimes went away wondering whether justice had actually been done.

I always felt uneasy when a rich or powerful man made a claim against a 'little' man. At Mumias I had to deal with an appeal involving members of a local tribal group which still maintained some sort of traditional form of chiefdom, along side the government-appointed chief of the location. A group of elders, acting on behalf of this 'chief' sued two men for land, which they had clearly cultivated for some time. The 'chief' did not at first put in an appearance. I was told that it would not be seemly for him to do so and that the case was therefore being taken on his behalf. I could not accept this and next day an unimpressive young man appeared before me who seemed to have little idea what the case was about. Broadly it seemed to be based on an assertion that all the land had once belonged to the chiefly family and he now wanted it back. I allowed the appeal.

My decision was clearly not popular among the local elders. Not long after that my then DC died in tragic circumstances and I took over the district. An anthropologist who was working in the Mumias area reported to me a local rumour that when someone in authority dies in unusual circumstances, one does not have to look further than to his successor to find out who had been responsible. Old East African hands may recognise this as a typical case of *fitina*, ie. spreading malicious gossip about someone you do not like.

One final case from the African courts may raise a smile. An ancient lady sued a young man for the return of her bride price that had been paid when she was first married. She explained with a wicked smile displaying a single tooth, that the young man had inherited her according to the local African custom, but that he refused to sleep with her. She therefore claimed that the marriage was at an end and she wanted the bride price back. Both lower courts had found in her favour but my sympathy was naturally with the defendant. After studying the African Courts manual, I eventually found a let-out and ruled that the lower courts' decisions were 'repugnant to British law and practice'. I am glad to say that my decision was upheld by an Appeal committee which had by then been set up to hear exceptional appeals from the decisions of DOs.

When I moved to Maralal things were very different. There were no African court appeals and only a small number of magistrate's cases to hear. The *moran*, ie. the young warrior class, having been deprived of their traditional manly pursuits, were left with little else to do to prove their manhood other than seducing the younger wives of the elders and the occasional stock theft from the neighbouring European farms. There was a long-established and well-known tariff for anyone convicted of stock theft: three years in gaol. Nevertheless, not yet having been contaminated by civilisation as we know it, when the culprits were brought before the court, they readily admitted their guilt. One did however, have to make sure that they were closely guarded as occasionally one of the accused, on being sentenced, would go into convulsions and have to be restrained. It was a great sadness to have to sentence such virile young men to lengthy periods in prison because one knew that they would probably catch TB there and some would not come back at all. However, one did not dare relax the sanctions against stock theft.

As a tailpiece I might add that, on my return to the UK, I found employment in the industrial relations Directorate of the Confederation of British Industry – hardly an occupation for which my colonial service experience had qualified me. However, I went on to specialise in industrial relations law. I served for eight years as an employer member of industrial tribunals, which were originally set up to provide a cheap, speedy and informal system of justice – 'something on the colonial model'. In this they failed dismally.

A Popular Judgement

TED ALLEYNE

I wonder how often a Kenya DO acting as a magistrate was loudly cheered after delivering a judgement in his court – not often probably.

The circumstances of this particular matter were common enough in the Kilifi District, where it occurred in 1961 or thereabouts, when I was stationed at Kilifi headquarters. An elderly woman in the south of the district contracted pulmonary TB and was sent to the Port Reitz Chest Hospital near Mombasa where she reacted well to the treatment. However, she did not appreciate being confined to the hospital and ran away after a few weeks. She was caught and returned by medical orderlies sent to find her. (It should perhaps be mentioned that such highly infectious patients were legally confined in hospital for treatment until cured, at the discretion of the MO). After this had occurred several times the MO apparently decided to leave the matter be, since she seemed to be reluctant to be cured, was less infectious and he had better things to do than chase one patient while many others needed and appreciated treatment. She had no children to infect and no doubt the MO acted in the best general interest.

Shortly afterwards the woman died of her TB at her home in Rabai. Her husband being long dead, her only son and heir sought out a witch-finder to identify the person who had so obviously caused her death by witchcraft. The witch-finder charged him one hundred shillings, quite a large sum in those days and pointed the finger at an elderly man living alone nearby, half-blind and rather wobbly on his legs, as I remember. He owned about half an acre of land, about a dozen goats, a few chickens, a couple of coconut palms and a few cashews and eked out the usual bare living. On being accused of his alleged crime by the son, the old man naturally denied it, whereupon the son filed a suit against him in the local African Court for restitution of the one hundred shillings paid to the witch-finder for the identification – but not for causing his mother's death, which was anyway well beyond the court's jurisdiction. Luckily for both of them he took no other action. The usual course of events in such matters was for the aggrieved party to get roaring drunk on palm wine, stoke up his anger and slash his presumed oppressor with a panga, usually killing him and attracting a death sentence as a result. These sentences were often commuted.

The local African Court decided in the plaintiff's favour and ordered payment by the defendant of the hundred shillings plus the court fees, at that time about three shillings, if memory serves. The aggrieved defendant appealed to the Southern Division African Appeal Court at Kaloleni, paying a further few shillings in fees, but the wise men there upheld the lower court's decision. After all, everyone knew witchcraft was rife, ought to be discouraged and witches exposed, and clearly the young man should have his money back.

Much aggrieved, the old man travelled the twenty-five miles or so to Kilifi to lodge another appeal with the District African Appeal Court, paying another few shillings in fees. In course of time the appeal was heard and again the elders agreed with the lower courts and dismissed it.

That is where I came in. As DO1 it was my job to supervise the African Courts and the appeal case file duly came up to be perused. At the same time the old man, now incensed and exercising his legal rights under the African Courts Ordinance, lodged a further appeal in the Magistrate's court against the finding.

What all the courts had ignored was that the African Courts Ordinance expressly prohibited the hearing by such courts of cases where death was alleged to have occurred in the events leading to the case being filed. Perhaps it was a fine point, but in this one I thought it was valid and the case should never have been heard. It was notable that none of the courts concerned had heard, seen or called for evidence from the so-called witch-finder whose accusation seemed to have been accepted as gospel truth, unquestioned and undeniable. Considering that the Witchcraft Ordinance did not admit the actual existence of witchcraft, and spoke only of 'pretending to practice witchcraft', the prohibition of African Courts hearing cases where death had occurred and common sense dictating, I decided to allow the appeal and award the full costs to the old man, amounting now to around forty shillings. There was also, of course, a letter from the Medical Officer at Port Reitz Chest Hospital laying out the condition of the deceased old lady, which effectively disposed of simple witchcraft as the cause of death. While there had not been a Police investigation or post-mortem there was no suggestion of poisoning or other physical method of speeding the old lady to her death.

The Magistrate's Court was next to my office, and was capable of seating perhaps fifty people in fair comfort on a cool day. When the case was called there must have been nearer a hundred attentive listeners, mostly young men and a few girls, including both the parties. Having listened to the judgement with great attention as I read it, the spectators erupted in cheers and were hustled out by outraged clerks and orderlies.

Why the decision was so popular I never really found out. The Court Clerk and the interpreter naturally said it was a just decision – they had little choice – and I thought so too. The elders in the string of African

Courts concerned were reminded of the provisions of the African Courts and Witchcraft Ordinances, and there it ended, leaving some rather upset court elders who still believed firmly in all the powers of darkness.

A Failure of Justice

ROGER HORRELL

Dipping randomly into the catalogue of infinite duties, I pull out the subject of courts and court work. In particular the case in which I had to ask the High Court to set aside one of my own Judgements. It appeared straightforward. A prominent local farmer was accused of watering his milk. Of course, he denied it vehemently. I cannot remember whether the official responsible for monitoring the quality of milk was a Veterinary man or a Health man. Let us simply call him the Milk Man. I do clearly recall that he had a state of the art instrument which, when dipped in milk, acted as a litmus test. The accused's milk had failed this test. Only water added after milking could cause this result. As magistrate I quizzed the Milk Man closely as to the accuracy of his instrument. With total certainly and, I believe, honesty, he assured the court that it was infallible. The farmer was convicted and fined. The papers were sent off to Nairobi. I took some pleasure from the Judgement because the accused was one of the most vociferous opponents of grazing control.

A few days later the farmer came to my office and said he wished to talk to me as his DO not as magistrate. Would I come to see his cows milked and bring the Milk Man and his infallible instrument with me? Early the next morning we three plus a small gallery of spectators watched as a boy milked a cow into an empty bucket. The instrument was inserted. It showed the milk to be watered. But this was impossible. Another cow and another. Same result. The Milk Man conceded he had never seen anything like it. The fact was that the grazing was so poor and the cattle so emaciated that the milk was sub standard without dilution. The High Court duly annulled my judgement. The farmer failed to draw the obvious conclusion about land management. But justice was done.

THE ADMINISTRATOR'S DAY

Sport and Education

ERIC GORDON

International recognition of the prowess of Kenyan athletes had its dawning with official encouragement of competitive sport in the early 1950s, when primary education was also spreading to the more outlying districts. However, as this sidelight recalls, such affairs did not just come, they had to be brought to pass.

A morning in May 1952 and it must have been a Monday, for both Dick Wilson, the DC, and I, his DO were together in the office (as Tuesday to Friday one of us was normally on safari). The setting is the West Suk (later Pokot) *boma* at Kapenguria, situated at about 7400 feet in the north-western part of Rift Valley Province. Beyond, the hill ranges of the district were well over ten thousand feet, incised by valleys and over to eastward, the precipitous escarpment down to the scrub and camels in the Rift Valley, at an elevation of some three thousand five hundred feet. Good country for exercise when, needs must, you got around on your feet, and for protection men carried a couple of spears.

Dick was going through the mail, and with a 'Would you like to deal with this one? Let me know after lunch what you propose', I was passed a letter from the Provincial Commissioner 'Monkey' Johnston, with a couple of roneod sheets from the colony sports officer, Evans, at Kabete. The tenor of the PC's covering letter indicated that this, as in his eyes any sport, should be taken seriously. It seemed that I had better organise something, especially as there was in prospect an outing to Nakuru with a district team for the Provincial Sports. I suggested that Bill Oglenby be asked if we could use the field of his Secondary School for district sports and preliminary heats for the nearer locations; that somewhere we should have a similar initial local sportsday for the locations to the north-east, when Dick and his wife might like a day out and perhaps Dottie present the prizes; and for which and sundry expenses could I please raid the 'goat bag'? (The last being the small reserve of petty cash variously accrued but unaccountable.) It was so agreed. I wrote some notes in my duplicate letter book and called for Barabara, the District Messenger, a small wiry man with a ready smile. I asked him to take the first note to the Chief at Sebit, some twenty five miles away down a bumpy road; the next day to go on to give my compliments to Chief Lokori up at Mbara; then to take the last note on to Sigor and return to Sebit, where I would meet him on Thursday and bring him back. As he

55

set off happily at his usual fast trot, I thought 'there's my volunteer for the marathon'.

The following day, I went down to Sebit with TP Daniel Awosit. He had served in 3 KAR in the Burma campaign, later in government service as a driver; then after a fall from grace (due to a taste for tippling) he was re-employed as a Tribal Policeman, and acted as my driver, interpreter, orderly and companion on safari. He came from the Sebit area and in later years became its chief. We pitched camp on our regular site, which I then realised was unsuitable for a sports ground – too many trees and the stream was an unnecessary obstacle. Then we were joined by Father Byrne, of the White Fathers' Mission at Tartar. He had come through the Marich Pass on his way back from Lomut, a location centre with a Somali *duka*, at the foot of the escarpment. He had been to make arrangements for the new Primary School there which the Mission had been given permission to open in September. His problem was to get recruits; particularly as most of the population in the school's potential catchment area sensibly lived on ledges thousands of feet up the escarpment, where it was cooler and free of mosquitoes. My concern was getting likely lads to the forthcoming sports, which, like schooling, was another new concept for the Pokot.

After supper we were about to play poker and Father Byrne suggested that if he won perhaps I could ensure that there would be twelve boys from upper Lomut enrolled for Standard One in September. Experience suggested that I would shortly have a new commitment. In return I was assured that the sports would have his blessing and he would see that the young men from Tartar would be competing at Kapenguria.

Next morning Daniel and I went a few miles along the motorable track to Ortum, where an Indian had a *duka* and a Somali traded. We stopped to have a look at the ground behind the shops; although it was sloping gently and bestrewn with largish rocks, it could serve as a sports field. It would be relatively accessible and also do for the evening *ngoma*, which I was advised would be the real draw. We resumed our drive to Marich, and then walked the seven miles up the path to Mbara, where we duly met Chief Lokori. He was an impressive old gentleman, who appreciated being called upon by appointment rather than summoned. Incidentally, I had heard indirectly that Lokori had been quietly impressed when he learnt that previously Daniel and I had climbed by its north side to the summit of Mtelo, the mountain behind his homestead. Now however, the important thing was to get his support for the forthcoming Ortum sportsday and to ensure participation of his young men; especially as the other chiefs in the area usually followed his lead. We parted in the evening with his assurance and an indication that he would personally come down and watch.

Although 'sponsorship' was then in my future vocabulary, I did call on the shopkeeper at Ortum on Thursday morning, to invite him to provide a few prizes, like blankets, cooking pots and beads. Then Daniel and I did a recce on the ground to check we could get a circuit of approximately 440 yards, with a straight for sprints. We also had a brisk walk around a potential course for longer events, along which some Tribal Policemen could be posted to deter chums from taking the short cuts, which I recalled from school cross-country runs. After some jottings in my field note-book, it was back to the land-rover, meet up with Barabara at Sebit, then back to the *boma* and to other jobs.

Ortum sportsday had been fixed for the next full moon, for a better *ngoma*. When the day came Daniel and I set off at dawn with a collection of kit: borrowed stopwatch, jump stands, javelin and discus; string, stationery, including the Kabete guidance sheets giving performance standards to aim for, and some useful afterthoughts like a couple of extra mattocks and pangas. On arrival, the large safari tent had been pitched by the advance party sent down the previous evening in the lorry, and a collection of stakes made ready as markers. The working party set to, with some early-arriving enthusiasts enrolled as extras to help shift a few offending rocks. By noon we had a steady stream of 'probables', curious 'possibles', others just curious, and present, but somehow out of the way, the girl friends. Then Dick and Dottie Wilson joined and we began to get some order into things, to cease the skylarking and introduce practise of such new evolutions as high jumping and discus throwing.

We started with one of the longer races, which got a number of people occupied off site; then, with space created, began the javelin. Except for a final, entrants used their own spears, and only the poorest failed to exceed the standard. Thus encouraged, and reasonably pleased with how it was going, it was on to the 440. A last briefing and a fair start, then half way around, the second runner decided that it seemed more sensible and clearly quicker to cut straight across to the finish, an example followed by most of the others. Cheers and uproar! Dick and Dottie convulsed into laughter, and I, whilst appreciating the performance, sought to restore order and try again. This somehow set the tone for the day, as people not only enjoyed these strange games but found that they could do rather well. The half-marathon lads loped in from a circuit around the nearer hills, also within the standard time. We somehow got through the rest of the programme, made sense of results for Dottie's prize-giving, followed by a good short speech by Dick, and words of encouragement from no less than Chief Lokori.

The later District Sports were an anti-climax in a way, the boys from the backwoods having learnt the form and the Education Department more in control. But it was good practice for those chosen to represent us at the Provincial Sports. Lest they got diverted, we kept that team at the *boma* for a few days, before they went in our lorry and the Livestock Officer's pick-up to Nakuru. There the team met their related tribes like the Nandi, and their match. They returned slightly chastened, but, having performed creditably, were happy. Some even realised that there was something in what the *Bwana Mdogo* was saying about training; others were already thinking of next year's party. The seeds had been sown.

Lastly, there remained the matter of Lomut School. Daniel and I later went to upper Lomut by walking across the Cherangani watershed, which was the Elgeyo border. That meant a three day safari over the tops, across a valley, then down to the huts of Puruwon perched along the ledge overlooking the Rift. Next morning we assembled for a *baraza*. I addressed them on the theme of change and the need for education, so leading to the necessary boys for Standard One at the *Dini ya Catholiki* school shortly to open at Lomut.

When we resumed after a break, the spokesman for the elders stood up, leant on his spear, spat and paused for effect. A natural and experienced orator, he addressed us all. He thanked me for coming, and for the manner of our journey to them; they had listened with interest to my message. There was however an essentially philosophical problem. They had taught their sons to grow up to be useful men, but how were they to know the benefits of this schooling thing? They had thought on this and had a proposition for me. They would arrange, as I had asked, for twelve good young boys to report for school. Further, they would see that they diligently attended; but no more entrants until their schooling had been completed and they became young men. Then if they were better young men than those who had not been to school, the point would be proven and 'education' would be fully supported. I thanked him for such a well-considered reply, and respecting his wisdom, agreed to the proposal. After all I had the schoolboys for Father Byrne, my undertaking was met, and by the following September, I would be posted elsewhere.

Athletics and the Administration

MICHAEL PHILIP

On first appointment I was posted to Kisii, which was then the Administrative Headquarters of South Nyanza District. On my way there I made a courtesy visit to the Provincial Commissioner, Harold 'Ngombe' Williams, a great sportsman in his youth. As I was leaving he decreed 'I expect to see you running in the Provincial Sports'. Sure enough the first task given to me by my District Commissioner was responsibility for sport. As an aside he mentioned that my duties would also include Traffic Magistrate, DO, *boma* in charge of the Tribal Police and assisting with Eastern Division. As the annual build-up to District and Provincial Sports was already under way, the running of sports meetings and the selection and training of the district team to compete in the Provincial Sports took up most of my time immediately.

The Kisii locations were all very keen on athletics; the Luo of the south rather less. Athletics in the Colony as a whole, and in Kisii in particular, had recently had a considerable injection of enthusiasm as a result of the relatively good showing of the fledgeling Kenya team at the Commonwealth Games in Australia. Two of the team were Kisii, Nyandika Maioro and Arere Anentia. The former was employed by the African District Council and the latter was a Tribal Policeman and I forthwith made him my orderly. Later, however, the Kenya Police lured him away to strengthen their team for the Colony Sports.

The routine in most districts was for sub-chiefs to hold Sub-location Sports; then the sub-locations would compete at the Location Sports. From this event would be chosen the location team to compete in the District Sports. In parallel to this the schools would hold their sports and usually a district would have several secondary school athletes in the team on merit. Although this routine was organised by the Administration, once the district team was selected it was the responsibility of the African District Council to house and pay 'subsistence' to the athletes. The level of subsistence allowance was always a cause of discontent and there were always agitators in the team who demanded more. Another cause of discontent was training. The athletes were very happy to be housed, fed and paid by the ADC, but not so happy when dragooned into circuit training and exercises.

The Kisii are very good middle and long-distance runners but very poor at field events. Thus, during training one spent more time with shot, discus, javelin and hammer throwers than with the runners. They would be left in the hands of the more senior runners, such as Nyandika, to pound the track and practice starts. Despite time spent trying to improve the technique of the throwers, the result remained poor. Although a 440 runner at University, I ended up for several years and for several districts and provinces, throwing things, *faute de mieux*.

At that time there was always a problem persuading competent people to assist with the judging and timekeeping. District Sports took up several days. Heats usually took two days before the finals. Departmental Officers would be loath to spend time at the heats but would be happy to officiate at the finals.

A popular event was the tug-of-war. At my first District Sports, the favourites, Nyaribari Location, were quite correctly disqualified by the Judge, a PWD Officer. Their chief, the venerable Senior Chief Musa

Nyandusi appealed to the ultimate authority, the DC, who luckily upheld the disqualification. Musa threatened to withdraw his team, but was eventually mollified. Nyaribari won the Sports despite the disqualification. A member of the Kisii team chosen that year was a son of Senior Chief Musa, called Simeon Nyachae, later to become a senior civil servant and politician. At that time he was a mediocre long jumper.

In those days, a further chore was marking out the tracks and throws. Later Community Development Assistants and District Council Sports Assistants were trained to do this, but in the 1950s the DOs did it.

That year South Nyanza came fifth in the Provincial Sports despite the middle-distance excellence of the Kisii runners. When the build-up to the next athletics season came I was in charge of the Nyamira Sub-Station in the north Kisii Highlands and much busier than the newly arrived Cadet of last year. The difficulties were much the same: finding officers to help in particular. A great plus was a new DC, Gordon Skipper, a keen all-round games player who let everyone know that the showing of the district at the Provincial Sports was important.

As usual the training of the district team was a losing battle for at least the first two days but eventually they settled down to an early morning and an evening session. That year South Nyanza pulled up to third at the Provincial Sports, but again the Kisii runners monopolised the middle-distances. Apart from the Kisii the acknowledged athletes mainly came from the Kalenjin group of tribes – the Nandi, Kipsigis and Tugen in particular.

By the time of the next athletics season, I had been posted to Baringo, the home of the Tugen. Once more I was 'volunteered' by the DC to run the Sports. As well as the Tugen the district had a small population of pastoralists, the Suk. They were great warriors when defending their stock, but were not athletes.

As with the Kisii, the Tugen were poor at the throwing events. To try to improve this, I chose the largest of the Tugen TPs to be my orderly and every morning, that we were not on safari, I coached him in the shot, discus and hammer before breakfast.

The major rival to Baringo at the Provincial Sports was the Nandi District. That year Baringo pressed them hard, but Nandi won.

One major problem for districts was the poaching of their best athletes by the Army and Kenya Police. At the annual Colony Sports the Army and the Police each competed as teams against the Provinces. The Army, in particular, took their athletics very seriously. Officers and NCOs from the King's African Rifles frequently attended District and Provincial Sports meetings spying on form. As I mentioned earlier the Police poached Arere, the Kisii six-miler.

After two athletics seasons in Baringo, I was posted to Nandi District, the breeding ground of many of Kenya's champion athletes. Again I was asked to be responsible for sports. In Nandi however, I was not alone. There was an excellent Community Development Officer, Ted Harris, who had been in the district many years. Kapsabet, the District Headquarters had a very good stadium. Apart from the usual School and Location Sports culminating in the Provincial Sports, a very popular biennial event was a Triangular Sports meeting between Kericho (Kipsigis tribe), Nandi and Kisii. Between them those three districts provided a large proportion of the best athletes in Kenya. My second year in Nandi was our turn to host the Triangular meeting. The district team was called into the *boma* a week before the meeting. I had hoped that the standard of athlete we had would be enthusiastic. This was not to be. They, through one or two agitators, immediately demanded a considerable increase in their 'subsistence' payment, and accused the DO (me) of working them too hard. The African District Council refused to increase their payment, so the team refused to train. Faced with this intransigence and after consulting the DC and Ted Harris, we called their bluff and sent them home. We were left with those who could not strike – these were TPs, Police and Army athletes who had been called in, and others employed by government in some capacity. This rearguard numbered fifteen with me. The spirit of this rump of the team was terrific. All volunteered to run or throw as second strings of events not normally theirs, so we managed to fill in every event. By sheer determination and guts the Nandi David beat the Kipsigis Goliath. The Kisii team were not in the reckoning that year, but were the final factor in the Nandi win. It all depended on the last event, the 4 x 440 relay. Nandi had a good chance of winning this event but to win the meeting Kericho had to come third. Thanks to an outstanding effort by Kisii's middle distance stars Nyandika and Arere, they came second to Nandi and the mighty Kericho team was beaten. The Nandi win did not prevent the ADC from blaming me for the strike, conveniently forgetting the subsistence factor.

Kenyan athletes have shone in world competitions for the last forty years and many theories have been put forward to explain this phenomenon. The majority of successful athletes have come from the Nilo-Hamitic tribes and the Kisii. Can physique or diet explain it, or what is the secret of their success? One answer to this question must be that Kenyan athletes were first encouraged to compete by passing through the system organised by the Administration, through inter-schools sports inter-location sports and Colony Sports. There are other factors. All their running was done at high altitude. All the children ran to school, up and down steep valleys. A factor that did not enter the equation until American universities tempted the athletes from Kenya with scholarships, was serious, scientific training. Without the early input of young, mostly British DOs, who passed on to the chiefs the spirit of rivalry and location and district esprit de corps that they had learned in their schools and universities, the whole network of athletics meetings would never have started.

There is a tongue-in-cheek definition of the Colonial Empire as being 'thousands of millions of browns, hundreds of millions of blacks ruled by a handful of blues'.

A Young Man's Job

PETER DEMPSTER

I have happy memories of Runyenjes, the northern division of Embu, where I succeeded Dennis Lakin. Emergency conditions prevailed, and 'Detention Orders' were in use for those believed to be actively supporting Mau Mau, but against whom no witness was willing to give evidence in court. These orders were signed by the DC, on the recommendation of one of his DOs.

Peter Derrick was DC during at least part of my time at Runyenjes, Frank Loyd being Provincial Commissioner at Nyeri. Frank's visits were helpful, though often alarming. 'What is the name of that school/hill/coffee factory/headman?' he would ask, with the air of already knowing the correct answer. At Embu itself, John Tennent and Roger Hosking, as successive DO1s, were both blessed with a dry sense of humour, and a thorough knowledge of the 'Book of Rules': they were more than capable of curbing the enthusiasms of those of us who were out in the bush. One of their standard phrases was 'I'll mention your view to the DC, but I don't see him agreeing'. John and his wife Peggy, as well as Roger and Armorel, were extremely hospitable and gladly provided accommodation if one had to stay overnight in Embu. On these visits we could have golf or squash at the Embu Club, and the 'Izaak Walton' hotel provided curry lunches.

Urgent communication between DOs in the field, and District HQ were by 'Morning Prayers'. The DO1 would call up each division in turn by radio. As well as giving our own reports and complaints we could all hear what was going on in other divisions.

Runyenjes was well developed. There were numerous small plots of high quality coffee in the upper areas. Terracing had been carried out and agriculture was, by and large, very progressive. Dan Kimani was my young and efficient Asst. DO. Amongst our chiefs was the outstanding Ephantus Njage of Ngandori Location. I have remained in touch and visited Ephantus and Dan over the years. Both of them continued to serve after Independence.

At Runyenjes I was able to indulge in my mania for building. Examples were a massive Community Hall, in the township, and a new TP canteen, both still in use thirty years later. Beautiful honey coloured building stone was bought from the local quarries, in blocks, ready for use. Our crowning glory was a memorial, fifteen feet high and vaguely phallic in design, to the memory of Chief Ephantus's father, who had first introduced coffee to the area. For this we somehow commissioned a Carrara marble plaque, depicting a coffee bush, with a suitably fulsome inscription, in KiEmbu. This unique edifice was still intact in the 1980s.

The Emergency ended during the latter part of my stay at Runyenjes. Over the years support for terrorism had dwindled. The bulk of the people were looking for a return to normal conditions, and for a lead from politicians who had not been involved in violence. Gradually we were able to concern ourselves with really creative projects, such as Land Consolidation, and the fostering of local government, through locational and divisional councils. It was now also possible for us to hold the celebrated drumming festivals, on the football pitch at Runyenjes, where teams of drummers would compete before an audience of thousands of vociferous supporters.

When I was actually handing over Runyenjes to my successor, there came word that a leopard had carried off a calf, but had now been surrounded in a patch of thorn-bush, 'Would I please attend to the matter?' I grabbed my shotgun (the best weapon I felt, for self-defence!) and set out in the land-rover, with a couple of TPs, leaving my successor to check the contents of the divisional armoury. At the scene I found an impasse. The half acre of scrub in which the leopard was said to be concealed was by now surrounded by spear-toting locals. Someone suggested that we set fire to the scrub. Amidst blinding smoke the leopard emerged, snarling horribly, and knocked down the man next to me. At point blank range I fired both barrels, luckily without effect. The leopard departed unscathed. When I got back to Runyenjes my successor, whose name I have forgotten, was brooding over some discrepancy that he had discovered in the armoury and was uninterested in the gripping details or our leopard hunt.

The Coloured Shirt

PETER DEMPSTER

I had been in Marsabit a short while, and Sheila was down in Nairobi awaiting the arrival of our first-born. A letter arrived from Provincial Headquarters, asking all DCs to bring down a team of the best shots amongst their TPs for the annual inter-district rifle competition. This was to be on a

Friday, and we were invited to stay on at Isiolo over the weekend, for various social activities, but to make our own arrangements for accommodation, which meant battening on friends in or near Isiolo. In my case, I think I stayed with Richard and Rose Luce: Richard was then a DO, later to rise to ministerial and cabinet rank in London.

I took it that the rifle-shoot, as well as the weekend, was to be a social occasion, and all would probably have been well, had I not suffered from colour-blindness. The weather was extremely hot, so I wore a shirt, khaki shorts and sandals. Other DCs were similarly clad for the shoot: no one was in uniform and some wore 'brothel-creepers' (desert boots). As the competition progressed I noticed a certain coolness towards me on the part of the PC's party, especially when it became obvious that we, the Marsabit team, seemed in the running for first prize. In the event we were third, as I recollect, which still entailed the presentation to our team of some form of trophy. Again I noted an atmosphere of unease, for which I could not find any cause.

The weekend went well, with drinks and dinner parties, and on the Monday we all set out to return to our districts.

About a week later a letter arrived, from someone at Provincial Headquarters addressed to all. It read roughly as follows: –

'The inter-district rifle competition has long been regarded as a social occasion. District Commissioners are however reminded that the custom has always been that appropriate clothing for such an event is khaki shorts, a white shirt, stockings and brown shoes. On no account will coloured, especially pink, shirts be worn, and the same prohibition applies to sandals.'

As I have said, I am colour-blind. I had no idea that I was wearing a pink shirt: the colour 'pink' means nothing to me! I believed my shirt to be buff, or some other inoffensive colour. As for the sandals, these were of excellent quality, well polished leather, and what I normally wore around the *boma* at Marsabit, other than on formal occasions. I was taken aback that what was in effect a rebuke to me should be mentioned, in a general circular, to all my colleagues.

My friend Johnny Balfour, DC Moyale, who generally stayed with us, on his way to Isiolo or Nairobi, also of course, received a copy of these 'instructions as to dress'. He was good enough to give me his opinion on the whole matter. Even after thirty-six years I must refrain from quoting what he said, which was both very reassuring and even combative!

I still, on occasion, wear pink, believing it to be some other and muted colour. But it has never since been the subject of an official circular, or even of social consequence.

Politics in Fort Hall

DAVID NICOLL GRIFFITH

In 1959, when we arrived at Fort Hall, once at the centre of the Mau Mau uprising, military operations against the gangs had finished and the Emergency was effectively over. There was, however, still a close administration in the locations and the people were still in the villages which had been set up at the start of the Emergency. There were here and there other reminders of what had gone on in this place but a few years previously. I shall always retain the memory of a wooden cross by the roadside not far from Fort Hall, with Mount Kenya in the distance as a backdrop. The inscription commemorated a District Officer killed by terrorists at Gakuruwe.

Even at the height of the troubles the number of terrorists had not been large and not all Kikuyu had supported them. Indeed, we all admired the courage and strength of character of the Kikuyu who remained loyal to the government; many were killed for their refusal to aid the gangs, their families massacred and their homes burned. Not that they may not have wanted to move towards Independence, but they saw that the bestiality and violence of Mau Mau were not the way to achieve anything. The Anglican Church at Fort Hall was the cathedral church of the Fort Hall diocese and its bishop was himself a Kikuyu, the Rt. Rev. Obadiah Kariuki. The church, dedicated to St James and all Martyrs, had been built as a memorial to the loyal Kikuyu who had fallen, many of their relatives and those who survived having contributed towards the cost. There is in it a set of superb murals, painted with an African motif by an African artist and depicting events in the life of Christ.

The ending of the Mau Mau Emergency heralded the beginning of a more acceptable expression of political aims, namely the formation of African political parties properly constituted. As far as Fort Hall was concerned this meant the Kenya African National Union (KANU); at the outset it was exclusively Kikuyu in membership, and there followed many months of campaigning by Kikuyu politicians. The theme was, of course, Independence for the country with KANU forming the government, and this message was promoted by all kinds of cajoling and propaganda at large public gatherings. Kikuyu would come from all parts of the district to attend these, and the police were fully extended in covering them.

One day I was returning to Fort Hall in our car with my wife and two-year old son. As we rounded a bend we found the road blocked by a huge crowd of Kikuyu who were making their way to a political gathering. They were already in an excited state, evidenced by their dance-like movements and ululations from the women. We edged our way through at a very slow pace, the entire car surrounded by the crowd; I knew full well that if a wheel had gone over somebody's foot we would have been in serious trouble. We emerged without mishap, but the experience was unsettling.

We would get reports of what was said at these meetings, and it was distressing whenever we learned of instances of those simple people being duped by false promises. 'You see those nice houses over there? If you vote for us you will all get to live in houses like that after Independence' was one such example. There were also cases of tribesmen from the Reserves being accosted on the streets of Nairobi and asked to select a car they would like from those parked nearby. The number of the car was then written on a piece of paper and handed to its new 'owner' in exchange for ten shillings, with the promise that when Independence came he could claim it. Anything we might have said on the matter would of course have fallen on deaf ears, since we were labelled as the cause of all life's woes, and our position had not been improved by 'fact-finding' visits from British socialist politicians. These rarely lasted more than a week or so and one cannot even begin to form a judgement of a country and its people in a couple of weeks, for in such a time it is only the most vociferous of agitators who are likely to leave their impression; I personally did not get the 'feel' of Kenya until I had been there several years. Yet on the basis of such visits articles appeared in the British press with such titles as 'Kenya under the Iron Heel' and a photograph of Nazi jackboots alongside. All of us in the service had in fact spent our entire working lives, and a great deal of energy, in trying to help the indigenous people to a better and more rewarding life; to educate them, indeed, to the point where they could safely manage their own affairs in the face of the complicated world outside. It was therefore particularly depressing to realise that the 'facts' as 'found' were not designed to present a balanced view at all, but only to gain political capital.

Things moved inexorably forward, and towards the end of 1960 I was given the job of organising the registration of voters for a General Election to be held in 1961. The government had laid down that all adults would be eligible to vote provided that they had achieved a basic level of education (I think it was completion of primary school).

Fort Hall was not a large district in area but it had a population of about four hundred thousand. There were four administrative divisions, each with a District Officer in charge and twenty locations, each with its chief, sub-chief and headmen. With such numbers it would have taken weeks to check everyone's educational credentials (even if they had had documentary evidence). The practicalities of it were that divisional DOs registered every adult who came forward. They had, in theory, been 'screened' by the chiefs beforehand but on my visits, I saw precious little evidence of this. Most would have qualified anyway, and I doubt that the rest would have had any significant effect on the outcome of the election.

We had registered eighty-seven thousand in the first three weeks (the highest for any constituency) and reached a final total electorate of more than one hundred and two thousand. The election itself went off smoothly and we recorded a ninety-two percent poll.

Although politics had become a matter of general concern, there was always a great deal of other administrative work going on. The Kikuyu at his best is reliable, intelligent and astute, and we were inundated with applications to run any and every sort of business venture. They ranged from selling produce to running an inter-district bus service. As far as the latter was concerned licences were issued not by us but by the Transport Licensing Board in Nairobi; but this meant that we had to represent the district's interests at their hearings. My predecessor, Peter Lloyd, had undertaken two surveys of buses (frequency, areas covered, economic factors) and these were valuable aids whenever I had to appear and state our case. As for trading licences, if one asks people to pay for the right to trade one has to be sure that there is reasonable scope for a livelihood to be made, without reducing prospects for those already licensed.

It was about this time that the government decided to vaccinate the entire population against polio, free of charge. I think it was the experience of all of us that almost any new project by government to improve the people's lives or environment was met with suspicion: they could not believe that we would spend energy and resources in this way without some sinister ulterior motive. Even with projects as obviously advantageous as dam-building it might take a lot of patience before co-operation was gained. The polio vaccination campaign suffered from the same mistrust, and word got about that it was a scheme to sterilise the entire indigenous population. As a result it was a disastrous failure, and on one occasion when my wife went out to help with a vaccination safari their land-rover was stoned as it approached a village.

Nevertheless, the government was not to be so easily deterred. Some months later it was announced that a new vaccination was available, but that anyone who wanted it would have to pay a shilling. They came in their hundreds and the scheme succeeded. The mistake on the first occasion had been to offer it for nothing.

3

Central Government

The Colonial Office	Charles Wilks
The Old Secretariat	Peter Gordon
The Secretariat in the early 1950s	Geoffrey Ellerton
A Stint in the Secretariat	Hugh Walker
Secretary to the Treasury	Kenneth Mackenzie
Clerk to the Legislature	Geoffrey Ellerton
Legislative Council	Kenneth Mackenzie
The Emergency Council	Geoffrey Ellerton
Ministry Work	John Ross
From Council of Ministers to Cabinet Office	John Ross
Government House 1956–9	Dick Wilson
Government House 1962–3	Peter Johnson
Internal Self-Government	Dick Wilson

Introduction

To many colonial administrators working in the capital was anathema. They joined the service to work in the rural areas, not to be 'pen pushers' in the city. But the power lay in the centre and the departments of government had to be staffed.

The direction of policy came from the Colonial Office in London, from the Secretary of State and British civil servants. But the need for cross fertilisation was recognised. Some mid-career officers, usually DCs, went on short attachments as Principals in the Colonial Office. They did not work on the desks concerned with their own territories. Charles Wilks gives his account of what it was like to be a 'beachcomber' in Whitehall.

The fount of power in Nairobi rested in Government House. The Governor was appointed by London to rule the Colony. In normal times, if he proved effective, he would be trusted to do the job with minimal interference. Four men governed Kenya in the period covered by this book: Sir Philip Mitchell (1944–52); Sir Evelyn Baring, later Lord Howick (1952–9); Sir Patrick Renison (1959–62) and Malcolm MacDonald (1963). Mitchell and Renison were career administrators. Baring was a patrician figure, an

Indian Civil Servant who later accepted eminent appointments in southern Africa. MacDonald was a politician sent to hammer out agreements with Kenya's politicians. Closely assisting the Governor was his Private Secretary, usually a DC who had proved his worth. Dick Wilson and Peter Johnson describe working with different Governors.

The Secretariat was the administrative hub. It was staffed by bringing in officers from the field, or from other colonies. Some with valid experience served a short stint, like Hugh Walker in the Ministry of Internal Security and Defence. Others came in, found themselves well suited to Central Government, and stayed. Kenneth Mackenzie came from Mauritius and went on to be Financial Secretary and Minister for Finance and Development. Geoffrey Ellerton joined the Secretariat in 1951 dealing with Home Affairs and rose to the top in the Ministry of Internal Security and Defence.

As Secretariat officers rose in seniority, they worked closely with politicians in the Legislative and Executive Councils. Some Permanent Secretaries became official Members and later Ministers. With the approach of Independence, the system of government evolved. Dick Wilson describes Internal Self-Government and the short-lived Regional Assemblies. John Ross provides insight into his work in the Cabinet Office with the Council of Ministers and the personal chemistry between two very different Governors and emergent African politicians.

The Colonial Office

CHARLES WILKS

To exchange life in a rural district on the lower slopes of Mount Kenya for the daily bustle of inner London, on secondment to the Colonial Office, came as a sudden shock to all the family, and the daily routine had quickly to be adjusted. But we survived, adding to our knowledge, not only of Colonial affairs, but also of what we saw as the oddity of the 'native' way of life!

At the time the Colonial Office (CO) was situated in the heart of London in rented accommodation at Church House, Great Smith Street, conveniently close to Whitehall and Parliament. As the annual List sets out: 'The essence of the work of the Colonial Office is that it advises, assists and carries out the directions of the Secretary of State on everything pertaining to his responsibility for the good government of Colonial territories'. To cope with the remarkable diversity of tasks, the CO had an establishment of some seven hundred and fifty officials, mainly home civil servants, but with a small proportion with experience in the Colonies, either those seconded for a period or already retired from the overseas civil service.

It was the practice at any one time for several officers stationed in the Colonies to be seconded, usually for two years. They were known as 'beachcombers'. To restore the balance, officers from the ministry would be posted for experience overseas. They in turn had to adjust: problems faced on the ground could look very different from what was set out in despatches to Church House.

On secondment to London, an officer could expect to spend a year attached to a Geographical Department, eg. Colonies in the Pacific and Indian Ocean (which included the Falklands and Antarctic), and a second year with a Subject Department, eg. Defence, Intelligence and Security. Within the African Department, Somaliland and Nyasaland fell to my lot. It so transpired that as things developed – the Independence of Somaliland and emergency measures in Nyasaland – I remained with these two Colonies throughout.

On the fourth floor of Church House was a huddle of small rooms, providing accommodation for the department's Principals. My room was just large enough for a table and a chair and, a Principal's privilege, a strip of carpet, a bar of soap, a towel, and an embossed despatch case, handy for carrying a lunch box. In one corner was a metal security cupboard in which stood an enormous kit bag. This was more than half full of security documents discarded by my predecessor. It was not long before the bag was stuffed to the brim and I was at a loss as to how to dispose of the contents. Contacting the CO Security Officer, he told me to call a messenger to take it away. Asking whether messengers had security clearance, he astonished me by his reply. 'But surely you have torn everything up so that it cannot be read?' Had I complied, I might have been there still, but we compromised and I accompanied the messenger to the shredder in the basement.

Next door to me was a beachcomber from Sierra Leone, concerned with Uganda affairs, and beyond him was the Kenya office. Understandably, no beachcomber was allowed to be involved with his own country, but this proximity kept me in touch with developments in Kenya. Not long after settling in, I learned from the Kenya office that Uganda was sending a high-ranking representative to press a claim for a slice of Kenya's western boundary. Known as Kara-Suk, it was for convenience being administered by Uganda, but, *de jure* it remained Kenya territory. For some years, Uganda's Governor, Sir Andrew Cohen, had taken a personal interest in this issue, even to making a special visit to Kenya's Governor, Sir Evelyn Baring; but to no avail. Kara-Suk happened to be an area with which I was well acquainted and I was able, surreptitiously, to alert colleagues in Kenya to this back door approach. (Thirty years on, Kenya holds Kara-Suk - now Karapokot – both *de facto* and *de jure*.)

It is perhaps worth mentioning that Sir Andrew was well known to the CO, where he had served for a number of years. Immensely active, he was known to save time by continuing to dictate to his secretary as he walked out of his office. It was not recorded when, on following him along the corridor, his secretary, hastily scribbling as she went, was confounded to see him disappear into the Gents!

Apart from what we saw of each other in the office hours, there was little or no social contact. Widely different from life in a *boma*. Two or three of us beachcombers tended to lunch together, in warmer weather taking sandwiches into St James' Park. Apart from the ducks and the pelicans, we were able to watch our elders and betters, putting the world to rights, as they strolled purposefully towards their clubs. The CO alternative was a canteen only patronised by beachcombers in an emergency. But there was a congenial pub close by, and the Crown Agents in Millbank welcomed overseas officers to make use of their distinctly superior facilities. On one exceptional occasion during a visit from Somaliland's Governor, I lunched as his guest, joined by Dick Turnbull, and enjoyed a notable claret. It was mid-afternoon before I was back at Church House; little inclined to dip into my 'In' basket, not even on the question of Somali Independence, which was now a priority.

I came to have a great respect for Alan Lennox Boyd, the Secretary of State. He assumed office in July, 1954, inheriting, as *The Times* later recorded; 'a bewildering variety of problems before which the most experienced politician could be forgiven for quailing ... He brought to his task the qualities of knowledge, vision, patience and firmness ..... (and) he took infinite pains with people, which was the core of his success.'

It was he who, following on the disaster at Hola detention camp when 'Taxi' Lewis, Commissioner of Prisons and former DC had honourably resigned his post, had him met on arrival at Heathrow with an offer of employment. On Sunday evening, an emergency meeting was called at his Belgravia house. After considerable discussion, as Ministers and officials made their way to supper, I was left to arrange for the CO to despatch several coded cables. There were steps down into the supper room and, as Lennox Boyd saw me enter; he rose from his meal. There was only one vacant seat, but he courteously saw me to it.

There were other occasions, which confirmed his concern and respect for his staff. His last gesture when, for family reasons, he had resigned in October 1959, was to visit each Department at the CO wishing everyone well before he took his leave.

In his place came Iain Macleod, transferred from the Ministry of Labour. He was a vigorous, dynamic personality, able to absorb problems with ease that most of us would envy. Given that you provided accurate information and useful proposals, it was easy to work in unison. Otherwise, he could react quite sharply. His wife, to whom he was devoted, was a wheelchair invalid and somehow, he always managed to find time to care for her needs.

Apart from its own major problems, the CO could also be involved with those of other Ministries, especially those affecting people from the Colonies. As the CO's representative, I attended monthly Whitehall meetings to consider the question of the current flood of coloured immigrants. They were arriving faster than could be assimilated and an insoluble housing shortage was foreseen. This growing social problem was thought likely to give rise to trouble in areas with concentrations of immigrants. There were those who saw the danger of a continuing influx, but they were few, and for what seemed essentially political reasons, the government was not prepared to grasp the nettle.

On another occasion, an Army task force was to hold a 'sand table' exercise at Colchester. Based on a Uganda background, the scheme was to contain any possible uprising, bearing in mind the need for minimum disruption of the local people's lifestyle. Representing civil authority, there was little for me to do, except to enjoy my host's generous hospitality!

It was by chance that I was seconded to the CO and it proved to be an interesting experience, adding a great deal to my knowledge of Colonial affairs and the major role that government played. Certainly their ways were not ours, and whatever the problems, there were other points of view than ours to be taken into account. Certainly government could be sympathetic to our needs but decisions could be swayed by the political climate of the day, sometimes one felt, with detriment to the core issue.

My stay was now coming to an end, I was asked if I would be prepared to remain at the CO. As we were all looking forward to returning to Kenya, I had to decline. It was only later that corridor gossip had it that the post in question would have been hard to resist. Fortunately I had not known and was not tempted.

And how did my wife and three young daughters take to this change of scene? Not easily to begin with. Caroline would come home from her new school complaining that she had nothing to share with other children as their chatter was confined to what had been on the TV the previous night. Ours was the only house in the row with no aerial. On our first visit to the seaside it was she who rushed ahead over a high bank of shingle, only to come running back dismayed. 'We can't picnic here,' she said, 'there are other people.' Oh for the vastness of Africa! Often, with snow on the ground, we made our way to isolated spots where we could relish potatoes hot from the ashes of a campfire. The word soon spread to our neighbours' children who clamoured to join in, even so, their parents thought us a bit peculiar.

We had a number of Kenya visitors, among them Mary and Geoffrey

Kariithi, who had been in England since the previous autumn, with overcast skies and with little in the way of greenery or growth. It was Easter when they came to stay, when they found me planting potatoes. Geoffrey could hardly roll up his sleeves quickly enough to get his hands into the wet, warm soil.

All in all, we enjoyed ourselves and, as we had not previously lived in England, there was much to be absorbed. The change was good for us, yet not as good as the prospect of returning to a 'land of far horizons'.

The Old Secretariat

PETER GORDON

After my first eighteen months – spent in Nyanza Province – I had an early posting as an Assistant Secretary to the Secretariat. This was a square, squat building, whose sides – it was easy to imagine – were distended by the weight of innumerable files crammed within. There were few separate Ministries in those days and almost the entire apparatus of government was housed within its walls. Files accumulated on one's desk at an alarming rate and, from certain of my colleagues, I gathered the impression that the object was to shunt them onto somebody else at all speed. In my portfolio, the channels led mainly to the Chief Native Commissioner, P. Wyn Harris, to the Minister of Agriculture (the venerable Cavendish-Bentinck of whom everyone stood in awe and to whose august presence I was, in the course of a year, admitted but once), or to the almost equally remote Chief Secretary (Rankine).

One channel to the latter was via an officer who had spent virtually his entire career, stretching over many years, in the Secretariat, and who, delightful old chap though he was, seemed utterly unable to reach a decision on any subject whatever. He dithered endlessly over every paper submitted to him. A barrier of files hid him from view as you entered his office, others, in neat piles, lined the walls, and carpeted the floor. It was deeply frustrating when a file you had passed to him perhaps two or three months before arrived back on your desk with the words, 'Please speak' inscribed beneath your painstakingly composed minute. You presented yourself. A minute's perusal, and then 'Ah, Yes. Now what was it I wanted to say? Perhaps I'd better have another look at it. Just leave the file with me, please'.

One was expected to take the file game with deadly seriousness. Any officer creeping out of the building before 7 p.m. on weekdays or arriving after

9 a.m. on Saturdays did so with a sense of guilt. On Sundays, it was tacitly accepted, I suppose, that you had been to Communion and breakfasted; so 10 a.m. was acceptable for clocking-in. Only a dedicated few, however, turned up on Sunday afternoons.

But not everyone conformed with this routine. At least one Assistant Secretary (ex Indian Civil Service) kept a proper sense of values, knocked off for a gin and tonic at noon, and never appeared at weekends. He was an enthusiastic race-goer and, during Nairobi Race Week, put in no appearance at all, but fixed a notice to his door stating, with perfect veracity: 'Gone to a Meeting'.

If the foregoing suggests a great deal of buck-passing and abnegation of responsibility, I have exaggerated. In the course of the mass movement of files, decisions were indeed reached and much achieved to the benefit of the Colony.

The Secretariat in the Early 1950s

GEOFFREY ELLERTON

In April 1951, on my return to Kenya after home leave and attending a Second Devonshire Course – middle management training – at Oxford, I was posted to the Secretariat. This was engineered, some said, because the Officials' cricket team, and Nairobi Club had need of a middle order batsman who could also bowl a bit.

At the time, the upper echelons of Central Government were in a state of flux. The Governor, Sir Philip Mitchell, was beginning his freewheel downhill towards retirement. His golfing acolyte, John Rankine, the Chief Secretary was about to depart to become, like his father before him, British Resident, Zanzibar; his successor, Henry Potter, had not yet arrived from Uganda. Colin Thornley, the Deputy Chief Secretary, already earmarked for Uganda as Potter's successor, seemed always to be acting as something else, as did Charles Hartwell, not long arrived from Ceylon as Kenya's first Director of Establishments. John Whyatt, with no previous African experience, had just succeeded Kenneth O'Connor as Attorney General and Member for Law and Order. Victor Matthews, ex-ICS, Financial Secretary was already canvassing for his future posting to London as Commissioner for the East African Governments. C.M. Deverell, Administrative Secretary, would very shortly be on his way to Jamaica, as Chief Secretary. Eric Davies had recently taken over from P. Wyn Harris as Chief Native Commissioner and, as head of the Provincial Administration, kept seconded administrative officers like myself in touch with the human race. Arthur Hope-Jones was about to be gazetted as Member for Commerce and Industry, which, again to seconded administrative officers like myself, seemed something of a joke.

On joining the Secretariat, I was posted to A 1 Section. A 1 dealt with traditional Home Department subjects – Law and Order, the Police, the Prisons Service, Immigration. It also provided the executive link with the Judiciary.

A 1 also dealt with the local implications of the 1948 British Nationality Act, which in Kenya were considerable. A large number of Kenya Asians, mostly Muslims from the Bombay states who were formerly British Protected Persons, were made legally stateless by the Act, because they refused, for political or religious reasons, to register under the Act as citizens of India, which was their right and a necessary first step to subsequent registration as citizens of the United Kingdom and Colonies. To acquire this latter citizenship, therefore, they would now have to be naturalised, a formidable administrative task in view of their numbers and the time-consuming nature of the local naturalisation process, after which each entitled person had to be submitted to the Home Office in a formal, individual despatch, signed by the Governor. Little did we, or the Home Office, foresee, as we persuaded HMG to accept a rubber-stamp naturalisation procedure for these people, how we should be adding later to the diversity of the UK's own racial mix.

A 1, like most of the lowest forms of Secretariat administrative life, was located in the 'rabbit-hutches' on the top floor of the Law Courts, the Secretariat's home since Jack Troughton (so it was said) burnt down the old Secretariat on the Hill in 1940 by leaving on an unfilled electric kettle. My nearby colleagues were Donald Baron, dealing with Defence and Labour matters, and Jack Adie and Gordon Hector dealing inter-alia with Education and Public Works. Jack and Gordon worked to the Deputy Chief Secretary (soon to be Charles Hartwell), through the Assistant Chief Secretary, who was initially L. A. Weaving and then John Webster. When either of them made a contribution to the file greater than crossing out his own name and redirecting the file either upwards or downwards, there would be a gasp of incredulity from B Section and we would all gather round to see these rare collectors' pieces. Ginti Tannahill had a classic story: 'We must get weaving on this, Tannahill.' Tannahill (after a short pause): 'Do you mean get cracking, Sir, or get Mr Weaving on this?' Thornley (without a pause): 'I mean get cracking, Tannahill.'

The greater part of A 1's work went to the Secretary and Member for Law and Order, Jake Cusack and John Whyatt, who were located in the Attorney-General's old wood and iron building, situated half-way up the Hill.

I took over the Section from Jim Pedraza, who left at once to catch a boat at Mombasa on his way to England on home leave, so there was no proper take-over. My own immediate concern was to find somewhere to live and it was a day or two before I went into my new office to start work. By this time the files requiring attention were stacked up in two enormous piles, bristling with red labels marked Urgent, blue labels marked Immediate, and yellow labels marked Legislative Council Question. My personal secretary, Madge Ainslie, a splendid lady, recently widowed and old enough to be my mother, came in with an armful of files from the Secret Registry, similarly beflagged.

The first file I took from the top of the pile was a letter from the Commissioner of Police, enclosing the Police Annual Report for 1950, a report of about 50 foolscap pages. It looked all right to me, but I had no idea what to do with it. In desperation, I turned to Madge and asked: 'What do I do with this?' 'Send it to Mr Cusack and ask if it may be sent to the Government Printer for printing.' I did as she directed and the file came back with a note from Jake Cusack: 'This report is quite unsuitable for public consumption. Please redraft.' I was appalled; how was I to find the time to redraft fifty pages of foolscap on a subject, the Kenya Police, about which, I knew nothing? Once again, I turned to Madge, and once again, she came to my rescue. 'Send it back to the Commissioner of Police and tell him that this report is unsuitable for public consumption and must be redrafted.' She paused: 'No, send it back to the Commissioner and tell him that the Secretary for Law and Order says the report is unsuitable for public consumption, etc. Then, with luck, the Commissioner will get in touch with Mr Cusack about it, and not with you.' I was learning fast the ways of the Secretariat.

A Stint in the Secretariat

HUGH WALKER

In September 1962 I was posted as Assistant Secretary to the Ministry of Defence in Nairobi. I took over what was known as the 'Somali desk' from George Webb. Geoffrey Ellerton was the Permanent Secretary and Sir Anthony Swann was then Minister for Defence. One of my most interesting jobs was that of Secretary to the Kenya Intelligence Committee. On taking over from my predecessor, my first task was to reset the combination locks to the huge steel doors to the Secret Registry. I made a complete hash of this and was faced with spending the night inside the Registry until a locksmith approved by Special Branch could be found. Fortunately, one turned up in time for me to get away by nine p.m., well after dark.

Much of my work was drafting Security and Intelligence appreciations, answers to Parliamentary Questions, which required almost clairvoyant anticipation of likely supplementary questions, and statistics on stock theft and incidents throughout the Colony. All this required close liaison with the Kenya Police and Special Branch.

Due to the troubled situation in the Northern Province, or the North Eastern Region as it was later restyled, I had to take daily Situation Reports to Government House and hand them over personally to the Governor, Malcolm MacDonald. He was a short man of huge intellect, and although formidable, he was also approachable. This enabled him to gain the trust of Jomo Kenyatta, not long out of seven years in jail and subsequent detention. Kenyatta later became Kenya's first Prime Minister and a year after Independence its first President. MacDonald became Governor-General and then High Commissioner. He had an amazingly quick grasp both of essentials and details and he did not suffer slower mortals gladly. He was, however, a modest man; he consistently refused a knighthood and often travelled in Economy Class rather than First Class to which he was entitled.

Localisation of the Civil Service was well under way by 1962, as were plans and preparation for Internal Self-Government. Many files in the Ministry of Defence were highly classified and all Top Secret and many Secret files were considered to be unsuitable to be seen by future local, non-European officers. These included all communications between the Kenya and UK Governments, all Intelligence material and many Personal Files. Consequently many were designated for 'UK Eyes Only' or otherwise marked. Also working in the Security Branch was a particularly capable African Assistant Secretary; it became most embarrassing to contrive that all such reclassified files were not passed to him. Or, if they had to be, that clearance was first obtained from me as officer in charge of the Secret Registry. The European ladies who ran the Secret Registry often had to tell him that the files he called for were with other officers; but if he went to their offices to trace the files, they could not be found. Sometimes two files on the same subject were compiled, one with the classified folios removed; but cross referencing soon revealed their absence and it did not take him long to realise what was going on. I know he found it hurtful, especially as he was an effective and able official, but he was too much of a gentleman to say so. Fortunately this situation did not last long as in the run-up to Internal Self-Government in June 1963 and Independence six months later, many of the 'UK Eyes Only' files were either destroyed or transferred to England and the rest reclassified as ordinarily Secret or Confidential.

During my time there, a charming, able Luo was attached to the

Ministry. His name was Robert Ouko, destined to become Kenya's Foreign Minister long after Independence and, sadly, to be assassinated in 1990.

Working to very senior officers was challenging and stimulating but also stressful. After only nine months during which events in Kenya moved very fast, I was quite glad to take my overdue leave in the UK.

Secretary to the Treasury

KENNETH MACKENZIE

I had returned to Kenya in mid 1953 and been appointed to the newly created post of Deputy Secretary to the Treasury in 1954, when I accompanied Verry Vasey (later Sir Ernest Vasey) the Minister of Finance and Development to London for discussion with the Colonial Office and the Treasury on financial assistance during the Mau Mau Emergency. It was the first of such visits which became annual until 1959 when we thought (optimistically as it transpired) that, the Emergency being over, Kenya would once more be able to stand on her own feet so far as ordinary expenditure was concerned. After some leave, I returned to Nairobi in the autumn and then in February 1955 succeeded Edward Petrie, as Secretary to the Treasury, at the same time becoming a nominated member of Legislative Council.

I had first known Vasey in the 1940s when I was the Secretariat representative on the Board of Coryndon Museum. Fortunately, we hit it off well together then and during the whole of my term of office as Secretary to the Treasury, and subsequently when he went to Tanganyika. We remained friends in later life until he died. I greatly admired his ability, both financial and political, and his loyalty to his government and to his staff, and still consider him to have been probably the ablest political figure in the Colony at that time. He benefited of course, as did we all, from the support of the Governor, Sir Evelyn Baring, whose knowledge of, and interest in, financial affairs and political instinct were exceptional among Colonial Governors at any time. Fortunately, Vasey also had good personal relations with numerous members on both sides of the House of Commons.

We were lucky to inherit a first class body of officers in the Treasury. First among them John Butter, who was with me throughout the rest of my service, following me as Secretary to the Treasury and staying on as Financial Adviser after Independence. He was ex-Indian Civil Service as was the late Andrew Hume, who went on to be Permanent Secretary of Forests and Game. Most were of course, from the Provincial Administration: Geoffrey Ellerton, who became Secretary for Internal Security and Defence; Donald

Brown, Oliver Knowles, Duncan Buttery and Gerry Pratt. Elizabeth Usher (now Blair) was of course a daughter of an administrator. Others came from the Kenya unit of the East Africa Statistical Office, notably Philip Haddon-Cave and at a later stage Michael McWilliam. Duncan Ndegwa, our first African Assistant Secretary joined at the end of the 1950s and became Permanent Secretary after Independence.

As a political appointee and former elected member, Vasey rightly left the normal running of the Treasury to the Permanent Secretary, an approach which I, knowing that I was almost certain to be the last official Minister for Finance, and probably the last with previous administrative experience, tried to follow in so far as I could. Of course, I always kept the Minister in touch with developments and enjoyed 'open house' to his office at all times. The same procedure was easily followed when I became Minister since all officers had enjoyed free access to me when I was Permanent Secretary.

Day to day work as Secretary to the Treasury was as varied as the whole spread of government business and was never dull. Fortunately, it was possible to delegate freely to experienced and reliable officers. This was essential on occasions such as when Legislative Council was sitting – probably some one hundred afternoons in the year. There were also the times when Vasey was away on business either in the United Kingdom or in the USA or on spells of leave, when I would find myself acting as Minister for several weeks. As I had to be sworn in each time, I must have taken more oaths than the most enthusiastic insurgent!

I was fully involved in all-important matters such as the Annual Estimates and obtaining agreement from official and ministerial colleagues on the probable content of future Estimates. There were regular meetings with the Ministers of Finance from Tanganyika and Uganda about possible changes in direct and indirect taxation, agreement being necessary since we were all part of the East African fiscal area and the taxes were collected by East African Departments.

Clerk to the Legislature

GEOFFREY ELLERTON

In about the middle of 1952, I was transferred from A 1 to Section D, which dealt with Constitutional Affairs and Finance. Included in the former was the job of Clerk to the Executive and Legislative Councils.

The job of Clerk to the Legislative Council was regarded as something of a sinecure – time consuming certainly, terribly dull usually, but the duties not particularly onerous. There was a full-time Assistant Clerk to do the real work: to make sure that other hirers of the Memorial Hall (where the Council then met), like the Kenya Horticultural Society and the EAWL, packed up their wares in time for Council to sit; to prepare the daily Order Paper; to write up the votes and proceedings (the Council's Official Record); to collate and edit Hansard for the Government Printer. The Clerk's own principal duty was to don a (borrowed) wig and gown; to walk in procession with Mr Speaker from his first floor office, down the stairs (pushing aside the fading blooms of yesterday's show on the way); to shout out 'Mr Speaker' as the procession approached the entrance to the Hall; and to read out the items of business as Council worked its way through the Order paper.

The Governor had recently ceased to preside over Legislative Council. A Speaker had been appointed – a retired puisne judge, Mr Justice Horne. As Clerk, I sat at the Clerk's Table with my back to the Speaker. In front of me was a low-tech lighting arrangement operated by Mr Speaker; one flash meant that he wanted a word (usually to check up on the name of the back-bencher who was jumping up and down and seemed anxious to speak); two flashes meant that he wanted to answer the call of nature and would I please quickly catch the eye of the Deputy Speaker; three flashes meant, for God's sake, get him quickly.

Voting was by way of a roll-call of members, listed alphabetically, the list starting with Dr (Farnsworth) Anderson, the Director of Medical Services, who sat on the back benches as government lobby fodder. When dealing with legislation in Committee of the Whole House, the question was often 'that the words proposed to be left out stand part of the question'. If you were in favour of amending legislation, you said 'no': if you were against amendment, you said 'yes'. This was all gobbledegook to the learned Doctor who, to the delight of the opposition and the groans of his own side, invariably voted the wrong way. I tried to help him by shaking my head appropriately; he still got it wrong and strongly suspected me of trying to make a monkey out of him by shaking my head in an indeterminate manner.

We had a team of efficient palantype operators and aimed to produce a printed record of the Council's proceedings within twenty-four hours. Members would get a draft of their speeches the same day or early next morning. They were supposed only to correct grammar and punctuation, not to put in what they wished they had said, or to take out what they wished they had not said. Arthur Hope-Jones, the Member for Commerce and Industry, sought to embellish his contributions in another way. Drafts of his speeches, even a short one about the internal price of cement, would come back liberally sprinkled with (laughter), (loud laughter), (applause), (loud applause) – and, at the end, (prolonged applause). The Speaker had to intervene.

I have said that the job of Clerk was a sinecure. Nemesis struck one early afternoon. We had just reached the bottom of the stairs in procession when a European Police Officer pushed his way through the main portal of the Memorial Hall, clutching a piece of paper. 'Are you Mr X?' he asked me in an officious voice. 'No, this is Mr X,' I replied, indicating my very efficient assistant, 'and we can't speak to you now: Mr Speaker will be late for prayers.' He utterly ignored me and, addressing my assistant, said, 'Mr X., I have a warrant for your arrest' – and arrested he was (for earlier malpractice in another department) and I never saw him again.

For the next two or three weeks I worked harder than I had ever worked before or, probably, since. I worked in the Memorial Hall until the small hours of the morning, struggling to understand, and to transcribe into my own portable typewriter, the mysteries of votes and proceedings (particularly mysterious when recording amendments to legislation in Committee). Nor was I helped by the Council experimenting with evening sittings – an experiment, fortunately, which was very quickly abandoned; no sooner did the sitting start than half the European Elected Members, and as many on the Official side who dared, crept off to the bar of the nearby Torr's Hotel, returning an hour or two later in a distinctly unparliamentary condition. And on top of it all, I had to do my job as Clerk to the Executive Council, cope with the routine D Section work, and to serve my turn as Secretariat night duty officer.

I did derive one small, very small, profit from the Office of Clerk to the Legislature. A German shipping company, with which I was later to have much to do in my shipping career, wanted to build a cement works and jetty at Bamburi, on the mainland opposite Mombasa's old harbour. As the jetty would affect navigation in the area, the promoters had to proceed by way of a private Bill, and they first had to petition the Legislative Council for leave to present such a Bill.

The Council's Standing Orders said that for reading out a petition, the Clerk should receive a fee of three guineas and in due course I received a cheque for sixty-three shillings made payable to the Clerk of the Legislative Council. As Clerk, I had no doubt that the money was mine; but as Section D Finance Officer, I felt no less strongly that the cheque should be paid into public funds – even more to the point, so did the Treasury. As Clerk, I consulted my near neighbour, the Solicitor-General (Eric Griffith-Jones); and never did a Law Officer give such an unequivocal or more popular opinion: the money was the Clerk's, he ruled – the only remuneration I ever received beyond my personal emoluments in nearly twenty years in the Colonial Service.

Legislative Council

KENNETH MACKENZIE

Legislative Council was the most regular out of office occupation during the final seven years of my service. As Secretary to the Treasury, I was in the position of a junior Minister supporting the Minister generally and particularly in the Budget Debate, Supply Days and Ways and Means Resolutions. I enjoyed Legislative Council. Discussions were almost invariably friendly – although the Elected and Non-Government nominated members (when I first joined, all the African members were nominated) sat on the opposite side from the government they tended to be friendly critics rather than opposition. The European Members, who were the largest body on the opposite side of the house, were generally able, well informed, and kept government members on their toes. I have no doubt that the conduct of business in the House during these years, when African Members were coming into the Legislative Council in greater numbers, was valuable formative experience for the continued working of parliamentary institutions at Independence, which came much earlier than we could have expected in the mid 1950s. This is certainly the impression I gain from reports on proceedings in the Kenya Parliament in the journal of the Commonwealth Parliamentary Association. It could be argued that if, largely through lack of time, when we were struck by the hurricane of change, we had not trained nearly enough senior civil servants at Independence, we had trained a fair number of Parliamentarians not least by the example of the European Elected Members during the later Colonial years. We were well served by the two speakers of those days, Sir Ferdinand Cavendish-Bentinck (later Duke of Portland) and Humphrey Slade.

The most effective African speaker from 1956 onwards was Tom Mboya. I suspect that most of us foresaw a prominent place for him in any post Independence government, although I doubt whether we expected to see that reached as quickly as it was. He became a Minister in the first post Independence government but was murdered too soon for any one to see whether he would fulfil his potential. The first Vice President, Oginga Odinga was always personally polite but also, to put it mildly, rather excitable and it was scarcely surprising that his term of office was short. Kenyatta only appeared in Legislative Council once whilst I was still a member and did not speak, so I did not have an opportunity to judge his effectiveness as a Parliamentarian. Few, if any, of the African Members showed much interest in financial debates and were inclined to leave the 'opposition' benches to the Europeans at those times. Generally, their contribution to debate varied in quality, reflecting the fact that proceedings were in English rather than in their native tongue. I would have been at an equal disadvantage in Swahili.

It is indicative of the assumption that Independence was something which would happen in the future but 'scarcely in our time', that the Europeans were prominent in the House until the end of my service in 1962. They had, of course, the advantage that our proceedings were in English and had the sort of background which one might have expected in any Legislature in the English speaking world or even in the United Kingdom itself. Michael Blundell was an outstanding performer as was Humphrey Slade before he became Speaker. During the 1956 to 1960 Legislature there was the almost legendary Ewart Grogan who had walked through Kenya on his way from the Cape to Cairo at the turn of the century, when much of the territory was virtually unadministered. My namesake Bruce McKenzie gained increasing authority in the later years when he played Box and Cox with Blundell as Minister of Agriculture during the run up to Independence and again played an important role as a European Member of KANU afterwards. Two of the Elected Members, S.V. Cooke and George Usher, were retired officials of the Overseas Civil Service.

Dick Turnbull and Wally Coutts as Chief Secretaries and Leaders of the House were both effective speakers on the government side. It is a pity that some of their speeches were not reported in the British press, particularly one by Wally when he was Minister of Education, effectively giving the lie to criticism that we had done too little to prepare the Africans for Independence. The facts were, he said, that in the period up to the First World War effective administration was only being introduced and education was looked upon with suspicion by most of the people. Then there was the Great Depression followed by the Second World War. It was only after 1945 that development could really begin the job, much less finish it. As a corollary to that, in 1961 I noted that expenditure on African education had grown from one to ten million pounds a year between the late 1940s and 1961.

The main issues throughout my last seven years in office were the implementation of an efficient financial system throughout the Colony, capable of withstanding the strings of increasing political control, insofar as any legal or procedural devices could achieve that; financing the Emergency whilst at the same time maintaining and extending development; and towards the end meeting the very much foreshortened time scale in the rush to Independence.

The financing of the Emergency involved regular visits to London for negotiations with the Colonial Office and the Treasury. We were fortunate that from the start HMG had accepted as priorities: (1) expenditure on Internal Security and Law and Order; (2) short term development, including Education and Health Services; (3) longer term economic development projects; and (4) if practicable, Social Security. It had also been agreed that the development of the peaceful majority in the Colony should not be made to suffer for the behaviour of the terrorist faction. Both for this reason and because our taxes had to be in line with those of our partners in the East African Market, we should not be expected to impose intolerable levels of taxation. As an incentive to economy, it was agreed that the assistance should be partly Loan and partly Grant but that we should be allowed to draw down the Grant element first, only using the Loans, which were interest free, if needed. Finally we were always given a large enough total to ensure that we should not have to return for supplementary provision during the year – on the sound principle that, once allowed, supplementing could become a habit. The pattern of the negotiations was that I agreed to details with opposite numbers in the Colonial Office and the Treasury, with Vasey coming in for a final session chaired by a top Treasury Official. A minor advantage of my previous secondment to the Treasury was that after 1955, I was trusted to conduct the official level preliminary meetings with the Treasury without a Colonial Office official in attendance.

As late as 1958, when a United Nations Trustee Committee opined that Tanganyika would not be ready for Independence before the 1970s, I was still able to tell a farmer friend that I expected Colonial rule to see me through to retirement in 1970. I should clearly have kept my mouth shut. 1960 saw the 'Wind of Change' speech, after which the pace became increasingly rapid, helped on by the sudden decision of the Belgian Government to abandon the Congo to its own devices. We continued to plan future development, following the Lugard dictum that it was our purpose to retain control until the Colonies were capable of standing on their feet in the strenuous conditions of this modern world. I had assumed that we would continue to rule until we could hand over to a cadre of senior African officers with educational qualifications and practical experience comparable to our own, which was broadly what happened in India. Given the changed political outlook throughout the world and not least in the United Kingdom, and the paucity of potential candidates at that stage in Kenya's educational development, that was impossible in the 1960s climate. Decolonisation was the chief imperative.

My 1960 Budget was prepared and delivered on the old assumptions. For the first time since 1954, it was balanced without UK assistance towards recurrent expenditure and this was seen as the future pattern. Similarly, our negotiations with the World Bank early in the year were based on the assumption that the framework for the plans for improving African agricultural development would remain as it was. However, the first Lancaster House Conference, held just before, had already cleared the path to Independence. Although there was no timetable attached, the climate was rapidly changing and adversely affecting not only our revenue but also the stability of local financial institutions. By mid-year, I was back in London discussing with the Colonial Office and the Bank of England how best to stop a run on our Building Societies which threatened bankruptcy to at least one of them, not a confidence boosting prospect in the somewhat febrile political climate already developing. The immediate problem was solved thanks to the intervention of the Colonial Development Corporation, chaired by our former Governor, Sir Evelyn Baring (by then Lord Howick of Glendale). It was also necessary to prepare for renewed Grant-in-Aid to make good our revenue shortfall. The readiness with which this was agreed was another sign that we must avoid anything which might jeopardise political progress.

In 1961 the tempo quickened further and my hope, expressed in my reply to that year's Budget Debate, that given moderation on all sides there was no reason why we should not achieve financial stability without outside assistance, must have sounded rather hollow. In fact, we were already planning crash courses for training Africans to take over if large numbers of expatriates left under the compensation schemes being prepared. Plans were in hand for buying European owned farms for resettlement by Africans: thought was given to annexing the Coastal Strip (the Protectorate, nominally subject to the Sultan of Zanzibar). And Kenyatta was being released and elected to Legislative Council. All was in line for the second Lancaster House Conference and the formation of an interim government as a prelude to Independence.

The Emergency Council

GEOFFREY ELLERTON

As Clerk to the Legislative Council, I sat through the debates which preceded the Declaration of Emergency in October 1952, including a major debate in July initiated by Michael Blundell on a motion condemning the 'increasing disregard for Law and Order within the Colony and Protectorate.' The government was heavily outgunned in Legislative Council at the time. Officials do not necessarily make good politicians. I used to watch Henry Potter, as Chief Secretary, Leader of the Government side, literally tremble before he got up to speak. John Whyatt, the Member for Law and

Order, hopped from foot to foot (the European Elected Members called him the 'dancing minister') as he delivered desiccated lectures on the rule of law, which seemed somehow remote from prevailing events. The member for Agriculture, Cavendish-Bentinck, would often have been more comfortable sitting on the Opposition Benches (from whence in fact he came); the Chief Native Commissioner, Eric Davies, seemed strangely reluctant to talk about the reports he was receiving, and which the European Elected Members knew he was receiving, from his own District Commissioners, and so was regarded by the Opposition as complacent and out of touch. Only Vasey, the Member for Finance, was prepared to give as good as he got, reminding the European Elected Members, in particular of their ambivalent attitude to increased Government expenditure, even for Law and Order proposals.

When the Emergency was declared, as Clerk to the Executive Council, I became Secretary to the first Emergency Council, which met at Government House in the early evening under the chairmanship of the Governor. My recollection is that my principal duty was to await the arrival of the Private Secretary (Henry Howard) with a tray of drinks and to help him serve them round.

The Emergency gave impetus to changes in the machinery of government. Vasey took the financial sections of the Secretariat out of the Law Courts and set up a reformed Treasury in the Accountant General's old offices. I went with them. He persuaded the Legislature to establish an Emergency Fund, a kind of enormous goat-bag from which disbursements could be made for Emergency purposes without prior Legislative approval. This stood on its head the principle hitherto governing public expenditure, namely that every public servant is a potential crook and peculator; instead, the assumption was that civil servants could be trusted. For nearly three years I controlled the Emergency Fund and we disbursed millions. I dare say I was had for a sucker from time to time, but I was knowingly let down only once (a district just 'lost' shs 50,000 in a week). Sometimes I had a twinge of conscience (as when we restocked all the trout streams in Kenya after someone had chucked a grenade into the Sagana and killed a few fish). And once I had a flaming row with the PC Coast Province, when I declined to top up his Entertainment vote – ('Ellerton, you people in Nairobi must understand that an Emergency is going on and I have to maintain morale,') – at Nyali, Diani, and Malindi – like hell!

CENTRAL GOVERNMENT

Ministry Work

JOHN ROSS

In early 1958, when I was running a district in Western Nigeria, a circular arrived from the Secretariat in Ibadan, inviting applications for transfer to Kenya. One had to be about thirty-five and to have had at least ten years' service. I was immediately interested. Nigerian Independence was now just around the corner and we were worried about the future, or rather the lack of it. Moreover, our children were of an age when they would shortly have to go home for schooling and the prospect of family separation was alarming. One of my colleagues in Nigeria was a Kenyan and I sought his advice, in particular on career prospects. He said I need have no concerns on that score – Kenya was not Nigeria, there could conceivably be some form of limited Self-Government by the late 1970s but full Independence would not be for some years after that. I decided to apply and in due course was accepted. (This assessment was not as ludicrous as it now seems. In his biography of Malcolm MacDonald, p.389, Clyde Sanger writes: 'Back in 1959 Alan Lennox-Boyd, then the Colonial Secretary, apparently posed this question (how fast to Independence?) to the three Governors in East Africa. The four agreed that a realistic timetable might be 1970 for Tanganyika, 1975 for Kenya, and some date in between for Uganda.

While I was on home leave in early 1959, the Colonial Office told me I would be posted to the Ministry of Works for six months, as relieving Assistant Secretary, an appropriate enough posting for someone coming from such an 'advanced' country as Nigeria, but one that did not fill me with enthusiasm. I travelled ahead of the family and on arrival was delivered to the Norfolk Hotel and left to my own devices. This was something of a shock as I had been used to the hospitality code of Nigeria, which ensured that no one was ever on his own for the first few days. Before dinner I wandered out to the veranda of the Norfolk for a contemplative drink. No sooner had I sat at my table than a figure emerged out of the darkness and asked in a polite and rather plummy voice whether I would mind if he sat at my table. I replied that on the contrary, I would welcome some company and offered him a drink. When he had finished it I waited a decent interval before offering another, which he took with alacrity. After this I said that I was intending to eat at the hotel and we might perhaps share a table. He said he would be delighted but that most unfortunately he had left his wallet at home. The penny dropped when we entered the dining room and

I had my first real sight of him – bloodshot eyes, grimy shirt collar, frayed sleeves. Yet, on that first night in Nairobi, I was grateful even for this strange company.

Things looked up when I reported to the Ministry next morning. I happened to be wearing my Trinity College Dublin tie and when I entered the office of the Chief Engineer, Tommy Garland, I saw he was wearing one too. So began a friendship, which lasted throughout our time in Kenya, and beyond. Tom Colchester, the Permanent Secretary, was helpful in all sorts of ways, not least in imparting to me his deep knowledge of Kenya. We soon established that we had a mutual interest in trout fishing which led to memorable weekend safaris to the Nyamindi and other mountain streams, during which Tom would continue my education. The work of the Ministry proved more interesting than I had expected and all in all I was quite sorry to leave when the six months were up.

I asked to be posted to a district but was told sharply that I had been brought over from Nigeria to work in the Secretariat and that anyway I did not speak Swahili. I did not protest – by this time we had started to enjoy the delights of Nairobi after the rigours of bush life in West Africa and the children had settled well into good schools. I was posted instead to the Ministry of Defence under Geoffrey Ellerton as Permanent Secretary and was given responsibility for Prisons.

A new Commissioner of Prisons, John Burton, had just been appointed. Tough, quick-witted and uncompromising but with an enduring sense of the ridiculous, Burton had spent his life in the UK Prison Service, which latterly had undergone what we now call restructuring. He immediately set about reforming the Kenya Service in similar fashion and, as a preliminary, decided to visit all the prisons under his command. To my pleasure he insisted that I should accompany him and off we set in his land-rover (complete with portable bar and other comforts). His ideas were innovative and liberal and aimed, broadly speaking, at improving conditions in the prisons and reducing the level of recidivism. Once, while inspecting the workshops at Kamiti, we came across an aged Sikh engaged in some delicate wrought iron work. Burton complimented him on his skill and asked why he was in prison. 'For forgery, Sahib' 'What were you forging?' 'Sixpences, Sahib' 'With that ability why on earth didn't you try shillings?' said Burton and passed on. For a time all went well but it soon became apparent that Tony Swann, the Minister, did not share Burton's reforming zeal, and there was, in addition, a clash of personalities which their differing backgrounds did nothing to alleviate. In the end, Burton quit, a disappointed man, his work unfinished.

For a spell I acted as Civil Secretary to the Prisons Service and in the process became unwillingly involved in the Peter Poole tragedy. In late 1959 Poole had shot and killed an African house servant outside his house in Gordon Road in Nairobi. He was sentenced to death and was being held in Nairobi Prison. It fell to me one day to visit him there, quite why I cannot now remember, and I came away impressed both by the comfort in which he was living and his polite and composed demeanour. In due course his Appeal was rejected and his only hope was that the Governor, Patrick Renison, would exercise his Prerogative of Mercy. At this desperate juncture Poole's father, Norman, an electrical contractor with a shop in Government Road, but by now a frail and pitiful figure, visited Prisons HQ to see if anything further could be done. We were unable to give him any comfort. As much, I imagine, for political as other reasons, Renison declined to intervene and the date of Poole's execution was set. The case had been taken up by the populist press in the UK and, with only days to go, a *Daily Express* journalist managed somehow to obtain an interview with Poole in prison – to our dismay, and of course the government's. The paper, with had played up the racial angle of the story for all its worth, followed this coup by flying Poole's wife to Nairobi from Britain, where she had taken refuge, for a last meeting with her husband. Poole died bravely on the 18 August 1960.

From Council of Ministers to Cabinet Office

JOHN ROSS

I returned from home leave in mid 1962 to find myself appointed Secretary to the Council of Ministers, to use the wording of the oath of secrecy I had to swear. The person in overall charge of the running of the Council was in fact Frank Loyd who was my boss and more entitled to call himself Secretary than I. Our office was located in the grounds of Government House and was headed by the Deputy Governor, Eric Griffith-Jones. Frank's title was PSGO and mine ASGO and between us an Under-Secretary, initially Terry Gavaghan and after him, John Cumber.

The Council met around a long table in a magnificent room in Government House. Renison sat in the middle with his back to the windows and I occupied a small half moon table immediately behind him. Opposite Renison sat Kenyatta and Ngala, with Mboya always pretty close to Kenyatta. Before each meeting I would help to prepare the briefing book for Renison, a huge tome containing all the memoranda under discussion together with our comments and advice on each, a task that took several days and involved much ringing around to the Ministries concerned. My main role was to take the minutes and have them circulated to Ministers a day or two ahead of the next meeting. The Council met weekly with every second meeting devoted to the drafting of the ultimately ill fated 'Regional' constitution, the framework for which had been agreed at a conference in London earlier in the year. I was kept pretty busy, especially during a brief but hectic visit by Reginald Maudling who had taken over from Iain Macleod as Colonial Secretary. But generally speaking there was little sense of real urgency on the Constitutional front and on the whole I cannot claim to have been been overworked.

Renison ran Council meetings in a business-like way, but without much in the way of humour or warmth, rather in the manner of an old-fashioned headmaster dealing with his senior prefects. The Africans for their part treated him in the main with politeness and deference. There was however, much at stake: KANU wanted a strong central government and KADU the precise opposite. Often the exchanges across the table became heated and bitter, but in the end good humour usually prevailed. Mboya made much of the running for KANU and Ngala, puffing away at his pipe, for KADU. Kenyatta did not take a leading part in the debates but when he did intervene, sometimes with some witty remark, he was listened to with great attention by both sides. Most of the time he just sat there in a relaxed way and once or twice it looked as though he was about to nod off. Occasionally he would stare expressionlessly at Renison, thinking heavens knows what – it was not so long since the Governor had described him publicly as 'The African leader to darkness and death'.

Looking back one can see that Renison's background (he had had no African experience before Kenya) and temperament did not fit him for the essentially political task that had been thrust upon him. I believe he had an innate distrust of politicians, whether black, white, or brown – at a time when the situation in Kenya called out for trust above all else. Certainly he was unable to relax with them and I do not think he had ever entertained his non-European Ministers socially in Government House. He could also be insensitive. Whenever a Minister proposed being absent from Kenya, instead of ringing the Governor or dropping him a note he had to fill in a cyclostyled form ('If Your Excellency approves of my absence .....'). I have one such form signed by Kenyatta, who had been invited to attend the Tanganyika *uhuru* celebrations. On it he proposed the names of Ministers to fill in for him, including at routine Council of Ministers meetings. At the foot of the form Renison has written tersely in Gubernatorial red ink: 'I approve – except that we do not have substitutes at routine meetings'. It would not have occurred to him to say have a nice time and I look forward to hearing all about it when you get back.

In November Renison was summoned to London for talks with Maudling's successor, Duncan Sandys, who was disturbed both by the slow pace of Constitutional advance and by clear signs that things were not as they should be on the ground in Kenya. While Renison was still in London the news broke in Nairobi that he had been summarily dismissed. Shocked not so much by the dismissal as by the brutal manner of it, the Council of Ministers headed by Kenyatta were at the airport to greet the Governor on his return, in a demonstration of sympathy and support. At the start of the first Council meeting after his return, Kenyatta and Ngala made impromptu and felicitous speeches. Renison, stoical as ever, was able to mutter a few words of thanks before turning briskly to the business of the day. For the rest of the meeting, and indeed for the rest of his time in Kenya, the African Ministers treated him with great sympathy and courtesy. A day or two before his final departure, Renison invited the Council of Ministers and officials such as Frank Loyd and myself, and our wives, to a farewell dinner and at the cigars and brandy stage Kenyatta and Ngala again spoke most movingly, as Africans can on such occasions. The Ministers had clubbed together for a present, which was handed over by Kenyatta. This time Renison was incapable of coherent reply and all I could hear was a few strangled phrases and then, quite clearly in a tone of wonder, 'and Jomo too.... and Jomo too... '.

Renison's successor, Malcolm MacDonald, arrived in early January 1963 with instructions to bring Kenya to Independence within two years. It was immediately apparent that things would be very different from then on. On the night of his arrival he threw a drinks party for the Council of Ministers – 'a relaxed, gay party which aided the foundations for our agreeable co-operation throughout the next important year', as he put it later. Within a few days he proposed to a startled Council, and to my personal horror, that we should forthwith meet, not once, but nine times a week with the aim of completing the drafting of the Constitution by March at the latest. Thus we entered a period of frantic activity. For three days a week we would have sessions in the morning, in the afternoon (when tea would be served) and in the evening. The evening session would start with a buffet supper and would continue often into the small hours. At some point during the proceedings a drinks trolley would be wheeled in and we would, myself included, fall on it. Sometimes I would get home at one or two in the morning and finding I was too het up to sleep would be back in my office an hour or two later trying to write up my minutes. MacDonald himself was tireless. Although now in his sixties, it was not unknown for him to work throughout the night dealing with matters he had been unable to attend to during the day. By dawn he would be out in the grounds of Government House bird watching and by ten we would find stacks of blue chits on our desks with instructions and comments of various kinds, the fruits of his nocturnal labours.

The Ministers entered into the spirit of things with a will and we forged ahead. MacDonald handled the meetings with practised skill. When tempers rose, as they often did, he would relieve the tension with some joke or reminiscence or simply move on to another subject. In stark contrast to Renison, he was friendly and relaxed in his dealing with the African and Asian Ministers and it was soon clear that they in turn respected and trusted him. At a late hour after the conclusion of one of his night sessions, I saw him holding forth to an attentive group of Ministers gathered round the drinks trolley. I wandered over and found he was talking about his father and describing in some detail the circumstance in which Ramsay had been born out of wedlock. Towards the end of this extraordinary story, Frank Loyd joined us and after listening for a minute or two said to me in a loud whisper: 'I don't get it – who was the bastard, Ramsay or Malcolm?'

Within a week or two of his arrival MacDonald proposed, and Sandys with some courage agreed, that the timetable for Constitutional advance should be further compressed, with the Election to be held in May, followed by Internal Self-Government in June and full Independence in December. To my relief Donald Hodge was brought in to share my duties and off we set at full tilt. The immediate aim was to complete the drafting of the Constitution by early March, except for those sections on which Ministers were simply unable to agree. The Secretary of State would then visit Nairobi and, if agreement were still not possible on these points, would decide them himself. Ministers agreed in advance of his visit that in these circumstances they would abide by his decisions. At the end of the final meeting before Sandys' arrival, when we were all sitting around in a somewhat exhausted state, MacDonald said that he wished to raise a delicate and confidential matter. Duncan Sandys, he said, was an immensely experienced and respected politician, and a personal friend. He had served over the years with distinction in many high offices. He was a brilliant negotiator. But, MacDonald said, Ministers should be aware that in the heat of debate he could, at times be outspoken to the point of rudeness – in short, he had a vile temper which sometimes got the better of him. Kenyatta gravely thanked the Governor for this timely advice and the meeting broke up.

After this the Ministers treated Sandys with kid gloves. His visit was a complete success and rather to my disappointment passed without incident, although once or twice it seemed to me he was on the point of explosion. All outstanding matters were satisfactorily settled, and our labours were at last at an end. Astonishingly only two months had elapsed since MacDonald's arrival.

The Council continued to meet up to the time of the Election and towards the end of one particularly difficult meeting I noticed with surprise that MacDonald could not stop yawning. The next day, he retired to bed and from there he wrote to the Council. 'My dear Colleagues, I send you warm greetings. Unfortunately I cannot convey them in person as my

Doctor will not allow me to leave my couch. I have got pneumonia, having been caught by a virus, which is flying around Nairobi, and accosting many victims. One of them was Jimmy Gichuru. He may have passed it to me across the table at one of our Council of Ministers meetings. So beware of Jimmy! I suggest that he should sit at a separate table of his own, in a corner.... I look forward to rejoining you before long. In the meantime I send you my best wishes for your great work for Kenya.'

He was out of action for two months, but was on hand in June to swear Kenyatta in as Prime Minister, KANU having won the election. We moved the Cabinet Office (as it was now called) to the Ministry of Works building in central Nairobi which became the PM's Office, with Geoffrey Ellerton as Permanent Secretary. Before the Cabinet's first meeting I prepared the Briefing Book for Kenyatta just as I had done for Renison all those months ago. An hour or so before it was due to start, I was summoned to his office. He said it was quite impossible for him to read and digest all these papers and would I please give him an oral briefing instead. This was a tall order but I struggled through somehow, at any rate this practice became the norm from then on. I knew of course, that my days in the Cabinet room were numbered and that sooner or later an African would be appointed, but it was certainly stimulating while it lasted. Discussion was in English and was often very lively. Kenyatta had clearly taken a new lease of life since the Election and there was no doubt who was in charge. Once when Mboya was too longwinded, Kenyatta brandished his whisk at him and bellowed, 'Shut up Tom!' – which he immediately did. I handed over eventually to Duncan Ndegwa (who later became Governor of the Central Bank), and for the remainder of my time in Kenya did various jobs in the PM's Office.

I had by this time worked with Kenyatta for over a year and had come to like him. I was, of course, aware of his darker side, but I had had no personal experience of that. Whatever the truth of the past, Kenyatta certainly had some endearing traits. When the time came for me to say goodbye he said how sorry he was that both Geoffrey and I were leaving but that he understood why. He asked about my family and then, to my surprise, said he would like to meet my two boys, to wish them well. An appointment was made and we dressed the boys in their Thomsons Falls school uniforms for the occasion. There was much activity in the outer office while we were waiting, telephones ringing and so forth, and I remember thinking there must be some crisis afoot. Kenyatta emerged and taking the boys by the hand proceeded to give them a tour of his office and its many treasures, all the while talking to them with great animation. After twenty minutes or so an aide came in and said something to him. 'Let them wait', said Kenyatta. When eventually we left, the outer office was full of British and African military top brass; and later in the day, I heard that the KAR had mutinied.

As a postscript, in 1976, I returned to Nairobi as a member of the New

Zealand delegation to the UNESCO Conference of that year. Kenyatta opened the Conference by reading an anodyne prepared speech (always a penance for him). Then throwing away his notes he gazed out on the sea of delegates and said that he knew they would be discussing weighty and important matters but that because they came from many different countries, they would sometimes find it hard to agree among themselves. But Kenya, he said, had a solution to situations like this – and within minutes, waving his whisk at the thousands of somewhat startled delegates, he had the entire Conference shouting *Harambee! Harambee!* for all they were worth. I tried to see him while I was in Nairobi, but did not succeed.

Government House 1956–9

DICK WILSON

Government House, Nairobi, a large and imposing building designed by Sir Herbert Baker and set in extensive grounds, is thought to have been destined, in the mind of its first occupant, to be the eventual residence of a British Governor-General of an East African Federation. This was not to be. However, many years later, this grand house provided an excellent base to meet some of the accommodation requirements of the long sequence of VIP visitors, conferences, etc, which was to follow from 1952 with the arrival, as Governor, of Sir Evelyn Baring and with the simultaneous declaration of the Mau Mau Emergency.

Throughout Baring's term of office (1952-1959), GH was the centre of intense political and social activity: Constitutional talks involving politicians of all races; visits by important personalities from UK and elsewhere such as the President of the World Bank; the conduct of operations against Mau Mau, and, of course, the day to day business of running the country. These were among the Governor's daily preoccupations.

I was the Governor's Private Secretary during the period 1956–9, the year of Baring's retirement from the Governorship. The Mau Mau's violent campaign had been largely overcome and the struggle for political power amongst the various factions was at its most crucial stage. The PS was mainly concerned with the Governor's daily business schedule: arranging his frequent interviews with Ministers, visiting VIPs, politicians and business leaders; taking note of important discussions; keeping Ministers and senior officials advised of HE's position on current issues; drafting speeches for social functions, for example opening charitable functions – major speeches were drafted by Ministries – and, not least, co-ordinating safari programmes. This last enabled the PS to keep in touch with the administration in the field, as often as possible accompanying HE, who was always armed with a small black notebook, in which matters of importance were recorded before being transferred into his photographic memory.

These were most interesting and educative times for this holder of the PS post, and recollections of that time are legion. Two of these must suffice for this note. The first is of historic interest. With the Mau Mau offensive over, growing unease was important enough to prompt a visit by the Minister of Defence, accompanied by the Chief of the Defence Staff, with the aim of impressing those concerned that it was no longer possible to maintain this major British commitment. Baring found himself faced with a tired and irascible Secretary of State, badly in need of a break. This was quickly arranged in the form of a game-watching safari in the Mara. The effect was dramatic and the Governor was able to face a jubilant Minister on his return from a thrilling safari, with a document, to be discussed that afternoon, on what he saw as the UK's responsibility for the security of the British population of Kenya at that time. The discussion led to the immediate despatch of the CDS to approve a site for accommodation of a British garrison in the Nairobi area. The Kahawa site, later to become Kenyatta University, was chosen and the project was approved. For me, the sight of an ecstatic Secretary of State, standing up in his land-rover as it drove into the portico of GH was truly memorable.

The second is on a different note. In his leisure hours, the Governor particularly enjoyed bird watching, botany, and rock climbing, in the pursuit of which he had a number of regular companions. He also needed regular exercise to make up for the hours he spent at his desk, and he would go for snap rides on his large and spirited horse. Also in GH stables was a grey child's pony, seated on which his 6ft 2inch Private Secretary would do his best, as they rode through Mitchell Park, to keep up with his master at the gallop!

Sitting one morning in my small office next to HE's, I was surprised to be visited by HM the Queen Mother, seeking a stroll in the garden and to be told about the people she would be meeting on that day's tour. She was particularly anxious that during her visit she should, if possible, be able to pay some attention to the morale of the British people who might be worried about their future in Kenya. Of course, HM's very presence was a tonic for all who met her. I could not have wished for a more wonderful recollection.

Government House

PETER JOHNSON

February 1962 saw the second Lancaster House conference in London in full swing under the skilful chairmanship of Secretary of State Maudling. He had only recently taken over the job from Macleod whose influence was still powerful. Jomo Kenyatta had been released from detention only a few weeks earlier but had been elected President of the Kikuyu dominated party of KANU whilst still in detention. The world watched to see whether the old aura of authority remained – it did, in very full measure. The main protagonists at the Constitutional Conference were the two African dominated parties of KADU led by Ronald Ngala and KANU by Kenyatta. The progressive European and Asian vote had formed the New Kenya Group, under the direction of Michael Blundell, following the first Lancaster House Conference in 1960 and were now virtually an integral part of KADU. The European voice, per se, centred on a small group with the misleading title of the Kenya Coalition whose principal members included Maconochie-Welwood, Cavendish-Bentinck and Clive Salter. The Governor, Patrick Renison, was in attendance at the London Conference and Eric Griffith-Jones was Acting Governor in Nairobi, providing a backstop and reference point for difficulties arising at the Conference, particularly those with Legal or Constitutional implications. For instance, he was required to find out the Provincial Administration's likely reaction if Kenyatta were offered a Ministerial position as a result of deliberations in London.

Michael Blundell, who had been in the forefront of European politics in Kenya for more than ten years was to retire from the scene after his second Lancaster House Conference. His business affairs required rather urgent attention and besides the pace of Constitutional development had left him rather high and dry. However he continued to have direct access to the Governor and Secretary of State.

It was a slightly strange world to be plunged into as Private Secretary. The Griffith-Jones's made me very welcome with invitations to tennis, go-carting with the children and golf. Eric Griffith-Jones' background both in Malaya and Kenya was as Solicitor General then Attorney General and this, perforce, had involved him in some clashes with the Administration over the years, arising from the various investigations he was obliged to undertake, where the Administration were suspected of having exceeded its remit under the Emergency Powers. As an ex-Central Province District Officer I was therefore a trifle suspect. However, after a slightly bumpy initial period, we became firm allies and I much appreciated his subsequent support and friendship. This period had a slightly phoney feel to it. Speculation was rife that Renison would not return because he had lost Macleod's confidence by his 'leader to darkness and death' speech in reference to Kenyatta and his alleged lack of political feel. Meanwhile, Griffith-Jones was getting a regular up-date on the London scene, not from Renison but from Bruce McKenzie, the white South African KANU member, who might be described as something of a political adventurer! The 'legal eagles' were regularly in attendance at GH but the Provincial Administration's influence was largely confined to Robin Wainwright's reports. On the other hand, Griffith-Jones had developed a good relationship with foreign diplomats, particularly the Americans, and his handling of the press was professional. His non-attributable weekly sessions with editors and sub-editors were well handled.

The Lancaster House conference eventually concluded with agreement to form a KADU/KANU Coalition Government with Ngala and Kenyatta appointed as Joint Ministers of State responsible for Constitutional Affairs and Economic Planning. The new Government was charged, in particular, with responsibility for working out the format for eventual Internal Self-Government to be followed by a General Election 'early in the New Year' Special Commissions were to be appointed to address such crucial issues as the land question and compensation, the Coastal Strip and the Somali secession problem. Griffith-Jones, as Acting Governor, responded immediately with the swearing-in of the new Minister and setting the scene for pursuing in earnest the Conference's objectives. He was on first name terms with all the Ministers, except Kenyatta who was always addressed as Mr. One difficulty that Kenyatta had was to balance within KANU the power and influence of Mboya and Odinga, the two Luo leaders, both in very different ways vital to Kenyatta's authority. But he was not granted permission to appoint Odinga as a Minister. A measure of teasing and light hearted banter between Kenyatta and Ngala was beginning to occur in the Council of Ministers meetings, so Griffith-Jones had every reason to be encouraged by his stewardship at the helm. This was to be reinforced shortly by the award of a knighthood in the Birthday Honours. It was therefore a surprise all round when it was announced that Renison would return to duty at the end of June, prior to a visit to Nairobi by Secretary of State Maudling in July.

Renison duly arrived back. Clearly he had benefited immeasurably from the leave break and returned with all his old poise, authority and charm. I was delighted to get to know him and discover such a fruitful and easy relationship. He moved smoothly into the role of chairing the Council of Ministers and was able to pull his full weight during Maudling's visit. From a personal point of view, it was particularly fascinating to watch the Secretary of State at close quarters. His high reputation was easy to recognise and his masterly grasp of detail ensured the success of the visit. Also he was at pains to strengthen Renison's authority.

In the period July-November, Renison was very effective and derived much practical benefit from the warm relationship with Frank Loyd (Permanent Secretary, Cabinet Office), who, in the absence of Griffith-Jones on leave, became his principal adviser. He not only pushed ahead with Constitutional matters in a dignified and sensitive way, but was pleased to continue his patronage of a wide range of worthwhile causes in the Colony.

There was considerable cohesion at this stage and Renison was in full charge. Then came Macmillan's 'Night of the Long Knives', out of which Duncan Sandys emerged as minister responsible for guiding Kenya's immediate future. It would be idle to pretend that this was widely welcomed in Nairobi; Sandys had a reputation at the time of being difficult to negotiate with and very longwinded. The matter of immediate concern, however, was to know what London's plans were for Government House in Nairobi. It was suspected that Macleod had had every intention of replacing Renison; then there appeared to have been a stay of execution during the Maudling regime. And now what? Apparently at the time of the Uganda Independence celebrations in Entebbe, Renison had been told privately of the plan to bring in a new man at the Internal Self-Government stage. This was duly confirmed by Sandys, and to take effect at the year-end, but no mention of the name of his successor. When the news broke Renison was in London conferring with Sandys. There was a general wave of sympathy and this was shared by the Kenyan Ministers too, who voluntarily paraded at Nairobi Airport to greet Renison on his return from London.

Renison was an officer and a gentleman for whom political manoeuvring had little appeal. He had generated much respect from the Administration, Police, and Armed Forces throughout his time in Kenya and this was given tangible form by way of parades and presentations prior to his final departure. The elevation to GCMG had been used to soften the blow.

For a month or more, speculation was rife about the succession. Lord Caradon (Hugh Foot) of Cyprus fame was canvassed as a likely candidate. Malcolm MacDonald's name came as a great surprise as he was thought to be far too 'senior', having been Colonial Secretary himself twenty-five years earlier and subsequently holding a whole series of prestigious diplomatic appointments round the world. However, Friday, 4 January 1963 saw his arrival at Nairobi airport with his charming Canadian wife, Audrey.

With the minimum of fuss he moved into Government House and immediately began organising a series of meetings with African Ministers. In passing, at an informal lunch on that first meeting, he stated clearly that whenever he was hosting a meal at GH he and his wife would be served last! That was the first of a number of gestures designed to show there was a new 'modern' power in the land. So, within two weeks of arriving he decreed that the Council of Ministers would meet on three days each week (instead of one) with up to three sessions per day to ensure that the format for Internal Self-Government was hammered out as quickly as possible. He was an absolute whirlwind – with a mixture of very carefully planned work schedules making great demands on his own and other people's time. Some deliberately provocative gestures such as filling the corridors of GH with so-called *objets d'art* with a strong erotic theme, and insisting upon regular *ad hoc* lunches on the verandah with invitations extended to chosen guests, to those who had signed the GH Visitors Book and to his old cronies from Asia who were passing through Nairobi. The rig of the day at these lunches ranged from hats and gloves to 'tackies'!

His mode of working was to shut out anything he considered inessential or marginal in order to concentrate on Constitutional matters. No small talk was encouraged and he expected anyone vaguely involved in the work of the moment to be available for discussion whether it happened to suit his own timetable or not. Bird watching provided his one great relaxation and to this end he commandeered all the resources of GH. His long-standing Malay/Chinese photographer friend Christine Loke was a frequent visitor and together they wrote and illustrated his wild life book, 'Treasures of Kenya'. His communication system with his Private Secretary – and I assume it went for all the different Private Secretaries he must have had in his long and distinguished career – was to fill his desk drawer every day with heaps of small blue chits, each carrying a question requiring an immediate answer. Examples: 'why did the Daily Nation reporter state that I was unshaven on arrival from Wajir when I had shaved as usual that morning?' 'What was the name of the bird Bruce McKenzie saw when motoring on the Kinangop last Saturday?' 'Who is the Secretary of State bringing with him and why?' Tony Swann was so intrigued that he 'stole' two of the used blue chits as souvenirs!

Alongside this high pressure work schedule he dealt with a mass of – often intriguing – private correspondence, wrote an obituary (prior to the event) on Pandit Nehru for *The Guardian* and insisted on a reduction in the Government House budget including a substantial cut in his own salary. Simultaneously with this, and unbeknown to MacDonald, the Colonial Office was seriously exercised by the fact that because he had moved from one prestigious job to another with such frequency, no proper provision for his eventual pension had been made.

At the time it was not easy to read this extraordinary man. He appeared to have a cast iron constitution and to operate on a minimum of sleep. He was clearly a superb strategist and never felt obliged to either explain or apologise for anything. As his book, 'People and Places' (published in 1969) subsequently revealed, he was in part of, if not the centre of, the pre-war London *avant-garde* 'jet set'. He had found himself a Cabinet Minister in his early thirties with a very heavy workload. If he was not to be denied his birthright of youth and excitement, he had somehow to learn to do without too much sleep. He forged very close relationships in the theatrical world. Among his intimate friends were Ivor Novello, Noel Coward, the Oliviers, Beatrice Lilley and many others. MacDonald too was perhaps an actor and showman first, and a politician and statesman second!

His hunch about intensifying the pace of working for the African Ministers certainly paid off. A markedly friendly purposeful atmosphere – created in part by the continuous provision of food and drink – enabled Maudling's original timetable for Self-Government to be achievable. By early March (barely two months in the Colony) MacDonald was able to produce an agreed outline of the Independence Constitution justifying the immediate presence of the Secretary of State to negotiate the finer points of difference. Duncan Sandys and party promptly responded and there followed a successful four-day Conference, which cleared the way for a General Election in May.

It goes without saying that the stage managing of this crucial exercise was meticulously planned by MacDonald, even to the extent of highlighting Sandys' personal idiosyncrasies and advising the African Ministers on how best to play their cards in negotiations with him. Although the two party leaders, Ngala and Kenyatta, had been charged jointly with the fashioning of the final Independence Constitution, everyone recognised that the imminent Election which would trigger it, would in all probability make one of the main parties the government, and all the others the opposition. Officialdom remained strictly neutral, but emotionally was inclined to support KADU, largely because of the Kikuyus' Mau Mau record. In the event KANU triumphed and Kenyatta, rather than Ngala, became Prime Minister of a self-governing Kenya.

MacDonald would claim that this was the solution he had worked very hard to achieve. One had to admire the clarity of thought and singleness of purpose. He had always been three steps ahead of the field and subsequent events, at least in a five-year period, reinforced his judgement of Kenyatta's character and capability. I would not wish to add to or subtract from MacDonald's own account of this period recorded in the Kenyatta chapter in his book 'Titans and Others', published in 1972.

In reflecting on Malcolm MacDonald as a person to work with and understand, I have always been intrigued by the following quotation from a letter he wrote from Nairobi in 1964 to Thelma Cazalet-Keir (a Conservative parliamentary contemporary of the 1930s): 'The older I get, the less importance I attach to acquaintances and the more importance I attach to real friends. So I try to sheer away from a lot of new human contacts here. In fact I have only made three great friends in the last twenty months – two African Ministers and one Russian film star. Of course, Jomo is the greatest of the trio.' Dare I say it – their personalities were so similar!

The Order of Merit never comes cheaply. Malcolm MacDonald earned his in the fullest measure.

Internal Self-Government

DICK WILSON

Following the Elections held in May 1963 to establish the framework of Internal Self-Government, those of us who were assigned to the Provinces, then under Central Government control, became regional officers answerable to one of the six Regional Assemblies. PCs became Civil Secretaries to their Regional Assemblies and DCs became Regional Government Agents. Departments were also 'Regionalised'. The Northeastern Region was separately put under a Civil Service answerable to the Governor direct. The post of Chief Commissioner was abolished and the Minister for Home Affairs assumed general responsibility for the Regions. I became Civil Secretary, Central Region.

The major development, which coincided with the return of Jomo Kenyatta to the political scene, resulted in much disruption in the Provinces and a serious diminution in the authority of the Provincial Administration at all levels. The effects were particularly marked in the Central Province/Region, where elections to the Regional Assembly resulted in all but one of the seats being won by candidates who had at one stage been involved in Mau Mau. (Fortunately the Members elected the exception as their President.)

The Assembly Members quickly took full advantage of their perks and powers. To start with they took over the Civil Secretary's official land-rover and set forth in small groups to visit the KANU hierarchy in each of the seven districts of the Region. The Transport Vote was quickly exhausted, as was the Assembly's Attendance Allowance Vote, which could not cope with the demands of almost weekly meetings of the full Assembly insisted on by Members. There followed numerous visits to Nairobi in the search for funds, invariably without success. Debates were chaotic, and the departmental officers were as unhappy as we were.

At an Assembly meeting in September 1963, a few days before my departure on retirement, it was decided that there should be a farewell tea party for me. I was asked whether the Assembly's vote could meet the cost of this. As the answer was in the negative, there was no tea party!

And so I handed over office to a perplexed Geoffrey Kariithi, who was, however, destined to become Secretary to Kenyatta's Cabinet, when Provincial Administration in its old form had been re-established under Central Government control.

4

The District Boma

Bachelor Life in Lodwar	Tom Watts
Married Life in Marsabit	Tom Watts
A Distant Boma	David Nicoll Griffith
Official Entertainment	Peter Gordon
Goans and the Administration	Mervyn Maciel
My Favourite Boma	Robin Wainwright
A Child's View	Veronica Bellers
A Night Alarm	June Peet
The Queen Mother's Visit to Narok	Dick Cashmore
Bill and Long Drops	David Lambert
Shades of von Lettow Vorbeck	John Williams
Literal Responses	Alistair Anderson
A Quiet Posting	W.H. (Tommy) Thompson
A Haunted Boma	Henry Wright
The Bush Telegraph	John Williams
Marmalade Brown	Ian Willis

Introduction

The *boma* was home, a comfortable base to return to from safari. If you were married you had a house of your own, usually spacious with two or three bedrooms. Bachelors often had to share. Most *boma* residents followed a tradition of welcoming newcomers. There were dinner parties and curry lunches at week-ends. Often a small club provided tennis, squash, golf and social events.

    Not all *bomas* were comfortable. Tommy Thompson and Henry Wright describe the harsh conditions and the fascination of Kipini which was abandoned in 1960. Many *bomas* were remote, with limited shops and public utilities. Yet Tom Watts and Mervyn Maciel both enjoyed life in Marsabit, a mountain in the middle of the northern desert.

    Administration in the *boma* was largely office and court work. The most junior DO, often a Cadet, would be responsible for the running of the *boma* and would be expected to listen to *shauris*. His duty was to do a tour of inspection before breakfast. In earlier days the DC did this himself as Veronica Bellers recounts.

The DC was the head of the *boma* community and was expected to demonstrate his leadership. Mervyn Maciel tells us how much the legendary Whitehouse was held in awe as DC Turkana. Some DCs were eccentric. Ian Willis has the last word on one such whom he nevertheless liked and respected.

Bachelor Life in Lodwar

TOM WATTS

District headquarters built on the rocks at Lodwar, against which the Turkwell River flows and turns east towards Lake Rudolf, was a hot, windy, dusty spot in the middle of the day. We got up before sunrise and attended the Tribal Police parade before walking round the *boma* to inspect the lines, the trading centre, the brick works, the slaughterhouse, the jail in the fort, the small hospital-dispensary, the pumping station with its sump deep in the sand of the Turkwell, the night soil area and any other activity requiring supervision. In 1942 we were well housed in brick built houses with flat roofs on which was a gauze covered cage in which to sleep. We spent the hours of darkness in the cool air on the roof. The houses were reasonably cool but dusty during the daylight hours. I grew quite good tomatoes on sand mixed with goat manure, provided the cook watered the plants whilst I was on safari. My kerosene refrigerator was a great boon except when the cook failed to trim the wick whilst I was away; he found it easier to remember to pour water over the charcoal of the cool box. The cook, a local Turkana, was liable to get drunk and when he forgot to clean his cooking pots the hyenas would chew them into balls of aluminium. The Principal of the school at Kapenguria, George Chaundy, used to send each of us, on the weekly lorry, a box of vegetables grown in the school's garden, which was greatly appreciated.

The office closed at two p.m. and we then cooled off in the tank excavated in the rock and cement lined under a high *makuti* shade. The water came from the piped supply from the well in the Turkwell and the tank itself was officially the *boma's* water reserve having been paid for out of the 'goat bag,' an unofficial account derived from the sale of skins of sheep and goats slaughtered for rations. At a time when we were slaughtering large numbers of animals for the forces and the civilian labour, the goat bag income was considerable. It was used to construct some of the brick buildings in Lodwar such as the store cum squash court and the shelter for tribespeople awaiting visits to the offices. The goat bag funded the start of the dried fish trade from Ferguson's Gulf on Lake Rudolf to the Kitale market for Kavirondo labour in Trans Nzoia. Pangrassio, a Luo fisherman from Uyoma on Lake Victoria ran a fishing camp at Ferguson's Gulf for poverty stricken Turkana who had no animals. They were encouraged to increase their catch and to dry it for export to Kitale, thereby earning some money to augment their fish diet with posho, sugar, tea and salt and chewing tobacco. Some were even able to purchase small stock sufficient to provide a dowry for a wife. Unlike many Kenya tribes, the Turkana preferred to pay dowry for a woman who had already proved her ability to have a child. I never came across a case in Turkana where a husband sought the return of his dowry because his wife bore no child, unlike many down-country tribes.

Married Life in Marsabit

TOM WATTS

I met my wife-to-be in Kakamega clubhouse 1when she lent me a nail file to repair a broken nail! Molly was a better golfer than me. After my posting to Marsabit came on VE Day we learnt that the Forces Auxiliary Nursing Yeomanry (FANYs) would be demobilised if married. We announced our engagement on 12 May 1945, were married in the Provincial Commissioner's office on 19 May and had a four-day honeymoon at Kitale Club. I left Kisumu for Marsabit via Nairobi and Nanyuki on 24 May. Molly stayed behind to complete her service, sell the car and pack up. I took the lorry down from Marsabit at the end of June to meet her at Nanyuki station and so we started a two-year posting in Marsabit.

The Martin-Johnson's published their book about Paradise Lake on Marsabit Mountain with excellent photographs of game and of the scenery. Their seaplane was shown to have landed on the Lake. This was in the early 1930s. Marsabit by 1945 was both a gazetted forest and a game reserve, but Paradise Lake no longer held water sufficient for a canoe let alone a seaplane. Years of drought had greatly reduced the supply of rain with which to replenish the water in the volcanic crater high on the mountain. It was said that either elephants or humans, in their search for water had pierced the impermeable skin of the crater through which the water had drained into the volcanic tuff below. When we first walked to the crater just after the 1945 long rains there was sufficient water to call it an overgrown swamp well used by elephants, rhino and buffalo and a haven for millions of butterflies. There were other volcanic craters within the forest reserve and also rock pools in the gorges draining the mountain into the lava desert to the south. There were large troops of baboons based in the craters. Whilst the leopard kept them in check these animals caused damage to the limited cultivation allowed along the northern edge of the forest close to the government *boma*. Our Game Warden, at that time operating from Isiolo, George Adamson, arranged for a culling of these troops. He once came across a dying leopard in the forest, which had been mortally wounded by baboons who had ripped open its stomach.

Game played a part in our daily life in Marsabit where our house was on the edge of the forest. Our water supply consisted of forty-gallon drums behind the house from which water was piped by gravity to the kitchen and our bathroom. These drums were replenished by water brought each morning in two-gallon buckets on the heads of prisoners from the township wells. During the prolonged drought in 1945, the elephants would knock the lids off these water drums and take their fill. They constantly raided our vegetable plot, especially the pawpaw trees. A barrier of rolls of concertina wire finally kept them away but not before one elephant got entangled in the mass of wire and became very noisy in protest. They wandered through the garden and also enjoyed the avenue of pepper trees, which lined the road down to the office. Later in 1946 Molly was shocked to see a large dog baboon peering into the pram where our baby daughter was asleep, fortunately under a mosquito net.

Apart from ourselves there were three European bachelor policemen based in Marsabit but responsible for patrolling the border with Abyssinia from the fortified post on Lake Rudolf at Ileret to Sololo in Moyale District. Their quarters too, were on the forest edge. They too had their problems with game. One early morning, one of the young inspectors opened the door of his hut to find a lion stretched across the threshold. After the initial shock he realised that it was dead. It must have been a member of a pride, which had been carrying off cattle from the township *kraal* to such an extent that the game department had to resort to poison. 'To stroke the lion' became the explanation for the need to go outside. During the 1945 drought, rhino moved into the forest and on one occasion everyone turned out to try to pull out a rhino which in its search for water had slid into one of the Sagunte Wells. We had no tranquilliser darts to quieten this large beast which struggled every time we pulled on the ropes. Eventually it had to be shot in order to remove it from the well. At that time there were large herds of oryx in the plains south of the mountain into which the Milgis River drained the seasonal rains on the Mathews Range and Ndoto Mountains. There were also plenty of giraffe and zebra. This was a tsetse area into which the nomads seldom took their livestock. There was a herd of beautiful kudu, which showed itself regularly around the *boma*.

Marsabit was a lovely station for a young married couple to live in. Situated on the forest's edge it had the magnificent view across the lava strewn low country to the Huri Hills and beyond to the blue mountains of southern Abyssinia. It was, of course, isolated, being over a hundred and sixty miles from Isiolo, the Provincial headquarters and over two hundred miles from the railhead and our source of supplies at Nanyuki. During the rains the lorries were often held up at Laisamis with the Milgis River in flood. At such times our fresh food supply was often ruined in the heat of this low country when the lorry was unable to cross the swampy area. By 1945 the fine dirt road from Isiolo to Marsabit built by the Army for the campaign in Abyssinia 1940–41, had greatly deteriorated as there were no maintenance funds available and so lorry traffic had reverted in many places to bush tracks in the dry weather. The same applied to the road constructed from Marsabit *boma* down the mountain north-eastwards across the lava strewn Hedad to the border posts of Sololo and Moyale occasionally used by the armed police who more often used lorry transport to travel to North Horr and the frontier posts of Sabarei and Ileret. Visitors to Marsabit came through Isiolo by lorry or flew to our large, undulating landing ground which had to be inspected for wild pig holes whenever a plane was expected, which was very seldom.

A Distant Boma

DAVID NICOLL-GRIFFITH

There were, apart from Administration and Police, no departmental officers at Marsabit in 1954, but there was a doctor at the Protestant mission. Unfortunately he had had a series of failed operations and the tribesmen had lost all faith in his powers.

There came one day to my office a Habash (from Ethiopia). He had walked from Moyale, one hundred and seventy miles across the Dida Galgalo – a lava desert – in order to be operated on for hernia! I was amazed that he could have got so far in such a condition and said that I would make immediate arrangements for him to be attended to. At this he shook his head vehemently declaring that on no account would he agree to that, but instead wanted a pass to go on to Wajir. This would have entailed a further hundred and seventy-five miles (at least) across the desert, but incredibly he got there and was operated on successfully.

There was always a trickle of people wandering in from Ethiopia and they would carry official rubber-stamped passes. At least, that is what we presumed they were: they were written entirely in Amharic, including the rubber stamp, and totally incomprehensible to any of us. When the visitor had stated his reason for coming to Kenya I would look carefully at the pass, countersign and stamp it, then nod at my interpreter in an official manner, who would tell him that everything was in order!

All the peoples of that harsh land were good walkers and ready to offer their services without thought of reward. Once, when all contact with Isiolo was cut off and we had to get a message through urgently, five volunteers appeared, all willing to walk there (and back) simply because the need was apparent. On another occasion a young Rendille came into my office to ask if we would arrange a livestock sale for them because by their calculation the time was due for them to pay their poll tax. He had walked 85 miles to make this request.

These two examples illustrate something which I first really observed when in Marsabit, that the fewer material possessions a man has and the harder his life, the less selfish he will be and the more concerned for his fellow man.

Our arranging of livestock auctions was not just to collect poll tax (at that time ten shillings a year) but to see that the sale was properly conducted and fair prices paid. The buyers were always Somalis for it was they who ran the butchery business in Marsabit, and generally elsewhere in the NFD. Although they were in competition with each other the sales were a buyer's market, the tribesmen usually being unsure what their stock was worth in money terms. The Somali butchers in Marsabit numbered only half a dozen or so, but they took up more of our office time than any other group on the mountain, with their constant *fitina*.

The DC (Windy) Wild told me that the best way to deal with them was to write down everything they said: the complainant would then go off satisfied that his story had been seen to be important and that action would be taken. But of course it never was, these complaints of one against another being simply malicious gossip and slander. One day Windy called me into his office, and as I went in I saw six Somalis waiting outside. He told me he had summoned them specially, then called them all in and told them what each had said about the others over the last several weeks. The result of this revelation was that they stormed out of the office and went back to the township shouting and gesticulating furiously at each other. We did not see any of them back again for some time.

At this period of the Emergency frequent circulars were sent to districts from central government, particularly from the Commissioner of Prisons. At the outset they were merely marked 'Urgent', but as the Emergency progressed we had 'Most Urgent,' 'Immediate' and even 'Most Immediate'. We did have a handful of influential Mau Mau in a sort of open prison, one or two of them being employed about the place, and many of these circulars dealt with prison security, requiring such things as electrical fencing, watch-towers and searchlights. Even if these things had been necessary – escape being effectively impossible – no suggestions were offered as to how we were to obtain them or generate the required electricity, being 250 miles from the nearest shops and electricity supply. There was one consolation: the mail would be brought in about once a week by a trader's truck, or once a fortnight by air during the rains, and amongst the sheaf of circulars there would sometimes be one (probably 'Immediate') which cancelled a previous one (probably 'Most Urgent') in the same mail delivery. We therefore saved ourselves time by reading the later ones first.

A central government department may perhaps be forgiven for sending the same circular to all districts regardless, but the same cannot be said of the Provincial Medical Officer (in Wajir). He once sent an urgent signal asking us to list our operating theatre equipment, oxygen cylinders, electrical massagers – and the list went on. All we had (as he must have known) was one African dresser in a hut with little more than first aid supplies, so Windy – suiting his words to our feelings – sent in reply, 'My father has a bicycle'. The PMO was not amused.

We once discovered some old files dating back to the early years of the century, at which time there was only one file for the entire year. One I recall had only three letters in it: a request from Nairobi for details of tribal movements, a reminder several months later and the DC's reply – much later still – in which he apologised for not having replied earlier but he had been out a lot on safari ...

Official Entertainment

PETER GORDON

Lugh Ferrandi was a pretentious little town on the Juba River. Evidently the Italians had had grandiose schemes for creating a miniature edition of Rome, as they had attempted to do in Addis. Certainly there was a marked contrast to the stark and austere architecture of our *boma* at Mandera. There was a triumphal arch (cracking) and an enormous fountain (dry) embellished with statuary (chipped). The official residences were on the scale of minor palazzi, but their walls were peeling; the bathrooms were tiled but many, if not most, tiles were missing; there was water-borne sanitation, but water had to be poured manually into the WC.

We were however, lavishly entertained and it was a somewhat inebriated weekend. Dinner was served on plates engraved with a golden 'S' and wine was poured into glasses similarly monogrammed. But the food was awful. We heroically ate our way through large creme caramels obviously made from camel's milk, out of gourds, which had been copiously swilled out, with camel's urine. After we retired for the night, we were serenaded beneath our window by the entire Italian (all male) population equipped with several guitars and were obliged to get up and put in an appearance on the balcony of our room. Entertainment the next day included a duck shoot; this involved a hair-raising journey jolting over stony roads in a jeep crammed with voluble Italians, all brandishing loaded guns pointing in all directions. We were quite glad to get home to Mandera.

Goans and the Administration

MERVYN MACIEL

It is worth recording that Goan immigration to British East Africa started towards the end of the 19th Century, the main influx being during the construction of the Uganda Railway (1896–1901). Unlike other Asians who also arrived in Kenya around that period, the Goans were not coolies or labourers, but educated and English-speaking and much sought after by the British. Successive Governors and politicians alike were, in later years, to extol the qualities of these men whose integrity, loyalty and industry underpinned so much of the development of their adopted land.

My father was employed as a stenographer at the Secretariat in Nairobi in the days before the advent of the female secretary; most stenographers of that era were in fact, male. Sadly, his civil service career was prematurely and tragically cut short at the early age of forty-two years, when, on the return voyage following overseas leave in Goa, during World War II, the ill-fated BI liner, the SS *Tilawa*, in which he, my step-mother, and their three very young children were travelling, was torpedoed by the Japanese a few days after they had left Bombay. My two brothers and I, who had been left in Belgaum (India) for our education, found ourselves orphans overnight!

Having completed my secondary education (there were no funds available for university education), I followed in my father's footsteps, arriving in Kenya towards the latter half of 1947. After a brief introductory period at the Secretariat, I was moved to the DC's office in Nairobi, to provide much-needed clerical assistance. It was here that my love affair with the Administration really began, and I seem to have developed a taste for working in such an environment in preference to being stuck in some ivory tower.

Following brief stints in Mombasa, Kilifi, Voi and Taveta during the next few months, I finally landed at Lodwar – a remote outpost in the inhospitable Turkana District of the Northern Frontier. During his restriction there, Jomo Kenyatta had described Lodwar as a 'hell on earth': as indeed it was. Strange though this may sound, I had personally volunteered for this posting, even though I was aware that Goan Godfathers at the secretariat could well have fixed me up with a transfer to a more salubrious district within the Provinces. From the outset, I had never felt the need to ask for preferential treatment or seek personal favours from anyone, even though I was aware of the many Goans my late father had helped. I was determined to prove myself through my own efforts.

After a few days at Lodwar, it soon dawned on me exactly what I had let myself in for. True, this could well be regarded as a God-forsaken region, but apart from the heat, sandstorms, flies, nude and scantily clad Turkanas, I must admit that I enjoyed my term at Lodwar immensely. Here I was also fortunate to work under one of that rare breed of British administrators, Leslie Whitehouse, whom many a District Officer held in awe. Whitehouse could be a real terror inside the office and lost no opportunity of chastising many a junior DO whenever the latter got the Goan staff to attend to some of their purely personal ploys. On such occasions, he would hurry back to his office in an obvious fit of rage, and quickly type out, on his portable typewriter, one of his many Office Standing Orders. Some of these were amusing and a real treat to read. Outside the office though, the story was quite different, and you could not have met a more pleasant gentleman. Most of the staff, including departmental officers, and even the township traders and tribesmen dreaded the man and looked upon him as the monarch of all he surveyed, as indeed he was.

Although we (the Goan staff) endured the same inhospitable climatic conditions and worked well beyond normal working hours on many occasions, we received no additional remuneration, nor were our hardship and separation allowances or local and vacation leave entitlements anywhere near the generous terms the European officials enjoyed. This, despite the fact that our lives lacked the variety of a safari. Social life was virtually non-existent, our only recreational activity at Lodwar being a game or two of squash and a quick dive in the nearby pool to escape the excessive heat. On such occasions, we mixed freely with our European colleagues, as also when we met socially for drinks at one or another's house.

A Goan clerk in the Administration had to be a jack of all trades, combining his own role of District Clerk/Cashier with that of a Police, Court, Prisons and meteorological clerk, and even army personnel on leave fell to his lot too. For this, he sometimes received a modest honorarium, but this was hardly in keeping with the volume of work or responsibilities involved. We were also required to submit any number of returns to various headquarters; whether these were ever looked at or studied at the receiving end remains doubtful, but send them we always did month in, month out. Ours was not to reason why in those heady days of red tape and Code of Regulations (the Civil Service Bible, which many a Goan senior clerk at the Secretariat delighted in quoting whenever an attempt was made to bend the rules. It was as though these were set in tablets of stone!)

From Lodwar on the north western Kenya/Sudan border, I was transferred in late 1950 to Marsabit in the north east on the Ethiopian side, a district, climatically at least, the direct opposite of Turkana. I got to love Marsabit and its people, and it was here that I returned after marrying my Kitale-reared sweetheart in 1952. Like me, Elsie too fell in love with the place, but it was also here that we experienced some of our happiest and not so happy days; happy because we loved the great outdoors, the wild life and simple lifestyles of the nomads who inhabited this vast district (of some 28,000 square miles). Sad, because it was also here that we were so often separated. We had a congenital-heart-afflicted baby son, Conrad, who had to be flown out to Nairobi, often at short notice, due to lack of adequate medical facilities locally. Here, I must once again record our thanks and appreciation for the work of the Kenya Police Airwing, in particular for that gallant and well-known pilot, 'Punch' Bearcroft.

Marsabit was also the district where, thanks to my then DC (the late Wing Commander 'Windy' Wild), I was invited to accompany him on many a safari throughout the district – a privilege not normally extended to the clerical ranks. In the absence of a DO (Marsabit was a one-man station when I first arrived), I also had to carry out duties well outside my humble calling. These included the weekly inspection of the Tribal Police and Station labour lines and prison inspections, when I dealt with problems raised by warders and prisoners alike. I also visited political prisoners in their camp and attended to their many grievances. This was all during the Mau Mau Emergency in 1952. In addition, I censored all their in-coming and out-going mail, and even helped write some of their letters home to their loved ones, as in the case of that likeable Mzee, Ex-Senior Chief Mbiu Koinange, who was also restricted to this district. (Some of those I visited were later to become senior Ministers in Kenyatta's first government in independent Kenya.) In addition, I also acted as a sort of Quartermaster to the Tribal Police – indenting and issuing their kit including arms and ammunition, since I held the keys to the armoury. On several occasions I attended stock sales and assisted with tax collection and also supervised road works. There were other occasions when I helped the DC compile the Monthly Intelligence Reports, which were submitted to the Provincial Commissioner.

What I most resented however, were the feelings of racial superiority and high-handed attitudes so often displayed by non-Administration European officials who often tried to interfere with the running of the District Office during the DC's absence on safari. One such occasion, which immediately comes to mind, is when I was obliged to commit a known Somali spiv to prison. The European Works Supervisor, who had in the past posed as the DC's assistant, and who was approached by a delegation of local Somalis, sent me a note asking me to release the man. I politely told him to mind his own business as I accepted full responsibility for my action. Happily, on his return to the *boma*, the DC backed my stand. On another occasion, again at Marsabit, I had to put a European PWD employee in his place for similar intrusion into what I regarded as my sphere of responsibility. His attitude toward me changed from that day! I daresay that some of my more timid Goan colleagues may well have suffered such bullying at the hands of some departmental officials, but I made sure that such individuals would never ride over me!

After my first period of duty at Marsabit, I served at Kitale and Kapenguria (during the Kenyatta trial), returning briefly to Kitale after an extended vacation leave in Goa, Bombay and Poona, and finally to the Marsabit I loved, in 1955. I never really wanted to leave Marsabit, but a promotion to a higher grading (in name only, with no monetary gain) meant that I had to move to a district compatible with my grading. For my part, I was prepared to sacrifice my promotion if only I could be left at Marsabit – a move incidentally supported by my DC. Alas, the powers that be didn't agree, so Kisii in the South Nyanza District of the Nyanza Province, is where I found myself a year later. Kisii was a challenging posting and my efforts to re-organise the office didn't go un-noticed. It was also here at Kisii that I was asked by the DC to replace a European officer. Despite holding down this job for several months, with added responsibility but no financial recognition, I was not confirmed in the post. This was because of the peculiar workings of the then Civil Service Commission, where seniority in the service seemed the dominating criterion. I was very disappointed also, since about the same time, our son Conrad, who had so bravely endured his heart condition, lost his fight for life and died a painful death in the Native Civil Hospital. What hurt us deeply was the lack of adequate care and attention he received, which resulted in him dying without the dignity he deserved.

Annoyed by this tragic loss, and frustrated over not being confirmed in a post I had now been successfully acting in for months, I applied, in sheer disgust, for the one and only promotional post advertised in the Ministry of Agriculture. I never really wanted to leave the Administration, but to my surprise, my application was successful. It was a promotion I couldn't turn down since it meant so much in salary and privileges. The DC tried unsuccessfully to retain me, and thus, alas, ended my days with the Administration.

My Favourite Boma

ROBIN WAINWRIGHT

Embu from 1946 to 1951 with home leave in the middle was a most enjoyable posting. The *boma* was fertile and lush, situated on a ridge high above the eastern side of the Rupengazi river which was in a deep steep-sided valley. It had been well laid out in the past and the two roads through the town-ship were both avenues, one with jacaranda and the other with nandi-flame trees. At this time none of the roads were tarred and so vehicles travelling through the *boma* threw up clouds of dust. As our house was on the lee side of the roads much of the dust came our way.

The district ran from the forest edge high up on the southern slopes of Mt Kenya at a height of about 9,000 feet down to the Tana River at about 3,000 feet. Its area was 5,000 square miles and the population just under 250,000. The house was not up to standard having been built, together with that for the DO, in about 1909. It was built of stone with a mud mortar. There were just three rooms in a row with open verandas front and back. That at the back was walled in at one end for the kitchen and at the other for the store and bathroom. Between the kitchen and the front bedroom was a spare bedroom for the children or guests, but it was in a dilapidated condition and full of bed-bugs which were hard to eliminate before the days of DDT. The only lavatory was a wooden privy in the garden with a long-drop. All the floors of the house were made of concrete but it had numerous potholes where the concrete had disintegrated. The corrugated-iron roof leaked and as it was inhabited by thousands of bats, the smell of bat droppings permeated the house.

As our two small sons had to use the bug-ridden room next to our bedroom and as, at that time, there was no hotel in the *boma*, any guests that we might have had would have been put in a very dark thatched hut behind the house, with a mud floor. One day I went in there for some reason and was attacked by a spitting cobra. Luckily it thought that my wristwatch was an eye. Soon after our arrival the PC provided just enough money to build a new double spare-room of mud-and wattle with a thatched roof.

Although the house was in a very poor condition when we took it over (largely due to the war when no repairs could be undertaken), the garden was a dream. The wife of my predecessor, Rita Gillespie, was a brilliant gardener and made the most of the deep red soil, ideal climate (at 4,000 feet) and a permanent water furrow running right through the garden which was shared by the DO's house. A vast lawn ran in front of both houses, divided by three jacaranda trees. There were wide herbaceous borders, a separate canna garden, a tennis court, a vegetable garden, a variety of fruit trees – avocado, mango, citrus, passion fruit, guava and pomegranate. Bananas could be bought for about a shilling a bunch from the local people. Rita had also planted flowering trees and shrubs, including bougainvillaea, hibiscus, datura and poinsettia. In front of the DC's house was the biggest bougainvillaea I have ever seen which had grown over the top of a full-size thorn tree and could be seen from miles around. Roger Wilkinson, who took over from me as DC had a bull terrier taken from under the tree by a leopard which had been lying up in the tree a few feet from the house.

When I took over Embu District the only other European, apart from the DO and his wife was an Agricultural Officer. My office staff consisted of a Goan cashier and, unusually at this time, a local Embu, Ndwiga Karanga, as District Clerk. There was no Vet, Police Officer, Education Officer, or PWD man, though I had a splendid Asian carpenter-cum-handyman called Jagat Ram. One of the first things I did was to set up a brick and tile-making workshop using the water out of the furrow that ran down from the forests. We produced excellent bricks and Brosely tiles and built, amongst other things, new houses for the Tribal Police. On a return visit I made to Embu in about 1980, I went to look at these houses and found them still in very good order. A local askari told me that they were the best houses he had had in all his service.

When we arrived in Embu in 1946 the nearest doctor and small African hospital was at Kerugoya, about twenty miles away.

Soon after our arrival, the PWD built a new District Office, the old one being so decrepit that a large termite nest had pushed up one of the mud walls so that there was a large gap between the wall and the roof. There was also an even larger colony of bats in the roof than that in our house.

A Child's View

VERONICA BELLERS

In 1949 we were a family of five. There was my father, Hal Williams, DC Kakamega and my mother Joy, diminutive, practical, shrewd and busy supporting Hal, whom she adored. There was my brother Richard, ten, often away at boarding school and hero-worshipped by his five year old twin sisters: Sue and me, leading a blithe and unrestrained life, vaguely aware of the fluctuating adult numbers of servants, parents and guests. Our major preoccupations were keeping the white rats away from the cats and the terriers and devising ways to evade our mother's lessons from the dreaded 'correspondence course'.

A rather fierce Kikuyu woman called Sissalia helped to look after us. As we played under the gum trees with the other European children in the *boma*, I held the lofty view that we were top of the social tree. This was because Sissalia was the only woman we knew who had a set of false teeth – or a *'duka* set' – and, what is more, she wore shoes.

The day began with morning tea and then Dad would drive around the *boma* to check that all was well. Dogs and children would scramble into the back of the box-body as the early sunlight flung its beams over the African morning. The first stop was the brick works. Lines of terracotta bricks lay under the long thatched roof. Later the prisoners would be turning out more. At the prison itself Dad would instruct us to wait under a tree while he disappeared inside. After one or two more visits, such as the water works, we would at last arrive at the grassy airstrip with nothing more than the windsock to show its purpose. Dad would yell out of the window to those of us who were sitting on the wooden benches in the back, 'Buckle your seat belts!' We had no idea what this exciting order meant but, clutching the dogs amid much shouting and excitement, we would 'Take off' at the exhilarating pace of some forty miles an hour. We would then cheerfully trundle back to the house where a hot breakfast would be awaiting us.

The house was set in spacious gardens surrounded by eucalyptus trees. There was a guesthouse set to one side, behind which was a long drop lavatory. I was certain that a hoofed devil dwelt down there and that, one day, particularly if I had not been good, he would spring up. I could not quite summon the courage to imagine what might happen next. Between the guesthouse and the main house was our own children's garden, where we successfully grew a few barberton daisies.

All too soon we were six and boarding school loomed. Sitting on the steps of the house, we struggled with the complexities of tying our shoelaces. We had never had shoes before. The night before we left, Joy Adamson came to stay and, to our fascination, drew a bush baby from her shirt as a gift to us. But the days of white rats, kittens, puppies, bicycling at full speed away from lessons and even hoofed devils, were about to end, and mum firmly refused on our behalf the offer of an addition to the household menagerie.

A Night Alarm

JUNE PEET

One moonlit night when we were in Kandara, Fort Hall District, during the Mau Mau Emergency, we were woken by our spaniel barking in an alarming way. He slept in a basket outside the front door of our bungalow, from where the land fell away towards a stream. He was a good watch dog. I crept to the window and saw a man lying in the long grass in what seemed to me to be a threatening position, and it looked as if he was armed. I woke Tony, who went to the window with his revolver in his hand. At that time we all slept with a gun under the pillow since the *boma* at Kandara had on one occasion been over run in a Mau Mau attack.

We watched the man who made no further movement. After some more furious barking by the dog, Tony cocked his revolver as he prepared to go outside to find out what the man was up to. This was enough to bring a very drunken Agricultural Officer to his feet, and he staggered off to his house next door.

The Queen Mother's Visit to Narok

DICK CASHMORE

The DC's house had a new loo added, and everything that did not move was painted or white-washed. It was December 1958 when I was posted to the Maasai District of Narok. Given its low population it was heavily staffed by the Administration. In part this may have been a hangover from the Emergency. At one time the district had six divisions: even in my time there were three outstations with European Divisional District Officers in addition to the DC and myself, together with Philip Masindet, the Assistant District Officer at headquarters.

Narok *boma* itself had a dozen European officers with a hospital and large Maasai government school. Nearby was the legendary Game Warden, Temple Boreham. Yet there was a curiously suburban atmosphere in the *boma*. Few wives went out on safari but looked longingly for an excuse to go shopping in Nairobi ninety miles away. They complained ceaselessly to the DO about the roster for sharing water from the furrow for their gardens (telling tales about each other's gardeners stealing water out of turn).

In the east of the district, there was an element of missionary influence (Africa Inland Mission) not unlinked with the strong presence of Kikuyu and *nusu nusu* (descendants of mixed Maasai/Kikuyu marriages). In the west in the Trans Mara division was the Catholic mission of the Mill Hill fathers established single-handedly by the remarkable Austrian, Father Ferdy Fent. To assist him he had the gentle Brother Hilary, with his badly broken nose, a relic of a beating up at the hands of the Nazi Youth Movement. There was also an Italian in the *boma*, a former prisoner of war, who had stayed on to run the African District Council workshops.

Our main preoccupation for the next couple of months was the forthcoming visit of the Queen Mother. Although the visit was for a day, preparations were intensive. The airstrip had to be regraded, the three mile road from the airstrip to the *boma* had to be watered daily against dust (even so the press complained of our dusty road). Everyone handling the food that was to be served at the buffet lunch for HM, had to go to Nairobi for a medical check up. Seating and precedence were endlessly reviewed and security measures were complex. The police file of security measures to be handled by officers from Nairobi was five inches thick and included a detailed fifteen page memo of measures for checking and rechecking the royal car at the airport and afterwards. (The local Police Chief doubted whether those in charge would know the difference between a bomb and a fire extinguisher.) Another branch of the police was nervous that one of the Asian communities in presenting a gift to HM would pass over a subversive petition. It was my job to 'disarm' him. In fact the dear old boy was so nervous that he found great difficulty in coping even with the present of a silver bowl as he spoke those famous lines, 'This district is noted for its wild life'. Some mistook his meaning and looked interested! We were also concerned that the Maasai *moran*, who were capable of throwing fits at the slightest excuse, might cause embarrassment. When HM asked what would happen all I could do was cross my fingers. But the Queen Mother made the whole exercise worthwhile with her charm and genuine sympathy. As her visit ended with much needed rain it was more than welcome, and the downpour was seen as an excellent omen.

Bill and Long Drops

DAVID LAMBERT

Bill was a Kenya Police Officer. Charming, persuasive and irresponsible, he left a trail of disaster wherever he passed.

I first met Bill during a Sunday lunch time session at the West Lake Naivasha Police Post. It was a regular occasion when the unmarried police and administration officers in the area gathered for beer and curry. At some stage the conversation turned to the relative merits of the personal firearms we each carried. One favoured the Patchet sub machine gun, another the standard police issue .38 Webley revolver, another a pump action shotgun and yet another an odd looking weapon called a Lanchester supposed to have been designed for use by the Royal Navy between the wars. I argued strongly for the 9mm Luger automatic which I then carried in its original wood and leather holster. In the way of such conversations more and more exaggerated claims were made until Bill suggested the time had come to test the accuracy and penetrating power of our arsenal. Looking round for a target away from the police lines and with a reasonably safe background, he suggested the station officers' long drop. This was the standard Kenya privy built of corrugated iron with a wooden thunder box over a deep hole.

A circle was quickly drawn on one of the walls and we took it in turns to aim and fire. At the end of each round an inspection took place and points were awarded. Returning to the firing point, Bill, who was losing, became bored and fired off a whole magazine. This was the signal for everybody to join in and for several minutes a hail of bullets and shot went into and through the building, leaving the walls looking like a mad colander and the thunder box a mass of splinters and a very definite health hazard. As the firing stopped the sound of several vehicles was heard. Coming in sight of the post the vehicles stopped and a camouflage-smocked platoon of the Police General Service Unit jumped out and deployed into the surrounding bush and began to advance on the post. Apparently a local farmer hearing the shooting had reported the post under siege, and the GSU were rushing to our rescue.

Some time later I moved to Gilgil and shared a bungalow with Bill in the grounds of Mrs Gamble's guesthouse overlooking Lake Elementeita. Mrs Gamble was an elderly lady renowned for the excellence of her cuisine and the high standard of behaviour she expected from her guests.

One evening as I prepared for bed, Bill took himself off to the long drop at the end of the garden. Suddenly he rushed back into the bungalow shouting that there was a snake in the hole. As he calmed down we discussed the situation and the difficulties of getting at the reptile with sticks or shot and were reaching the conclusion that the only answer was to fill in the hole when I had a brain wave. Bill always travelled with a small armoury and when he was unpacking I'd noticed a phosphorous grenade among his socks. Drop the grenade down the hole, kill the snake and fumigate all at one time. The perfect solution we agreed, and without further thought inserted a detonator into the grenade and set off down the garden.

Bill held open the door; I pulled the pin, lifted the lid and hurriedly dropped the grenade down the hole. We both then ran back up the garden and turned to watch the results of our handiwork. Nothing happened for a few seconds then suddenly there was a flash and an explosion. Bill and I threw ourselves on the ground as the wooden lid flew out of the roof and disappeared into the night whilst pieces of the thunder box sprayed through the walls. This was followed by a flame of volcanic proportions.

As Bill and I picked ourselves up, the flames died down and with a sigh, the remains of the building subsided slowly into the ground. At that moment the dressing gowned figure of Mrs Gamble appeared and in a quavering voice asked, 'What's happened Mr Lambert?'....

'Well Mrs Gamble it was like this ...'

Shades of Von Lettow-Vorbeck

JOHN WILLIAMS

I cannot, at this distance in time, recollect the precise occasion which was to be commemorated. Whatever it may have been, all former *askaris* were to be given a 'celebratory' handout of some twenty shillings and the word had been sent out by way of the chiefs and headmen for the old warriors to present themselves at the DC's office at a given time on a given date.

It was 1959 and I was DO *boma* at Isiolo, headquarters of the Northern Frontier District, which was actually a Province but continued to be affectionately referred to as the 'NFD'. On the date and at the time specified, I was seated behind a table strategically positioned under what little shade was afforded by a straggling thorn-tree outside the DC's office, with a small pile of twenty-shilling notes in a metal box in front of me. The District Clerk sat beside me with a sheet of paper in front of him, already ruled up so that names, service numbers and 'signatures' could be inserted into the spaces provided as each payment was made: a violet inkpad was ready for the majority of the old askaris who would undoubtedly use a thumbprint as the appropriate method of recording their signatures.

The dubas (Tribal Police) sergeant presided self-importantly over the whole proceedings, trying to impose some long-forgotten military drill formations upon the haphazard line which had slowly been forming in front of me. At last, he was satisfied that he had full control of his charges and, marching ostentatiously up to the table and giving an exaggerated salute (obviously intended to impress the old *askaris*!) he suggested that we were ready to begin.

I had hardly time to indicate my assent before an order was barked out and the first old soldier came slowly up to the table, offered with a broad smile what he remembered of a salute (which drew what was obviously a sarcastic comment in Boran from the sergeant) and handed over his tattered service record. The latter I passed to the clerk who entered the details on the ruled-up sheet of paper and obtained a thumbprint 'signature' before I handed over a twenty shilling note and shook the hand of the grateful recipient.

And so the process went on. There were in all perhaps thirty or forty former *askaris* now in the line: the Boran and Samburu tribes had always been well represented in the KAR. Many were proudly wearing Second World War medals on their chests and some sported campaign medals whose ribbons I had never seen before. Of most of them, the *dubas* sergeant had no cause to criticise their military bearing, old though they were.

One wizened old man in due course appeared in front of me and proffered his service record. It was all in German. This old campaigner had been one of General von Lettow-Vorbeck's men down in German East Africa (Tanganyika) during the First World War: what on earth was he doing up there in Isiolo?

And of course he got his twenty shillings.

Literal Responses

ALASTAIR ANDERSON

When I arrived in Kenya in September 1954, I was posted to Kikuyu Division of Kiambu where the District officer was John Campbell. Very soon after I arrived, I was sitting in my office, when a young man came in with an application form to join the Surveys Department, on which he required a recommendation from his District Officer.

As John Campbell was not there, it was up to me to deal with this case. So, I had a good look at the form, which was quite long. I quickly noticed that in one section, in answer to the questions;

'What is your father's name?' – he had written 'Never the less'
'What is your father's place of birth?' 'Never the less'
'What is your father's date of birth?' 'Never the less'.

I looked at the man carefully, as I suspected that this was some joke being played on me, a new arrival, by some of the DOs KG in the division, but there was nothing to indicate that it was a joke. So, I looked at the form again and there at the bottom of this particular section was a note in small print which said 'if your father is dead, these questions should be answered "never the less"'.

A Quiet Posting

W. H. (TOMMY) THOMPSON

In October 1957 I was away to England for my first Christmas at home since 1940. This was the first of my new shortened leaves by air. At the end of it in January 1958, I flew into Entebbe, drove to Bungoma to get all my household and personal effects on the train to Mombasa and set off on the long, dusty, bone-shaking six hundred and fifty mile journey to Mombasa en route to my posting as DC Tana River based at Kipini.

My new PC was affable and over gins and tonics said the Tana River was quiet, backward, and just what a 'chap like you Thompson' can get his teeth into. He failed to mention that up-river was a large Mau Mau detention camp at an insalubrious place called Hola, which I had indeed heard of but knew nothing about. A name that was to ring around the world and cause me much grief.

My instructions were to drive north passing through Malindi and, somewhere after the hundred and eightieth mile, look for a wooden signboard labelled 'Ngua'. If I found it (what if I had not?) I was to follow a track through the bush to a rusted lorry and cast around for a footpath to the left. There I would have to abandon my car and proceed on foot – 'Take care of buffalo – nasty beasts buffalo!'– to the riverside village of Golbanti where, all being well, I would find the DC's launch. I could not drive all of the 260 miles to district headquarters because the Tana was in flood and the main and only road was under many feet of water.

On board the 'MV Pelican' my DO was waiting to greet me with a jar of cold beer. Built in 1950 as a prototype for the Burma Government, which

THE DISTRICT BOMA

rejected her, the launch was comfortable with a two berth sleeping and dining cabin, galley, paraffin refrigerator and shower room under the canopied upper deck. Driven by two large diesels she was not a handsome vessel but well suited for the job she had to do. Designed to slip over the ever-changing sandbanks she could get up and down the hundred and eighty miles or so of river in all but the driest weather. Twelve days to get up against the current and three to get back with it.

I was to be the last but one Sanders of the River of Empire, though we did not then know it.

The journey down river to headquarters was fascinating. Large herds of elephants, hippo by the gross and crocodiles on every sandbank: overpowering heat and a hundred percent humidity. The people in the villages waved and seemed happy enough. There was a lot of riverside cultivation which looked good, but as I was to find out later was anything but. The housing was of grass and thatch and there were no obvious signs of trade. Again I was in a different world far away from the thrusting Kikuyu and Nyanza tribes.

We arrived at Kipini after dark where the outgoing DC, his wife and daughter were waiting to depart. They hated the place, swore it was haunted, looked ill and said they would like to go up river the next morning. This I could not agree to: the hand-over had to be done.

That night I lay dripping sweat, listening to strange sounds compounded of rustling palm leaves, the sea and noises from the nearby village. I also had a glimpse of what appeared to be a row of white graves lined up just below. Daylight brought a view of a brick-red, flood stained Indian Ocean, palm trees, sand, a few thatched huts, a two-storied office from which flew the Union Flag and a flagpole on the ground flying the red flag of Zanzibar. And, confirming my nightmare glimpse, six or seven whitewashed gravestones of some of my predecessors.

In my memoirs I filled several pages with descriptions of the district, its peoples and problems plus a great deal of history. Here I have to collapse the whole lot into a few sentences. In essence the Pokomo tribe inhabited the riverbanks living in often quite widely spaced villages. The Orma who were owners of large herds of Galla stock kept themselves almost exclusively to the dry hinterland. Right up to my time very little was known about them. Ignorance of geography, especially on the river, before the 1914–18 war was probably responsible, and until the 1940s there was no road into the dry areas.

Johnny (R.R.) Rowlands one of my fairly recent predecessors had done a lot of research which he had committed to paper, a copy of which was held in the district files. Though the Tana River had never been of importance its available history from 1860 to 1960 was absorbing. The comings and goings of missionaries, the influence of Germany, including the activities of a Nazi cell, and the mainly failed schemes for agricultural exploitation are worthy of a book on their own. It seems I was the thirty-sixth DC and the last one, for I was to close down Kipini on my removal to Hola in 1959.

It was a lonely posting with only two other white officers on station; Henry Wright my DO and Peter Back the Agricultural Officer. Equally lonely were Marcus de Souza and his wife who made up our entire Goan community. For the rest the entire staff was African or Arab. The medical establishment consisted of one Hospital Assistant – and a very good one I must say. Supplies were difficult to obtain. Communications with the outside world consisted of a twice-weekly mail lorry (except when the floods were out) and a single telephone wire, which hooked into the Malindi – Lamu line at Witu some miles away. Only once in my entire tenure did I get through to anyone, and then it was the PC, in Mombasa with neither of us being able to hold a conversation above the crackle.

I have said supplies were difficult. We had but one shop which sold matches, paraffin, flour, tinned beans of a peculiar and very nasty Australian variety, together with tinned Christmas puddings of which there was a large stock. Apparently Johnny Rowlands had told Salim Ali, the proprietor, that the British loved Christmas puddings and a job lot of vast proportions had been obtained. Unfortunately at a sale rate of two a year, the tins had rusted to danger point. Alcohol was out. Muslim drivers would not carry it. Luckily the PC let us send our one and only vehicle, a lorry, to Mombasa twice or three times a year to buy 'essentials'. For most of the year we could only allow ourselves a couple of Tuskers on Saturdays and Sundays. We were perforce abstemious.

With crocodile on every mud bank, screaming baboon in the trees, hippo in hordes, elephants in herds, sightings of leopards, rhino and buffalo, safari on the river should have been tremendously exciting, but it was not so.

Pushing against the flood made it a hot sticky business in the launch, which was a dreadful hot box made only bearable by the breeze of the vessel's movement. But if there was a following wind (which there nearly always was when proceeding upstream) there was nothing for it but to sweat it out and douse oneself with prickly heat powder.

Loaded with camping equipment, safari boxes, cash boxes, food and spare fuel there was little space to spare. A canopy on the upper deck provided but little shade, for with the twists and turns in the river the sun was forever presenting itself from different angles and directions.

Looking up my frayed copy of handing over notes, I see I wrote to my successor as follows:

'Most of the Pokomo only see the DC on the river safaris about three times a year and you will have to cope with a vast amount of work and *shauris*. You will have to:

Check all the work of the tax clerks and the chiefs' tax collectors.
Hear and certify all claims for exemption from tax, bearing in mind that everyone will plead absolute poverty (and poverty is very real when the up-country rains fail).
Inspect and license all shops in villages outside the four main trading centres.
Clear up all land case appeals from the African Courts (twenty six registered for hearing).
Hear sundry other appeals.
Check on all Court Elders' attendances.
Take five cases awaiting you as Magistrate.
Visit all schools.
Inspect and check on the new authentication of their land boundaries.
Inspect all villages for cleanliness and make suggestions for improvements.
Chase up every chief and headman (they do need chasing!)
Hold *barazas* in every location.
Check on African District Council licensing of produce exports, cattle sales and boats.
Visit both Mission Stations and try to cheer them up. They need great help.
The RC Priest is all alone miles from anywhere and under enormous stress.
The Methodists under the Rev. David Livingstone (no relation to the famous one) run a hospital and are often cut off by floods for several months at a time.
Take with you: the Assistant Cashier,
  your interpreter,
  a good Tribal Police Orderly,
  the Medical Assistant (there is no doctor) or a dresser,
  licenses of every kind,
  court Registers and the Penal Code,
  Magistrates files, as much beer as you can muster,
  a library.'

To this I added, 'If you take visiting officers with you make sure they limit their kit. There is nothing worse than a mass of boxes and luggage all over the cabin and upper deck. Last year the Provincial Education Officer who came with a retinue of six had enough packing cases to fill the boat. It was most unpleasant.'

The Tana River posting was well worth a book in its own right and these brief recollections can do no more than scratch the surface.

As the graves at Kipini illustrated it was a most unhealthy posting. I went down with malaria several times and became infected with amoebic dysentery which led in a strange way to my getting the job I most desired – but that was in the distant future.

A Haunted Boma

HENRY WRIGHT

After service in the British South Africa Police in Rhodesia and action in the Embu District of Kenya during the Mau Mau rebellion I was posted to Kipini at the mouth of the Tana River in June 1957.

My main task at Kipini was to administer the riverine tribe, the Wapokomo. A river launch, the Pelican was the only way to visit these people and if the river was low, local wooden canoes were used.

Kipini is almost on the equator and conditions were always trying to the one, two or three Europeans who lived there. Up river, away from the coast, it was hot and humid most of the year. Mosquitoes were abundant and escaping into a mosquito net or cage by 6 p.m. was essential. Malaria and other tropical diseases were rife amongst the local Africans.

Whilst at Kipini, I walked and explored nearby Arab cities which were deserted or evacuated by their residents in the 16th century. Every spare moment I had, and there were many, I walked the beaches and hinterland.

At Kipini, near my house, there were three European graves. Two were of particular interest:

K.D.J. Duff
(Duff committed suicide in Garsen and was buried at Kipini in 1919.)

In very dear Memory
of Clifford George Pitt, Oxon
Born at Lyddington Rectory, Wilts. England
Entered into Rest
February 1st, 1915, aged 26.

Pitt was on safari on the Tana River, in a barge. He seems to have got severe sunstroke, which drove him raving mad. He jumped in the river, threw everything out of the barge, and was only pacified with difficulty by Juma, his personal servant. He was taken to Masabubu, slightly recovered but lost consciousness on the way downstream and died near Kibusu.

The DC had the small graveyard correctly maintained and duly white-washed. Almost daily, I walked past these graves and wondered about the deceased's background and family.

I decided to try and trace the Pitt family in Liddington, Wiltshire. I went into Liddington Church, and behind the altar was a big stained glass window of C. G. Pitt wearing a cloak and holding a spear, and looking as though it was a photograph taken yesterday. On either side of the altar, were stained glass windows of his father, William Baker Pitt, and his mother, Alice Mary Pitt.

Kipini is and was a fascinating place. It was renowned for the Kipini ghosts which have affected many people who lived in this isolated place.

There appeared to be two authentic ghosts who haunt the DC's house which is now in a ruined state and since the Colonial administration left in 1959, Africans do not go near the house due to the tormented spirits who haunt it.

The first ghost is said to be C.G. Pitt who has been heard and seen by Africans and Europeans. The second ghost is a European woman. Legend has it that she is the mother of Duff who committed suicide, and she had hysterics partly against the DC who is supposed to have sent him on safari when he was unwell. Mrs Duff and Pitt have been seen together.

I tell this story about the ghosts because local Africans still talk about old Colonial administrators and the ghosts and it brings together Duff and Pitt who are buried there. They must have been completely different characters, but did the same job.

The Bush Telegraph

JOHN WILLIAMS

One of the unfathomed mysteries of Africa, and probably also of other parts of the world, is the operation of the bush telegraph.

How is it that information, which in principle can be known to so few people, travels, as though telepathically, over great distances of both time and space to others who would seem to be very unlikely to hear about it? Let me give two examples from my personal experience in Kenya.

During my national service when I was a platoon commander in 23 KAR in the early days of what came to be known as the Mau Mau Emergency, I had as my cook/general batman, a delightful Kikuyu *askari* by the name of Githogo. There has been much debate as to the genuineness of so-called 'loyal' Kikuyu during those times but I had no hesitation in trusting myself, and my life, unreservedly to Githogo. I used to 'tell off' those of my *askari* from other tribes who were constantly teasing him about Mau Mau.

Now Githogo had one principal ambition in life – to become an army driver – and when I left 23 KAR at the end of my national service in September

1953, I put his name forward to go on the relevant course. I went back to four years at Cambridge before coming out to Kenya again in the administration in the summer of 1957. I served first at Bungoma (Elgon Nyanza District) then at Isiolo, Thomson's Falls and (by 1960) Kapsabet.

One evening at Kapsabet, while I was playing tennis after work, I caught sight, out of the corner of my eye, of a three-ton KAR Bedford truck lumbering and swaying down the eroded track, which led to the club. Nobody ever drove to the club! The KAR periodically undertook recruiting safaris in Nandi District, of which Kapsabet was the headquarters, and one was currently due to take place. I naturally thought that one of the trucks had taken a wrong turning.

I was surprised therefore when, on going over to the vehicle, I found a beaming Corporal Githogo at the wheel, proudly pointing to the two stripes on his arm! How on earth did he know that I had come back to Kenya and was now a DO at Kapsabet, four years since I had last seen him? Of course I asked him but he just smiled enigmatically as though I could not be serious that I did not know.

I mentioned earlier that my first posting when I came to Kenya in the Administration was to Bungoma, known to all of us (except perhaps the DC Peter Gordon) as 'Bungle Boma'. I had an excellent local Bukusu cook/houseboy by the name of Moses – why were nearly all cooks called Moses or Abraham? – but he positively refused to go with me when I was posted, after about eighteen months, to Isiolo in the Northern Frontier District. He had heard too many stories about the wild tribes in those parts.

So, on arrival in Isiolo, I had to find a new cook. Gerry Pryer, the DO whom I was relieving, was very intent on taking his own cook with him to his next posting but the cook (almost certainly by the name of Moses) said that he had a relation who was a good cook and was looking for a new post. Word was passed back to the Kikuyu Reserve at Fort Hall and, a day or so later, Muthenge duly arrived in Isiolo. All his belongings came with him and there appeared to be no doubts but that he would be taken on. His references at any rate were all quite laudatory and there were not any of the nature of: 'Muthenge is looking for a new berth – give him a wide one!' which I always thought was a cowardly way of giving a bad reference.

Muthenge stayed with me throughout my time at Isiolo, even sticking it out for six months when I was sent by the PC 'Pious Paul' Kelly, to open a sub-station at Garba Tulla, some seventy or eighty miles along an eponymous track (notorious to anyone who ever served in the NFD) in the direction of Wajir. The purpose of the new sub-station was to be closer on the ground in order to prevent Somali incursions into Boran territory: while Isiolo District was reserved to the Boran and Wajir District to the Somali, the 'powers that were' in earlier times had unfortunately settled the border between the two districts along a line of wells which were consequently under continual dispute as to which side of the border they were located. I had many an interesting safari with John Deverell, my opposite number from Wajir, in trying to resolve the problems, which our predecessors had left for us when they ruled the lines on the map – but I digress from the story of the bush telegraph.

Muthenge also accompanied me on my subsequent postings to Thomson's Falls and Kapsabet, from where I went on home leave early in 1960. I told him then that I had no idea where I would go on my return and advised him to return home to Fort Hall where I could contact him if need be in due course through the DC's office.

When I returned from home leave in the middle of 1960, I had no idea where my next posting would be, but learned on arrival in Nairobi that I was to take over one of the 'special camps' at Mwea in Embu District. When I arrived at Mwea camp two or three days later, I discovered that my predecessor had already departed and I was too preoccupied with getting the hang of my new role of 'psychiatrist/prison warder' to worry about my domestic arrangements: fortunately, one of the cook warders was able to boil an egg or roast me a chicken as an interim measure.

Some four days later, when I was engaged in my 'psychiatrist' role in a long debate with one of the detainees about the woes of the world, a warder interrupted to say that somebody at the gate was asking for me by name. Who should it be but Muthenge! It is true that Mwea was not far from Fort Hall where Muthenge lived but how could he possibly know that I was there, and so soon after my arrival? I had not even known myself a week before where I was to be posted. Needless to say, Muthenge stayed with me as cook for the remainder of my time in Kenya: he has not yet turned up at my house in London but I sometimes feel that he might!

There is no doubt a simple explanation to the apparently mysterious ways in which I was tracked down both by Githogo and by Muthenge. There must be, unless one believes in thought transference but, even then, on neither occasion was Githogo or Muthenge uppermost in my thoughts. To me, such occurrences will always remain one of the unexplained phenomena of Africa.

Marmalade Brown

IAN WILLIS

George Huntley Hilton Brown, my District Commissioner in Samburu District was a stickler for the rules. In October 1962 I took delivery of my plane, an Auster VP- KBA from Campling Brothers at Wilson Airport,

Nairobi. I flew up to the *boma* at Maralal with the instructor. George took exception to his arrival because I had not asked for permission for him to come in, Samburu being a closed district. So I took off immediately for Nairobi, returned the instructor and flew back solo. The flight time was 1 hour 40 minutes. By road the journey took six to seven hours.

I enjoyed serving under George. Not everyone did. He had been a naval officer and was aware that the senior police officer had been a stoker. At a Provincial meeting in Isiolo he told the police officer to 'get below'. Relations with the Kenya Police became even more delicate after the DC's dog had sat on his police hat during breakfast.

George's nickname 'Marmalade' came from his frugality. He ate bread and marmalade for breakfast and expected his guests to do the same. On Safari, he made do with a pocketful of raisins. His dogs posed a problem for visitors too. He had a fierce ridgeback and a little dog called Kahli which had belonged to his father in India. No one could enter George's home or his office in the *boma* unless George came to the door to let them in.

In 1963 I flew George to Wajir for the ceremony to mark the end of Ramadan. The Governor, Malcolm MacDonald came up for the occasion and wore full dress uniform with helmet and plumes. He was accompanied by his Malaysian friend and photographer whom the chauffeur called 'Bibi China'. Trouble had broken out in the Somali areas of the North. Somalia had become independent in 1960 and claimed the NE corner of Kenya. *Shifta* fighters had killed two administrators, a Kenyan, Daudi Wabera, the DC Isiolo, and Neville Judge, the DC Wajir. Neville was on safari and was shot in his tent at night, his profile being illuminated by his paraffin light.

Outside Baragoi, George and I had an unpleasant experience with both Samburu and Turkana Chiefs getting very close to warfare between them; shields were out, a sure sign of war. George had a revolver hidden but I was unarmed. No tribal police were at hand since George and I accidentally arrived to witness the meeting. George was relaxed and patiently listened to both sides' grievances going back many years of cattle rustling. George sent me back to the land-rover to await him. After four hours of talking both sides went back to their separate ways.

George was a good administrator. He commanded the respect of his staff and of the Samburu people. After the incident of the flying instructor we got on exceedingly well. But my wife and I always took great care not to dilute his single malt whisky with water!

5

Development Work

Policy in the Northern Frontier District	Gerald Reece
The Dam Builders	Peter Gordon
The Furrow	Jeremy Lunn
Development in Moyale	David Evans
Land consolidation in Kiambu	John Golds
A Revolution in Land Tenure	John Johnson
The Creation of a New District	Peter Gordon
Orderly Administration	W. H. (Tommy) Thompson
Reporting from the Bush	Eric Gordon & Johnnie Rowlands
Controlling Migration	Dick Turnbull

Introduction

Economic and social development was a high priority for all administrators, especially in the rural areas. The need for schools, health facilities, water supplies and roads loomed large. The institutions of Local Government had to be built up. The government, then as now in Independent Kenya, relied on the District Team, the Departmental Officers under the chairmanship of the District Commissioner.

The constraint was money. Development had to be financed from the budgets of Central or Local Government. Only in the 1950s did substantial funds become available first from Colonial Development and Welfare (now CDC) and later from Aid donors. The solution was to eke out the limited resources with ingenuity, local participation and prison labour.

Sir Gerald Reece lays down simple principles to guide progress in remote areas of the Northern Frontier in the 1940s. Sometimes the results were disappointing. Peter Gordon recounts how the forces of nature destroyed the efforts of the District Officer and the community. Almost every *boma* in Kenya had its furrow. Jeremy Lunn charts the uncertain course of one in Maasai country. A real test of enterprise was to put up modern buildings in far flung places as David Evans did on the Ethiopian frontier at Moyale.

Agricultural development accelerated in the 1950s. Land consolidation, beginning in Central Province, created freehold land tenure and rapid progress. Kiambu District was the first to complete the process. John Golds describes how it was done and John Johnson tells us how Embu District followed.

Local Government, through African District Councils, was seen as the road to national political development. People expressed their wishes vociferously. Because of this a new district was created in Elgon Nyanza, and Peter Gordon recounts how the DC managed the transition. Tommy Thompson came straight from the Emergency situation in Fort Hall to the peaceful progress of western Kenya and points out the contrast.

Finally, to return to the pastoralists, Eric Gordon introduces Johnnie Rowlands' report in verse on bringing development to the arid lands. And to complement Sir Gerald Reece at the beginning of the chapter that other great administrator of the Northern Frontier, Sir Richard Turnbull reflects on the value of strict grazing controls.

Policy in the Northern Frontier District

GERALD REECE

Our present intention is to try to make some progress with what is regarded as Civilisation.

The purpose of it all must be this:

a. to make the NFD more productive and profitable;

b. to improve administration and to aid the government of the people by the people, so that their policing and control will not become unduly troublesome and costly as sophistication and detribalisation increase;

c. to make the tribesmen more healthy and happy. As elsewhere in the Colonial Empire, we strive to improve, but not always to change, the way in which the people live. Whether we desire it or not, changes will inevitably come in the manner of their living and it is clearly better for us to give the lead. What we hope to see here is not a greatly increased number of semi-detribalised town dwellers wearing European clothing, but a leavening in the tribes of stock-breeders who, while still and necessarily nomadic, will acquire some modern knowledge that will enable them to live more healthily and happily.

DEVELOPMENT WORK

The Dam Builders

PETER GORDON

One of my first tasks in Kisii was to build a dam. I had not the remotest idea of how to start. However, I selected what seemed a suitable site on a small stream. The chief arrived with an eager band of workers and, after a week, I gazed complacently upon a structure that, to my mind, might well have served as a model for some future Barrage across the Nile. Only a few finishing touches remained for the following day.

Alas, that night a storm broke of typical Kisii ferocity: spectacular lightning, prolonged rolls of thunder and torrents of rain. We were lucky my tent was not washed away. At dawn I walked down to the stream below the camp. It gurgled as merrily as before, almost uninterrupted in its flow by a few heaps of mud and stones. The chief and the workers appeared. We all gazed at the ruin in silence. Then someone laughed and the laughter spread and the women began to ululate and move in a swaying dance, clapping their hands. The men joined in, stamping their feet and one of them began to sing. It was a recitative punctuated by a chorus chanted by the rest – all clearly quite impromptu. When this 'celebration' ended I dished out the small payments, which I was glad I had been authorised to make 'on completion of the dam'. I forget how much; probably enough to cover tax for that year. They dispersed still singing and dancing. Marianne and I, a bit shame-faced, but happy enough, made our way back to the *boma*. On the way, my Interpreter told me the words of the song had been along the lines of: 'The *Bwana* and his *Memsahib* came to build a dam. But *Mungu* (God) told the dam to move. Now it has run away into the Lake.' I am sure this was a bowdlerised version.

The Furrow

JEREMY LUNN

Nairage Ngare is an unfrequented corner of Maasailand extending from the Mau plateau to the Kedong valley, and its jagged craters of Longonot and Suswa, down to the southern Uaso Nyiro river and Lake Magadi.

This is the stamping ground of the Kekonyukie section of the Maasai, and home to huge herds of wildlife, until recent times including all the Big Five (elephant, rhino, lion, leopard and buffalo). The Kekonyukie Maasai hold their Eunoto age-grade ceremonies in the folds of Suswa, where the warrior *morani* have their heads shaved as they graduate to Elder status. This was weekend camping and walking country to (amongst others) Dick Turnbull, prior to his becoming the last Governor of Tanganyika.

Intermarriage with the Kikuyu in the hilly country bordering Ngong and Naivasha produced a sub-tribe, to all appearances more Kikuyu than Maasai. The little cluster of *dukas* and huts that constitute Nairage Ngare District Office and Township was lived in by people called Kamau ole Njeroge and Stephen ole Tiambati. For several years after the ending of Mau Mau in 1956, the occasional dread-locked terrorist was winkled out of hiding places in the forest above the Township, apparently unaware that hostilities were over.

Many of the Nairage Ngare folk were agriculturalists, clearing a few *shambas* of maize on the hillsides around the village, and setting wire traps to discourage wild pigs and other predators. Water was a limiting factor for most of the year. The Township itself was served by a stagnant pond for a few months after the rains in what constituted a flat and rather fetid *vlei*. This quickly became puddled and a source of ill health for one and all. Hence the idea of the furrow.

Furrows in East Africa have come and gone. The Nairage Ngare furrow was initiated in the early 1950s in a professional manner with a view to it being one of the survivors. It would tap permanent spring water from two miles up in thick forest on the edge of the Mau Plateau, bringing it down by stages into the Township via the *shambas*, giving birth to a brave new vegetable nursery on the way. Water engineers were called in, and a volunteer workforce of villagers, armed with buckets and spades, put to work.

Regrettably, like many another enlightened field engineering project, the furrow never realised its potential. The small trickle of water that was coaxed into the top of the furrow had a short and inglorious journey of a few metres before losing itself in the deep soil of the upper reaches of the forest. Nick Scott, the District Officer at the time was posted, and none of his successors had the heart or motivation to resurrect it.

Before being mercifully shrouded by the forest, it remained as a visible rebuke to a number of otherwise promising young District Officers' careers.

Development in Moyale

DAVID EVANS

The District Commissioner, Bob Otter wanted to transform Moyale District (about twice the size of Wales) into a showpiece pastoral area, in spite of its 'Sanders of the River' image, on the Ethiopian Border. During one of our frequent evening rides, mostly along the border near the *boma*, he once commented, 'I prefer to be a large frog in a small pond'. Clearly, he was referring to the years spent in more advanced districts, particularly in Central Province, where he had been one of many DOs under a DC, who chaired the District Team comprising a Medical Officer, an Education Officer, Veterinary, Agricultural, Livestock, Forestry, PWD and Police Officers, all of whom were trying to establish working African District Councils prior to Self-Government and eventually, Independence. None of them knew how very little time there was in which to build up ADCs across the country! Many of them had been told, during the Fifties, when recruited, 'Independence is over thirty years, or more, in the future!'

Unlike districts in southern Kenya, with good soil and agricultural management, Moyale's pastoralists were always on the move. They believed that livestock – cattle, goats or camels – were the only wealth a man should have. This view was held by all the Northern Frontier tribes, except for one very small one, the El-Molo, which lived by fishing in Lake Turkana. The pastoralists tended to overgraze. Endless schemes, with and without penalties, were introduced in order to keep stock at a level which the parched northern districts could sustain.

In Moyale, we had no 'District Team' embracing the numerous government departments represented down south. We had the DC, the DO (myself) a Police Assistant Superintendent and a number of junior Inspectors as well as a doctor – all very basic. I was the first DO to have been appointed to that district and, perhaps because, in some quarters I might have been regarded as surplus to requirements, I was determined to justify my existence. Consequently, when the DC said that the district's budget had been allocated £10,000 (a lot of money in those days – enough to buy two good detached houses in either Marlow or Surbiton) to build part of a new hospital, I accepted the challenge with alacrity. Before national service and the Oxford Devonshire Course, I had been articled to a Chartered Architect and was experienced in building.

Not only did we build the main part of the 'cottage hospital' – with a splendid operating theatre the like of which our Brahmin doctor had not seen – we also built a whole new garage complex with guardroom attached, an attractive Tribal Police (*dubas*) residential block, two comfortable bungalows (one for the doctor and the other for Mr Khosla, the Asian District Clerk) and a small covered – but 'open' – market used primarily by milkmaids. Before I left I designed a Secondary School building. As work went on the DC managed to extract more funds for the building of the two houses and the school, based upon what we had managed to achieve with such limited funds. On a flying visit the then Minister of Health, described the building development as like a piece of southern Italy.

Moyale boasted only one trained carpenter/joiner, he was a cheerful Boran who was not dismayed by what was planned: he trained a few other Boran to do the more repetitive work and, eventually, was taught to read plans. When preparing plans I listed all the materials required and then arranged for vehicles to collect the materials from Nanyuki, a rail head 450 miles to the south. We trained the prisoners (there was a prison in Moyale for about 40 offenders) to work on a seemingly endless production line of concrete blocks of different shapes and sizes suited to the programme. Some prisoners became so skilled that, on release, they came to the office for letters of recommendation before looking for work further south.

Terracotta bricks were a problem. We excavated inside a dozen or so large anthills and made sensible 3" x 6" x 9" bricks which, after being dried in the sun, were baked inside all the hollow anthills. The ants had done most of the mixing work for us. Similarly, kiln workers, some of whom were prisoners, also sought letters of recommendation when their time was up.

The Boran and Somali chiefs were proud of their impressive new district *boma*. Practical roundabouts, bursting with colour, and dual carriageways were constructed to minimise the churning up of dirt roads in the *boma* during the rainy season.

One of the DC's many interests was tree planting. Hundreds of trees (produced from local seedlings) were planted around the *boma* and along parts of the escarpment where soil erosion was anticipated. Bob Otter was also concerned that the prisoners could become bored by the concrete block and brick production line, so they became planters of seedlings as well. In time, they specialised: some preferred being associated with building materials and others with trees.

DEVELOPMENT WORK

Land Consolidation in Kiambu

JOHN GOLDS

I was variously, District Officer, Kikuyu Guard and later, Divisional District Officer in the Kiambu District of Kenya from 1953 to 1959. As the Emergency began to quieten down I was given the opportunity by the District Commissioner Douglas Penwill, and the Provincial Commissioner Frank Loyd, to take on a new challenge, new not only to me but also for Kenya. That challenge was to become responsible for creating and carrying out Land Consolidation (LC), in Kiambu. This district of Central Province had the huge advantage that its Kikuyu inhabitants were personally ambitious, economically conscious and knew a good thing when they heard it, particularly if it appeared to promise benefit for their own pockets! This job turned out to be the most worth-while and enjoyable I have ever done.

The objective of consolidation was to measure up the tiny pockets of land owned in the district, pre-plan the area location by location, siting the villages, the common areas (schools, roads, churches, clinics etc), combine the tiny pockets of land created by inheritance and dishonesty over the generations and issue a registered and marketable title deed. The average ownership in Kiambu was twenty pieces of land to make up one registered site; the amount of land to be deducted from each owner averaged about 7%. At the same time, it aimed to settle all outstanding land ownership disputes, which was one of the single most important causes for lack of agricultural development in Central Province. A side advantage, not fully apparent at the beginning, but which the Kiambu Kikuyu very quickly seized on, was that these registered and marketable land titles enabled them to borrow money from banks to improve their new farms.

But first the whole idea had to be sold to the Kikuyu as, in spite of rumours still being published from time to time by ill informed press and sociologists, the whole scheme was voluntary. The first location selected was Komothai in Githunguri Division where Chief Magugu had already expressed to me strong support for the whole idea. I held widely scattered and often very vocal *baraza*s throughout the area. A vote was then taken to decide if there was a genuine wish for the process. If the answer was yes, elected committees for each sub-tribal grouping were formed by public election to act as liaison groups with the LC staff and, more important, to act as land 'magistrates,' to settle all land ownership issues ahead of the survey teams.

The most important part of the whole system and indeed the most difficult, was the need to keep the land adjudication committees honest. The officers in charge failing to control these committees almost always created the failure of consolidation in other districts. It was for this reason I employed many non-Africans who could not benefit from dishonest decisions, and it worked. These officers, such as David Slater, Leon Fouche, Bobby Cade and many others originated from the cadre of the Kenya Regiment, DOs Kikuyu Guard and short contract District Assistants. They did a wonderful job and worked all hours. One of them when he wanted his unpaid adjudication teams to work extra hours to settle a difficult case, would amuse them by playing his trumpet. There was a route of appeal against their decisions to myself, but my decision was final. This was tested in the courts and upheld.

Typical cases of dishonesty arose by Kikuyu getting together and disputing between each other for a piece of land that had not been occupied for some years (owner abroad, in prison or often as a Mau Mau fighter in the forest). If their claims were not defended, one side or the other would, they hoped, win their claim, and divide the proceeds. This was a form of claim that became increasingly common and had to be most rigorously investigated. Other members of the land owning community who had to be carefully defended by my staff were the Mau Mau members either in prison, detention or indeed still in the forest, these we felt had equal rights with the more law-abiding members of the community. This risk we covered by sending many of the adjudication committees to visit the inmates at all the prison and detention camps in Kenya.

Every piece of land was surveyed. I think survey teams measured well in excess of half a million and in the end I had over one thousand persons on my pay role. These teams consisted of labourers, clerks and survey assistants with a District Assistant in charge of each group including the volunteer adjudication committees who were not paid. The Kenya Survey Department prepared base plans and my district staff fitted in all the consolidated pieces into the original area, less a percentage, normally about 7%, for the common land. The next problem, and again where the adjudication committees were so important, was to decide where, with this jigsaw puzzle, each new farm should be sited. One had to take into account the need for effective road access, did the owner previously own good or poor land, the need for some form of water access, being within their tribal family grouping etc.

Fortunately Kiambu District largely consisted of long ridges with water sources in each valley bottom. With roads along the top of the ridges and water at the bottom the general pattern was long narrow farms stretching

DEVELOPMENT WORK

from the top of the ridges to the valley bottoms, giving access to roads and water, with each piece consisting of some good top flat land, steep land and flood plain.

One had many arguments on the common land percentage. Each committee wished it to be as small as possible. The beneficiaries wanted it to be as large as possible. The education department wanted lots of school sites on the best level land. The Ministry of Works wanted excessive road reserves. This was something that had to be most tightly controlled as their need was to have these roads along the top of the ridges and this adsorbed the best land available. I became most unpopular with the churches and missionaries, all of whom wanted their own faith represented in every area even though they knew finances would make it impossible for them to build a church or mission station. They also did everything possible to keep out their rivals!

The view of any location or tribal area that by clear majority vote, turned down the offer to consolidate their land, was accepted and their area was left out. In every case they asked, before the end of the Kiambu consolidation process, for us to return and consolidate their area and this was eventually done. After I had been doing this for about six months the District Commissioner, Douglas Penwill, called me into his office, where he was consuming a choc-ice with his feet on his desk. As he offered me one, I knew something was up. He enquired how long I thought it would take to complete LC in Kiambu. I said my plan and budget was based on three years from start to finish. He said he wanted the whole thing completed in two years and asked if it could be done. I assured him that we could, providing the finance could be speeded up and I could obtain sufficient staff. He agreed and simply told me to assume the new target completion date as from tomorrow. I in turn invited Frank Ratzburg, my most co-operative liaison officer in the Survey Department, to a good lunch. The outcome was agreement on the importance of these new targets, and he quickly provided me with thirty survey assistants to the fury of every other district in Kenya, which was waking up to the importance of land consolidation. Interestingly, about twenty-five years later I met up with Frank in St Lucia and many other old Kenya Survey department colleagues of my Kenya LC days. They were now doing a similar operation on that island and were rather strangely, employed by an American group, at I hope and assume, generous salaries.

While all this activity was under way in the locations we were also setting up a permanent land registry building, creating village plans (hugely helped by Thornley Dyer the Government Town Planner). Also, and something which did not enhance my popularity with the Agricultural Department, we were creating a follow up to land consolidation. We pressurised the Agricultural Department to produce more and more farming plans, I even wrote a picture book and made a video on better agriculture; after all I was a farmer myself. We educated the banks on the security of our land titles for the purposes of lending money but at the same time persuaded them not to lend money unless it was to be solely used for farm improvement. Such actions encroaching on the sphere of the Agricultural Department did not improve my popularity with some senior agriculturalists but I felt most strongly that to simply issue land titles with no follow up was to waste a most wonderful opportunity.

At the end of the consolidation process we made every landowner dig around their boundaries a wide swathe of tilled soil and then we made aerial photographs of the entire district from, I think, 15,000ft. These boundaries had already been marked by hedges and at corners the traditional Kikuyu land 'peg' of the deep-rooted matoka lily. From this the Survey Department produced accurate plans for the permanent record of everyone's land, and from this record every boundary can be resurveyed and a record of ownership established. The difference in the standard of Kiambu agriculture was immediate and persists right up to today. During this task we created 1,860 miles of new roads, 285 school sites, and 225 sites for, churches, tea and coffee nurseries, cemeteries, sports grounds, markets and cattle dips. The final figure of new consolidated farm units in Kiambu District was 37,139, made up of:

Small holdings less than four acres	17,316
Farms, four to seven acres	10,359
Farms seven to twenty acres	7,975
Farms over twenty acres	1,489

A Revolution in Land Tenure

JOHN JOHNSON

Land consolidation and freehold title created a rural revolution. In the mid 1950s there was no private ownership of land in Embu district. All farmland was vested in the *mbari*, an extended family group. Most farmers owned scattered pockets, some on the ridge-top, some on the slope and some in the valley bottom. This was a time-consuming way of farming, but it was the traditional way. I was appointed DO Land Consolidation in Embu in 1956, six months after my arrival in Kenya. It was my first proper job after learning the ropes in the *boma*. Working with me were Geoffrey Kariithi an officer with local roots and Ludwig Kolbe, an Agricultural Officer. It was Geoffrey who decided how it should be done. He had been sent to look at the consolidation already in train in the neighbouring Kikuyu districts. He recommended that we should work through committees of Elders from each mbari and we accepted his judgement. Kolbe and I had recruited and trained the survey teams and co-ordinated the operation. But convincing the people was Geoffrey's show, and he made it all work.

The Elders marked out the boundaries of each *mbari's* land and these were cleared. A recording team then made a map. Inter-*mbari* disputes were resolved by a higher committee.

New legislation, the African Courts (Suspension of Land Suits) Ordinance 1965 stopped all existing cases. Public purpose land – roads, schools, churches, coffee and tea factories, medical centres – was discussed for each area and put on the maps. The demand for future school plots at twelve acres apiece was amazing as all contributed to a percentage cut off the land available for allocation as farms. Finally the Elders drew up a record of existing rights in conjunction with the potential right-holders. A survey team put these acreages on the map trying to plan each farm as a strip extending from the ridge down to the valley.

I soon moved on to be a Divisional DO, handing over the supervision to Geoffrey. But I saw how quickly the enthusiasm of the people translated the maps to working farms. Thirty years later I was able to go back and look at the results. The high parts of my division, on the edge of the Mt Kenya forest had been transformed. A carpet of tea in smallholdings averaging ten acres covered what was formerly grazing land. The scale of the economic and social change was impressive.

The Creation of a New District

PETER GORDON

For many years, the seven locations in the northern half of North Nyanza (formerly North Kavirondo) had campaigned to be hived-off as a separate district. The reasons were partly tribal and partly economic. These locations (the majority of whose population was Babukhusu) were the producers of more than half of the district maize crop and they bitterly complained that they did not receive their proportionate share of the maize cess. This was collected by the Maize Marketing Board on behalf of the North Nyanza African District Council, based at the District HQ at Kakamega. Some 70% of this cess was allocated by the ADC to meet the nigh inexhaustible demands of the people of the southern locations who, on account of their numerical superiority, dominated the Council. The latter made lavish grants for schools, health centres and other services to the south where Central Government schemes for agricultural and other development also tended to be focused. Understandably, the North felt neglected not only by Central Government, but also by its own local Council.

Even before the 1950s the Central Government had not been entirely averse to the idea of dividing North Nyanza into two districts. It had long been recognised that administration of the seven northern Locations, comprising some 1,250 square miles, with a population of over 250,000 (ie. half the area and a third of the population of North Nyanza) could not be adequately effected from Kakamega, far to the south.

But largely for financial reasons, the proposal for division had been repeatedly shelved. Its revival, in 1955, was partly in conformity with the general policy of closer administration throughout the Colony following the Mau Mau Emergency. But mainly it was due to the enthusiasm of the Provincial Commissioner, C.H. 'Ngombe' Williams who had long favoured the split. He finally overcame the financial objections by undertaking to effect the change 'on a shoe-string' without calling on the Government for new funds – at least not in the initial stages, With this assurance, the Council of Ministers decreed, by Legal Notice, that the North Nyanza District should be divided into two on 1 January, 1956.

Mainly in order to curb the subversive and violent activities of the *Dini ya Msambwa* sect which had erupted in the Kimilili area in the 1940s, a Sub-Station had been established at Bungoma in 1950. This comprised a District Officer, a Medical Officer with a small hospital, and an Officer from each of the Agriculture, Veterinary and Education Departments. This was to form the nucleus of the HQ of the new district at Bungoma.

In April 1955, I was appointed District Commissioner, Designate, of the new district, charged with responsibility for planning and establishing it. An early priority was choosing a suitable name. After extensive local consultations, the suggestion finally adopted was that put forward by the PC: 'Elgon Nyanza' – an appropriate salute to Mount Elgon as the dominant geographical feature of the area.

Eight months remained after my appointment before the district came officially into being and, clearly there was a lot of ground to be covered in that period. But the task ahead was made so much easier by the fact that the wishes of government and governed for once coincided. Every step in the process was supported with enthusiasm by the overwhelming majority of the peoples of Elgon Nyanza. For the moment anyway, politics were relegated to the sidelines.

The first priority was to set up the administrative structure. The build-up of DO strength was gradual. There was already a DO in place in the Western Division. Early in 1956, another DO, W.H. Thompson, took over the triple duties of DO1 and DO Courts and DO Kavujai Division. Later, he acted as DC for two months while I was on leave. Before the end of the year, a DO was posted to the Kimilili Division. Construction of the Busia Sub-Station, as specifically requested by the people of the Western Division, began in May 1956. An indication of the measure of improvisation necessitated by financial stringency was the fact that the DO was housed for most of the year in the nearby Leprosarium! The building of the Sub-Station close to the Uganda border let loose a flood of rumours. During the year, the Uganda Government was obliged to issue at least two denials that this was the first step in the process of Kenya taking over the Eastern Province!

The most urgent need for funds was for the Sub-Station at Kimilili – ever a potential trouble spot – but it was not till the end of 1956 that money was forthcoming and a start made on housing and offices. Meanwhile, the DO roughed it in a rest house.

When the day came for the official opening of the district, an enormous amount remained to be done. Bungoma resembled more a refugee camp than a District HQ.: at one time, five officers were sharing an economy house; three, an African dwelling; a family of four lived in a servant's quarter; and many more were under canvas. But it was a case of 'coming, ready or not'. On 10 January 1956, the Inauguration of Elgon Nyanza was symbolised by the Governor, Sir Evelyn Baring, raising the Union flag at a colourful ceremony at Bungoma. The new district was blessed by the Bishops of Mombasa and Kisumu. Four hundred invited guests and some 15,000 jubilant Africans watched the proceedings, which included the laying of the foundation stone of the new African District Council by the Governor.

The establishment of this Council was the second major task, which had had to be accomplished in the months preceding the official opening. 'In my considered opinion,' wrote the Senior Crown Counsel, 'the proposal to wind up the present North Nyanza African District Council and at the same time to establish two African Councils one of which bears the same name, is fraught with complications and difficulties'. An understatement! Indeed, in the end, it proved impossible to effect the change under existing legislation and an amendment to the African District Council Ordinance was found to be necessary. The amending Bill was passed through all its stages in record time.

Apart from the legal complications, another problem was the natural reluctance of a majority of the North Nyanza ADC to lose the goose that laid the golden eggs, ie. the contribution to Council finances made by the locations in the north. However, after protracted negotiations, conducted by the DC North Nyanza, Jock Leslie, the Council unanimously accepted on 4 July 1955, the division both of the North Nyanza District and the ADC.

But the old Council was, at first, totally unable to agree upon the division of its assets. Proposals put forward by a Local Government Inspector were rejected. In the end, it was the Finance Committee of the Council itself which, to its great credit, reached a compromise: the North Nyanza Council would pay the Elgon Nyanza Council £50,000 to compensate for under-capitalisation of assets; the remainder of the surplus balances would be equally divided.

On paper, this seemed admirable. But implementing this decision was an entirely different kettle of fish. The actual release of funds ran into snag after snag and, as a temporary solution, the Ministry of Local Government eventually suggested a special Loan of £5000. This was approved by Legislative Council in November, 1955. However, no instalment of this loan had been received at the start of the new Council in January. The Elgon Nyanza ADC therefore began life with not one penny in its coffers – and a single clerk.

It was clear that, if the new Council was to come into physical existence on the appointed day and a hiatus in Local Government avoided, it must, somehow or other, be constituted beforehand. It was decided that elected membership should be on the basis of one member per 10,000 of the population (a total of twenty-six) and that the unit of a constituency should be one or more complete sub-locations. In addition, there were to be nine nominated members (all the chiefs plus two others). Elections were held throughout the district during the first such elections to be held in the Colony – and passed off without incident. The only objection to the propriety of these proceedings was raised in Legislative Council by Hon W.W.W. Awori who wished to know whether such 'elections' were valid before the Council had been legally constituted. He had a point, of course!

By the end of the first year, in spite of much frustration and many setbacks, something resembling the framework of a district was more or less in place. A full divisional organisation existed in the field with a District Officer and Agricultural Officer in each of the three Divisions; Bungoma had become a lively *boma* with twenty-four British officials (and two banks!); the African District Council was up and running; building to the value of some £200,000 was in progress in the district.

Above all perhaps, the people felt that, at last and for once, they were getting what they wanted, and the overwhelming majority were accordingly grateful and showed this by their ready co-operation.

Quite an exciting year! I enjoyed every moment.

DEVELOPMENT WORK

Orderly Administration

W. H. (TOMMY) THOMPSON

In 1956 I was posted to be the senior district officer (DO1) at Bungoma in the Elgon Nyanza District far away in Nyanza Province bordering on Uganda, which had until a few months previously been part of the large North Nyanza District, the home of the Abaluhya and the sub-tribes thereof. I could not have been sent anywhere more different from Fort Hall.

My new DC, Peter Gordon had obviously hoped for someone with greater experience and I cannot blame him for his obvious wariness. Given the choice he would not have accepted anyone from Central Province, and who could blame him? Far away from the Emergency areas, Nyanza had carried on very much as it had wanted to. Cowboys and strong-arm men, of which I was probably one, were not wanted. Furthermore we in Kikuyuland had been soaking up the money and that had not gone down at all well. Gordon never lifted his air of disapproval though, as time went on, he softened a little. Of course, I was being over-sensitive and very scared of having to get down to much more desk work than I had been trained to do. I had been too long a member of the inner Fort Hall family and Central Province clan. Though I did not know it I needed the change and new direction.

Peter Gordon had done a tremendous job setting up his new district and the important and well-financed District Council that went with it. His knowledge of African local government was considerable and it was soon clear that by Central Province standards Nyanza was years ahead. Unrestricted by the exigencies of the Emergency there was money in the coffers, capable African officers in positions of authority, and a greater independence from the administration than we 'Kikuyulanders' could have possibly imagined.

When I had found my feet I began to go out on safari. The change was fascinating. Not only were the Abaluhya richer and enjoying their new found freedom away from Jaluo dominance, they also had a wonderful district stretching from the lushness of Mount Elgon to the arid plains. Often doing ten miles a day on foot, I was in a new world. My great joy was the African Courts. Not held back by Emergency restrictions DCs and DOs had put in a lot of time to very good effect training Court Clerks and Elders. I learned a great deal about training and organisation which was to stand me in good stead later on.

In August 1956 Gordon and his family went home on leave and I took over. Princess Margaret visited the Province and I had the chance, at long last, to wear my ceremonial whites. We had a local sculptress, Flora Avuaguto, who, though completely untrained produced breathtakingly beautiful models in baked local clay. The Governor told me to commission a piece for the Princess. She sculpted a head but HE decided there were already too many busts dotted around Royal Residences and selected a minor piece of a man winnowing corn. The lovely head became mine for a modest payment and now graces our own mantelpiece.

When Gordon returned we had the first colony-wide election to organise and control. It took a lot of doing especially as we were not helped by the shenanigans of the candidates. Given space this would be worth expanding upon but it cannot be. Let it suffice to say that many of the older and illiterate voters did not, and could not, comprehend that if they voted for the candidate with the motor-car symbol that they would not receive one in return. There were tantrums and tears. Such was the volume of voting that the ballot boxes overflowed and at one polling station I found forty-seven ballot papers posted into the local community radio set.

Reporting from the Bush

ERIC GORDON & JOHNNIE ROWLANDS

In 1957 the Provincial Administration in most of Central Province was in overdrive; pressing on with urgent programmes of rehabilitation, Land Consolidation, livestock improvement, rural health and education etc. Districts and sub-Districts were required to report every two months, in a prescribed format, on their progress on such matters. I was the Personal Assistant to the Provincial Commissioner at Nyeri, and one of my duties was to check the due receipt of those reports and pass them to the PC with any 'staff' comments. The reports from Ndorobo Sub-District of Nanyuki were adrift. In response to a friendly but firm reminder, I was delighted to receive (by return so to say) the following from the late Johnnie Rowlands, and to pass it to Frank Loyd to cheer the end of a rather vexatious day.

Bi-Monthly Report – Ndorobo
There's a forest, Mukogodo, with dead cedar but no podo
For the rainfall here gives timber little luck.
On the Isiolo border there is sometimes law and order,
But on the whole we're living in the Muk.

DEVELOPMENT WORK

We see the storm clouds pass to overlook our grass
Which we admit is often very shocking.
And confounded geep and shoats that have never eaten oats,
Just aggravate a state of overstocking.

We have lions; we have lambs; and we're building several dams,
Which elephants are trying to destroy.
Though we plough no seed, we scatter alien tribes by the manyatta
And there are lots of pretty views we can enjoy.

Nerve centre and metropolis, a place by name of Dol Dol is
Where lie the borehole and too many bores.
Here we marshal all our forces, the riflemen and horses
And sally to shoot guinea fowl in scores.

I am a local Fuhrer from Il Polei to Tura
But all the same the elders don't keep quiet.
Though the Council has no money, men live on milk and honey
(Monotonous and such old-fashioned diet).

We've just begun a school but one will seem a fool
If there's no Standard One next year to use it.
And though a new health system can treat the sick and list 'em,
There's very few who care to pay or choose it.

It's a pity rates and taxes don't run to prophylaxes
And soap and vim to rid oneself of flies.
For the dudus humans wear around the head and hair
Do appear a halo smudged up to the eyes.

Folk are picturesque, but yet they are given just a Vet
To tend the beasts and cattle's prior claim.
And an infant washed in water yells like a piglet slit in slaughter
And to wash *Moran* of war paint is a shame.

So begins the March of Mind (lagging mentally behind
Sophisticates in rest of Central P.)
But since most people nod and in the land of Mukogod
They really do not miss what they don't see.

For were I born Ngwesi I would probably be lazy
And take four weeks of leave instead of one.
And if we were Ndigili it really would be silly
To work instead of resting in the sun.

But from Anadanguru plain to the Uaso Nyiro drain
No longer are we hidden and forlorn:
What with roads and ALDEV service, now this so-called reserve is
Just dragged awake from nightmare into dawn.

Controlling Migration

DICK TURNBULL

Unlike the constantly repeated pattern of seasonal stock movements from grazing area to grazing area, long-range migrations must, at some point in time or in space, come to a stop. Either the supply of migrants exhausts itself; or the receiving country turns out to be so unwelcoming in terms of the health of the livestock or by way of violent opposition from rival claimants to the local water and pastures that a halt has to be called. Or the migrants themselves, their characters modified and their determination blunted by inter-marriage into one or other of the more stable communities with which they have made contact during the move, or by experience of the luxury of running water for the stock instead of the harsh discipline of the deep well, deciding that fighting is not, after all, the only proper pursuit of man, and that the hardships of the enterprise are no longer acceptable.

Of those factors it was the operation of the second that brought the Darod invasion to an end; though the passage of time would, doubtless, have seen the third, and perhaps even the first, taking effect. It was not so much the violent opposition of the Boran and the Sakuye that stopped the Darod; for the amount of power that could be exercised by these unhappy demoralised people was not such as to deter a man of the quality of, say, Abdurrahman Mursaal. But the decision of the Government of the Protectorate to exclude the Aulihan from Wajir, and the heavy fines collected in the course of the Aulihan campaign of 1918 were quite a different matter; and although the second half of the 1920s saw a good deal of manoeuvring by the various Ogaden sections between the Wajir and Garissa Districts on the one hand and Italian Somaliland on the other, there were none of the massive incursions that, ten years earlier, had so jeopardised the peace and good government of the district.

1909 saw the start of a systematic administration of the Northern Frontier District. 1934 is a year of equal importance; for it witnessed the introduction of the Special Districts Ordinance, and enactment that enabled the Officer in Charge of the district to allocate certain pastures and certain grazing ranges and certain waters to specific tribes, and to prohibit other tribes from trespassing on these preserves. At the same time he was empowered to prohibit the use of particular grazing ranges and water supplies by specified tribespeople, and in this way not only to protect the resources of the region against overstocking and other forms of bad land use but to ensure that in times of inter-tribal tension, known trouble-makers could be kept out of areas where their presence might be expected to spark off a serious incident. Admittedly the Ordinance could have been criticised by a disgruntled, dispossessed Boran or Sakuye on the grounds that it sealed the stable pump after the pump's water-supply had been spirited away; but for the twenty-eight years since its introduction it has proved itself to be a versatile and easily handled legal weapon, as efficacious against the long-distance 'invaders' as against the local 'grass-poacher'. Independent Kenya will, I hope, find it as valuable a chapter of the Statute Book as has the Colonial regime.

6

Safari

The First Safari	Tony Peet
Among the Turkana	Tom Watts
Ethiopian Raiders	Tom Watts
Coastal Travels	Anna Osborne
Getting to Know the Kamba	Alan Liddle
Keeping the Peace	Hugh Walker
Hard Pounding	Henry Wright
A Self Reliant Man	Peter Dempster
A Punishment Posting	Roger Horrell
Launch Safari on the 'Pelican'	Henry Wright

Introduction

In many minds, the word safari conjures up images of wealthy big-game hunters in the moulds portrayed by Ernest Hemingway in *The Green Hills of Africa*, or by Clark Gable and Ava Gardner in Hollywood epics such as *Mogambo* which was filmed in Kenya.

To the colonial administrator in Kenya, the reality was quite different. It was part of the job. An administrator's 'working' safari in the Northern Province could have some of the imagined romanticism: travel by camel, horse or on foot in the cool early hours of the morning, rest under the shade of a *doum* palm or thorn tree during the heat of the day, a camp-bed under the clear night sky with the occasional grunt of a lion in the distance. But mostly it was a case of getting on with routine chores: tax collection, supervising the building of small dams or the terracing of hillside *shambas* to prevent soil erosion, visiting the scene of a crime or boundary dispute, surveying or map-making, inspecting the conduct of African Courts.

If the safari had to visit remote areas for a week or more, it entailed taking home and office with you and living in tents or simple rest houses. Sometimes the family came too. Up to the 1950s, supplies were usually carried by a string of porters: there was never a shortage of willing manpower, as the service provided a useful means of earning some ready cash. In later years, lorries took over, often hired from local traders.

The outbreak of the Mau Mau Emergency accelerated the government

Plate 1: Porters on foot safari, Turkana District.

Plate 2: DC's house, Thika.

Plate 3: Tax collection, Turkana District.

Plate 4: Dam construction for drinking water, Turkana District.

Plate 5: Fort and boma, Wajir.

Plate 6: DC inspecting dubas, Wajir.

Plate 7: Harambee: DC's lorry in sand lugga, NFD.

Plate 8: Luo fish market, Lake Victoria.

Plate 9: Queen Mother with Sir Evelyn Baring amd Coast officials, Mombasa.

Plate 10: Queen Mother and Maasai moran, Narok.

Plate 11: Fortified village, Embu District.

Plate 12: Captured Mau Mau fighter and Tribal Policeman.

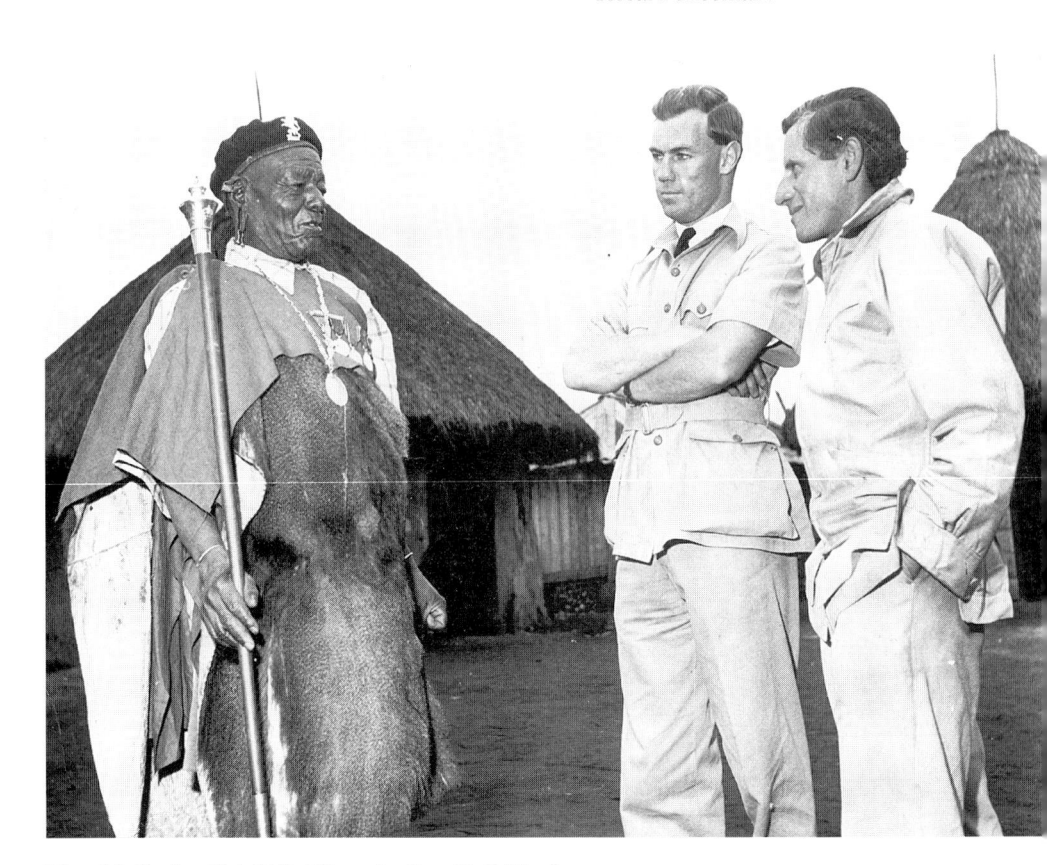

Plate 13: Senior Chief Njiri Karanja, Fort Hall District.

Plate 14: Land consolidation: measuring with elders, Kiambu District.

Plate 15: Governor, Sir P. Renison greeting Chiefs, Kiambu District.

Plate 16: Jomo Kenyatta visiting settlement scheme, Escarpment Forest.

Plate 17: DC Isaac Okwirry and family.

policy of 'closer administration'. More DOs were established away from the district *boma*, living in the divisions over which they had responsibility, in daily contact with the local chiefs and headmen. In the more populous areas, and especially in Central Province, there was less need for long safaris. Land-rovers were provided so that time was not spent on long journeys. For most officers life became physically easier, but much busier.

Safari could be testing for a young District Officer. Tony Peet recounts his first experience. Tom Watts revelled in safari life in the NFD in the 1940s and faced trouble on the Ethiopian border. In Coast Province Anna Osborne and her husband enjoyed more peaceful travels. The added bonus of outdoor living was meeting the people on congenial terms as Alan Liddle tells us. Hugh Walker and Henry Wright describe working among the Somali in their harsh environment. Peter Dempster records his visit to a Development Officer on a remote mountain top in the north. Another project, this time for the reform of elephant poachers is described by Roger Horrell. Some districts were unaffected by modern trends, and Henry Wright delights in a journey back in time down the river Tana.

The First Safari

TONY PEET

The first safari on one's own can be a test for any new cadet. After I had been in Kitui for a few weeks in 1949, I was sent off into the district with instructions to hold *barazas* in three or four locations with a view to arranging the construction of more dams to provide extra water supplies in the dry season. The DC, Paul Kelly had begun this excellent scheme, which was most popular once its value had become apparent. In one location I had long discussion with the chief and his *wazee* (elders) as to the best way to provide a dam in a slightly difficult area where there were several water courses which had clear signs of a good flow of water in the rainy season. We deliberated at length and looked at some six or seven possible sites. Having been a sapper during the war and responsible for building several bridges over rivers during the Italian campaign, as well as for preventing rain and flood water destroying roads, I was confident, having taken levels, that my proposed dam site was sound. The chief and his *wazee* appeared to agree.

Dick Brayne-Nicholls, who was DO1 in Kitui, went out shortly after I got back from my safari to check on what I had done. On his return he called me into his office and said that he had found an unhappy chief and *wazee* in the one location already referred to. They had told him that the new *Bwana*

Mdogo was '*hapana mzuri*' (no good), because he did not even know that water will not run up hill! What a 'damning' criticism, and I wondered if Paul Kelly would have any further use for me when he came back off leave! Meanwhile I had to go back and agree a different site with the chief, since he would have to organise all the work and must be confident it would be worth while.

Among the Turkana

TOM WATTS

I enjoyed safari life in Turkana. One was close to the tribespeople and their daily life. The administrative safari included the syces with the baggage camels, the Tribal Police escort, the hospital dresser with his box of medicine, the tax clerk with his register, the interpreter who looked after the tobacco, the ostrich feathers, the calico cloth and the maize flour. Either one or both of my Kitui Kamba servants accompanied me. We followed these nomads during the dry season from one set of wells to the next, meeting with the local headman at each campsite. The government chief in each area would accompany the safari but at the *barazas* tribal elders would do the talking. The chief would only intervene if he wanted to show that whilst he was following government instructions such as grazing control or frontier security policy, his people were not!

In those wartime days, we were concentrating on the maintenance of tribal discipline and security by stopping intertribal raiding, killing, and stock theft between nomadic tribes along our Uganda, Sudan, and Abyssinian borders. There was tax to collect, an efficient way of keeping tabs on the male tribesmen. There was livestock to purchase with which to feed the troops down-country. Early on in my service with the Turkana, I received a basic lesson in economics from an elderly tribesman who had been asked whether he had paid his tax. He looked at me disapprovingly and replied, 'When have I had the chance to buy some money?'

On a tax safari we carried, on our outward journey, boxes of one shilling pieces known as *rupia nyeupe* and returned generally with not so full boxes but large numbers of sheep, goats, and a few cattle. The full tax was three shillings. The price of a reasonably good condition sheep or goat was three shillings with an extra one shilling for a large ram or he-goat. A good young steer would be worth twenty-five shillings. I would stand with my interpreter with a box of two thousand shillings and the taxpayer would hand over his animal, if in good condition, to the tax clerk and purchase his tax receipt, which was, I think, embossed with an aeroplane in 1942. The tax year was known by the symbol on the receipt such as a cockerel, cow or train engine. In Kitui I found that the Wakamba would base their dates on their famines the year of the *Nzige* (locust), or *Mchele* or *Mahindi* and so on, that is the cause of the famine *Nzige* or the famine relief provided by the government, rice or maize.

After the tax collection for the day was completed and the livestock taken off to be branded with the government brand, the elders would line up to receive their generous pinch of chewing tobacco before gathering in the shade of the baraza at which they presented their petitions. I passed on matters which the DC wished to have discussed, such as grazing control along the territorial and district boundaries, stock theft, and inter-clan fighting, stock sales, and news about the North Africa campaign. There were a few Turkana in the Army. These tribesmen bemoaned the fact that the military boreholes had been abandoned though generally water was well distributed in the many sand rivers which flowed from the western highlands across Turkana eastwards to Lake Rudolf. Finally the interpreter would sell the much sought after ostrich feathers, brought from South Africa, the calico cloth and perhaps even some maize flour.

I was always attracted by the activity around the wells in the sand rivers. The goats always looked more intelligent and inquisitive than the sheep. The camels were so often awkward and grumpy. As the men placed their wooden dugout troughs in the sand beside the well so the small stock gathered under the control of the women and children. Small groups of animals were then allowed to go to the troughs to drink followed by cattle, camels, and donkeys, those patient beasts of burden for the nomadic Turkana. These wells were usually sited by rock bars running across the river and holding back the water. After the war when there was money and manpower available there was a very successful programme of building sub-surface dams by constructing concrete walls tied into these rock bars across sand rivers thus holding back millions of gallons of water within the sand.

At all barazas there was a plea for dispensaries to be built, which at the time was impracticable. The dresser who accompanied me with his box of medicines could deal with the usual round of cuts and wash out the eyes of those suffering from conjunctivitis and trachoma. Only in the later years was it possible to organise eye camps and to fly up surgeons from Nairobi to operate on those blinded by trachoma and cataracts. Having no lorry transport it was not possible even to move the really sick to the small hospital in Lodwar, looked after by a hospital assistant (a paramedic in modern parlance) let alone move a patient to the care of a doctor in Kitale hospital. The DC and I shared an old Bedford truck, OHMS 1066, and needless to say I seldom had access to it, as it was required in Lodwar and for the DCs visits to Lokitaung.

During 1942 we were carrying out a re-organisation of the tribal administration which the DC had worked out with the elders based on the Turkana system of clan divisions and livestock brands. This kept me on foot safari most of 1942 with the tax clerk re-registering the tribe's adult males. We went all over Turkana district from the Sudan border down to the southern district boundary with Baringo, Samburu and Suk districts.

We always had mountains in the distance when we followed the Turkwell and Kerio rivers fed from Mount Elgon and the Cherangani Mountains. I wish that I had had grounding in the botany and geology of the Rift Valley as we walked through a great variety of bush and over many types of rock. There was little game to be seen though one heard elephant, lion, and even leopard in the riverine bush of the Turkwell and Kerio. The inevitable hyena could be heard most nights.

I was once laid up with a bout of malaria in camp close to the Kerio river. I gave my orderly my old shotgun and two cartridges and asked him to get me a bird. He returned with a guinea fowl and a duck – and one unused cartridge! A remarkable piece of shooting.

Ethiopian Raiders

TOM WATTS

The frontier with Ethiopia (then referred to as Abyssinia) was a constant problem due to the inadequate administration in the south.

The nomadic Boran, whose cousins were in the Isiolo and Moyale Districts, lived around the foothills of Marsabit Mountain. There were some Gabbra nomads who followed the grazing back and forth across the Abyssinian boundary, enjoying the better seasonal grazing in the Huri Hills on the northern edge of the district. Apart from these nomads with their camels, cattle, sheep, goats, and donkeys there was a small group of cultivators around the *boma*. These Burji, who had escaped from feudal subjection in Ethiopia, enjoyed the educational and medical facilities provided by the Bible Churchmen's Missionary Society.

There was a small loyal group of fishermen living on the edge of Lake Rudolf at Loiyangalani where there was a fresh water spring from Mount Kulal. These El Molo fishermen lived a primitive life catching fish, some of which they were able to dry and sell. Their great need was to collect together sufficient small stock with which to provide a dowry for a young Turkana or even a Rendille or Samburu woman in order to inject fresh blood into the inter-bred community.

Molly, my wife, and I took a lorry safari across the Chalbi desert to spend a few days at Loiyangalani and in the Kulal area with the Rendille. On our first morning at Loiyangalani there was a half-eaten carcass of a zebra, which had been killed just down stream from the camp. No one had heard the attack. We had spent the previous night in the lee of the lorry amongst whistling thorns overlooking the Chalbi. We were covered in dust.

This area of the district around Mounts Kulal and Nyiru near Lake Rudolf was much favoured by the Rendille, who were also inclined to trespass into the plains north of Baragoi in Samburu District which we visited for inter-tribal *barazas* on two occasions. Spending a night in the DC's guesthouse at Maralal, a large sturdy caravan, we were woken when it suddenly swayed. Next morning we were reassured that it was only one of the local elephants scratching itself.

The administrative interests in Marsabit District were very different from those in the more populated area of Turkana on the western side of Lake Rudolf. There were the same security problems of raiding gangs crossing over from Ethiopia mainly to kill our tribespeople but also to steal livestock which were not easy to move quickly over the lava strewn northern part of the district. The worst raid in my time was when a party of the Gelubba attacked a Gabbra *manyatta* killing indiscriminately old women, men, children, and babies. This was at Sabarei and the raiders were back in their Abyssinian administered territory before we came upon the *manyatta*. Fortunately we were able to get a wireless message back to Marsabit for a lorry to collect the wounded.

On my return to Marsabit a week later, I found an old woman who had had her right calf blown away by a dum-dum bullet sitting outside. More remarkably a young boy who had a hole blown in his skull had survived the long journey on top of the lorry and was recovering. The Gabbra *manyatta* had moved far beyond the grazing line and had paid the penalty. There was a constant demand that the armed police should be permanently encamped at *manyatta* sites rather than along the frontier.

Coastal Travels

ANNA OSBORNE

I left school in England to join my parents on their coffee farm near Kitale. So for some years I saw the scene from the settlers' side of the fence. Now, I think that I was very lucky to marry an administrator – although it did not enter my head then.

We were married at the little church in Limuru. It was so small that we could not walk up the aisle side by side. The reception was at Brackenhurst, a lovely hotel kept by the Hudson-Caines. We had become engaged there. There was a large contingent of Kitale settlers, all Paul's settler friends from Machakos and a sprinkling of Administration representatives.

We returned to Machakos after our honeymoon in the Usambara Mountains, as Paul was posted to Malindi. What a joy!

We packed and decided to motor to Mombasa: the road then was very basic, a couple of tarmac strips if you were lucky, and you got stuck if you weren't. We slept at the rest house at Voi. The road from Mombasa to Malindi was a 'Great Adventure'. We all came to know it well.

There were two ferries, one at Nyali and the other at Kilifi, where the DC lived, far enough away for Paul to be fairly independent. The ferries were unique: they consisted of a large raft that held three cars, chained into the bank so that the cars could get on. There were two thick ropes on each side of the ferry and we were pulled across relying on African muscle power. This was accompanied by loud and very rhythmic song in dialect, blowing of conch shells and stamping of feet.

At sea the waves were breaking on the beach, and the estuary stretched inland, to palms and *bundu*. It was a variety show that never palled: there was laughter, gaiety and shouting. We were to cross these ferries many times in our three years at Malindi and only once did I not find it amusing. Paul, in a hurry, tried to mount the ferry before it was chained up. Consequently the car pushed the ferry before us and only stopped when we sat waist deep in seawater! The old Ford was never the same again.

All this was long ago in the old days of 1938. Malindi was then an ancient Arab township; a village of corrugated iron huts with mud walls, one or two Arab or Indian *dukas* and the *Liwali*'s and DO's houses. The only other white resident was the schoolmaster who lived outside the settlement.

The DC's office was an imposing building with a flight of steps down to a drive and the seashore. The two offices with disused fans were downstairs and a wide staircase led to our flat above. The wide hall gave onto the courtyard and the boys' quarters behind. The flat upstairs consisted of four rooms with a wide, airy verandah all around. The back verandah was the kitchen. The front verandah looked over the sea, the sparkling sand and waves breaking gently on the reef. From the right side you saw Vasco da Gama's pillar perched on a rocky promontory complete with date of first landing. Beyond it ran Silver Sands.

To the left was the surfing beach, which stretched away to the Sabaki River, bright red when the rain came. There were two hotels and two private *bandas* only. The snag to perfection was the bats which lived in the roof in large numbers, and because of them we slept and lived on the verandahs.

The *Liwali* was a lovely old gentleman in flowing robes with a long grey beard. He was consulted on all Arab affairs. His house was quite near and on occasions such as the King's Birthday, we were asked to tea. We drank our tea with him outside the house, after Paul, in sparkling white uniform, had taken the parade on the office steps, and the ladies had been shown inside to talk to his wife and daughters. Luckily I had been learning Swahili with Paul, who was studying for his exam and could speak a little. We were given sweets and black coffee and then the great moment came – a small silver vessel, perfumed with incense and smoking strongly, which was held under our skirts. The fertility rite!

Another joy was the *kitetes*. Tiny creatures much smaller than the Indian mongoose, they were about nine inches long, with pink noses and ears and long tails like a mouse. The Africans would bring them in on a string, very miserable and half-trained. Soon, with good feeding and lots and lots of petting, they became as tame as a dog and would run up inside your trousers or jump onto your lap. It was enchanting to see two of them on their hind legs wrestling together in play. Given an egg, they would put it between their front paws and then shoot it backwards against the wall to crack it. Then they would suck away.

I left Malindi to go up country to my mother to have my baby – the *Liwali's* charm must have worked!

Quite half the time we were out on walking safaris. We were lucky, they were coming to an end. Our camping kit would be loaded onto a lorry, I would put out the stores and we would be off to the farthest part we could get to by road, probably Marafa. Sometimes we had to cross the Sabaki. The Sabaki was deep and wide: in the rains it was red-ochre with all the mud from up-country. We had to cross in frail dugout canoes paddled by two local Giriama. They only held four and you didn't dare move and rock the craft. When we had the baby, he came too in a basket slung on poles.

At camp the headman would come to report all *shauris* and see that all the porters were there. Then Paul would hold a *baraza*. The next day we would set off before daybreak accompanied by *askaris* and a guide, leaving the camp to be packed up.

We went by native paths connecting tiny clusters of mud huts where the women and *totos* would come out and stare and giggle. Most had never seen a white woman before; they were naked to the waist except for bead necklaces and bangles in their long pierced ears. They wore straw skirts made of reeds, full like ballet dancers' and very attractive. The Giriama were a jolly people, always singing and laughing.

We arrived at camp hot and tired and the headman would come with chairs. Two Giriamas were sent climbing the palms to bring down *madafu* (green coconuts). They were cut in half and given us to drink. Wonderful cooling drink! The sun would be up now and the porters would have arrived. Our tent was pitched and the fire was lit and we could sit down to a slap-up breakfast, feeling that we had earned it. Paul would hold a *baraza* to collect the *kodi*, head tax which all had to pay, and to hear the cases which were brought forward, and generally to advise. In the evening, we would walk round to see the *shambas* and to look at the crops – cotton was a new crop.

We were in camp one day when we were alerted by loud shouts and a man staggered in with a gash six inches long where his brother had slashed him with a *panga*; blood was pouring out. In desperation, I got out a large needle and thread and drew the edges of the wound together; he never made a sound but my fingers were trembling desperately. He was sent to the nearest dispensary on a stretcher and we heard later that he was fine.

In the camps there was the *choo*, a small grass hut approached by an entrance passage. It had a large wooden seat and was completely dark. I stood in the passage pulling my trousers down and as I moved forward to sit, I found myself confronted by an erect puff adder, which had been coiled up on the seat. I halted. It was later killed by the boys.

Another time we had left the path and were pushing through the long grass when the askari in front jumped back and shouted, *nyoka!* Paul went forward with his gun. Luckily the python had just swallowed a goat and was unable to do any more damage. Once there was a python in the office courtyard, it had crawled there during the night. It was shot.

Looking back, those three years in Malindi were my deepest memories of Kenya. We returned for holidays, but it had grown and changed and become a tourist attraction.

Nearly half a century later, the house, the *kitetes*, safari, and our African servants come back like old friends. Yet again I hear the smash and withdrawal of the waves, breaking on that silver sand.

Getting to Know the Kamba

ALAN LIDDLE

In Kenya's bigger districts, safari was an inescapable part of one's working life. It was also often enjoyable, always interesting, sometimes surprising, and on occasions rewarding. It enabled the DC or DO to know and speak to a greater number of people and, equally important, to listen to them. A visit on the spot to obtain a first hand impression of progress on projects in hand, or to identify local needs for new projects such as markets, water supplies, land reclamation, anti-soil erosion measures, livestock marketing arrangements, tree planting, roads, to name but a few, was always more likely to lead to better judgement than relying on papers and reports in the District Offices. It set up the DC in his district, or the DO in his division, as the visible symbol of government, to be knocked down or worked with according to the political winds that blew. To avoid the former fate the administrative officer had to pit his wits, no less than his statutory authority, against those of the politically active, who did not necessarily wish him well. For 'politically active' read, as a general rule, 'against the wishes of the government'.

The bigger districts also had outstations, with a resident DO in charge, for the same reasons. In my outstation, Mwingi, the centre for the Northern Division of Kitui District, I found it necessary to be on safari for some three weeks out of four. Mwingi was sixty miles northeast of Kitui, the District Headquarters, and the Northern Division had a population of a 100,000 Akamba in 2,600 square miles. For the most part this, to put it mildly, was not a politically conscious population, but even in these distant locations by 1960 the pace of change was accelerating and with it the heightened need for contact, communication and explanation – in short for closer administration. There were eight chiefs in my division, each one in charge of a location, and each location had its centre with a chief's office and accommodation for a small staff, also a rest house for the use of government officers on safari. Rest houses – the bigger locations had several in strategic places – were built of mud and wattle, whitewashed, with thatched roofs, and in Kitui were kept spick and span. Of my chiefs, four had held senior non-commissioned ranks in the King's African Rifles (Kitui was a great KAR recruiting district) and one in the Kenya Police. One of them was a member of Kenya's Council of State, a sort of powerless but advisory upper House which met from time to time under the Governor. He was both progressive and comparatively modern in outlook. All of them accepted, more or less, the changes that were coming but equally all resented the indecent haste with which they were brought about. Macmillan and Macleod would have won few votes in Kitui.

Most safaris meant leaving my wife and family behind at Mwingi in the small pink washed house with its long views to the east. The lot of the Colonial Service wife could be a very lonely one, and quite often was. Exceptionally, however, if a safari was likely to be based in one centre, my family came too and then quite a number took to the road. My usual safari retinue had some interesting characters. James Muthusi, my driver, formerly a corporal in the East African Armoured Car Squadron, was an entertaining source of local lore and gossip. He was a good looking, light skinned, Kamba, reputedly the by-blow of a nearby Baluch trader, with a jaunty air and a cavalry swagger, which had rubbed off on him from the

British officers of his army days. My Tribal Police sergeant at Mwingi, Ndinda Kitonga, sometimes came too in order to generally sharpen up the TPs stationed out in the chiefs' centres. He was a first rate NCO, with a good army record, a retired 11 KAR sergeant and veteran of 11 EA Division's famous advance down the Kabaw Valley in Burma against furious Japanese opposition in 1944 during the monsoon. Then there was my safari cook, Kabubu Musanga, formerly my orderly in 23 KAR and an askari of long service, who came as much as anything else for auld lang syne and to cheer me up with his flashing grin and infallible good humour. On the night of our arrival at Mwingi, there had been a knock at our front door. Outside stood the broadest smile in Africa beneath a red KAR *tarboosh* – Kabubu. By some combination of bush telegraph and Mwingi gossip, he had heard that we had been posted to his home district and had walked in to welcome us with a chicken. I offered him a job on the spot and he jumped at it. Finally, and usually, there was my TP Orderly, Mutinda, a smart young Kamba with all the charm and manners of his tribe. Added to these, when the family came too, were our ayah Teresia, who rather surprisingly enjoyed these occasions, and last, but never least, Cindy, our black and tan dachshund.

A family safari would be typically to Ngomeni, a big location on my far eastern boundary, where, from time to time, I could spend a week working in that location and the eastern halves of Endui and Mivukoni locations. The area had a number of projects in progress including a school building programme, a new market being set up, road improvements, water supplies with a pipeline being run from the big rock catchment dam at Ngomeni itself out into the cattle country towards the Eastern Crown Lands, and African Court of Kyuso – plenty that needed attention. The Crown Lands were a buffer between the Kamba of our eastern locations and the Orma of Garissa District and, while in theory occupied by neither tribe, in practice, and in periods of drought, were occupied by representatives of both, accompanied by their cattle, competing vigorously for scarce water at water holes. This at times could lead to undignified scenes of inter-tribal strife, though fortunately not during my time in Kitui.

Since, within six months of our arrival at Mwingi, our second son had been born, the need for his rather cumbersome cot on safari meant that it had to be fitted into the back of our long wheel base land-rover, with Sam in it, and our retinue seated around it. All the safari's kit and baggage went into the trailer towed behind. Arriving back at the rest house below the huge bulk of Ngomeni Rock, over five hundred and fifty feet high, after my day's work at dusk, I found hurricane lamps lit, Sam tucked up in his mosquito netted cot, and Sue bathing Nick, our senior son, in a metal *karai*. This was a sort of wobbly tin basin used by Africans for a variety of purposes from cement mixing to ablution. Sue found it an ideal baby bath on safari.

SAFARI

As I prepared for my evening bath, a one-foot high canvas affair with wooden battens in the sides, we heard a lion coughing and grunting on the sandy, shrub covered and now darkened plains below our camp. His voice was magnified and echoed by the huge looming rock behind us. That was an evening scene Sue and I remember as clearly as if it was yesterday and one beyond price.

Bathed and refreshed, both sons asleep, and the chief would come round for a drink and a chat. In this case it was Chief Henry Musyoka Mboti, nicknamed Smooth Harry by my predecessor. He was the ex-Kenya Police Sergeant Major, a man of considerable charm, polished cocktail party chat, and a certain comfortable indolence. When on safari on my own, he, and some other chiefs, would stay on for supper with me from time to time, and regale me with reminiscences and gossip, often hilariously entertaining, as well as with local intelligence. My Kamba chiefs all had prodigious memories and most were great and inspired raconteurs. Senior Chief Kasina Ndoo MBE, full of years, even remembered the initials of the officers under whom he served in 3 and 6 KAR in the First World War, and later in Jubaland. He and Chief Kathuru Nyaga, of the Tharaka, a small sub-tribe on the Tana River were the pick of the raconteurs and Kathuru's account of the battle of Jambo Hill in Burma in which he won the MM – he had been a sergeant in 11 KAR – was a tour de force.

We were up soon after dawn to the spectacular daily East African awakening, with rapidly warming sunshine coming into the front of the rest house, birdsong in the bushes between us and Ngomeni Rock, and often peregrine falcons flying from their perches high up on its east face, their high pitched chattering screeches echoing off the rock. On several occasions we arose before dawn, leaving the boys with Teresia and TP Mutinda, and walked round the north of the rock, past the big dam, to its west end where it sloped gently up to the summit facing east. The trick was to get to the top before dawn and then to watch dawn break in the east, with the sun's rays gradually spreading towards us across the plains below. One of Kenya's great sights, and one which never failed to evoke in my mind the appropriate passage in Dvorak's New World Symphony. Then back down the rock, sometimes setting off the shrill cackle of a flock of vulturine guinea fowl, cobalt blue necks and chests flashing in the sun, and on to breakfast. This would be laid on the camp table outside the rest house, under a small thorn tree, in the bright morning sunshine.

At the right, tactful, interval after breakfast Sergeant Ndinda would materialise from the bush, immaculate in starched khaki drill shorts, maroon jersey with sergeant's stripes on the sleeves, khaki pillbox cap with its brass lion badge, blue puttees and sandals, stamp to attention and salute, with a *'habari za asubuhi, memsahib'*? to Sue and *'yote tamaam, effendi'* to me. Time to start the day's work.

With Kenya's approaching independence, it became vital to focus administrative efforts on the activities most likely to contribute to the progress of the Kamba. I saw these as being the African Courts and the Location Councils, and these were to have extra attention on every safari. Naturally education and its expansion would go on being sought, livestock marketed, roads being maintained, and so on, but the African Courts would increasingly become the dispensers of local justice, and the Location Councils would have their fingers in every development pie and project in their areas. After the conferences in London on Kenya's future in early 1960, therefore, safari work brought more contact than ever previously with the African Courts to attempt to enhance both their standing and their skills and so to broaden their scope. The Location Councils had so many meetings with me when on safari that they were giddy with their own efforts and perhaps in the end surprised by some of the results. In a short space of time they were drawing up estimates, allocating capital to projects, matching capital to *mwethya* (self help) schemes on projects, controlling modest budgets, ordering and controlling supplies of materials for simple projects, and generally showing the first signs of being able to move their locations forward with their own energies rather than place a total reliance on a DO who would not necessarily be there much longer. So each day on safari wore on, with rarely enough time to fit in all that was necessary. Looking through some old safari diaries and letters one can see the great increase in the pace of activity in 1960 in Kitui as compared with 1959.

Occasionally the reason for a safari was outside one's normal purposes. While at Mwingi I had two Governor's safaris, which guaranteed a huge turnout in the locations to be toured. The differences in style of each of those safaris reflected to some extent the character of the two Governors concerned, but this was also because of the changing climate at the time. In 1959 Sir Evelyn Baring travelled around Migwani and Mutonguni Locations, and spent the night at Migwani. Senior Chief Kasina, Chief of Migwani, was a veteran of Governor's visits and had a well-practised sequence. His guard of honour of retired KAR *askari*, as immaculately turned out as when under the colours, medals proudly worn, received HE on his arrival at Migwani. Local notables were presented, at night Kamba dancers performed their spectacular acrobatics to drums and whistles, and in between there were visits to improved farms and local notables. Time had to be found for some walking, and Sir Evelyn, a keen amateur botanist, loped up hillsides with his long strides to pluck sprigs of greenery from shrubs which caught his attention. There was then much discussion about identity, and the whole entourage was required to contribute to that. Sir Evelyn appeared to have time and charm for everybody, and his safari had something of the flavour of a proconsular tour. Over a year later life had become a touch more urgent. When Sir Patrick Renison visited Kitui's

Northern District it was to add to the explanations the DC and I had given at successive *barazas* of the implications of approaching Independence. The same guard of honour turned out, and HE dealt with the occasion that arose with a charm equal to his predecessor's. But one had the distinct impression that there were not going to be many more Governor's safaris in Kitui, in fact the post-colonial shadows were drawing in. In the evening, after a big *baraza* at Migwani again, HE returned to the *boma* at Kitui. Perhaps another small sign of changing times and accelerating pace.

In the end Internal Self-Government came to Kenya, followed soon after by full *Uhuru* some eighteen months after my departure from Mwingi on home leave. The arguments about the pace of change and the readiness of the Colony to take its place, on its own feet, in the world have been fully aired over the years. Probably no administrative officer in any colony approaching self-government felt it was ideally equipped to run its own affairs, just as every local man of the rising generation believed we were too tardy about handing over Independence. In March and April 1960, *barazas* were held in every location in Kitui district explaining what the approach of *Uhuru* would mean. I was on safari for a number of days running eight *baraza*s in my division, while the DC and other DOs did the same in the three other divisions. Senior Chief Kasina at Migwani made plain his views, and probably those of most of the older generation of Akamba, at the end of my *baraza* at Migwani as he delivered a ringing endorsement of Britain's sixty odd years of running Kenya. Several younger men had put points to me after I had spoken, fair enough points in their way, but considered impertinent by Kasina. Finally he lost his patience and leapt up beside me and, in his curiously high pitched voice, said; 'Do you know what *Uhuru* is? I'll tell you what *Uhuru* is. When I was young there were those of the Akamba who still remembered Arab slave raiders. The British came and stopped that. I remember as a boy the Maasai raiding our land to try to take our cattle. Then the British came and stopped the tribes fighting each other. The Kikuyu, Embu, and Meru combined and caused the barbarous Mau Mau rebellion. The British stopped that. The British brought us education, showed us how to improve the use of our land, brought us water supplies, and much else. What did we do for the British? We gave them askaris for the KAR and the Kenya Police. We fought for them as our friends in their wars. We can be proud of that. Today we have peace and improving conditions. Do you see that? (pointing at the Union Jack flying above his office) That is *Uhuru!*' The young smirked, the old looked embarrassed, Kasina looked defiant. I could have hugged the old boy, but it would probably have been against Queen's Regulations.

Keeping the Peace Among the Somalis

HUGH WALKER

In 1957 I was posted as District Commissioner, Mandera District in the extreme north east of the Northern Frontier District (NFD). I was twenty-six. The title was a trifle pretentious as I had only one other District Officer working with me and three European Police Officers for the whole district. Although fifteen thousand square miles was a large area, the population was only thirty thousand nomads, or two to the square mile.

Administration in the Northern Frontier in 1959 was relatively straightforward. It was peacetime, being almost sixteen years since the war in East Africa had ended. Disarmament of the clans (tribes) had been completed about ten years earlier. No one openly carried a rifle and inter-clan stock theft was containable. A DO's job entailed minimum office work and maximum safari work; we were meant to be out of the district HQ for at least ten days a month. Also we were supposed to complete one hundred miles each month on foot or camel. Few reached this target but I once spent three glorious weeks on foot in the bush. My in-tray was almost up to the ceiling on my return.

Camels were used for the remote and inaccessible areas and lorries where there were roads. Camels are the most uncomfortable creatures to ride, particularly over long distance. The Somalis have a saying: 'First God made the land, next he made the Somali and after that the camel – and then he laughed!' Others say that the camel is so ungainly that it must have been designed by a committee. We used wooden saddles which, even with cushions, are not like horse saddles. Your thighs are parallel with the ground, so you cannot grip with your knees as you can on a horse. A camel walks at two and a half miles per hour which can be quite relaxing, but when it trots, you bounce! After riding one camel for a hundred miles I developed a splendid boil on my rump and had to walk the hundred miles back. It was certainly a healthy outdoor life.

Most of the safari work involved the maintenance of peace between the Somali clans, the enforcement of grazing boundaries, providing water supplies and collecting poll tax. To ensure that enough money circulated for that important purpose, stock sales of camels and cattle were held regularly, except during periods of quarantine for foot and mouth disease or prolonged drought.

Mandera was remote. The nearest doctor was two hundred and fifty miles away in Wajir. All we had was a small dispensary with an African dresser. He performed marvels with the few drugs he had. Crocodile bites and clap were his specialities – and there were plenty of both. Nairobi, the capital, was six hundred miles away: a three day journey by lorry over mainly dirt roads. When it rained these became impassable. Mail and fresh vegetables were flown up once a fortnight. The life was lonely and not everyone's cup of tea. Indeed, over the years there had even been an occasional suicide; but for those who enjoyed it, and I was one, it was the experience of a lifetime. I spent some two and a half years there.

The northern border with Ethiopia was half a mile away from Mandera *boma* and District Headquarters, as was the eastern border with Somalia. There the Mandera airstrip ran right up to the boundary so that planes taking off flew straight into Somalia's air space.

Young camels were often snatched by hyenas. In order to poison them, we issued strychnine to camel owners. I kept the strychnine in my office safe, and was always petrified I would get some on my fingertips and later bite my nails without thinking. Once all but one cub out of a pride of lions was poisoned, by mistake or on purpose I am not sure, as lions did sometimes take young camels. I rescued the surviving three-month-old lioness and took her back to Mandera. Being near to Ethiopia, I christened her Sheba.

Sheba grew fierce as she became fully-grown. One day, she knocked me face downwards and stood over me growling. Luckily her mother had not had the time to teach her to break her prey's neck, and I was able to roll over and push her off me. I offered her to the Whipsnade Zoo. Although its owner, Sir Robert Tyrwhitt-Drake, accepted her, it was on the condition that I pay the necessary airfreight to England. But in 1958 that was eighty pounds, or two months salary. So, sadly, I asked the Assistant Superintendent of Police to shoot her whilst I was on safari. To rear a lion cub safely (if, indeed, that is really possible) it should not be more than three weeks old.

Later on safari, I found another lioness that had been poisoned, leaving three of the cutest cubs. They were so small that I was able to hold all three in my arms at once; but again, they were too old to tame and, as they could not have survived without their mother, I hardened my heart and shot them all.

The Somalis in Kenya's NFD had never felt they belonged to Kenya and rudely called the Bantu Kenyans 'the horse-nosed people'. They wanted no part of Kenya's future Independence and saw secession as the only alternative, by joining their independent cousins in Somalia with whom they shared a common border. Although there are only some two hundred thousand Somalis in the NFD, there are – or were as they have multiplied despite war and famine – some five or six million Somalis in the Horn of Africa. The majority were, and still are, nomads. All are Muslims of the major Sunni branch of Islam; all claim descent from illustrious Arab ancestors connected to the prophet Mohammed. In Kenya they used to claim that they were not really Africans and for many years they were treated somewhat differently by the colonial government.

Every Somali child is taught to recite his genealogy through the Somali clan tree right back to some remote ancestor. Although all Somalis speak Somali, they are fundamentally disunited by their clan system. Competition for grazing and water for their livestock also causes intense rivalries and this, too, hindered any real sense of nationhood or unity

Living in an extremely harsh natural environment, Somalis are very volatile. In the 1950s and 1960s their lives centred almost entirely round their camels, sheep, goats and cattle. A man is a lifelong slave to his camels. Every camel has his pedigree, which its owner can also recite for generations past. Without camels the Somali nomad cannot survive, and in droughts when camels die for lack of grazing and water, sometimes their owners die too.

They spend their waking hours herding and watering their animals, searching for grazing and moving wherever the sparse rains decree. In Mandera the rainfall was only eight inches a year. They care for and treasure their animals as much, if not more, than their women or children – and their women are some of the most beautiful in Africa. The search for grazing and water is always in conflict with other camel owners of other clans. To protect his stock from wild animals as well as humans every clansman is armed with at least a spear, a knife and a knobkerrie – and in more recent times with a rifle, often a Kalashnikov.

All this inevitably leads to fighting which can spread rapidly from a minor skirmish over water to inter-clan warfare on a wide scale. And it can erupt very quickly. In such vast areas government forces could not be everywhere; often news came in that stock had been looted and a number of men killed and that the fighting was spreading. Then Kenyan and Somali Tribal Police had to speed to the spot. Sometimes they arrived too late, but always camels were seized and inter-clan meetings held to thrash out who had done what to whom. Finally a balance sheet was drawn up and the clan which owed most had to pay up – one hundred camels for a dead man but only fifty for a woman. Often they took months to pay and more fighting resulted. Somalis are probably the only people whose standard greeting is '*Maa nabad baa*' – is it peace? Camel theft is their idea of manly sport, often with fatalities.

Nomadic life bred in every Somali a basic independence and an aggressive self-confidence. They have a traditionally open contempt for other people and a defiant scorn for anyone who seeks to impose dominion over them, be he Somali or foreigner. Displays of superior strength often earn only temporary respect as they bide their time. They have a proverb – and they are skilled at composing proverbs and beautiful poetry whilst herding their camels – which runs: 'One kisses the hand, which one cannot cut off.' Their reputation that 'every man is his own sultan' suggests that any would-be leader may argue or cajole but can never securely command, except perhaps, when he has complete control through overwhelming strength. And that can lead to immense cruelty. This was evidenced in the early part of the century by the Somali hero, Mohamed Abdille Hassan, the so-called 'Mad Mullah of Somaliland' and more recently by the military dictator, General Mohamed Siyad Barreh, who used to stand his opponents ankle deep in acid. A Somali's personal independence is compounded with an unpredictability even in routine situations; but they are brilliant improvisers and entrepreneurs although less successful in humdrum tasks. These qualities and characteristics have always impressed foreigners in their relations with Somalis. During the campaigns against the Mad Mullah, one British colonel, later Major-General James Lunt, said of his men: 'Somali excitability is probably due to the climate he lives in – intense sun by day to cold at night, combined with a life of constant motion and unrest. Though impatient of restraint he soon learnt the necessity and value of military discipline. His volatile impetuosity gave him tremendous elan as a soldier. He has physical courage, extraordinary endurance and is a faithful, gallant soldier, at his best in times of scarcity and hardship.'

A Self-Reliant Man

PETER DEMPSTER

Mount Kulal rises to over 7,700 feet on the eastern shore of Lake Turkana, known as Lake Rudolf in the early 1960s. The mountain towers more than 6,500 feet above the lake, and has two peaks split by a deep and dramatic gorge, home to the Lord knows what beasts. In my time at Marsabit the upper slopes of the mountain were densely forested with hardwoods, including some magnificent stands of cedar. Kulal, viewed from the eastern lakeshore, and from the Loiyangalani fishing lodge and encampments of the El Molo people, was an awesome sight. The mountain was feared: rightly or wrongly, it was believed to be the source of the ferocious winds, which would sweep down and turn Rudolf into a savage and stormy place. Tents and trees were often flattened and sudden thunderstorms amongst the peaks could bring torrents of rain.

Near the top of Kulal, and with only a few African labourers, lived Gordon Plant, a Development Officer. He was then in his mid-forties, and was in charge of one of the more sensible development projects in Marsabit District. Kulal had some permanent springs amongst its forests, and Gordon's task was to pipe out this spring water to the low country, where it could be used by the nomadic Rendille and their stock. The Rendille had become accustomed to setting up camp high on Kulal and to taking their camels, sheep, and goats through the forest and right up to the springs, causing severe damage to the young trees, ground cover, and to the water sources themselves.

Gordon was by nature charming, but very shy, and solitary. He generally came the 140 or so miles to Marsabit once a month for supplies, leaving the next day. When I first met him on Kulal, having driven to his camp up an appalling track on the northern shoulder of the mountain, I found that he had no radio, and thus no way of contacting us in Marsabit, were he or his men to fall ill or require urgent supplies. There was also the chance that he might receive news of movements of the Gelubba warriors from Ethiopia, who had carried out some very unpleasant raids on the lakeshore.

I reached his camp in the evening. The weather was crisp and clear, Rudolf glistened below us to the west, and we could see South Island. Next morning we were enveloped in clouds, drizzle and mist, with visibility reduced to a few yards. I was told that this was normal and that things would probably improve in two or three hours, as indeed they did.

Gordon had made himself and his men reasonably comfortable in timber houses with corrugated roofs. Three things made life difficult. The first was the track up the mountain, frequently impassable in wet weather. The second was the almost inevitable cold mist and rain every morning. The third was mice. These creatures had never before had access to warmth or shelter, or to the delights of maize meal, flour, or sugar. In Gordon's house, which I shared with him on this first visit, the night was made hideous by the constant snapping of mousetraps, up to twenty of which would be set, and then re-set, through the hours of darkness. Despite this campaign, the mice were winning, or so it seemed to me.

On my next visit I took more mousetraps and a reliable radio-transmitter up to Gordon, and used the radio, in his presence, to call up the Police at Marsabit. But it was obvious to me that there was little chance of the set ever being used, and so it proved. Gordon was self-reliant and I had the greatest admiration for him and his men, perched remotely on top of Kulal, and in what they were trying to achieve. By the time I left the district his scheme was near completion. I have often wondered whether it was ever finished, or whether anyone knows or cares about the magnificent forest and cedars of Kulal in their uniquely remote setting.

SAFARI

Hard Pounding

HENRY WRIGHT

I was stationed at Wajir in the Northern Frontier District of Kenya in 1960 to 1961. The tribe we administered was Somali and the clans were Mohammed Zubeir, Degodia, and Ajuran. The Somali population numbered approximately 30,000, and they were nomadic with camels being their domestic stock.

Wajir was a Beau Geste station as we lived in and around a big fort. The annual rainfall was perhaps five inches per year, but this was irregular over the Wajir district of 30,000 square miles. Being dry and virtually on the equator it was always hot and dusty with magnificent sunsets.

The Wajir wells were the only source of permanent water in the district. There were hundreds of wells within ten square miles of the fort. When the district became dry and barren, all Somalis and stock converged on the Wajir wells for their water supply. With a 100,000 camels, 50,000 goats, 1,000 cattle, plus 30,000 Somalis living a short distance from the fort, the intrigue and our workload was enormous. As soon as the rains came they left for the hinterland for fresh food and grazing.

We had an armed Tribal Police force of fifty-six Somalis. They were called *dubas* because of their red turbans. The *dubas* were mainly illiterate and came evenly from the three clans. They were chosen from the best families in the district, and were much admired by the young Somali boys. My personal *dubas* orderly was called Abdulla, and he was from the Degodia clan.

The Somali is inclined to appear lazy, for his dignity does not allow him to do manual work. Treated with confidence and consideration, he is cheerful, intelligent and willing to learn. Treat him harshly however, or unjustly, and he becomes sulky, mutinous and obstinate. Unlike other Africans, he can treat European authority with disdain as European government officers could not react like Somalis in the desert or bush, and would appear to be weak and second-rate.

District Commissioners in the NFD expected loyalty from their *dubas*. Without it, administering a district would be difficult, as the *dubas* could be their eyes and ears, making it easier to solve difficult problems. On safari they would act as interpreters, guards, escorts and companions around a campfire in the evenings. They respected discipline.

My DC, Peter Fullerton asked me to organise a safari to a big hill near Tarbaj, a small trading centre, which had a few domestic water wells. This hill, which was a landmark in the flat district, had a small rifle range. All fifty-six were to participate in this training exercise.

Two trucks took us to Tarbaj. The *dubas* were divided into two equal groups. Peter and I each assumed command of a group. Over the next three days a friendly competition was held between the two groups consisting of various shooting trials on the rifle range, running, marching, and other physical exercises. The last test was a long race up Tarbaj hill, then to the rifle range for an immediate shooting competition. Peter and I joined in all these events and a happy atmosphere prevailed. This was a good way to get to know our *dubas*.

At dusk on the last evening, we were drinking tea outside our tent, when Peter challenged me to walk back to the fort. I readily agreed. After a short discussion, we called the Sgt. Major and told him the plan. The running and walking over the past three days had made him appear weary and he looked surprised.

The track back to the fort at Wajir was sandy and a distance of thirty-four miles. As Wajir was on the equator and at a low altitude, the conditions would be hot and trying. My group of twenty-eight *dubas* was to leave first at four a.m., and Peter with his group to follow thirty minutes later. We all carried a rifle and a water bottle that contained one pint of water. The truck carrying our equipment would pass us and prepare one cup of tea each at the halfway mark. This was to be a stop for fifteen minutes only.

The first two hours whilst dark was easy going, but I had developed sore feet due to unsuitable shoes. This amazingly did not worry me for the entire walk. My *dubas* appeared fit and strong up to the halfway mark when we had our tea. The Somalis loved their Brooke Bond tea. Just as we were about to commence our walk after the tea break, I could see Peter and his group in the distance. They appeared to be walking strongly. I did not see or talk to Peter until he came to my house on his return.

It was becoming very hot. I felt fit, but carrying the rifle was a problem as it was difficult to find a comfortable position. It went from hand to hand and shoulder to shoulder. The last six miles into Wajir a few of my *dubas* became weak and dizzy. We put them in the middle as we were marching and pushed them along. It was a dangerous practice, but I was determined that every *dubas* should walk to Wajir.

My group of *dubas* arrived outside Wajir fort at twelve-thirty p.m. The duration of the march was eight and a half hours, which included fifteen minutes for tea. This was an average of four miles per hour. Considering the conditions, the heat, the sand track, wrong footwear, one pint of water and one cup of tea, I was pleased with the effort. I congratulated the *dubas*; we clapped each other and I dismissed them and proceeded to my house for a much-needed cup to tea.

Peter and his group of *dubas* arrived about forty-five minutes after me. I believe he had six *dubas* drop out and he was disappointed. Thirty minutes after Peter arrived he came to my house with his squash racquet, dressed in white sports clothes and challenged me to a game of squash. By this time my feet were really sore, but with his persuasion and for the good of the Empire, I went with him across the square in the front of the fort to the open-air squash court. We played for thirty minutes in the afternoon sun. The squash court was like an oven. We made plenty of noise but did little running.

Every Somali in Wajir either saw us or heard of our escapade and thought we were mad And their respect for us was total.

During the *shifta* uprising in 1964, I flew into Wajir from Garissa, and met my ex-Orderly and other *dubas*. We talked about the past. They seemed happy even though these were troublesome times. They had served the Crown loyally and now they were serving independent Kenya.

A Punishment Posting

ROGER HORRELL

I returned to Kenya as a cadet in 1959. The glorious summer of that year, and the diversions which Oxford affords, helped to ensure I did not pass the Devonshire Course Swahili exam with much credit. As a result I was posted to Kilifi. There may be an unfortunate moral here. My fellow cadets were rewarded for their diligence on the course by postings to politically interesting districts in Central Province and Nyanza. My 'punishment' for slacking was consignment to paradise.

Eric Risley was temporary DC pending the arrival of Paul Kelly. An early visitor was Sir Evelyn Baring on his farewell tour of the coast. He met a line of district officials in royal fashion, boomed a few words, and moved on rapidly to Malindi, there to fish. Shortly afterwards I was introduced to the Progressive Dinner – nine courses of it from one extremity of the *boma* to the other. Sherry with the first course at the first venue, port at the last, wine at the intervening seven. Black tie. One casualty from a broken glass.

Our Game Warden was Ian Parker, whom we shared with other districts. He was passionately advocating a scheme, which combined human and environmental features in controversial tandem. The Waliangulu, a small tribe sparsely spread over the districts of Coast Province, were supremely skilful at hunting elephants using poisoned arrows. They were inveterate poachers and a principal objective of the scheme was to turn them into gamekeepers, harnessing their natural inclinations to constructive and legitimate ends, without, of course, the poisoned arrows. In essence the

Waliangulu would be encouraged to cull elephants under direction and benefit from the sale of what we might now call 'elephant derivatives'. Ecological arguments were cited persuasively in favour of the case with particular reference to the Tsavo Park.

Parker thought it would further my education if I could witness the 'production' process from execution to dismantlement. Accordingly, at dusk on the first night of a short safari together, he shot an elephant. The great creature sank slowly to his knees. A tragic sight compounded by the poignant sound of trumpeted pain. Next morning, a team of Waliangulu expertly set about the butchery. Huge intestinal tubes gurgled loudly as the carcass was systematically sundered. The acrid smells linger in my memory to this day, though fortunately not in my nostrils. Meat, feet, skin, and tusks were (fairly) swiftly and carefully separated. So much for the product. Other aspects of this putative commercial operation, such as marketing, sales, bookkeeping and storage were yet to be developed.

Parker also took me to meet David Sheldrick, Warden of Tsavo, who seemed open minded about the idea. But while tribal lien on hide and flesh posed no problem, the sticking point was ivory. Without the proceeds from ivory (or at least some) the scheme was not viable. Elephant theologians were, naturally, divided on the merits of the proposal and there were sufficient political and legislative obstacles to ensure no such project advanced in 1960.

In late 1959, Richard Meinertzhagen was in Kenya prior to finishing his book 'Pirates and Predators'. He was then about eighty. Parker was asked to make arrangements at the coast. For whatever reason no DC was available in Kilifi to put him up so it was agreed he should stay in the modest bungalow I shared with another bachelor. I confess I had never heard of him. Parker told me about his involvement in the death of the Nandi *Laibon* in 1906 and also that Meinertzhagen had known T.E. Lawrence (they were both at the Paris Peace Conference). This was of interest. A newcomer could be ignorant of Meinertzhagen, and for that matter the *Laibon*, but not of Lawrence of Arabia.

Launch Safari on the 'Pelican'

HENRY WRIGHT

After discussions with my DC, Tommy Thompson, it was decided that I should do a launch safari on the 'Pelican' to cover the lower reaches of the River Tana up to Garsen, which is about ninety miles by river from Kipini.

SAFARI

The river was at its lowest at this time of the year, as the rains up-country around Mount Kenya do not start until mid-April and flood water usually reaches the lower Tana around mid-May. It is not possible to go much further than Garsen during April.

The purpose of the safari was to show government presence, and to check various projects. Also, to liase with chiefs, headmen, Tribal Police, Game Scouts, teachers, artisans and health workers. A visit to the old European house at Belazoni Estate was required, as permission had been granted to utilise some of the house for building requirements at Kipini.

Personnel were chosen for the safari: a few Tribal Policemen, a Swahili/Pokomo interpreter, a Tax Clerk, a couple of Game Scouts, and my cook. There was always a headman or chief wanting help to return to his village.

I can never really remember the food I took on safari. Tea was essential and perhaps rice and potatoes. Fruit was always available from the local Wa-Pokomo, as were fish and meat. On the 'Pelican' there was a galley, shower, two bunks and a toilet. This was probably the most luxurious form of safari transport in Kenya and envied by many, especially as the launch had a crew of six: coxswain and assistant, engineer and assistant, and two deckhands.

After each safari it was necessary to submit a report to the PC in Mombasa, so that he would be aware of happenings in his province. Most DCs and DOs were not diligent in their safari reports and the PC could get upset if reports were not forthcoming. From my notes I would submit a report in detail. Looking at these notes after forty years, my handwriting has not changed. Apart from the paper being yellow, it is as though they were written yesterday.

The first night we stopped at Kau. I remember my night there. I sat on the top deck alone and watched the hippos coming to life, snorting, bellowing and preparing to leave the river to graze. They were supreme. At dusk I went below to my cabin, safe from mosquitoes. I recall writing to my parents and describing the scene.

Next day we left Kau for Belazoni. This stretch of the river was straight, being the canal that connected the old Tana and Ozi rivers

We arrived early at Belazoni estate, which was a German rice plantation started before the turn of the century when Germany laid claim to the area, and it was vacated in 1940. The first part of this safari we crossed old canals, which were covered with sparse dried grass. We then came across savannah grass, which was about two to three feet high. I believe the plantation got their heavy supplies from *dhows*, which anchored just the other side of these high sand dunes. They probably loaded supplies into carts, which were pulled by steam tractors. There was still a rusty steam tractor near the house at Belazoni in 1958. I decided to do something unorthodox. I had always from this part of the river marvelled at the high sand dunes, which I could see from Belazoni. They were on the coast and probably about seven or eight kilometres away by foot. With a TP and Game Scout, I decided to walk to the coast. There appeared to be just savannah grass and small clumps of trees to traverse. My footwear was sandals and I had a .22 rifle. My TP and the Game Scout each had .303 rifles. I had broken one of my sandals and was dragging my foot. The two *askaris* were about fifty yards behind me. Suddenly five yards in front of me a lioness stood up and looked at me for perhaps seconds. She then turned away and loped to some trees fifty yards away. From these trees, about thirty buffalo appeared and ran past us. My two *askaris* were amazed. It seems the lioness was asleep and wakened perhaps by my noisy broken sandal, ran away and frightened the buffalo. If my sandal had not been broken, I might have trodden on her. I often think about this incident and consider I must be lucky. At times I can still picture the lioness looking at my confused expression.

7

Nomads and Borders

A Posting for a Non-Cricketer	Oliver Knowles
Locust Control	Tom Watts
The Kolloa Affray	Eric Risley
A Samburu Circumcision Ceremony	David Shirreff
Trying to Understand the Maasai	Dick Cashmore
An Isolated Posting	Hugh Walker
The Ethiopian Border	David Evans
The Turkana Move	Michael Wasilewski
Divination and Rustling	Robin Williamson
Tax Collection in Turkana	Robin Paul

Introduction

There were clear differences between the populous districts of agricultural potential and the semi-arid areas where life was dictated by water and grazing. They presented varied challenges for administrators. Some were drawn to the wide horizons and the blue hills in the distance. They preferred to work with the nomadic peoples who were often chary of development and followed the age-old pattern of livestock movements. They embraced the relative rigours of safari and living in hot places. These districts were largely in the north and on the Maasai steppe to the south. In these regions borders were important because of potential conflict and nomadic wanderings. Territorial security was at stake then as now.

Oliver Knowles went to one of the most remote districts, Turkana, on his first posting. Tom Watts had to deal with the scourge of locust invasion. Eric Risley describes a conflict, which had erupted into violence and was long remembered in the Kenya Administration. Areas like Samburu were peaceful and David Shirreff was able to study local customs. The Maasai, close relatives of the Samburu people, held special status in colonial annals as they staunchly resisted change. Dick Cashmore underlines the sensitivity needed in dealing with them. The Northern Frontier was hard country, a posting for young men. Hugh Walker and David Evans recount what it was like to work on the borders with Ethiopia and Somalia. Movement of people across tribal borders searching for better grazing was common.

Sometimes they had to go back and Michael Wasilewski escorted one enforced return. Cattle rustling was endemic. If it could not be settled by meetings of elders, punitive action had to be taken, and Robin Williamson describes hot pursuit in Turkana. Even there tax collection was a regular chore for the District Officer. Robin Paul tells us how it was done outside the cash economy.

A Posting for a Non-Cricketer

OLIVER KNOWLES

I arrived in Mombasa in early 1949 with the annual draft of about six Cadets who had completed the Devonshire Course. We were met on the ship by Dennis Hall, then PA to the Chief Native Commissioner, Percy Wyn-Harris, who asked, 'Which of you chaps plays cricket?' Postings of cricketers were then arranged according to the needs of various station cricket teams eg. a slow bowler to Nyeri, a wicket-keeper to Kakamega. There was then a call for bird watchers to go to the station where Myles North - a famous collector of bird song - was DC. Finally he turned to me and said, 'and what can you do?' I said I had served in the Indian Army, so was posted to the outlying, arid Turkana District.

We all stayed for our first weekend with Wyn-Harris, who had just bought a light aircraft with a legacy from an aunt, and was busy at an aero-show at Nairobi West. It turned out that he was involved in an argument with Charles Hartwell, the Director of Establishments, as to whether he could claim road mileage or the shorter direct air mileage when he used his plane for NFD safaris. Navigation was not his strong point. He used to put his secretary in the back seat with a map, with instructions to follow the railway line to Nanyuki.

I went by train to Kitale, where I was met by a lorry of the contractor, A.M. Kaka, which took me to Kapenguria, where I spent the night with the DC Pat Hughes in the 'spare' guest house. In the morning I was awakened by three sheep known as Abraham, Esau and Isaac, who apparently lived there when there were no visitors. Leaving Kapenguria we arrived in Lodwar in a dust storm in the middle of the afternoon, and I reported to 'Wouse' Whitehouse, the DC in his office who showed me to my house (a Sudan pattern with a sleeping cage on a flat roof). Shortly after, four old metal ammunition boxes were delivered to the house, which, I was informed, were for safari use. I was to take over from Peter Barker, who was due to take leave to be married, and in a hurry to depart. So the next day we left by lorry on a handing-over safari to South Turkana. Immediately after leaving the *boma*, we got stuck in the sand, crossing the Turkwell riverbed, and all hands got out to push. One of my new Turkana servants decided to stand in the back, and push on the driver's cab. Our safari lasted about five days.

Back in the *boma* early mornings were filled by taking the Tribal Police for PT, drill and shooting practice; mid mornings by petty cases, and Preliminary Inquiries. As my Swahili was still rather hesitant, and I had to work through two interpretations - from Turkana to Swahili (by my interpreter), and from Swahili to English (by me) – some rather creative translating undoubtedly took place. Later on I was placed in charge of the brick works.

Wouse judged DOs by their performance on foot safaris, and it was not long before I was instructed to carry out a month long safari along the Uganda border with camels. This was an enjoyable, if tiring, experience, rising an hour before dawn, walking until nine, camping under a thorn tree until four, and walking again until dark, making sure that one camped up wind of the camels. After about two weeks I reached Lokichoggio, where a lorry should have met me. So, I walked back for another seven days to Kakuma, where I managed to shanghai the anthropologist's lorry to take me back to the *boma*.

Getting married in September and having just uncrated my new piano (a wedding present from my wife), I was posted to Lokitaung. My predecessor, Pat Crichton an ex - RNVR officer, had been very keen on being saluted, and the Turkana decided that they might take the mickey out of the new DO by carrying out this instruction to the absurd. We slept in an open-sided sleeping *banda* outside our thatched house. A few nights after we arrived, we were awakened at five am by a loud 'eyes right'. It was the camel *syces* delivering our daily water supply and saluting the DO in bed. A few days later I sent a TP up from the office with a message for my wife. She was in the bath. The TP walked straight into the bathroom, saluted and handed her the message. A little later I was sitting in meditation on our long drop, which did not have a door and was in a small rondavel overlooking the Lokitaung gorge, when I noticed a small goat-herd standing in the gorge at the salute: After that I gave orders that the DO was only to be saluted outside the office. We had in Lokitaung a turkey, which laid a very fine clutch of eggs. Going on local leave to Nairobi, I instructed our Turkana servant to look after them. On our return he beamingly told me that 'the eggs are very safe, *Bwana*, I put them in the fridge every night'.

Locust Control

TOM WATTS

The year 1942 saw the initial invasion of desert locusts, which in Turkana enjoyed the ideal breeding conditions of widespread rain and warm sand for their eggs. As Kenya was providing an important amount of food for the North African Campaign a great effort was made to kill the newly hatched 'hoppers' before they reached maturity in the warm desert areas and flew away to devastate the crops in the agricultural areas of East Africa. A large expensive transport organisation was set up to bring in poisoned bait (the husks of the coffee berry) by the thousands of sack loads and water with which to damp them before laying the bait across the path of the marching hoppers. Companies of the East African Pioneer Corps were employed not only to lay the bait but also to dig trenches across the path of the marching hoppers. Their density was so great in places that they smothered each other in the trenches before they could crawl out. The last line of attack, when the hoppers were reaching the final stage by developing wings, was to use flame throwers to scorch the almost mature beast before it could fly away in its vast swarms. It was deemed necessary even to burn wartime petrol in the attempt to protect the crops.

The Administration was the buffer between the tribes-people and the pioneers. Every effort was made to warn these simple people of the dangers of the poisoned bait. Nonetheless women gathered it up and boiled the coffee husks as food for their families, fortunately with no apparent fatalities. This campaign kept me in the bush for many weeks. I dreamt of these hoppers, with their large eyes peering at me. During one night a band of them marched through my camp and tackled the bags of maize meal rations - and they ate the puggree on my helmet.

The Kolloa Affray

ERIC RISLEY

Kolloa had been the scene of the tragic battle, in 1950, between the *Dini Ya Msambwa* Pokot and the Government. Sandy Simpson as the outgoing

DC Baringo was taking his successor on a routine safari around the district. When they came to Kolloa they found that the *Dini Ya Msambwa* army was in the neighbourhood and threatening battle. The *Dini Ya Msambwa* (Faith of the Spells) was an outlawed religious sect responsible for much violence and disorder in both East Pokot and the western side of Baringo. Sandy sent immediately to Nakuru for reinforcements and another DO came with a contingent of Kenya Police led by a European police officer. On arrival the whole force went forward to meet the *Dini Ya Msambwa*. The police deployed themselves, but very stupidly; the officer in charge only issued five rounds of ammunition per man. Old Chief Ngeleyo who was himself to show me the whole detail of the battle at Kolloa went out in front to parley with the *Dini Ya Msambwa* army. There were about two hundred of them and they had spread out in the usual sort of formation in which the Pokot were accustomed to come to a *baraza*. They spread out in a long line each man carrying his two spears and coming forward chanting. This might well have been the way in which they would come to attend any peaceful *baraza* for they still had their ostrich feathers on the sharp ends of their spears. Sandy took it as that but Ngeleyo was out in front trying to talk with them. Very late in the proceedings, it became clear that this was to be an attack and not a peaceful approach to a baraza and Sandy countermanded the police order to open fire to give time to get Ngeleyo back and for no other reason. The police then opened fire and a total of twenty-eight Pokot were killed on the spot, but they came on and overwhelmed the government force. The incoming DC, the DO and the Police Officer and a number of police *askaris* were killed. Everyone ran away and the police reinforcement lorry was captured by the Pokot. Sandy himself told me that the only reason that he escaped was that he was carrying a double-barrelled shot gun. Having fired it twice as he ran away, he had reloaded and was able to shoot two men just about to spear him.

I only write from hearsay but I had heard both Sandy and Ngeleyo describe the whole battle to me. But of course there was a long inquiry afterwards and the tragedy of it was that Sandy did not come out of this inquiry particularly well. I always felt strongly that the inquiry was not altogether fair and particularly not fair to Sandy for it made him look as though he lacked courage. Sandy was to be worried by this report for the rest of his life and I think it put a deep shadow on him, but there was no question of his courage in 3 KAR. At the battle of Kulkabar he had been recommended for an immediate field award of an MC but all the recommendations for decorations got lost immediately after the action and when it came to sorting them out later, Sandy did not get his MC.

On safari to the area in 1954, I took Ngeleyo along to show me exactly how the battle had taken place. The skeletons and skulls of the dead Pokot still lay around the battlefield: they had never thought of burying them. Kolloa lay close to the Kerio River in the bottom of the Kerio Valley. As part of the reconstruction following the battle a road had been built to Kolloa from Baringo and a bridge built across the Kerio river with a road made to the West Pokot headquarters at Kapenguria.

No one had expected the Pokot to continue their attack after losing twenty-eight men killed, and the whole thing was a most tragic business. I was really the first person since Sam Slater had withdrawn his punitive force about three years before to have gone through all this East Pokot country. I had walked quite a long way and come right round that great mountain, Tiati. I stayed at Kolloa for three or four days thinking all the time of the wretched Sandy who had gone on with his administrative career and was then DC Kajiado. For Sandy had been my particularly close friend in 3 KAR, and whenever it came to sharing a room or tent we had always done so.

A Samburu Circumcision Ceremony

DAVID SHIRREFF

When I was appointed District Officer, Samburu, in 1947 the last age grade circumcised had been the Il Mekuri in 1936. Before them the warriors were the Il Kileko who had been exceedingly troublesome, raiding for cattle and blooding their spears on Kikuyu cattle herds in Laikipia. Tribal tradition then still demanded that they must prove their manhood by some exploit before winning a wife, and the taunts of the girls were behind many of the raids.

Government policy had been to encourage the Il Mekuri to marry while still *moran* but this had had only limited success. This was because the girls were circumcised at the same time as the boys, so there were few marriageable girls and many Il Mekuri *moran* were still unmarried.

In 1948 the circumcision of the boys (*laioni*) of the new Lekeh age grade took place. Precautions against possible trouble were taken by the posting of a European Police Officer to the district with a detachment of Kenya Police, and by *barazas* all over the district warning the tribesmen not to emulate the Il Kileko. In fact there was no trouble. Disputes over grazing and water as the tribesmen gathered were settled by the elders. I was kept informed as the ceremonies progressed. The rites were protracted.

The first requirement was to test the strength of the *laioni* to see if they were capable of strangling an ox with their bare hands. After some false starts the required white ox was found on Mt Nyiro and strangled by El Masula *laioni* in September 1947.

Early in 1948 the Samburu started to concentrate by sections in *manyattas* to up to eighty families. In the low country the heavy rain falls in April-May, on Leroghi plateau in July-August. By May 1948 the low country Samburu were concentrated and ready to start their ceremonies, but traditionally had to wait for the El Masula on Leroghi. This put a heavy strain on the low country grazing and I recommended in my report that for future circumcisions the low country Samburu must be allowed to start without waiting for the Leroghi people.

After the ox strangling, the *laioni* start to don the ceremonial dress, the *El Kilani*. These were long black robes made by their mothers of sheepskins, sewn together and dyed with charcoal. They then sent parties off to collect the gum of the *silali* tree, a type of acacia which produces a black, sticky gum. Each boy then walks about with a lump of this gum on a stick until he is circumcised.

The surgeons (*lamuraten*) were mostly Dorobo with a few Rendille and one Kikuyu. They received one sheep or goat for each boy circumcised.

Circumcision can only take place during the fifteen days when the moon is waxing. The El Masula and Nyaparai started in July and the whole of the rest of the tribe completed their circumcising in mid August.

After circumcision the *laioni*, still in their black robes, make small bows and arrows, tip the arrows with lumps of the *silali* gum, and wander about shooting small birds, mainly crested barbets and mouse birds. The birds are skinned and stuffed and hung on a band round their foreheads, amongst black ostrich feathers. They do this for about a month. They then go through the ceremony of the *aiterangwen*, ('throwing off the feathers'). They take off their black robes and feathered head dresses and put on for the first time, the red *moran shukas* and red ochre. There is much killing of cattle and feasting.

I had been invited to attend a ceremony. I left Maralal at first light on horseback and reached the Nyaparai *manyatta* just as the sun appeared over the Karissia hills. I arrived after two *laioni* had already been circumcised and stayed to watch five more being cut. I quote from my diary:

'The boy is first stripped naked of his black robe and stands on an ox skin in front of the door of his hut. In the centre of the ox skin is the skin of the sheep or goat, which was slaughtered for him the previous night. A *kibuyu* (gourd) of cold milk is poured over the boy's head so that the liquid runs over his whole body on to the ox skin. He is then told to sit down.

One man sits behind him, holding him round the chest. Two others sit either side holding each leg. The man who sits behind him is a sort of 'godfather' to whom he can always turn for help. The boy's legs are straight and slightly apart.

The circumciser squats opposite the boy while a circle of elders and moran gather round. The women stay in their huts and are not allowed to watch.

The circumciser, in this case was an elderly Wamba Dorobo called Lengalawepi, who looked, inspite of his blanket, very like any professional doctor or dentist of any race. He had a rather smug expression on his face as though he told his victim, ' I know this is going to hurt, but it is good for you and anyway I'll get my fee afterwards.'

His weapon was a short bladed steel knife with a long wooden handle. It looked fairly clean. He started by rolling back the foreskin to expose the end of the penis. He then inserted his knife between the foreskin and the penis and cut all round it to free the foreskin.

A slit was then made in the top of the foreskin through which the surgeon drew the head of the penis. This was the crucial moment when the boy becomes a *moran*. Most of the foreskin was then cut off; leaving a strip, which would hang until it dried off and then became part of the penis.

During the operation, which lasts for fully five minutes and must be absolute agony for the victim, the boys sat silent with their eyes shut, almost as though they were drugged. Not one winced or showed the slightest sign of pain. Any such sign would have condemned the boy to be an outcast from the tribe for life.

After the water has been poured over him the boy starts to sing, 'I am a warrior. I did not show fear or run away. Bring me blood to drink.' He is then helped to his feet by his 'godfather', who dresses him again in his black skin. He is then led into his hut and spends the rest of the day in the care of his mother and sisters.'

Trying to Understand the Maasai

DICK CASHMORE

The Senior Chief of the largest section, the Purko, was Ole Sangale, most influential among the Narok Maasai. Each generation had turned up a powerful leader: Lenana, Ole Masikonde, Ole Legalishu, Ole Lemein, and now Ole Sangale. He was a small squat man with suspicious eyes. Most Maasai in Narok were on the lookout for the trap, which they believed government set at every opportunity. Government and all its works were distrusted and it would be a matter for celebration if government went away, taking with it the doctor, the schoolmaster, the policeman, the vet, the taxman, and the District Officer. All too often in every proposal for progress and development, the old matter of the 1911 Treaty would be brought up as a reminder of our bad faith and as an obstacle to any change. Perhaps the most disliked department of all was the Forest Department which was always suspected of trying to steal more Maasai land.

And yet Ole Sangale was never slow to use western methods when it suited his book. In a clash over the timber co-operative, owned by the Maasai, he determined to wreck a promising scheme by resorting to a European lawyer (as had the Maasai in 1912 in challenging the legality of the 1911 Treaty). But then, as John Ainsworth had said in 1912, at least this showed that the Maasai were not without virtue by opting for peaceful processes of the courts rather than the more traditional way of war and rebellion.

Many Europeans said that the Maasai were now cowards, were decadent, and had run to seed. I myself doubted it at the time, and doubt it now. The Narok Maasai had had an extraordinarily chequered history, faced with administrative policies that alternated between an iron fist and a velvet glove. They had been hammered by punitive expeditions, by levy forces, and still they did not change their ways. In the 1920s the whole *moran* system was banned and the young men were forbidden to carry the warrior spears. After ten years the ban was lifted as unworkable and the *moran* system re-emerged unchanged.

The elders from their vast cattle herds freely and willingly paid compensation for any stock that *moran* had stolen - provided the cattle tracks led into the Maasai reserve. There was no haggling over this. But equally the Maasai insisted on compensation being paid by European settlers who entered into the reserve in anger to shoot Maasai cattle in revenge for lost stock. In every instance, up at Olokurto, the elders won. Their willingness to pay for the faults and crimes of the *moran* was a reflection of the whole tribe's attitude to their young warriors. These were the spoilt darlings of the Maasai, and stock thieving - with occasional murder - and lion killing was a sign of bravery or high spirits. Indeed the *moran* killers were looked up to by their fellows and called 'stars'

One of my regular duties was the hearing of court cases involving cattle theft. With sentences of two or three years at a time I put away some sixty young *moran*. I also imposed fines, which in one year totalled £3000 which the families paid. In addition, the Purko paid a similar sum in voluntary compensation for stock thefts. They also surrendered some five hundred head of cattle as part of the punitive collective fine for the misbehaviour of their young. In that single year some ten *moran* died; killed in various stock thefts. Yet the thefts went on, nor were the thefts solely from European farms. The Kamba, the Kikuyu, the Luo, Kisii and Kipsigis were also victims.

With the last named - as with the Kuria - it was often a tit-for-tat affair.

And all the time many of the neighbouring tribes looked on with envy or hunger at the large and seemingly vacant Maasai lands. At the same time that Kipsigis and Maasai raided each other for stock, they would happily meet on the borders to settle up the balance of gain and loss (with the Maasai usually the gainers), and promise to pay off in cash any outstanding balance. Sometimes cash was paid but not too often, for the whole process was rather like a home-and-away football fixture. The dichotomy was that all the time the Maasai were adopting Kipsigis young men as 'acceptees' (strangers) into the tribe.

Cattle and 'shoats' (sheep and goats) were the mainstay of Maasai life, save for some agriculture around Nairage Ngare, and in previous years also in the Melili area by Kikuyu squatters. These last had been removed during the height of the Emergency. Although the Maasai were wealthy in terms of cattle, drought and disease frequently played havoc with their herds. Probably the harshest fate to face a Maasai family was an outbreak of disease followed by a veterinary order to move into the Quarantine Ground. Since this had been in use for years and was thought to be saturated with cattle diseases, the chances of getting out after eighteen months with any cattle left were slim. No wonder that families often tried to hide evidence of diseases or diseased cattle rather than be ruined by a stay in the quarantined area.

On the other hand it was ironic that an attempt to set up a progressive co-operative, the Purko Sheep Ranch was saved from financial ruin by converting it into a wheat growing area cultivated on contract by European farmers from the neighbouring district. This they did on a yearly contract for which a hefty fee was paid to the Narok African District Council. As for the sheep they never flourished on that ranch.

The Maasai also had a clan of medicine men know as *laibons*. The great Lenana, at the beginning of the century, who Government had considered the paramount chief of the tribe, had in fact been a *laibon*. His brother, Sendeyo, defeated in a tribal civil war, had been something of a thorn in Government's side but had finally settled down to respectability on the Loita plateau. There his descendants and members of the Enkidong clan continued to live and to cause some trouble. The *laibons* were believed to bless and foretell successful stock theft raids. Also the clan, back in the 1940s, had been responsible for the spearing of the DC Hugh Grant. It was typical of the Maasai that not only did they accept the execution of the young *moran* responsible, but they paid for the education of Grant's young children.

Grant made a fatal mistake with the Maasai, which cost him his life. When I served in Maasailand, I think I did one of the most stupid things I ever did in Kenya, and I was lucky to get away with it. The Loita had been indulging in stock theft and I went over one day to preach the virtues of restraint to the elders. I warned the few *moran* present at the time that if it went on they would be disarmed. The African District Officer, Philip Masindet was with me and an anthropologist from Makerere happened to tag along. As we moved into a valley after our session with the elders, I came upon a band of their *moran* in single file, with spears, crossing my path. Rightly or wrongly I instinctively felt that this was a deliberate challenge by the young, following our *baraza* condemning stock theft. Without thinking I stepped forward, greeted the leader, then laid my hand on his spear. For a second, I felt him freeze and then he let go. I immediately ran down the line disarming all the others and planting their spears on one side. My Tribal Police orderly, without hesitation had brought his rifle up to the ready position to cover me. All hell then broke loose as the *moran* started to throw fits and scream abuse. Philip Masindet, who could understand what they said, went pale and shook with anger. We slowly drove them back and I told them the spears would be left at the tax office in Loita and would be returned if they behaved. I took their leader with me, until some miles away I turned him loose to walk back home unarmed.

The Ethiopian Border

DAVID EVANS

In 1957/58 Kenya's border relations with Ethiopia were, generally speaking, satisfactory in spite of border raids by Ethiopian *shifta* (bandits) whose main aim seemed to be to steal camels, goats and women - in that order. The *shifta* were armed with World War II Italian rifles and, occasionally, with Lee Enfield .303s. Mounted on Boran ponies, the *shifta* crossed the border on moonless nights heading south in search of campfires and unwary herdsmen. They aimed to be back over the border before dawn, if possible, with their stolen stock. Unlucky *shifta* were caught by either the Kenya or Tribal Police mounted patrols and brought to trial. Their ponies became a prized bonus for us as the mounted sections were always up to (and often over) strength: we did not have to buy new ponies if we were vigilant. This caused embarrassing audit queries at times to which we responded that the steady increase was due to our mares always being in foal.

The District Commissioner of Ethiopian Moiale, was Major Deselanny, who apart from his native Amharic only spoke 'survival' Italian. Being of the select aristocratic caste of rulers in all Ethiopia's provinces, Major Deselanny had not wished to change well-established procedures for visitors going into his office. On entering, 'all' visitors had to bow low (as the

Japanese do) and, once more half way across his office as well as, finally, when standing directly in front of his desk. Members of the local *Burji* (slave) tribe had to crawl across the room, face down, until they reached the DC's desk whereupon, after a while, they were instructed to stand up and ask for permission to address 'His Excellency, the most honoured *Dedyasmach* (Provincial Governor). The poor *Burji* were treated far, far worse in Ethiopia than any 'untouchable' in India today.

In spite of following such mediaeval procedures - which also involved extremely harsh 'discipline' for wrongdoers - Deselanny appeared to be reasonable and used to ask permission to visit Kenya's Moyale from time to time, accompanied by a few henchmen who always seemed to be taking copious notes. In theory, he came for 'shopping' although we had no real shops - just Somali *dukas*. He appeared to be fascinated - and perhaps a little suspicious - about the apparently frenetic building on the Kenya side of the border, as well as the layout and maintenance of the roads in and around the *boma* and township. On the Ethiopian side, no building and no maintenance had been undertaken since the Italians had been driven north during World War II.

Deselanny had an embryonic sense of humour and occasionally teased us about British colonialism and its quaint ways, to which I invariably replied, with a satisfied smile: 'But look around you. We do have something to show for our presence here' as I pointed to, for example, the almost completed new hospital's operating theatre or some similar edifice, as well as at the accurate district maps which had been prepared without aerial photographs or Ordnance Survey assistance.

'You won't be here for long!' Deselanny used to say. 'And, by then, your Moyale will be part of our Ethiopian Moiale'. By that time - also primed by what we junior District Officers had been taught on the Devonshire A Course in the United Kingdom - we suspected that he was right about impending *Uhuru* in Kenya. But, there again, when Emperor Haile Selassie's corrupt regime was overthrown by Colonel Mengistu's leftwingers in 1974, Major Deselanny and his high caste Habbash colleagues had also disappeared - without trace.

In order to keep an eye on potential border trouble the British Government had maintained a Consulate in southern Ethiopia at Mega, just seventy miles north of the border. John Bromley, the Consul, was a frequent and welcome visitor to Kenya Moyale and was fascinated by all our building activity. He invited me to go to Mega and I accepted. One of my reasons for having accepted a 'weekend break' was that I had been told in Moyale that one of the most notorious shifta bandits responsible for raids into Kenya was based in Mega. His shifta name was 'Abu Mega', but he was also known as 'Buru Tunye' among the Habbash. One of our *dubas* claimed to have wounded him as he crossed the border with stolen stock.

By a stroke of luck I not only managed to photograph this notorious *shifta* leader, inside the Consulate compound, sitting at a campfire, but also spoke to him briefly before I returned to Kenya. I asked how he was convalescing. He smiled slowly and shook hands with his left arm. His right arm was in a sling, confirming that our Tribal Police rifle practice had not been wasted.

Shooting a rifle from the saddle at a gallop, or even at a trot, is not as easy as it appears in Hollywood movies. The *dubas* graduated from 'ground' target practice, firing on the rifle range, to drawing their rifles from saddle buckets while riding at speed to catch the shifta before they crossed over into Ethiopia. We even made them competent at 'tent-pegging' - at a gallop. They loved every minute of it. It improved their macho *heshima* (prestige) both in the ranks and among their clan.

I mentioned the Abu Mega incident to John Bromley, not wishing to embarrass him about having a murderous *shifta* leader inside the consulate compound, sitting at a campfire. John commented that Abu Mega was a respected local resident and a very reliable source of both ponies and fresh meat. Rumour has it that Abu Mega 'retired' soon afterwards to graze his stock not far away from Mega, never to return to Kenya, watched by the Consul's askaris and their informers.

The Turkana Move

MICHAEL WASILEWSKI

On arrival in Isiolo, the Provincial Commissioner, Paul Kelly, told me that I would take over as his Personal Assistant when the incumbent went on long leave. Until then I was to help the DO Isiolo, Gerry Pryer, with the Turkana move. The Turkana and their livestock were already assembled at Kipsing, by the Uaso Nyiro River. When I joined Gerry there, he explained the background more fully. The Isiolo Somalis for years had used Turkana as herdsmen, illegally. What I had glimpsed of the country round Isiolo struck me as arid, but to a Turkana it was a land flowing with milk and honey compared with the volcanic, almost waterless and barren regions they came from. The well-off Somalis liked having servants, or, more accurately, serfs, but for the desperately poor Turkana, it was a good deal to work for the Somalis, as they were allowed by their masters to keep their own herds, which prospered in the relatively benign Isiolo country. From a government viewpoint, leaving aside the fact that the Turkana had no business to be living outside their own district, their stock intensified the over-grazing problem, about which the Somalis were always complaining to the authorities. Plans to move the Turkana with their cattle, sheep and goats had been drawn up long before and approved by Nairobi, but somehow reasons had always been found at the last moment to postpone action. Paul Kelly was determined the move should at last take place.

The orders stated that the intention was 'to move some three thousand, five hundred Turkana men, women and children squatting in the Isiolo native leasehold area with livestock estimated at fifteen thousand head, back to south Turkana.' The document instructed that 'every care must be taken that they suffer no unavoidable hardship in the course of the move and that they arrive in Turkana in good heart and with their stock in the best condition possible under the circumstances.' It said that 'the conditions at present prevailing are the best that have been experienced for several years.'

An outbreak of foot and mouth disease postponed the start of the move. The optimism about the good water and grazing conditions was based on the situation in Isiolo and on reports from Samburu (the district separating Isiolo from Turkana), and from Turkana. Nobody had actually reconnoitred the whole route of some two hundred miles. Advantage was taken of the delay to despatch me to double-check. I went with two Tribal Policemen in a land-rover to carry out the survey as quickly as possible. At Wamba, about fifty miles on, I picked up the Livestock Officer, Tom Powell, and we did the rest of the journey together. I was able to rely on his judgement and returned confirming that the conditions were good. The move had already started the day before.

The move itself, mostly took place over the plains between the mountains of Maralal, far to the west of our route, and the Mathews range to our east. Game of all kinds was abundant but it was scared off by the huge procession. We met some Samburu from time to time, usually *moran* (warriors) painted in red ochre, spear in hand who, standing on one leg, gazed at us with an air of puzzled superiority. Gerry Pryer asked me to lead the column. The pattern was to set off at sunrise and walk for about ten miles, which was as far as the sheep and goats could go, stopping at a river and resting there the next day to give the livestock time to recover. We had dry weather but the rivers were flowing thanks to rain in the Maralal area. Our baggage was borne by camels. Although I slept out in the open, a tent was needed, to provide some privacy. I stuck to curry day in and day out; that made catering simple. When we stopped, the main task was to check numbers, first of people, then of livestock. The former was relatively easy, thanks to the rations register; what-ever the Turkana may have felt about the move, free and ample food was a great boon for them. Checking of livestock was more complicated, as it involved putting up pens and then patiently counting the various herds as they passed through.

The Turkana were undemanding. Their few possessions, mostly cooking pots, were carried by donkeys. Though from a nomadic tribe, their settled years in Isiolo had had the result, the report of the move notes, that they 'seemed remarkably unprepared for safari conditions and none really carried adequate containers. Had water not been found so frequently along the route the Turkana would have suffered the greatest difficulty and thirst. Some Turkana women carried an open saucepan of water on their heads from Kipsing to Kangetet'. The Turkana did not wash, which was hardly surprising as water was usually scarce, but they kept clean by rubbing themselves with animal grease.

Although others took part in the move from time to time, Gerry Pryer, Tom Powell and I were the three who were the most involved, though I had to go back to Isiolo in order to take over as PA from Dudley Winter. The journey ended in Kangetet in south Turkana. Some two thousand people left the Isiolo area, with their stock (nearly two thousand cattle, over nineteen thousand sheep and goats, and over eight hundred donkeys).

One hundred and three aged and infirm Turkana were transported, on lorries, by another route. Their journey, which took five days, was beset by mechanical and other difficulties. John Deverell, DO Wajir, who was put in charge of that party, reported that the convoy got through only by great good fortune, all spares having been used up. All the road party Turkana reached Kangetet in reasonably good spirits. Their families were, however, most depressed to see them, having hoped that they would die en route. No compensation for loss of stock was offered and the primitive Turkana were either too innocent or too frightened of government to think of asking for any. The reaction, no doubt, would have been that as their illegal settlement in the Isiolo area had necessitated the move, there could be no question of making good any losses. Whether that attitude would have been sustainable had a more developed tribe been involved is questionable. Indeed, the whole operation, although carried out humanely, smacked of authoritarianism. In 1958, there were not many parts of the British Empire where two thousand harmless people, many of them long resident in a particular place, could have been ordered out and escorted to far worse conditions without questions being asked.

Was the migration justified by its results? I do not know, for although I later served in Turkana, I was not responsible for the south of the district. The report on the move said that at the time the Turkana re-entered their home territory 'Both DO Gardner and LO Hall were of the opinion that the move was now a good thing for Turkana District. The Isiolo Turkana were bringing with them a knowledge of veterinary work, previously treated with the greatest suspicion by the Turkana. There was also a real chance of the Isiolo Turkana establishing shops in the local district which would begin to teach the Turkana the value of money and encourage attendance at stock sales.' I trust that those hopes were fulfilled to some extent at least, but the news that reached me was that the livestock of the arrivals was not faring well in the inhospitable conditions of south Turkana, and that some people, much impoverished, were filtering back to Isiolo.

Divination and Rustling

ROBIN WILLIAMSON

Had the *imuron* foreseen unseasonably early rain or was it chance?

Together with a small escort of Tribal Policemen in a land-rover we were making our way across south Turkana. Our purpose was to arrest Akelerio Lodip, a reputed *imuron* or seer.

A Turkana stock raid on the Samburu had roused the Security Forces and the District Administration into a flurry of activity. We had set out as lightly provided as possible since there had to be room for our captive in addition to my escort and such necessities as we required. As evening was falling, we reached the Kalapata *lugga,* brim full of water. Without full safari gear we had to spend the night either inside or under the land-rover. What our evening meal was, I do not recall, but the following day our fare was a shared packet of biscuits.

By next morning the Kalapata had gone down to a trickle. We crossed and then leaving the road, struck out through the low thorn bush using raised gravel strips between the numerous watercourses that cut across our path. Progress was crabwise. By late morning heavy clouds had gathered and the rain soon swept down upon us. Every gully and stream quickly filled in spate and we were unable to proceed further. We sat it out until the afternoon and then made our way cautiously towards Akelerio's *manyatta*. Surprisingly the area around his homestead was dry and we found the huts empty. A quick search led the TPs to a small earthenware pot in the middle of one of the huts. They were convinced that this had been used by the *imuron* in his rites of divination and in his blessing and cursing. They insisted that before we arrested the man, his source and symbol of power, the pot, should be destroyed by rifle fire in his presence. There had been mutterings about our being held up by streams in flood already. Now it had come to this!

We seized other incriminating objects, such as the skins of recently slaughtered stock, what appeared to be Samburu possessions and an empty tortoise shell. We then made our way to a small *lugga* adjacent to the homestead where Akelerio, his cronies and members of his family were taking their ease from the mid-afternoon heat in the shade of the trees. After the charges had been put to Akelerio through a TP, he was removed from his group to witness, in the sight of his friends, the destruction of his 'source of power'. The earthenware pot was placed on the opposite bank of the *lugga* and each TP, rifle to his shoulder, attempted to blast the pot to smithereens. Their confident looks soon turned to distinct unease as the small pot defied their aim. Had this man not only influence over the elements to block our way to his home but also power over the bullet? In desperation the TPs turned to me to do the job. I had hoped to keep myself out of this charade. However, as a National Service marksman and the one who had been deputed the task of training our Reece Shield TPs, I would have been ashamed to miss. This act of wanton vandalism displeased me, but at least it restored a degree of confidence in my party.

As it was now late, we had to make camp with our prisoner in the vicinity. This too proved unnerving for my escort. Equally, on the following morning the two TPs who were directed to seize sixty-four goats and sheep from Akelerio's flock and walk them to Lodwar were not at all happy. After two days we drove back to Lodwar. Thoughout the night at Kalapata and during the following day's drive, my escort muttered about what the old man might have in store for us. Sure enough we were on the final leg of the journey when a half shaft in the land-rover's four-wheel drive broke. We limped homewards to Lodwar only to find the river Turkwell in flood. We abandoned the vehicle on the south side of the river, waded across and entered the *boma* with Akelerio unceremoniously, on foot. Had this been another tease in the old man's game?

Akelerio languished in prison at Lodwar before and after his trial. What the Regional Government Agent, as First class Magistrate, determined his sentence should be, I am not able to recall in detail. However, I do know that his confiscated goats arrived in Lodwar as directed but seemed to spend their time grazing around my house prior to their sale to meet the fine imposed. Daily I had the uncomfortable feeling that Akelerio's stock watched me with the old man's baleful defiance, and certainly the drought that lasted from the time of his imprisonment to his release was ascribed by the local Turkana to my rash action in arresting an *imuron*.

Tax Collection in Turkana

ROBIN PAUL

In the 1960s the cash economy was still largely foreign to Turkana. In the area where tax collection was going to take place the local headman was advised to produce volunteers. The heads of those families who owned few animals, were not expected to pay tax.

On arrival, those who had elected to pay tax would gather, sing and dance, and then make a mock charge on the seated District Officer. A sack of tobacco would be produced by the DO and sufficient to satisfy the taxpayers was distributed. Each head of household would then lead his tax to the DO. Ideally this would be a sheep or goat (shoat) big enough to meet the value of the twenty shillings per annum poll tax. A bigger animal would fetch a higher price and the cash balance would be available for the purchase of tobacco or beads from local retailers.

Volunteers to pay tax were not hard to come by, as people were keen enough to demonstrate their wealth. Some tax animals were allocated as rations to Kenya Policemen and the *dubas* on the basis of one animal per man per month. Other animals were effectively purchased from the government with funds emanating from famine relief sources, the shoats being, in turn, given to the poor in the famine camps. Twenty shoats were given to each family, with advice to leave the camp and increase the numbers of their new herd. In this way it was possible to redistribute stock from those who had a surplus to those who had none.

8

The Mau Mau Emergency

The Outbreak of Mau Mau in Fort Hall   W. H. (Tommy) Thompson
Confronting Mau Mau in Embu   Peter Johnson
Encounters with Mau Mau in Meru   Fergus Mc Cartney
The Forest Tracker   Roger Horrell
District Officer Kikuyu Guard   Christopher Barnett
The Battle of Lake Naivasha   David Lambert
Trouble at Hola   W. H. (Tommy) Thompson
An Unexpected Role   John Williams
Releasing Mau Mau Detainees   John Johnson

Introduction

The term Mau Mau was first mentioned in 1948 in intelligence reports from the Rift Valley Province. In October 1952, a State of Emergency was declared in the face of a growing insurrection. Its origins went back fifty years earlier to opposition to European settlement in the empty terrain of what is now Kiambu district and parts of Nairobi. It was exacerbated by the dissatisfaction of the landless, especially returning World War 2 veterans. Jomo Kenyatta used the nationalistic fervour in his climb to political power, though his actual role in the movement is contested.

Mau Mau was a seminal event for Kenya. Although confined largely to the Kikuyu, Embu and Meru ethnic groups, it posed a direct threat to the Colonial Government in general and the Provincial Administration in Nairobi District and Central and Rift Valley Provinces. Law and order was a paramount duty. Government was put on a war footing.

W. H. (Tommy) Thompson describes being thrown into the thick of the Emergency in Fort Hall, one of the most volatile districts. Trouble was slower to develop in Embu District and, as Peter Johnson recounts, was heavily influenced by Nairobi residents. In Meru District, big and more remote, there was a more favourable balance: the 'loyalists' proved to be the key to winning the battle with the gangs operating from the Mt Kenya forest. Fergus McCartney shows how important the Home Guard was in the contest and so does Christopher Barnett who began his service as a DO (Kikuyu Guard) in Ngong Division.

After big security operations in the urban areas in 1954 removed 35,000 men to detention camps, the forests became the battleground. The most effective operations were mounted by 'pseudo-gangs' of turncoat Mau Mau. Roger Horrell highlights the role of a tracker in the forest. David Lambert's description of the battle of Naivasha epitomises the frustrations of fighting Mau Mau.

From 1955, the war was virtually won. The Administration turned to the battle of hearts and minds with enhanced funds and a focus on development and land reform. Political pressure for Independence was in the hands of the African Elected Members in the Legislative Council. The Governments in Nairobi and London were struck by the tragedy of Hola Camp. Tommy Thompson makes it clear in a graphic account how woefully the aftermath was handled. The pressure was on to release the remaining detainees and return Central Province to normality. John Williams and John Johnson describe their experience in the special camps and at the receiving end.

The Outbreak of Mau Mau in Fort Hall

W. H. (TOMMY) THOMPSON

I began my career in Kenya in 1946 as a Civil Reabsorption Officer. I was posted to Fort Hall District where the DC was Wally Coutts. He was a wonderful man with great command of the Kikuyu language and knowledge of Kikuyu affairs. In 1948, I became a Community Development Officer. Frank Loyd replaced Coutts as DC. All the while storm clouds were darkening. Jomo Kenyatta loomed large on the scene and, from our point of view, threatening. I left in 1952 to go home and be interviewed at the Colonial Office. I was appointed an Administrative Officer with the rank of DO and posted back to Fort Hall District.

An increasing number of murders, oathings and appalling acts of intimidation were taking place everywhere, and in Fort Hall we were at the centre of it. On the declaration of the Emergency on 20 October 1952, I was sent to Kandara in the south of the district there to do whatever could be done, or had to be done, to bolster morale and deal with the worsening situation. It is worth recording that my first home in Kandara Division was a small marquee erected inside-out by one Sergeant Idi Amin, who, to me and my Tribal Police in particular, was a clumsy oaf no matter how much he was lauded by the officers of his KAR Company who were posted there. It is also worth recording that the very first shooting of a local Kikuyu, a woman, was done by Sergeant Amin who was supposedly on patrol. At that time it was impossible, to know who might have been Mau Mau and who was not. The shooting was totally unjustified.

The influence of Nairobi was strong. When the forest gangs were formed, we suffered greatly. Oathings increased and the murder rate went up savagely. I had to make up my mind – what was I to be?. Where should my strengths lie?. I came down in favour of continuing to be an administrator, wholly rejecting the idea of being a para-military. Sanity had to be held on to as strongly as possible, whilst, all the time, getting to know as much as we possibly could about the oathing system and the organisation behind it. Back at District Headquarters, Frank Loyd kept his strong hand on the tiller, encouraging, backing us up, cursing us when necessary and keeping the drive going.

There were several nasty happenings. Only a few weeks after my arrival at Kandara, a Kenya Police patrol was attacked by a large crowd at a market gathering. The Police fire killed fourteen. I was only a mile away at the time and hearing the shots was soon on the scene which was chaotic and angry. Then a gang hacked to death thirty women and children in a village on the forest edge. My own headquarters was attacked by a large, well-armed gang that had filtered down from the Aberdare Forest along riverbeds. They had at least one Bren gun and several rifles stolen from the Army before the Emergency. Two gallant Kenya Police constables defended and saved our armoury. The local school and two houses were burnt, but saddest of all, three of the Tribal Police wives and four of their children were hacked to pieces. The heads of the four children were laid out in a row beside their disembowelled mothers. Let it be said that in this and many other actions there were many examples of great bravery and fortitude amongst the Kikuyu themselves and the whole array of the security forces.

A vital part of the effort was the bringing together in 'District Teams' of district and departmental officers, the local commanders of the Army, Police, and Home Guard. An arrangement that paid handsome dividends.

Two of my colleagues Jimmy Candler and Jerome Kihori were ambushed and killed with their escorts. On another occasion, I was luckier. My driver, seeing a tree across the road, did a violent swerve with his foot hard down and only a few shots were fired at us. A short while later when visiting a local Presbyterian Church, I and my escort of three TPs came under fire from a heavily armed gang commanded by General Kago. As was recorded by his scribe in a document captured some months later, 'We met up with the DO Thompson and started abusing each other facing one another' We certainly did, and between bursts of automatic and rifle fire exchanged language not fit for gentle ears. He had a wonderful command of what might be described as language on the coarser side. My driver, Maina said his Mission education had been set back several years!

The document was obtained in 1954 whilst taking an evening stroll with my Tribal Police Sergeant-Major Andrea Muturia. We had decided to look at a closed school not half a mile from my house as the crow flew. A window, which should have been nailed shut, was open. Suspicion then being a part of our lives, we moved quietly alongside to hear voices. Stupidly we had a go. Andrea had size 11 boots with a physique to match and I was then thirteen stone and fit. He ploughed through the nearby door and I followed. Five persons were around a table writing. Two went out through the window, Andrea sat on two, and, I think, I held the other. In addition, we recovered a rifle, hand-grenade and a fascinating diary entitled 'A Book of Forest History and War and Attacks Here and There,' - the title was written thus in English though the content was in Kikuyu. It told us a great deal about attacks on farms and villages and, most importantly, an almost complete breakdown of Mau Mau organisation within Fort Hall District.

Looking back, I believe I can see where our true success lay. Under Frank Loyd's guidance we were of one mind in our desire to get rid of the evil holding back the breakthrough into self-government, which, as we all knew, was the sole, though not clearly seen, goal at which our stewardship was aimed. Kikuyu thinking had to be behind us because, unless it could be put over by Kikuyu for Kikuyu, it would have very little chance of realisation. We spent hours and hours in discussion with those we could trust and had thoughts to offer. The great, indeed magnificent, Senior Chief Njiri Karanja said at this time, 'All are but sheep who will follow anywhere. In every hundred only five think. If out of that five three think evil thoughts, the flock will follow. But if you can change the minds of only one of those three so that he joins those of good thoughts then the flock will follow them.'

Confronting Mau Mau in Embu

PETER JOHNSON

In September 1952 Embu was still a hopeful and relatively cheerful district – unlike its Kikuyu neighbours. Chiefs and others were still prepared to speak out and denounce the poison of Mau Mau. It was indeed a brave thing to do – and alas too many paid the ultimate penalty later – but at that time it seemed that business was much as usual. However, on the night of 22 October, I was to find myself with half a dozen Tribal Policemen in a pick-up truck manning the Karatina/Kerugoya road junction on the Embu/Nyeri border. We were there ostensibly to intercept Nyeri Kikuyu fleeing for refuge to Embu to avoid the Emergency Regulations which had come into force at midnight and which applied to the Kikuyu districts only. How delightfully naïve we must have been to think along such lines. The only person we apprehended was an Embu Agricultural Officer making his hiccoughing way back from an evening with his girl friend in Nyeri! However it was not long before Embu and Meru districts were also designated as Emergency areas.

It was interesting to witness the Missions' differing reaction to the State of Emergency. The Catholics were outstandingly practical, supportive, and disciplined; the Protestants, in contrast, were hesitant, unsure, and sometimes even critical of Administration initiatives specifically designed to protect their flock. It was through the persistence of Catholic witnesses that we quickly recognised that Embu expatriates in Nairobi were the greatest source of danger to peace and good order in the Embu Reserve. Hence a series of expeditions to Nairobi were mounted with those stalwart witnesses in tow (sometimes disguised) and a search made for known troublemakers. By March 1953, over a thousand arrests had been made in the squalid African townships of Nairobi. The Indian lorry owners made a fortune as this surly and truculent bunch of thugs had to be transported and held on remand in Embu gaol. Inevitably a gaol break occurred and we lost 200 who made their way straight to the nearby forests. However, it had the effect of encouraging the neighbouring Kikuyu districts to follow suit and pursue their very subversive Nairobi element. In Fort Hall, my opposite number was Jimmy Candler who, alas, was to be murdered by Mau Mau a year later.

Because of the magnitude of the problems consequent upon holding such large numbers of unconvicted persons in detention, it was a further fifteen months before Operation Anvil could be launched. This was a full-scale co-ordinated exercise, involving all security forces, to clean up Nairobi. It was largely successful and caused the planning and directing of Mau Mau from then on to be switched from Nairobi to the Aberdare and Mount Kenya forests.

Four special Magistrate's Courts were set up on Embu golf course and a host of Police CID drafted in to mount prosecutions. The success of the venture depended upon how the group of witnesses could be switched from one court to another as the need required. Convictions were secured on the lowest common denominator charge of 'membership' of Mau Mau, so we were able to ensure that this hard-core of terrorists were out of circulation for a minimum of one year and thus to provide the necessary breathing space to encourage and develop the Loyalist movement. In fact, this was the turning point so far as Embu was concerned. From then on security forces' initiatives began to pay off. Villagisation, crude though it was in the early stages, met with ready response and there was a marked improvement in the quality of Intelligence. Undoubtedly Mau Mau provided the excuse for settling some old scores, but despite the temptation, there was not too much miscarriage of justice.

Roger and Renee Wilkinson's Christmas card that year showed a photo of Roger emerging unharmed from an overturned land-rover in the forest during the long rains and the caption '200 prisoners escape, 14 crown witnesses murdered – quite a year'.

In those days, there was an endless stream of VIP visitors – Governors, Generals, Ministers, Bishops, journalists and hangers-on. Some came with outriders, flags, and escorts. Some did not. A favourite was General 'Loony' Hinde who moved about without any formality and with barely adequate protection. He came to listen, not to preach, – also to fish our trout streams!. Some visitors bordered on the mischievous – well known journalists Marjorie Banks and Edward Ward (Lord and the 4th Lady Bangor in private life) seemed anxious to dent our cause and appeared generally unsympathetic with what was being done to restore law and order. Many of them stayed at the Izaac Walton Inn where Geoff and Eva Keates kept the flag flying.

Encounters with Mau Mau in Meru

FERGUS McCARTNEY

I was posted to Meru District in 1955 as a DO Meru Guard and drove to the *boma* across the northern slopes of Mt Kenya.

My District Military Intelligence Officer was Captain Geoff Dowse, and it was to him I reported next morning after a comfortable night at the delightful little Pig and Whistle Hotel, run at that time by Mr and Mrs Stephens and their daughter Mrs Barbara Payne. Captain Dowse was not quite sure what to do with me, so he suggested I went on a three- day patrol high up on the mountain.

The District Officer 1 (the DC's Deputy), John Trestrail, Victor Burke (Agricultural Officer), and several others set off before dawn next morning. It was hard going, even harder where the forest gave way to moorland because of the tussocky grass.

On our second day out on the edge of the moorland, we suddenly stumbled upon what must have been a fairly large Mau Mau gang. We were totally unprepared and so were they. There was utter confusion as our accompanying Home Guards loosed off in all directions with their shotguns. The Mau Mau managed to get off a few shots in reply but nobody was injured. We set off in pursuit but the gang had distanced itself from us in no time at all. We returned to the scene of the action and, to our pleasant surprise, found that we had stumbled across a factory producing home made guns, with nearly a score of weapons on the stocks. Also captured were a number of useful documents, a lot of meat and a lot of smelly bits and pieces of equipment, all of which had been abandoned in the headlong flight. The documents told us that this was General Kaggia's Haraka 65 Battalion. They also gave us the real names and 'bush' names of all the northern Meru gangs – a Mau Mau 'Who's Who'. Thereafter we were more cautious but we didn't encounter any more Mau Mau.

A few more days in Meru and I was sent on detachment to a DO (Meru Guard) by the name of John Berning, at a place called Egoji, about thirty miles south of Meru, on the road to Chuka and Embu. An African Agricultural Instructor, a particularly good man I was told, had recently been murdered by Mau Mau nearby and there seemed to have been a spate of incidents in the area. It was my job to interrogate Mau Mau suspects and find out what was going on in regard to gang activity and disposition. Berning and I were under canvas at Egoji, but, we were given the facility of having hot baths, whenever we wanted, at Chogoria Mission not far away. It was there I had the pleasure of meeting that renowned missionary doctor, Clive Irvine and his wife. They were the essence of kindness, and I shall always remember them. Their son Geoffrey followed in their footsteps and it is to the Irvine family, and many other dedicated missionaries, Agricultural Officers, like Jack Benson, the father of the Meru coffee industry, and Administrative Officers, that the people of Meru owe a great debt. This can be safely said of all districts throughout Kenya, and the officers who served unstintingly in them.

Later on, I was asked to go up to Katheri in Upper Abothuguchi to help the DO Alan Pyne. Alan had built a comfortable log cabin of timber off-cuts with a concrete floor and corrugated iron roof. He had the added luxury of a bathroom. This house was situated inside the Home Guard Post and was surrounded on three sides by circular thatched huts in which the Tribal Police and Home Guards lived. The whole was surrounded by an earth rampart beyond which was a deep trench full of barbed wire and sharpened bamboo stakes. Entry was by way of a drawbridge and a crow's nest in a very large eucalyptus tree overlooked all.

Katheri was not far from the Kazita River, a little beyond which, and all around the Mount Kenya forest, lay the one mile strip, an area which had been cleared of all cultivation and habitation, and into which only security forces were allowed. It acted as a no-man's land and anybody moving in that area risked attack by the security forces.

A very different situation prevailed in Meru District from that in the Kikuyu districts of Kiambu, Fort Hall, and Nyeri. Their cousins the Meru were by no means one hundred per cent Mau Mau, and a fair proportion remained loyal to the Crown. One could, therefore, when planning an operation, count on the support of the Loyalists. This factor was to play an important part in the mounting of two big operations, Schemozzle I & II, later in the Emergency. These resulted in the killing, capture and surrender of many Mau Mau militants but, more importantly, identified the locals - and there were nearly 70,000 men and women involved in these operations – with the Forces of Law and Order.

Forest Tracker

ROGER HORRELL

One thing leads to another. As a National Serviceman commissioned into the Devonshire Regiment, I first went to Kenya in 1954. After night stops in Benghazi and Khartoum, the RAF Hercules reached Nairobi mid afternoon on the third day. I was taken to the Muthaiga Club for tea.

The Devons were stationed at Embu then, and my own Company was camped at Irangi, twenty miles north of Embu on the edge of the forest. Patrols into the forest were usually accompanied by a native tracker. The most impressive one we had was Musa, a survivor of the Lari massacre and far more motivated to hunt down Mau Mau gangs than the average British Tommy. However, it was not so much his enthusiasm for the task that made him stand out, nor his stretched, deeply sagging earlobes (remarkable as these were by any standards); it was his awesome ability to read microscopic detail into a broken twig, a turned leaf or the merest toe print in the mud. 'Six men passed this way about two hours ago. There is a woman with them carrying food,' he might pronounce. Such was his proven record, we never doubted him.

After only six months in the Colony, I had no doubt that I wanted to return. I do not think I travelled beyond the borders of Central Province and Nairobi, but I liked what I saw, loved the forest itself and, then as now, was entranced by the sight of Mount Kenya's snow capped peak.

In 1957 I joined the Colonial Service and returned as a DO.

District Officer Kikuyu Guard

CHRISTOPHER BARNETT

Having just begun duty with the Kenya Regiment, I saw an advertisement. District Officers (Kikuyu Guard) were wanted. They were to take command of Tribal Police combat units. They could be posted anywhere in the Kikuyu, Embu, or Meru Reserves. A 'working knowledge' of Swahili was required. I went for an interview in Nairobi. One of those interviewing was Charles Wilks, (years later my District Commissioner at Kisumu.) I was offered the appointment. It was 1955 and I was eighteen. I accepted.

I was posted to Kerarapon. That was part of the Ngong Division of the Kajiado District in the Southern Province. The District Officer was then Roger Peacock. The District Commissioner was Sandy Simpson. The Provincial Commissioner was Eric Sweatman.

Kerarapon was to the south of Embakasi Forest. To the north was Dagoretti Forest. That was in Kikuyu Division of Kiambu District. The District Officer Kikuyu was John Campbell, M.C., and Bar. He had served in Popski's Private Army during the war.

Kerarapon guard post was tiny, surrounded by a waterless moat, filled with sharpened wooden staves. The next line of defence was a high barbed wire fence, beyond which was a building, which had two rooms. About twenty Tribal Policemen slept in one. I was in the other.

To begin with, I had no bed. Government regulations (I was advised) did not permit such furniture to leave the *boma* at Ngong. I was short of money. The first month I bought a camp bed and a blanket and later added a pillow and sheets. Later still, when Duncan Buttery became DO Ngong, all this changed. His interpretation of such regulations was purposive. I got a bed. That seemed a luxury.

We oversaw the process of 'villagisation.' The local population, whose little round dwellings had been close to their holdings, were placed together in rows of huts next to the Guard Post. They had not wanted to move, but they could see it made them less vulnerable to attack. The change was effected rapidly.

The headman was Mureithi, a small, energetic, Kikuyu with a sharp intelligence. He had been described by Geoff Mackley (formerly DO Ngong) as 'rabidly' Christian. He lacked formal education, but could read, and he read and reread the Swahili translation of the Bible. The result was, his

Swahili was good. I talked to him for many hours and fairly soon had a working knowledge of Swahili.

Mureithi greatly admired Geoff Mackley. He would often regale me with tales of how Bwana Mackley had run the division. He would sit at a meeting, saying little, but when he made an utterance it would be interspersed between carefully gauged puffs of his pipe. He did not eat much 'lunchie' as other white men did, but would content himself with *'ndisi tu'* (just bananas.) His words were invariably wise, (*'akili sana'*)

Second in command to Mureithi was Ndirangu, another Kikuyu, who had reputedly been a cattle thief as a youngster. One day we were following the trail of a Mau Mau gang, who had stolen cabbages from a nearby patch of sand. I wanted to follow the apparent direction of the footmarks, but Ndirangu said they were misleading. The men had walked backwards. He could tell by the way that the sand had fallen. He was right. We followed the trail. Then came rock and I said I could see nothing. He was exasperated. 'Can you not see the way the dust has moved?' he said. I could not. Again, we followed his lead. Again, he was right. We found a burning fire which the gang must have just left. We followed, but the birds had flown.

There was an operation called 'Royal Flush.' It was a joint Police, Army, Tribal Police, and Home Guard initiative. Effectively the Home Guard were to act as beaters. The scheme was that when the gang was 'flushed out,' the Police and Army would do the rest.

Numerically, the largest number of men I could call on were seven hundred Home Guard, drawn from the eight villages on the Nairobi side of the Ngong Hills, whose Chief was Simeon ole (son of) Pasha. He was a good and wise old Maasai. He once offered me milk from a Maasai gourd. They rinse these with urine to curdle the milk. I had to go behind his *manyatta* very rapidly after drinking it, to avoid discourtesy.

These Home Guard were variously armed with spears, bows and arrows, and pangas.

I also had fifty Maasai *moran* (warriors). I decided to take their names. They wore the traditional *shuka* or blanket, were covered in red ochre, and carried a spear. They were young. They were both amused and amusing. As I called out a name, so as to be able to write it down, they laughed. My pronunciation convulsed them. I thought the joke must pall with repetition, but they laughed just as much at my rendering of the fiftieth name! That this number of men, drawn from all parts of the local population, was willing to confront Mau Mau was impressive. The tide had turned. They were on the run. They had lost the argument. The families from which the Home Guard was drawn wanted an end to the insurrection and they were prepared to run risks to achieve it. The Government had won the hearts and minds of the bulk of the population. Popular feeling and the readiness to use force to defeat Mau Mau now ran hand in hand.

Towards the end of my time at Kerarapon, the Deputy Governor of the Colony, Sir Frederick Crawford called. He was escorted by Kenneth Cowley, by now PC Ngong. Sir Frederick said the Guard post was one of the least comfortable to live in he had seen. I replied unconvincingly that it was 'not too bad.' He said to me: 'Young man, what would you like to do when you finish here?' I said that I would like to be a District Officer. But I added there was no chance of me doing this. I was not Oxbridge. I did not have a degree. He replied: 'Young man, you apply.' I repeated the problem but he said with finality 'Young man, YOU apply.' I achieved that ambition as DO Maseno from 1961–2.

Eventually it was decided my presence at Kerarapon was no longer required. I was called back into the *boma* at Ngong. That ended a year or so amongst some fine men. They taught me more than I taught them. There was a great spirit there. I often think back to those extraordinary days. I do not miss the pit that passed as a sanitary arrangement. Nor the lack of running water. But the comradeship was exceptional and remains my most enduring memory.

The Battle of Lake Naivasha

DAVID LAMBERT

Early in January 1956 a large Mau Mau gang was tracked from the Aberdares into the twenty square miles of papyrus swamp at the north end of Lake Naivasha. 70th Infantry Brigade was called in and a cordon of Police and Army was thrown around the area whilst ways and means were worked out to flush the terrorists into the open. Operation Bullrush was born and soon the UK press was reporting (from the New Stanley Long Bar) 'black clad terrorists are charging British troops firing automatics as they run.'

On the ground things were somewhat quieter and after several days the only haul was a shivering food carrier who had wandered into the line of troops from the wrong side. Still convinced the swamp contained at least a hundred terrorists, a plan was made to divide it into sections by cutting lanes from the shore to the edge of open water. Stop lines would then be set up in the lanes and the troops would sweep and clear each section in turn.

At first it was thought bulldozers could do the work, but these soon bogged down and I was volunteered to take charge of a force of minor offenders from Naivasha jail to finish the job by hand. Each morning I collected my prisoners and we drove as far into the swamp as we could get.

From then on, whilst I tried to keep a straight line, they cut a way through to the lake edge, usually knee deep in water and sometimes having to swim. It was tiring and unpleasant work never knowing when we would disturb a hippopotamus and always having to remove leeches with salt or cigarettes.

One day, after we'd been working for a week or so, we stopped for lunch in a dry spot. As we settled down, several shots were fired in our direction. In spite of the fact that we were in the middle of a military operation, it took a long time to register and only during the second burst did we start to take cover. Looking round and taking stock, I realised that we had lost our escort and I was on my own with fifty prisoners, of unknown sympathies, armed with *pangas*, and one elderly prison guard who was wisely beginning to retreat taking his shotgun with him. It was obviously time for action so I reached for my newly acquired Luger automatic. Unfortunately, when I opened the flap I found the holster was half full of water from a week's floundering about in the swamp. Emptying the holster, I pulled out the gun and pulled back the automatic cocking mechanism. Not surprisingly it stuck and I had to force a round into the breech. Loosing this off, I had to repeat the slow process to reload. Realising that I could not respond with an appropriate show of rapid fire, I decided on a psychological approach. Still in cover, I shouted for the terrorists to surrender, offering them hot food and warm clothes as an inducement. There was no reply from the papyrus but I could see some of the prisoners looking at me and thinking this was the best offer they'd heard all week and wondering how they could cash in.

I tried a second time and received another couple of shots for my efforts, which persuaded me it was a good time to leave and find our escort.

The next morning was a Saturday and when I arrived at the jail, my workers were reluctant to go back into the swamp, believing rightly that the army were paid to chase armed terrorists and that their minor peccadilloes did not merit being shot at. Feeling my reputation was at stake I promised to supply an ox for roasting if they completed the task, and, in a moment of inspiration, added that if any of them captured a stray terrorist they would be given a free pardon.

Later that morning a message reached me that Noel Hardy had been taken ill, and with Peter Johnson and others out of the district, I was the senior administrative officer, so would I please attend the Brigadier's daily conference. Arriving, I found the meeting wanted to hear all about our adventures of the previous day and was very interested in my plan to keep the prisoners working. When I'd finished, the Brigadier asked if the PC knew what was happening and if he did not, suggested I might put him in the picture. This seemed like a good idea and I returned to Naivasha and telephoned Robin Wainwright, the Provincial Commissioner, in Nakuru.

When he came to the phone, it took a few minutes to explain who I was and how I had come to be in charge of one of his districts for the weekend. He concealed his surprise and was suitably encouraging so I went on to tell him about the arrangements I had made with the prisoners.

'Ah!' he responded, 'I suppose you do know, David that the only person who can grant a free pardon is Her Majesty the Queen through the Governor?'

There was a pause and I saw my career in the Administration coming to a very quick end. 'However,' he continued 'I'm sure that if it becomes necessary, the Governor will support you.'

We never did capture a terrorist but then neither did the Army or Police, but we did have the roast ox and even a small quantity of beer to wash it down.

Trouble at Hola

W. H. (TOMMY) THOMPSON

The Hola Detention Camp was within the Tana River District, remote from any centres of population and a long way from the actual village of Hola. It was a three-part establishment. First and foremost, it was in 1959, a place of detention for the hard-core and most vicious Mau Mau . Secondly, under the same umbrella of Prisons Department management , it was a jail for medium term and general offence prisoners of all tribes. Lastly, it was the base of a large-scale experiment in irrigated agriculture using water pumped from the Tana. Under the superintendence of an ex-Manager of the great cotton-growing scheme at Gezira in the Sudan, it was hoped that some thousand acres of hitherto dry, barren land, would eventually produce marketable crops of soya bean, dates and anything else that could be made to grow. Unfortunately for the planner's, labour from the local Pokomo tribe turned out to be scarce and unreliable. Thus it was that gangs of prisoners and detainees were used to keep the work going. By and large, something they were willing enough to do.

Although the Camp was within the geographical bounds of my district, none of it was under my jurisdiction, the whole area having been excised by Emergency Decree. My only function derived from my powers as a First Class Magistrate. Thus I was able to hold Court as might be required, to act as a Visiting Justice to the Prison and, but only if called upon, to inspect certain aspects of the Detention Camp. In fact, because the Prisons Department was barely aware of my existence, and of the difficulties of travel, distance and communications, my visits had been very few and far between.

The staffing of the Prison and Detention Camp was entirely the responsibility of the Kenya Prisons Service. The only non-Prisons personnel were the Irrigation Manager, a Public Works Officer, a newly arrived and very young Medical Officer, and a junior District Officer who had recently arrived 'to do something about rehabilitation.'

One morning I was up-river on safari, sitting under a tree, surrounded by Pokomo litigants and onlookers, attempting to unravel the mysteries of land inheritance when, to my annoyance, a young white Prisons Officer drove up in a great cloud of dust which swept all over us and, without as much as the courtesy of a salute, (thereby causing a great deal of tut-tutting amongst the assembly) demanded to speak with me. Whispering, he said a detainee had died at the camp. Would I please go there? I said I would as soon as I could. Away he went. Twenty minutes later, he was back to say two were dead: would I please go soon? Ten minutes later a senior officer appeared with the information that something dreadful had taken place. His words were 'Perhaps as many as six might have died.' Adjourning the case, I hastened to the camp where I found nine dead and several wounded, two of whom died later in the day. What I was told, what actually took place, and why, are separate stories, and must be told as such.

The bodies lay on an open and bare piece of land just outside the perimeter wire of a compound housing the very worst of the detainees, who had always refused to co-operate in any way. The Senior Officer in charge of the Camp was there together with several other Prison Officers both black and white. In the middle of all this stood a portable water cart in the form of a tank on wheels.

The story was that a party of detainees, who had refused to work, had been removed from the compound and told that, whether they liked it or not, they would have to clean up their own rubbish around the place. This was part of a specially authorised and very careful plan to impress upon them that they could not continue to cock a snoot at authority, together with a somewhat faint hope that it might get them to accept a first step or two towards rehabilitation. I was told that all had gone well until several of them had collapsed 'probably because of the heat,' whereupon their guards had panicked and had thrown buckets of water over them.

I seemed to be the only person present who realised that a keg of political dynamite had just been exploded. I knew I had to assert myself and take command.

When I asked what action had been taken to inform Nairobi, I was told no message had been sent. I thereupon gave explicit orders that all was to be left to me and that no matter what the eventual repercussions might be, for which I would take responsibility, nothing was to be sent out on the Prison Service radio network, which everyone involved in the Emergency knew could be received on a domestic radio. The local Kenya Police had a

VHF radio, which was 'safer', and this I would use to make what contacts I thought to be immediately necessary. It was now about 1 p.m. Nairobi was at lunch.

Using the Police Radio I called Nairobi Police Headquarters, told them who I was, and requested that the Police Commissioner himself, or his immediate deputy, come to the set. This latter officer came on within seconds and I gave him a message something on these lines: 'We have met before, you know me. Something I cannot safely tell you about over the air requires your personal presence here pronto. Bring a senior CID Officer with you, contact the Chief Native Commissioner (who was also the Minister for African Affairs), tell him either to come himself or send his Permanent Secretary (both these luminaries were old friends of mine) and most importantly bring the Commissioner of Prisons with you. I cannot remain by this set, but a land-rover with a driver can get me within a few minutes. In any event, I will call again in exactly one hour.' I repeat 'get here today.' The Kenya Police Air Wing made all these demands feasible.

I returned to the scene only to discover that the Prison Officer in charge had 'disobeyed' my instructions, not only telling a garbled story but stating quite definitely that the deaths had been by drowning. The message was picked up, hit the British newspaper headlines, panicked the Kenya Government into making what I can only describe as a daft statement of what was taken as confirmation and resulted in a dreadful tangle of deceit.

The Kenya Police were magnificent, doing almost exactly what I had asked and doing it so quickly that by 4 p.m. they had flown in. The Prisons Department sent an officer in the same aircraft but I regret to say he never consulted me. He accepted the story of drowning which his department stuck to, to its own detriment. My own ministry came up with a weak message that they would try to send someone as soon as possible – which meant late the next day. I was on my own.

The white Prisons Officers closed ranks and the black ones of all grades kept their mouths shut. The Police Officers and myself had no sleep that night as we worried, debated, and theorised. Both as DC and Magistrate I had no option but to give my view but, as far as facts were concerned, I had not witnessed any actual assault. At that stage the young doctor had not expressed the medical doubts that came to him as he progressively tackled his new and fiendish workload.

I was far too busy to make notes, so all I write is from memory, which I am absolutely sure is accurate in all but time scale. It may have been the next afternoon or, perhaps, the morning after, that I was summoned to Government House in Nairobi and an aircraft placed at my disposal. Wearing my far from pristine safari clothes, I somewhat apprehensively found myself in the presence of Sir Evelyn Baring.

'Tell me all you know' he said. What I knew was this. A group of very hard-core detainees had been taken out of their compound against their will. Every one of them had a history of absolute non-cooperation. The plan to take them out to work had been made at the highest level in the Kenya Council of Ministers inner 'War Cabinet' and approved by the Governor himself. Success depended on very careful briefing of all concerned right down to the lowest Prison Warder . It also required sensitivity of handling and control. I gave it as my view that neither the Senior Prison Officer nor his deputy spoke anything approaching good or adequate Kiswahili and that, as far as I had been able to ascertain, the issuing of instructions to the African Officers and staff had been fragmentary and unclear. As short term contract officers, they certainly had no knowledge of the tribal backgrounds of those under them. They had never visited any tribal areas or received any expert instruction and background training on tribalism from the time they had entered the Prison Service.

The Nandi who made up the bulk of the warder strength were of haughty warrior stock, totally contemptuous of the Kikuyu whom they saw as irritating little men of the forests incapable of fighting. Added to this was a deep local hate brought about by the habit of this particular group of detainees throwing the contents of their latrine buckets at, and sometimes over, their warder guards.

Told in bad Swahili to take a tough line, the Nandi took their chance. Out came the truncheons and old scores were settled. Prison Officers on the spot lost control and it was at least five minutes before any order was re-established. Half-a-dozen Kikuyu who had been either at the scene or very close to it all gave eyewitness accounts, which tallied, but, because of their fear of being beaten up by hard-core detainees, they did not agree to give evidence. The story about drowning came after the warders had been restrained and others nearby had thrown bucket after bucket of water over the dead and wounded in an effort to revive them.

The whole thing was as simple as that. There were no political machinations and no sinister designs. If the truth had been told and action taken against the offenders immediately the whole awful nonsense might have been capable of explanation.

The Governor, and an hour later his 'War Cabinet', to whom I had to repeat the tale, was naturally exercised about the drowning story which had been put out in the world's newspapers and repeated in the House of Commons in London. No matter how or why the Prison Officers had said what they had, they had said it and that was that.

Whilst we sat around the table the Governor put in a person to person call through to the Secretary of State in London. I remember being surprised how quickly it went through, and being more surprised to overhear the Governor being told that it would be politically unwise to alter the story. I distinctly remember the words (indeed I noted them at the time) 'You would put me in an untenable position in the House.' As a result out came a statement from Government House to the effect that senior officers were on the spot gathering evidence and that a further press notice would be issued in due course. The one chance to clear the air had been lost and Hola became one of history's black marks. At the subsequent inquest and full-scale enquiry, the truth never became clear. Such blame as was apportioned was not, in my view, correctly placed: nor were the lessons of briefing and lack of background knowledge emphasised or acted upon.

Sir Evelyn gave instructions that I was to take over and supervise all that went on concerning detainees at Hola and leave my district in the care of a junior District Officer. The 'take over and supervise' part of my instructions was vague, I suspect deliberately so, but this gave me considerable freedom without tying my hands too much.

The real task before me was first of all to re-establish trust with the staff and the many detainees who had not been involved. Whilst, at the same time, to begin the run-down of the vast detention camp by rehabilitating and repatriating as many of the incarcerated 'malefactors' at such a speed as the safety of the Colony would bear, taking into account that all the other major detention camps elsewhere would be doing the same thing. One thing was certain, the improving situation in the home districts meant that neither the District Commissioners nor an ever growing and already large proportion of the population were with me. They were going to fight tooth-and-nail to keep the detainees locked up and far away for as long as possible. However, under direct orders from the Governor, arrangements were made to send me small screening parties of carefully selected loyalists from each district in Central Province and the Kikuyu dominated areas of Nairobi. I also made my own personal selection of a special inner team of advisers all of whom were known to me from Kandara and Fort Hall days.

Faced with just over 2000 detainees the task before us could never have been easy and, with the extra hate and bitterness flowing from the killings, our chances of any success seemed to be scant. What I did not want, which was the same as my colleagues back in the districts, was to have a politically dictated timetable of releases forced upon us by totally misinformed government sources back in the United Kingdom. In this respect, the pressure was already on.

My first priority was to make it clear to the detainees that I, and all my team members, were working independently of the Police and Prisons Departments.

We had to give the strong impression that we knew everything there was to know about each detainee plus a lot more, which was not by any stretch of the imagination true. In some cases, all we had to go on was a copy of the original dossier, which contained but the single line: 'Known to have been a member of a gang and present at oathing ceremonies.'

We worked on the easy cases first, which not only gave us a lot of information on the past history of those being interviewed but also quite a lot on the Mau Mau organisation within the Camp itself. Within a very few weeks, we sent off four hundred to conditional freedom. In theory, should they misbehave, they could be reconfined, but that was politically impossible to enforce and I cannot remember any coming back. Then we bit into the remainder with considerable success. Messages coming back from Kikuyuland proved that the early releases had reached home without being 'murdered on the way by the Government' and in each postbag there was an ever increasing number of letters from families urging the recipients to spill the beans and get home as soon as possible. Even so it was a wearisome business and I was near to exhaustion both physically and mentally. Constant visitors, newly created Panels of Inspection, Members of Parliament from Britain, Departmental Heads and Deputy Heads who had hardly heard of the place. A Commission of Enquiry added to the burden.

The house which had been hastily built for me – two rooms up, two plus a kitchen and shower down – became a hotel and place not so much where I lived but where I lectured, cajoled, pleaded, fed and watered a human flood. Incidentally, when I asked for an increase in my £80 p.a., DC's entertainment allowance I was shot down by the Secretariat in Nairobi. I think, in the end, I did get an increase, but I am not at all sure about it.

By January 1960, the numbers of detainees in camp had been reduced by half, but there was still a long way to go.

An Unexpected Role

JOHN WILLIAMS

I returned from my first and, as it was to be, only home leave in the middle of 1960. It was normal practice (or so I learned from colleagues) for officers to receive notification shortly before the end of their leave as to the district to which they were to be posted on their return: it was a notification received either with some relief or with great displeasure!

However, my instructions were simply to report to the Secretariat in Nairobi upon my arrival in Kenya and I had no reason to think at the time that there was anything odd in that. Perhaps the officer in charge of postings had a number of vacancies to be filled and it had not yet been decided which pawns were to be moved to which squares: at least I would have some opportunity to express a preference if I were there on the spot.

Feeling uncomfortably pale-skinned after my summer in England, I duly presented myself one morning at the Secretariat in Nairobi and was eventually ushered into the office of Frank Goodbody. He began by explaining (the way he put it implied that it was 'for his sins') that he was in charge of what were known as the 'Special Camps.' Did I know much about them? I had to confess that I knew very little – why should I admit to knowing virtually nothing!?

Undismayed by such ignorance, Frank recalled that responsibility for several thousands of Mau Mau detainees had been taken over by the Administration from the Prison Service following the unfortunate Hola incident when several detainees had been killed during a riot. The vast majority of the detainees had by now been released back into the reserves but there remained a few hundred who were still in the Special (or rehabilitation) Camps.

Four of these camps now remained in being under the charge of Administration Officers, and policy was that an all-out effort should be made to release the last detainees as soon as they were fit to go home, which meant in effect, as soon as they themselves opted to go home and as soon as it was certain that they would be welcomed back by their local communities.

So, this was where I came into the picture. The officer in charge of the Mwea camp, on the huge expanse of black-cotton plains below Embu, had recently been posted elsewhere (which sounded mysterious in itself) and I was to take over. Any questions?

There were lots, but regrettably, as so often happens in such circumstances, most of them came to me as I was already speeding up the Nairobi – Nyeri road in a brand new Special Camps land-rover. One statement and one question I was able to put to Frank Goodbody before he wished me luck and showed me out of his office. The statement was to the effect that I had read economics at Cambridge and not psychology and the natural question which followed was therefore – why me? The answer came back readily enough: the personal reports of various District Commissioners under whom I had served during my first tour had one feature in common, that I 'got on well with the natives.' With such a qualification, academic background was irrelevant to the process of persuading the remaining 'hard core' detainees to co-operate in seeking their own repatriation!

The great redeeming feature of the Mwea plains is the magnificent view of Mount Kenya towering overhead on a cloudless early morning. Otherwise, it is hot, dusty, and oppressive. The Mwea camp was set in the middle of nowhere, perhaps some twenty miles or so east of the main Nairobi – Nyeri road, down a rough track across endless black-cotton soil: it was fortunate that I arrived during the dry season, for the track must have been impassable during the rains.

My first impression of the camp was that it was a set from a war film about Stalag III. A large square barbed-wire perimeter enclosed three or four rows of huts, numbering about thirty in all. Also inside the enclosure were a latrine block and a cookhouse. Entrance to the compound was through a massive wood and barbed wire double gate above which a watchtower perched precariously. There was no searchlight or machine-gun in view but the warders on sentry were armed with old .303 rifles. The first thing I learned from the Prison Service warrant officer who showed me round on my arrival was that, although the camps were under the authority of the Administration, they were still manned by Prisons Service personnel.

The Camps were obviously never intended to be permanent and the accommodation for the warders and myself reflected this ephemerality, but it was adequate and certainly more agreeable than the huts of the detainees, which, I soon discovered, were uncomfortably hot during the heat of the day. A section of my 'house' also served as the camp office and it was there, on the day after my arrival, that I went through all the records of the detainees with the warrant officer who was, in effect, my deputy and who had been left to 'explain everything' to me: he was a Kamba, very efficient and conscientious.

There were at Mwea camp some fifty 'hard core' detainees, described as 'hard core' because they had all been convicted of Mau Mau associated offences and because they had consistently refused to acknowledge their guilt or to repudiate the activities of Mau Mau. They had all been told, and I told them again as I visited each one of them during those first few days, that they were free to return to their villages as soon as they wished to do so and as soon as their families agreed to have them back. The process of getting this two-way agreement was for detainees' chiefs, headmen and/or relatives to be brought to see them at Mwea (for which purpose I would send out transport from the camp), often staying in 'guest huts' within the compound for days at a time, so that they could try to persuade them to agree to go home and rejoin normal life. It may sound a simple process – why should anyone not wish to be released from prison to rejoin their families? But it certainly was not. Several of the particularly difficult inmates were, for example, in the habit of welcoming visiting relatives by emptying their latrine buckets over them, while others would go on hunger strike so long as their relatives remained at the camp. Some – I remember one very likeable and well-educated detainee with whom I would spend hours discussing history and world events – the chiefs or family would not have back. The reasons given were always that their crimes had been so shameful that they could never be forgotten or forgiven. But was this really the case? What was perhaps more likely, in many cases, was that someone back at home had used the opportunity to take over the absentee's land, cattle or wife. On a number of visits to the homes of detainees in Fort Hall or Nyeri districts, it was made very clear to me that the return of a detainee would not be welcome. It would not be the joyous homecoming of a 'freedom fighter': it was late 1960 and the world had moved on.

Early in my days at Mwea, and in my innocence, I questioned the need to keep the detainees' huts locked at night. If they were to be made into sociable beings again in preparation for a return to their communities, would it not be helpful if they could mingle among themselves and talk to each other? I learned that this had been tried on a number of occasions and had always led to fighting and near riots: I accepted advice and did not try it!

Over several months, there was a steady trickle of departing detainees, released back to their villages. Most went with a handshake and a sheepish smile (much as though to say, 'why have I wasted so much time being locked up here?') Some went with obvious uneasiness as to what the future held for them: life in an institution (and some had been interned for seven or eight years) can have its reassurances. One even came back on a visit, having joined his brother in running a transport service from Fort Hall to Embu, almost proud to show off where he had been incarcerated for the last few years!

Then, one day, a message arrived over the VHF from Nairobi headquarters to say that the Camp was to be closed by a particular date. It was not that I had been lost and forgotten since my posting to Mwea some months before: Frank Goodbody and other visiting dignitaries had looked in from time to time to see how the process of releases was progressing. But now, as the end of 1960 approached, political decisions had been taken that the 'Special Camps' should be disbanded.

The dozen or so detainees who remained at Mwea were to be sent home whether they wanted to go or not, and whether their chiefs/headmen/families wanted them back or not. Never have I had a clearer movement order! Four buses and two 3-ton lorries were sent to Mwea one afternoon. All stores were to be loaded onto the two lorries and sent back to Nairobi. That evening, I called a meeting of all the remaining detainees – to my surprise all but two of them attended quite voluntarily and those two I visited separately in their huts – and announced that they would be going back to their districts the following morning. They were to pack up their personal belongings and take them with them: one bus would go to Kiambu, one to Fort Hall and one to Nyeri and they should indicate to the driver whereabouts they wished to be dropped off. The fourth bus would take the warders back to the Prison Service headquarters in Nairobi.

And me? I was to proceed to the Special Camp at Nyeri where I would take over from Don Clay, who had been District Officer at Kimilili, in Elgon Nyanza District, when I had been at Bungoma on my very first posting, in 1957.

The instructions were simple. But what if some of the detainees refused to go? Several of them were still refusing even to see or speak to their relatives when we brought them to visit the camp. I did not dare to contemplate such an eventuality, with the thought however at the back of my mind that a fall-back position would always be to take any such problem individuals with me up to the Nyeri camp.

To my amazement, the camp was empty by 10 o'clock the next morning, all three buses gone to their different destinations, all the warders and stores departed for Nairobi, my cook/houseboy and myself left alone to pack up my land-rover and head off to Nyeri. If it had all been so simple, why had this solution not been considered before? And was it in fact so simple? I never heard of the reception which those thus released received on their return to their own districts.

And what of Mwea camp? I never returned there but assumed that it was in due course dismantled if not otherwise stripped of its more valuable or useful articles (such as the barbed wire) by enterprising locals.

It is very difficult to analyse my reaction to the ten months or so, which I spent in the Special Camps. They were not prisons, but they were surrounded by barbed wire and were patrolled by armed guards. They were not 'Broadmoors,' but many of the inmates behaved as though they were in an asylum. What were they? They probably have no parallel elsewhere in our colonial history, but then Mau Mau probably had no parallel either. I certainly never expected to serve in such a capacity, but I did not regret it or resent it. Whether I had the right qualifications to be asked to take it on, I cannot say – what, after all, were the right qualifications? Perhaps in the long run it gave me an experience of how to deal with some of the characters whom I was subsequently to meet in civilian life back in England!

Releasing Mau Mau Detainees

JOHN JOHNSON

My first independent command came in 1957 after I had been in Kenya for over a year. I moved from Embu boma to take over the most westerly division, Ndia, from Eric Gordon, who went to Nyeri. The division (now in Kirinyaga District) was a slice of country stretching from Mt Kenya to the Tana River. The population was 75,000.

I was exhilarated. My father responded to my enthusiasm by pointing out that the population of districts in India was often in millions. That did not matter, I was in charge. And I had competent colleagues: two Administrators, a Police Inspector, an Agricultural Officer and a Livestock Officer, Africans and Europeans.

The job priorities in Ndia Division turned out to be a mix of development and security issues:
 building local democracy;
 the completion of land tenure reform;
 agricultural progress and cash crop development;
 the return to the land from the Emergency villages; and
 the release of Mau Mau detainees.

All the Kikuyu, Embu and Meru districts were under pressure to accelerate the release of detainees. At the peak of the Emergency 70,000 were incarcerated. Fortified camps mushroomed. The biggest were down in the low country on the Mombasa road, Manyani, and Mackinnon Road, but many were in Central Province. The Special Camps, Gathigiriri, Kandongu, Mwea, Thiba and Wamumu (later to become a reform school,) were in Ndia. The detainees were building the Mwea Irrigation Scheme which was destined to provide work for landless Kikuyu.

Every week in 1959 I sent a screening team down to the Detention Camps to interview and classify detainees for release. The team members were chiefs, headmen, and an Anglican cleric, Rev. Johanna Njumbi. Category A detainees were 'hard core' and were at the end of the release queue. Categories B and C were released as soon as they were cleared by the rehabilitation process in the Special Camps and in Aguthi in Nyeri.

The teams would see a screening report. This would normally be based on a full confession of Mau Mau activities. I kept one typical report. The detainee was arrested in Operation Anvil in Nairobi in 1954. He took the first oath in his late teens. He then became a member of a sub-location committee from his home district, rising to be a district committee member. Selection as a central committee member usually involved the third (leadership) oath. The Mau Mau organisation replicated the colonial hierarchy. His duties included collecting money and supplying food, clothing, arms and ammunition to the fighting arm in the forest.

The release operation went like clockwork. Virtually everyone, except those who had been recalcitrant and were still considered a danger to security, came out in monthly lorry loads to the location centres. They returned to their homes and were swallowed up in the community. Fortunately, the progress on land consolidation usually meant that a piece of land had been demarcated for them. They got on with it and built a house. Few people in Embu District in those days emerged landless; unlike in Kiambu District where there was a serious shortage of available land.

Two years later in 1961 in Kikuyu Division of Kiambu District, I witnessed the end of the process of releasing detainees. Eight men were brought to my office. They refused to move, so had to be carried from the lorry and deposited on the floor. They refused to speak so I delivered my usual homily about changed times, reconciliation, and the approach to

Independence. These were among the last of the 'hard core' detainees who had refused to co-operate in the rehabilitation and release process. I felt sorry for them, but there was nothing I could do. Office work was out for the afternoon. I went to my home across the road and had tea. When I came back, they had all gone.

In 1986, I was driving alone through the small farms in Kikuyu to look around my old stamping ground. I lost my way and asked directions from a group of farmers. We talked and I told them I had once been DO Kikuyu. One then said: 'I know you. I lay on your office floor. After we had made our protest we all decided to walk home to our families.'

9

Preparing for Independence

A Political Dilemma   John Johnson
Elections   Anthony Merifield
Staffing Problems   Wally Coutts
The Progress of Africanisation   Nick Scott
My First African DC   Tony Stephens
White to Black 1   Terence Gavaghan
White to Black 2   Patrick Crichton
Training the New Administration Colin Fuller
Last Post   Roger Horrell

Introduction

From the mid 1950s the pressure for greater involvement of Africans in running the country grew fast. This was primarily about constitutional development. The first African Members were nominated to the Legislative Council by the Governor after local consultation. Elections in 1957 under the Lyttleton Plan (Oliver Lyttleton, Secretary of State for the Colonies 1951–4) resulted in eight African Members elected on a qualified franchise. Under the Lennox Boyd Constitution (Alan Lennox Boyd, Secretary of State 1954–9) a further six Africans were elected. From then until 1960, the African Elected Members Organisation provided the main drive towards Independence.

The unity of the African Members broke down in 1960 after the formation of the Kenya African National Union (KANU). Seven tribal organisations opposed to the Kikuyu-Luo leadership of KANU met and formed the Kenya African Democratic Union (KADU). The Lancaster House Conference chaired by Iain Macleod (Secretary of State 1959–61) early in 1960 increased the tempo. John Johnson describes the beginnings of party political campaigning in Kiambu District.

After the 1961 elections, the majority party KANU candidates refused to take office before the release of Jomo Kenyatta, which happened later in the year. A Coalition Government of KADU and the European-led New Kenya Party was formed. This pressed for a new structure of government giving greater powers to the tribal areas in the form of six regions. A second

217

Lancaster House conference in 1962 chaired by Reginald Maudling (Secretary of State 1961–2) led to a Coalition Government. The pre-Uhuru elections, which took place in May 1963 resulted in a decisive win for KANU led by Kenyatta. Anthony Merifield describes the process of the complex polls in Kisii District and makes a contrast with earlier local elections in Kilifi district.

The other major development was Africanisation, particularly in the high-profile Administration. The first African District Officer, Isaac Okwirry, was appointed in 1955. But mass recruitment of Africans to that rank did not get going until 1959 and after. Until then the personnel policy had been to give Africans experience first in support grades. Nick Scott recounts this process from his service in districts to a job in the Ministry of Home Affairs. The imminence of Independence after 1959 accelerated developments. Tony Stephens served under Geoffrey Kariithi, in Taita District and is full of praise for this notable African administrator, who rose to the top of the Civil Service in an independent Kenya. Wally Coutts, the Chief Secretary, laid down future staffing policy. In the early 1960s, a crash programme for the promotion of Africans to top posts was begun together with the creation of a training institute. Terence Gavaghan and Patrick Crichton recount how this great change was managed. Colin Fuller describes the training process and sums up the Africanisation of the civil service.

For most of the British officers, this was the end of their careers in Kenya. Roger Horrell looks back with satisfaction and nostalgia on Meru District, his last post.

A Political Dilemma

JOHN JOHNSON

Everything changed in January 1960. The Lancaster House Conference and Iain Macleod shortened all the time frames. The Emergency legislation had been lifted. European politicians were in disarray, with Michael Blundell's New Kenya Party challenging the traditional forces. African politics exploded exuberantly. *Uhuru* was in the air.

In March 1960, I was posted from Kericho back to Central Province, to Kiambu District, the cradle of Kikuyu politics. Economic and social development was in full swing. The farmers of Kiambu had been the first to get freehold title to their newly consolidated shambas. Each year they planted more coffee trees. Grade cattle were being bought from settler farms and stall-fed on tiny plots. Gone were the mud and wattle thatched rondavels. In their place, rose timber, even stone, houses almost overnight. It was exhilarating to see hard work rewarded by rising prosperity. There were landless people, but they at least got a plot in one of the newly planned villages. And jobs in those days were only a few miles down the road in Nairobi.

There were no doubts about political allegiance. In my division, Kikuyu, everyone was staunchly pro-KANU. But the party wanted to mobilise the masses willy-nilly. After all, they were the masses and it would be fun for everyone to turn out on Sundays. My duty was clear. The basic tenet of any administration is the preservation of law and order. How that was to be done in the event of trouble was not clear. The Kenya Police Inspector thought he might be able to provide about a dozen constables. There were a few more of my Tribal Police. But they were all local KANU supporters and looked forward to joining in.

I duly turned up at the school playing field an hour before the rally was timed to begin. A platform had been erected, and a flimsy roof for shade. Several thousand people were sitting on the ground waiting. I thought I would stand under a big *mugumu* (fig tree). My TP Sergeant elected to keep me company. The speakers arrived in an elderly Mercedes. I went to talk to the KANU candidate, Dr Mungai Njoroge. He told me that a seat had been reserved for me on the platform. I had grave doubts. If I sat there, I might forfeit my official impartiality. I dithered. The rally began.

After the initial slogans, Njoroge began his address by calling out: 'There is the DO Kikuyu who must ensure we meet in peace. He will sit here on the platform so that he may do his job.' My doubts were resolved. I sat in the shade for two hours and listened with interest. Every speaker emphasised the need for early progress to Independence coupled with the immediate release of Jomo Kenyatta. Next, in order of priorities came universal adult franchise. And then the bread and butter issues of political speeches everywhere in the world: education, health, jobs. I never once felt threatened. There was no untoward disturbance. In any case, if I had been obliged to invoke the Riot Act – a drill we all had to learn – I would have been hard pressed to gain control. I cannot remember whether there was an opposition KADU candidate. But I am sure that he did not risk holding a rally.

The most important event during my time in Kiambu was the release of Jomo Kenyatta in August 1961. My minor role was to collect the senior KANU politician, James Gichuru, from his home before dawn and drive him to Eastleigh Airport to meet the plane bringing Kenyatta from Maralal. A few weeks later *Mzee* paid a visit to my division. He walked up the drive of the *boma* and I greeted him. After a while I asked him what he thought of the newly consolidated farms, including his own twenty-five acres at Gatundu. 'It is good,' he said. I breathed a sigh of relief. The future looked more promising.

Kenya Elections

ANTHONY MERIFIELD

In 1958, when I arrived in Kenya fresh from Oxford, elections were not a top priority. They had not featured in my one year Colonial course, though I had been told how to build a bungalow with windows low enough to enable you to lie in bed and still look out at the surrounding bush, how to map a new road and why a rural economy was less susceptible to change than an industrial one. ('You can always change the jig on a machine but you can't muck about with a cow.') Nor did elections feature in my initiation into the work of a District Officer at Kilifi in Coast Province, where my tuition had been entrusted to the wise and dignified Gideon Ngetsa, the District Commissioner's driver, who escorted me on my first tax collecting safari. At Vitengeni, Bamba, Sokoke and Ganze, the chiefs waited with their poll tax collection and a host of assorted petitioners. When in doubt, a glance towards Gideon offered reassurance, or a gentle warning.

But nine months later I was enjoined to supervise the election of the members of each chief's Advisory Council – one representative per sub-location. The system was simple: proportional representation, the single transferable vote and other variations beloved of today's television pollsters were then not in vogue. At a chief's *baraza*, as the name of each sub-location was called, the candidates, two or perhaps three, stood in front of my camp table and I invited the residents of that area who were present at the *baraza* (all of course male) to come forward and stand behind the candidate of their choice. The sub-chief and chief checked to ensure that no stranger had joined the lines, and I then counted the numbers of men standing behind each candidate, declaring as the winner the one with the longest support. First past the post would hardly have been the most apt description of this rather static procedure. I well recall the final contest of the day – two candidates advanced and when the preliminaries had been dispensed with, some seventy men stepped forward, all behind the same candidate. With a note of sympathy, I enquired of the unfortunate loser why he had no support. 'Ah *Bwana*' he replied, 'I did not want to stand, but there was only one candidate and the chief said that this was not enough for an election so he told me that I would be the second candidate.' I was glad to know that no deposits were lost for such a selfless gesture in the interests of democracy.

By 1963, within only five years, all had changed and on the eve of

Independence, Kenya was poised for the election of a new Central Government and Regional Assemblies. The areas of South Nyanza, where I was then working, were mainly KANU in allegiance, strong supporters of Jomo Kenyatta, then Minister of Constitutional Affairs and expected to emerge as Kenya's first Prime Minister. The urgency and excitement of the occasion had been trailed by the registration of voters, men and women, in late 1962, which required the compilation of lists of those qualified to vote throughout the district. This involved me and my colleagues in long days at each of the voting areas, approving the entry of individual names onto a new register by a Registration Clerk. Surprisingly, there was little dispute as all applicants had to pass the scrutiny of his or her chief and sub-chief acting as assessors, and pretenders were quickly warned off. In some areas, the registered voters represented over 100% of those estimated from the recent census to be eligible, but on the whole, the outcome was satisfactory. Indeed, the only problems I recall at this distance in time, were the embarrassments caused to the under age women aspirants, whose amour propre was severely damaged by what I loosely but authoritatively called '*Mheshimiwa Mzee* Kenyatta's rule that, whether or not you had two or even three children, you had to be twenty-one to qualify.' Before driving home along South Nyanza's corrugated murram roads, we discussed local events over a chicken curry provided for the Registration party, with customary African hospitality, by a local shopkeeper from the market where the Registration had been conducted.

The elections themselves, in May, were more demanding. The constitutional pattern had evolved from the inter tribal rivalries and aspirations, or fears, of the two main power blocks – KANU and KADU. The latter secured a Regional structure, which proved time consuming, and wasteful of scarce trained African leadership. By the end of 1964, it had largely disappeared.

Two days were allotted for each election; to the House of Representatives, the Senate and the Regional Assembly, to follow each other without a break, with the count beginning after a seventh day of rest. As deputy to the Returning Officer, Fionn Holford Walker, my District Commissioner, I recall retiring for several days to consider the siting, manning and preparation of polling stations; the arrangements for securing the ballot papers before use and the sealed ballot boxes after each day and each two-day election; liaison with the Police and deployment of our own district Tribal Police; the count; the selection of election staff and their training. (Sadly, I no longer have a copy of the instructions which were given at day training sessions to my DO colleagues and to the teachers, Agricultural Officers and assistants who, with the supervisors of the Count, made the election work in acceptable fashion.)

The most testing administrative issue, apart perhaps from the staffing, was the preparation of the sites for the Polling Stations. As is customary in

England, schools were chosen, but there the similarity ended. Expecting two or three thousand voters at each station in the first few hours of polling, the entrances and exits had to be separated and the entrance made impregnable against an early morning tidal wave of enthusiastic voters. Because the schools were low rectangular constructions of mud and wattle, or loosely laid concrete blocks, albeit with a corrugated iron roof, and each of four or five adjoining classrooms, it was possible to punch out the rear window of the classes to construct an exit door. Across the front of the building, a heavy wooden fence provided the main line of defence, with similarly stout wooden channels leading to the entrances of the classrooms where voters with family names, say, A to F, G to L, M to P and Q to Z would queue. Those familiar with entry to old time football grounds will understand the format.

I am glad to say that on only one occasion during the Kisii poll was this protection over-run. On the first day of voting several hundred exuberant voters at one station could not be contained by the polling staff, who wisely decided to remove the ballot papers and let the crowds stream through the station before being directed back into line at the front of the fences. Thereafter there was an orderly progress past the controller at each entrance, into the classroom where the polling officer sat with the register of voters and his ballot papers, forward to a booth where a cross was entered on the paper by the voter (or if they could not write, by a polling helper), and then past the ballot box where the paper was placed and into the open air. There, with little of the reticence of English voters, many announced their choice to the waiting crowds. One old man took this a step further. Each political party had its own symbol – a cockerel for Jomo Kenyatta's KANU, an open hand, I think, for KADU, an umbrella or bicycle and so on, for other groups. On the first day of polling, as I toured the stations, it took me some time to realise why the roads were filled by platoons of people sporting open umbrellas under a clear blue sky, or why cars were passing with cycles or guitars strapped to the roof. On such a visual occasion, one old man had no hesitation about arriving with a cockerel under his arm. Perhaps understandably on his first voting experience and in his late seventies, he misunderstood the arrangements and demanded the right to make his vote clear and unassailable by placing the cockerel in the ballot box. The polling officer, with commendable presence of mind, decided that this was not the time to give instruction on the niceties of electoral practice; nor should the completed forms be spoiled. So he opened the box in which, at the start of the day, the unused ballot papers had been stored, and into this, the bird was happily deposited, en route no doubt, to the polling officer's evening meal.

When, much later, I was working in Northern Ireland, several people reminded me of a traditional heavy vote of the dead (names left on the registers and claimed by others who attended more than once). In the 1963 Kenya election, the validity of one man one vote was strengthened because, on collecting a ballot paper each voter had a fingernail stained in a red dye, which could not be washed out for at least a week. Three fingers were chosen, one for each of the elections. This proved a strong safeguard, and in Kisii, where inter party rivalry was not an overwhelming issue, all appeared to go well. The greatest threat to propriety came from the young people who had been sent to vote for those of their elders unwilling to make the, sometimes lengthy, journey to the polling station. Many of these young boys, wearing an old and usually too long overcoat, and hat pulled over their eyes, would be unmasked as they waited in the queue to the polling station and sent home. Persistent offenders were more severely dealt with. Electoral law may have had procedures to deal with the offence of 'fraudulently pretending to be a registered voter,' but undoubtedly the process of law would have been long and costly. One candidate, three days later declared as the Senator elected for the Kisii District, simply upended one offender, and administered justice with his fly whisk. Elsewhere polling officers used their red dye to mark the errant boys clearly on the nose – to universal delight and significant deterrent effect.

My story has an epilogue. Two or three months after the poll, the Prime Minister/President-designate, visited Kisii. The *Mzee* and his entourage were entertained to lunch by the local Asian shopkeepers led by Ebrahim Kassam (whose strikingly elegant daughters, I recall, were welcome guests at our Kisii Club dances). Laurence Sagini, a local MP and the Minister for Education, took the DC as the senior government official present to sit with the Prime Minister, and after lunch Tom Mboya invited the district staff to join him at the rally in the stand of the Kisii football stadium (where an unknown schoolboy, Naftali Temu, won the District Sports 5000 metres before going on to win a Gold medal at the Commonwealth Games in Jamaica in 1966 and Kenya's first Olympic Gold in 1968, at Mexico City). Peter Kenyatta, a rather shy visitor from Cambridge University, was introduced to the crowd and bidden to say a greeting in Swahili. Tom Mboya, whose later pamphlet on African Socialism I much admired, and whose premature death was such a tragedy for Kenya, introduced the Prime Minister. Then Jomo Kenyatta began to speak. He teased the crowd by pointing out to them the 'white' District Commissioner and Superintendent of Police, 'our DC,' and 'our Superintendent.' He then told an astonished audience that, having heard of the increasing incidence of stock theft from the European farms of neighbouring Sotik, he had instructed the Superintendent to ensure that the thieves went to gaol for a very long time. '*Harambee*' he added, 'does not mean that you can lie in the sun and wait for the money to drop into your mouths. It means working for Kenya, white or black, together.' It struck me afterwards that had I been asked to write a draft of his speech, I would never have dared to be so outspoken.

I was probably too busy at the time to realise that this was history in the making, and to fully appreciate that the act of voting was a landmark of self-affirmation for the Kenyan people. More recently, the striking experiences in South Africa have underlined the potency of the vote to those for whom it was not a commonplace. Conversely, sharper rivalries in Africa have no doubt put pressures on the administrators of the electoral processes that were hardly felt by those of us who in the early 1960s heralded the next phase of Kenya history.

Staffing Policy

WALLY COUTTS

It is the aim of Government:

1. To increase the supply of qualified local candidates for every grade of the public service by expansion of facilities for local education and training, and the award of bursaries to enable local men to obtain essential qualifications overseas which cannot be obtained in East Africa.

2. To ensure that local candidates for Government service with the necessary basic standards of education should not be rejected for lack of immediate vacancies. This applies particularly to graduates from Makerere; and local students, who have acquired suitable qualifications, in higher education overseas.

3. To increase the tempo of in-service training by provision of training posts, supernumerary when appropriate.

4. To review the position of Africans in the lower grades of the Service and ensure that any whose experience and proved merit qualify them for more senior posts of greater responsibility, but who were previously held back by the operation of the pre-Lidbury racial scales and conversions based on racial scales, should be considered for promotion together with officers of no greater experience serving in higher grades.

5. To safeguard the conditions of service and recognised promotion prospects of local officers of whatever race, who are already in the Permanent Service.

All officers who, in the course of their duties, are required to make recommendations regarding appointments and promotions are requested to assist in putting this policy into operation.

The Progress of Africanisation

NICK SCOTT

I joined the service as a DO Cadet in Kericho in late 1953. There were on this station at this time no Africans in the Provincial Administration in anything resembling an officer grade, though shortly before my arrival there had been a representative of the small group of African Assistant Administrative Officers (AAAO), in one Washington Ombito. This grade had been created quite recently, at the instigation of Kenneth Hunter, a Provincial Commissioner, and was endorsed by the previous Governor, Sir Philip Mitchell. It contained some half a dozen officers, three more of whom I refer to below. I have no specific information on their backgrounds but believe some to have completed secondary education and others to have been appointed on the basis of long service in clerical grades who had distinguished themselves by outstanding character and capacity.

One of the capable African clerks in the DC's Office at Kericho, reappeared a dozen years later as a District Commissioner himself on one of my courses at the Kenya Institute of Administration.

Occupying a next door office for some time was Taita arap Towett, a well regarded Community Development Assistant of the local Kipsigis tribe, who distinguished himself both as editor of the government-financed Kipsigis paper and as sports organiser for that district, which had already produced a number of notable performers at Commonwealth Games. He went on to make a career in politics.

The expansion of the Provincial Administration on account of the Mau Mau Emergency brought a development that could have greatly set back advancement of African officers in the junior ranks of the service. This was the creation of the grade of District Assistant (DA), non-graduates brought in direct from Britain without prior training (many of whom, I hasten to say, gave valuable service). However, the demands for manpower meant that many Africans were soon recruited into this grade as well, and I have always felt it fair to say that this unexpected outcome of the Emergency went far towards producing a cadre of seasoned African administrators, who were to become the core of the capable civil service of early post-independence Kenya. I would speculate that the creation of a corps of junior African staff for the land consolidation and land registration programmes also brought a crop of able officers into the administration around the time of Independence.

In 1955, I moved to Narok District, the western half of what was then the Maasai Extra-Provincial District. Here there had been for some time another of the AAAOs I have referred to above, Francis ole Lemeke, a Maasai. As I served in outposts all my time in Narok, I had no direct dealings with him but understand he was the DC's adviser on Maasai affairs and liaison officer with the principal elders. Tony Stephens, a colleague from that time, adds that Francis particularly helped the DC with two large cooperative schemes supported by all the sections of the Narok District Maasai, one a sawmill to exploit the rich cedar forests of the Mau and the other, a sheep ranch.

A posting after leave in 1957–8 brought me to the Ukwala Division of Central Nyanza District. Another AAAO, Sam Josiah, was of great assistance to the District Commissioner and to the DO of the neighbouring Maseno Division in the matter of land consolidation.

I moved to Nakuru as DO1 at the start of 1959 and found already there, a notable African Officer, Geoffrey Kariithi, who had just been made a full District Officer. He was highly respected by all staff, and was chiefly concerned with African affairs in this major industrial and railway town. Within four years, he was Permanent Secretary in the Prime Minister's office, and remained in that role to serve both President Kenyatta and President Moi with great distinction for many years.

A year later, I was in Nandi District as DO1 and for the first time found myself in the same station as an African DA, who worked alongside two European officers in this grade. This was Sila Boit, son of a Nandi senior chief who had retired some years before. His brother Paul Boit, another DA. at this stage, I met when he was home on leave in the district. Both brothers had just secondary education; Sila was one of the notable Kalenjin athletes at Commonwealth Games level. Both made rapid progress from this point on and both were well regarded Provincial Commissioners by the early years of Independence.

Knowing that Africanisation of the service was in full swing, and that Independence was imminent, I wrote to the Secretariat before the end of my leave in late 1962 to ask if I could be posted on my return to duty as DO1, to one of the new African District Commissioners then expected to take up their positions. The idea was accepted in principle and I found myself posted to Homa Bay, headquarters of the newly-established district of South Nyanza, (recently separated from the former district of the same name which had included, and had its headquarters at, Kisii). However, I was to find myself for three months under an old hand expatriate DC who had undertaken to be one of the first to leave the service under the initial limited compensation scheme. When he was leaving I learned that my request was after all to be granted and that my new DC was to be one Ezekiel Josiah. I wondered how much I was going to have to teach this 'new boy', until I looked him up in the Staff List and found that he had joined the service in the year I was born! A salutary lesson for me. He was, of course in no way daunted by taking charge of a huge district, but in fact within a few weeks he was seriously injured in a road accident and I found myself running the district for him, until I was posted away as DC Bungoma, a couple of months before the pre-Independence General Election of 1963. Nevertheless, he was to have a great influence on the course of my life.

My time at Bungoma, March to November 1963, was a blur of election upon election, crisis upon crisis. First three Elections with universal franchise within ten days, for the Regional Assembly, House of Representatives and Senate, then furious bargaining between the parties over the final Independence constitution; also serious inter-communal violence within the district between tribes supporting the different main national parties; then local council elections. In July, a KANU government led by Jomo Kenyatta took office, and the Provincial Administration had an African Minister in Oginga Odinga, as Minister for Home Affairs. Nevertheless, the only event bearing directly on the theme of this short paper was the posting in of an African District Officer, Onesimus Mtungu, one of the many ex-secondary students who had gone to the USA for university education under a scheme promoted by the late Tom Mboya (commonly known at the time as the Mboya Airlift), and who arrived back at an opportune time to fill the gap left by the retiring expatriates. I survived this period of turmoil for nine months but, with concern for the safety of a very young family, I decided that I no longer wanted to serve in the field and asked for a Nairobi posting. My wish was very promptly fulfilled when a former Education Officer, Matthew Mwenesi, arrived to take my place as DC (or rather, under the short-lived Regional Constitution, Regional Government Agent). A number of capable Education Officers found their way into senior positions in the Provincial Administration.

My Nairobi posting was as an Assistant Secretary in the Ministry of Home Affairs, in a greatly changed Secretariat, working for a most capable African Under-Secretary, Jeremiah Kiereini, who in turn reported to an African Permanent Secretary, who I shall just call XYZ. This PS was a London-trained barrister; he threw his predecessor out of the building the day he arrived to take over, and was big-headed enough to put on his door the inscription, 'The Honourable and Learned XYZ, Permanent Secretary'. His incapacity and vanity were the despair of the Under-Secretary. Long after my time, XYZ came to a bad end while Chief Justice, a post in which he performed very badly. He aspired to the Presidency and backed a coup attempt which failed. He suffered the penalty for treason.

My main responsibility in the Ministry was the maintenance of the strength of the Provincial Administration. Under the Independence constitution, this cadre was to have been split up and assigned to the new Regions. This never happened, and the KANU Government maintained their influence throughout the country to a considerable degree by their control of this capable corps of officers, now mostly African.

Early on in my year in the Ministry, I decided that I must keep a close track of the level of experience amongst the staff (District Commissioners and District Officers) in each of our 41 districts. I inherited a large board with slots for cards with the names of the districts and the names of the officers serving in each. I devised a colour coding system to highlight such factors as how long each officer had been in the service, what his level of education was, and how long he had been in the particular post.

As the year progressed all such indicator levels were falling alarmingly, and at one point, I passed word to the Prime Minister's Office that I believed our Minister was deliberately giving away experienced officers to any para-statal organisation that asked for them so as to weaken the Provincial Administration. The upshot was almost immediate. The Prime Minister said he must approve any transfers of Provincial and District Commissioners out of the department.

The great source of recruits was the Mboya Airlift, already mentioned, of African graduates returning from the USA. They reported to our office and had an interview with the Under-Secretary. He decided where they should go, and typically, they were on their way to their various stations the same day. Most fitted in happily, though I well remember one unfortunate whose life's ambition was to be an archivist and whose degree was in that field. Willy-nilly, he was posted to a district bordering on some of the wilder parts of the country, where he was most unhappy. In the end, by virtue of, to all intents and purposes, going on strike, and even feigning madness, he managed to get the department to let him leave and go into his chosen field.

My First African District Commisioner

TONY STEPHENS

About the end of 1961, during my second long leave, I was informed that my next appointment would be in Taita District as the DO 1 under one of the first four African DCs, Geoffrey Kariithi – whom I had not previously met. It was not immediately apparent that this post (which would less grandiloquently be termed DO HQ, as the only other DO in the district was at Taveta, seventy miles away) would be as onerous or challenging as my previous job of Divisional DO in Vihiga, where I had two other DOs in the division – including the excellent John Njoroge Michuki – and where two of the five locations each had as many occupants as the whole of Taita. Nevertheless, I gathered that the appointment was intended as a compliment and I certainly took it as such.

When I arrived at Wundanyi in March 1962, Geoffrey was in the course of taking over as DC from Bob Otter, who was about to retire from Kenya.

From the outset, and throughout the next fifteen months, I was never in any doubt that Geoffrey had what it took to be a fully effective – and in some ways, outstanding – District Commissioner. He very soon won, and retained at all times, the respect of his own staff, the departmental officers, the handful of 'unofficials' at Voi and Taveta and, not least, the people of the district: respect which was accompanied by a good deal of affection. He took in his stride his administrative or governmental duties. It goes almost without saying that he was keen to see educational progress. But what particularly stood out was the importance he attached to economic improvement and the energy and determination with which he set about achieving it.

This latter was no easy task. The Taita did not lack intelligence, but they were sadly lacking in drive or enterprise – as was well illustrated by the deplorable fact that, although much of the district was suitable for growing vegetables and was only a hundred miles from Mombasa (and on the railway line), most of the vegetables marketed in Mombasa came from Kikuyuland, three or four times further away. Not even Geoffrey could transform that situation in the time he had available, but it was not for want of trying.

Something else which especially impressed me about him was that, when he learned that a few of our European residents were misbehaving among themselves (there is no need to go into details), he did not shirk dealing firmly with the matter, even though he clearly found it a distasteful task. He saw that as his duty and there was no question of leaving it to me or to any other of their compatriots.

I suppose the one negative feature was that he only had his wife and family with him for a few very short spells when they were able to visit him from their home in Embu. This was clearly unavoidable and no doubt continues to be so for a large proportion of African officers in the field, but it does make for a fairly lonely existence and detracts from *boma* life, as we knew it.

My abiding feeling is one of regret that, however understandably, the system had not been equal to making him a DC years sooner. The counter-argument, of course, is that no one could have foreseen the speed at which political change was to occur. Without that foreknowledge, the policy was to allow the emerging African administrators to gain experience gradually. That may well have been sensible in other cases, but was not so in Geoffrey's case because his quality must always have been there to see.

Be that as it may, my most lasting memories of that period are two-fold. First, of watching Geoffrey conducting a meeting of the District Team, while (at some risk to my minutes) I watched the other faces around the table, the majority of them white, growing ever more impressed. And second, of the Kariithi children and our own racing round the lawn on their battered bikes – memorable because sadly, it happened so rarely.

Geoffrey left Taita at the end of May 1963 and moved to Provincial Commissioner, Nyeri. He was at least spared the indignity of being transmuted into an RGA (Regional Government Agent). Which befell me a few weeks after I was gazetted as DC on succeeding him. In September, I, in turn handed over as RGA to a young Arab who, it is fair to say, had absolutely none of Geoffrey's qualifications. The appointment could only be explained in terms of the prevailing drive to regionalise the Government of the country and, for the Taita, reinforced their resentment at being treated as part of a KADU – dominated region despite their strongly KANU alignment. No doubt, they welcomed the subsequent abandonment of the regional policy; and, for those of us who cared and still care, about how Kenya is administered, it was glad news that the Provincial and District structure was restored soon after Independence. It is said that the newly appointed Minister of Home Affairs made it abundantly clear that he expected to preside over proper PCs and DCs. His name was Oginga Odinga.

White to Black 1

TERENCE GAVAGHAN

Africanisation of the civil service, albeit innocuously introduced as 'localisation', was the most creative and exhilarating work entrusted to me after sixteen years of mixed fortunes in the Provincial and Local Government Administration of Her Majesty's Overseas Civil Service in Kenya. It signalled a final advance towards the objective which had been our lodestar since the Devonshire Declaration of Paramountcy of African interests back in 1922. The mills of colonial policy since the Second World War had ground through successive Inter-Territorial civil service Commissions: 'Holmes 1947/8 had pronounced the time 'not yet ripe' for racially integrated grades: 'Lidbury 1954' had ruled that grading by race, namely into A, B and C scales 'should disappear' as African colonies moved towards self-government: 'Flemming 1960' had only recently introduced a new colour blind, escalator of A, B, C and Z scales with emphasis on standards of performance and recruitment.

PREPARING FOR INDEPENDENCE

There had been one oblique but historic outcome from the contra-flow between discriminatory civil service pay and the staged increase of African political representation. The Maasai elected member for the huge Rift Valley constituency, J. Ole Tameno, who I had entertained at Maralal Club when DC Samburu in 1956, was also an Edinburgh Dick Vets' graduate and a serving Vet. He was still ineligible for the salary scale enjoyed by his expatriate peers which naturally undermined his status and morale. By a consensus at the next (1958) elections the Rift Valley seat was won by a young Tugen (of the Kalenjin group) Headmaster, Daniel Toroitich arap Moi.

Two informal but indispensable supports of the existing Colonial Civil Service system merited careful attention in any Africanisation plans. One was the proudly cohesive, assimilated community of (Indian) Goans in the executive and clerical services - *'Mabwana Karani'* - to be found almost anywhere sustaining the administration from bush station to railway services; without my exemplary friend Caesar Lobo in Maralal, I for one would have been quite lost. The other was the leavening of expatriate officers' wives and locally recruited career secretaries - *'Mabibi Weupe'* perhaps - who were a vital, sometimes dominant, influence in District and Secretariat, without which comparable support our successor Administrators would be severely constrained.

European, Asian and African representative Staff Associations, roughly coinciding with respective A, B and C scales, had come to see that the time was now 'ripe' for fusion of real interests in place of definition of status by race. In 1959, by then DC Kiambu, after completing the Rehabilitation Programme of Mau Mau detainees, I was, for no apparent reason, invited to take a lead in negotiations for the formation of a unified, non-racial, Civil Service Association (the current European Association chairman being the unsighted but far-seeing Ray Cuthbert, Assistant Secretary in the Treasury). A mass meeting was finally held in the Nairobi City Hall, at which the Senior Civil Servants Association (SCSA) was launched with acclaim. By an electronic count, I was elected President with a widely representative Committee, employing an ideal qualified Executive Secretary, Betty Annesley, in rented premises.

The SCSA, for which I took the 'scandalous' precaution of seeking registration as a Union carried on the negotiating role of Staff Side of Central Whitley Council with the Chief Secretary, Wally Coutts, (including conditions of retirement and compensation). We moved up a notch, via the reportedly (by incoming Governor Renison) 'nose out of joint' Colonial Office emissary, Philip Rogers, to a formal call on Secretary of State Iain Macleod, who assured the puzzled mixed delegation that 'one must look after one's own.' Before light could dawn on Betty Annesley, Aquil Quraishi, Fred Eddleston, Chris Malavu and myself we were ushered out by Rogers, but good PR and London press coverage resulted.

Beyond Civil Service concerns, it was a time of intense jockeying for position between, across and within the many political and 'tribal' parties, African, Asian and European. 'Multi-racialism' was enjoying a brief post Capricorn Society hey-day fronted by elected settler leader, Michael Blundell, ostensibly favoured by the Colonial Office (Hugh Fraser and William Gorrell-Barnes visiting Maralal had told me he was an 'Instrument to hand')

Colourful characters abounded. Old Etonian grocer, Derek Erskine; Churchill devotee and look-alike Air Commodore Howard-Williams; stiff-necked Group Captain Puck Briggs, and United Kenya charmer, 'Gaby' Sheikh. More weightily loomed the towering Kenyatta and fractious un-Communist Jaramogi Oginga Odinga of KANU. Pipe smoking coast MP and KADU leader 'Noddy' Ngala and the brilliantly unsuppressible loner Tom Mboya were too soon to fall victims to 'car crash' and bullet.

Along the corridors of power, firm but slackening old hand Philip Mitchell had marched on; superb, Emergency drained Evelyn Baring had been elevated as Lord Howick, to be replaced at length by Patrick Renison, a professionals' professional, out of the different experience of British Guiana, having himself run a staff association. Conservative leadership hopeful and bridge expert Iain Macleod, Colonial Secretary after larger than life Lennox-Boyd, now held his honours and discards close to his heart and called the bidding or did not.

Most discriminatory obstacles to planning 'staffing of the public services from within a self-governing Kenya's own resources' (Lidbury) having been set aside, despite some remaining foibles of social prejudice in famous New Stanley hotel or exclusive Muthaiga Club, the time and space were more than ripe for affirmative action. I was not, of course, privy to preparatory government discussions, but I at once responded to a circular advertising a new senior position of 'Localisation and Training Officer' and to my delight I was appointed in October 1960, thirty-seven months before not only Internal Self-Government but actual Independence.

The new office module was set within the power-house of the Treasury, under the Director of Establishments (and *'eminence grise'*) Tom Skinner, and his deputy, Cyril Claude (but Peter) Rickets, both generous and tolerant supporters, closely linked with Under-Secretary for Finance, whirlwind Tasmanian, Philip Haddon-Cave, (later Deputy Governor of Hong Kong). Our module was staffed by two outstanding colleagues (who would have been on the old B scale), Elizabeth Saldhanha, impeccable in all respects, and Nisar Mir, who would have made a hero of Indian film, but gave his all to creating order from chaos. Kenya owed them a debt.

The population of Kenya was then over eight million and the total Civil Service establishment numbered approximately sixty thousand (not including local councils). It had been agreed that the seventeen thousand or so posts above a certain salary level (C6-5) should be eligible for The Senior Civil Servants Association while those below E scale, nearly all African, chose to form a new negotiating union to represent their somewhat divergent, even conflicting concerns. This attracted the interest of the feisty Labour MP for Rugby, James Johnson, who was keen on having a monolithic Union. In the top ten thousand posts only a sprinkling were Africans, while in the next seven thousand the majority were locally recruited Asians and the rest Africans. The potential for 'Localisation' but in reality for 'Africanisation' was obvious and urgent.

The immediate requirement was a concise draft plan covering the entire government service across all departments, presenting realistic action in regard to finance, recruitment and, vitally, the putative time scale up to the deadline of Independence. Within six weeks, on 30 November 1960, with kind help from my former colleagues, local government Inspectors, Fred Altorfer and Joe England, we presented a slender foolscap sized paper in pink card covers entitled:

'First Interim Report on Localisation.' 1960 (copy now in Rhodes House Library).

(This concluded that) 'Localisation must have as a definite aim the introduction of a minimum proportion of Africans at all levels in which they are not adequately represented … A decision on this matter, which is fraught with political and economic hazards, cannot be long delayed'

We cited three levels of urgency of action: a crash programme of appointments under severe pressure; selective displacement with accelerated replacement; controlled replacement of normal annual wastage. In the event we acted on the basis of the possible, revealed by our research, and set an arbitrary target of three thousand Africans in the top ten thousand posts by Independence which was assumed without guidance to be from three to five years away. (Constitution making went on all round and above our heads!)

Without delay the report was followed by a Chief Secretary's Circular (which I was asked to draft) emphasising that the future composition of the service would aim to reflect the proportionate racial composition of the whole population. There was a vast amount of detailed work involved and the pace of international interest was accelerating from all sides. Nisar Mir rounded up all his Executive Officer colleagues and put together a hundred page analysis of the entire staffing position serving as a ready reckoner for Africanisation, or indeed Localisation, by which any department's needs and opportunities could be identified at a glance.

I was attempting to perform at speed a delicate balancing act, which achieved a certain useful equilibrium in the circumstances; as President of the SCSA, I was elected to represent the concerns, including displacement, compensation and pensions, of the body of expatriates from whom three thousand places were to be found for Africans, while maintaining and furthering standards. As the officer responsible for planning and accelerating Africanisation I had to facilitate and advance to a timetable the policies and processes leading to that result. It helped for a time that I could usually agree with myself without debate after consultation!

Appointed to the Joint Supervisory Committee, Tom Mboya quite rightly beat the table. Without commotion but with a handsome tribute from my superiors, I moved on from both positions: from Africanisation to the Cabinet or Governor's Office handing over to dynamic Dick Lake, Senior Education Officer, who later handed on to pragmatic and perceptive Patrick Crichton from Provincial Administration, who acted on the essential need for efficient secretaries: The Presidency of SCSA was taken over by Eric Prince of Education, and later by Alan Simmance who had been with me as No. 2 in Kiambu.

Preparations were put in hand for the most significant project of all, the training of a new cadre of Administrative Officers, both Provincial and Central Government. It involved many co-operating agencies, and imaginative contributions. The core element irradiating the entire Africanisation programme was the foundation of a Kenya Institute of Administration (KIA). Uniquely it was planned without a limiting P, for Public, so that its remit and appeal could extend to the private sector. About this time there was also talk of an East African Staff College, but the impetus for a Kenya Institute came from a seminal paper by Tom Neil. Tom was Permanent Secretary to the Chief Secretary and thus more equal than others, having also been a Lieut. Colonel with staff experience. He told me in his curl of the lip, throw away, manner that he had knocked it up over a long weekend, but the concept had found its time and our new unit was put to drafting a full-scale plan and estimates. Vital to success was external assistance over which we all had quite a time.

Mindful of the forthright advice of E.V. Mamphey, Director of Establishments in Ghana, we were already aware of the tussle for influence before Independence, between American 'generation' of dollars and ideas and the questing Russian and Eastern European Communist ideology, with Tom Mboya tugging on both kite strings with his University 'Airlifts'. Displaying great enthusiasm were the US Consul General, Dudley Withers: USAID Bob Powers and Gavin Lawson; Stephen K. Bailey, visiting Dean of Syracuse University and confidant of J. F. Kennedy; Professor Fred. Burke from Syracuse at the University of Dar es Salaam; John Sergeant visiting Deputy (to Raymond Nottage) Director of the Royal Institute of Public Administration, with Colonial Office Principal, Hobden, spurred on by the formidable Under-Secretary W.A.C. Matheson, (having been seconded Education Minister in Kenya)

In this favourable climate and under pressure of time we were able to strike many favourable bargains. Together with Bob Powers and Gavin Lawson, I put together a mid-Atlantic language version of our and their requirements for early processing by USAID Headquarters in Washington, which usually took over two years. The main factors were finance, plant and staff. The US Government and Syracuse University, as our 'Contractor', wanted a substantial staff complement (about which we were ambivalent); we and they needed a campus and premises; we needed their money in plenty set against a somewhat phoney pound for pound contribution by Kenya. It is not entirely shameful to reveal that we bargained US staff input against dollars contributed for a large token figure each since everything was done to satisfaction!

The campus requirement was met by appropriating a splendidly verdant sixty-eight acre site near Kabete (seven miles from Nairobi) from or with under funded occupants and installations of a socially creative kind. The first permanent Institute buildings were a brilliant revamping, by PWD Engineers Pat Garland and Jim Graham, of the unused blueprints of a once projected European girls' boarding school at Nakuru. With plans, costs and quantities immediately produced on spanking new blueprints, the coffers of USAID opened in astonishment and the Kenya Institute of Administration took shape on the ground by the end of 1962. Much of the detailed work in establishing the KIA up was done by an agriculturally qualified administrator Eric Gordon, with Institutional experience in Nyanza, seconded from the Provincial Administration as Interim Principal. He vigorously set format and tone before handing over to Peter McEntee, a Senior DC, returning from a visit to Syracuse University to formalise relations with them.

This is where I bowed out to the Cabinet Office, happily leaving Africanisation to progress toward the substantial targets set, with confidence that Civil Service standards would be maintained under the future Government of Kenya.

White to Black 2

PATRICK CRICHTON

R. A. (Dick) Lake was appointed to the Africanisation schedule when Terry left. It was a brilliant appointment. Dick was an Education Officer of great integrity, keen intellect, and almost unlimited energy. Under Terry's guidance, an analysis had been made of the racial composition of the Civil Service, the foundations of the Kenya Institute of Administration had been laid, and promises of help obtained from many sources. Further, Terry had been instrumental in negotiating the early retirement scheme for expatriate officers, without which it would have been well nigh impossible to begin with the Africanisation of the senior grades.

Almost the first task Dick was faced with was to find all the Kenyans who had been granted scholarships, largely in the United States where a variety of colleges had offered help, on the initiative of Tom Mboya. Also a few in Iron Curtain countries to which Jaramogi Oginga Odinga appealed as a sort of counter-balance to the Mboya initiative. (Sir Richard Luyt, later to be Vice-Chancellor of Cape Town University told me that Tom Mboya was the most intelligent person he had ever met.) Dick went to America and travelled from coast to coast, managing to trace most of the students. He told me that the exercise was immensely tiring, not only because of the distances he had to travel but because the students ignored time differences when telephoning, so that many calls were received in the early hours of the morning.

Dick arranged for the students to finish their courses, where possible, before returning to Kenya, by which time I had succeeded him. Another of Dick's tasks was to evaluate the standing of the American colleges, which vary from the excellent, as in the case of the state colleges, to the scarcely credible, in the case of some of the private institutions. It was also becoming clear that the structure of the Kenya Civil Service was too inflexible to absorb, satisfactorily, students who had, say, done two years in college but not been granted a degree.

By this time, early 1960s, it was also clear that there would be three universities, one in Dar-es-Salaam and one in Nairobi, as well as Makerere, but naturally the financing body, in this case the UK Government wished to avoid overlap and the provision of post-graduate studies for which there was but a small need. There were a number of issues:

How many surveyors were needed?

How many geologists?

Do we train citizens or is the short-term need better satisfied by recruiting expatriates on contract?

Most postgraduate medical courses were provided in the UK; eg. cardiologists to London and Glasgow.

Some first degree courses were also provided in the UK such as foresters to Bangor and Aberdeen.

Digressing a little, Frank Kalimuzo, Mr. Obote's Permanent Secretary got his degree from Aberystwyth. He told me that in the first summer, when walking in the hills with Welsh friends, he was induced to enter a 'Teas with Hovis' hostelry and greet the proprietor with 'Bor y Da, Mrs. Jones', to be answered with 'Bor y Da, bless you; fancy a black man talking Welsh! Better than those English foreigners.'

I have not mentioned the work of the KIA, which, by this time was training Africans in a multiplicity of disciplines, still largely financed by USAID. Although nominally within my fiefdom, the KIA was almost an independent body lacking only its own revenue raising powers. The full story is told elsewhere.

With the number of students returning from America, and others resident in UK universities, we needed a Students' Adviser in London and were lucky enough to find Tom Colchester, at one time our Commissioner for Local Government.

We had our excitements with the students going abroad, or returning. Once, Tom rang me to say that he had 147 students returning from America and would I hire a 'plane for onward transport. EAA offered me a Comet for seven thousand pounds and then withdrew the offer, demanding full fare for each traveller. BOAC would do no better, so Tom hired a larger, and therefore much better plane for the job, from Caledonian Airways for three thousand pounds. BOAC and EAA opposed landing rights, but the Airports authority ruled that both these companies had acted unreasonably, and we got our men back for three thousand pounds. We never again had any trouble. The Commonwealth countries, too, offered specialist training. One student set off for Australia and was well on his way going onto the runway at Embakasi airport but somehow managed to turn up in London, much to Tom's surprise and irritation.

I do recall the dates when Tom Skinner and Peter Ricketts left us. For the greater part of my time with responsibility for Africanisation, the Director of Personnel was Titus Mbathi who was rarely to be found in his office. After Peter left I was also acting as Deputy Director, but the greater part of the work remained in continuing the process of Africanisation, and in policy I worked directly to the President's Office. On the money side, David Pean and Frank Gilboy of the Treasury could not have been more understanding and helpful. When we were setting up the Secretarial College in Nairobi I put in fifty thousand pounds as the first year's expenditure figure and David asked where I had got the figure from. I said that I had gazed at the ceiling and the figure just came to me. David replied that it was as closely worked an estimate as he had seen in many cases and accepted the figure.

When I first took on the schedule it appeared that the one great gap to be filled would have to be the replacement of the *Mabibi Weupe* to whom Terry has referred. Peter Pitman gave unstinting help and advice, and with extra money from Sweden we started two schools, one on Hospital Hill in Nairobi, and another in Mombasa; in the process I lost my excellent secretary Ann D'Sa to be a teacher, and a splendid teacher she proved to be.

In my contacts with the President's Office, my normal contact was Duncan Ndegwa as, for instance on the day when Oginga had let fly in Cabinet about the slow progress of Africanisation and Tom Mboya had said, 'But Oginga, you are the Minister responsible!' As soon as the Cabinet meeting was over I got a call from Oginga instructing me to report to his office in the Secretariat. He had called in his PS who conducted me to a large and prestigious office with a desk and a telephone and told me that was to be where I worked from now on. I rang Duncan who asked me to wait and I heard, *'Aiee Mzee'* repeated three times; and then Duncan came back to me and said, 'The President says you are to ignore his Deputy and return to your office in the Treasury. You will not be troubled further.' And I was not.

I can recall only three occasions when the President spoke to me personally: once, after he had made a speech in which he had said that all citizens of all races were to be treated equally, I asked him whether white or brown citizens were to be included in the Africanisation programme. He laughed heartily and said 'You know perfectly well what I want Mr Crichton, I want BLACK MEN, BLACK MEN' On another occasion, after the establishment of the secretarial school, the President had heard that I was receiving visits from Ministers who were presenting very personable young girls to me, with a recommendation that they be admitted to the school. I received the strictest instructions that pupils be admitted on merit alone.

Most of the returning students were well qualified for employment, although finding the right niche was sometimes a problem; one candidate said that he had majored in central heating, which I suggested was hardly the discipline for a country on the equator, but he replied that heating and refrigeration were only the two sides of the same engineering problem. He prospered.

The third occasion when I had the direct support of the President related to a Machakos Mkamba who had been awarded a Ph.D. at Oxford (I do not know to which branch of human knowledge he extended the frontiers) who, on his return was appointed Chief Executive of the Local Authority, a post which he did not hold for long. Suffice it to say that he was eventually appointed as a clerk Grade 1 in the Police and, one day, I had a plaintive call from the Police to say that he was quite useless, that he was never at his post, and what were they to do. I called the man to my office and asked him to explain his behaviour and he told me that he had no time to work at Police Headquarters because it took him all his time to fill in applications for promotion. So I rang the President's Office and posed a hypothetical case. The President came back to me on the 'phone to assure me that it was our job to get Africans into posts, but not to keep them there if they were incompetent. So it was up to the employing department to take such disciplinary action as was deemed necessary, which they did. There were a few similar cases, but in general the reabsorption exercise went smoothly.

Although this paper deals with the Africanisation of the Civil Service the whole fabric of society was changing and needed to change. In many cases the wives of expatriate officers, through the East African Women's League, for example, were able to help the wives of newly promoted African officers. The arrival of well educated Ghanaians in the shape of Alasdair Adu, lately head of the Ghanaian Civil Service and the new Chief Justice helped leaven society. In the case of the Scouts, we introduced a new constitution and I insisted on retiring as Chief Commissioner, to the chagrin of Jeremiah Nyaga and Musa Amalemba who felt themselves to be politically exposed. I think I was right; but the creation of a multi-racial society is another story.

I recall being told by the Colonial Office that my task was to work myself out of a job so, to my mind at least, it was in the success in carrying out this programme that we, the Administration, fulfilled the mission for which we were recruited.

Training the New Administration

COLIN FULLER

The Kenya Institute of Administration (KIA) was founded on the site of a former Community Development Training Centre called Jeanes School. Initially, training was for Administrative Officers only and the first course began in July 1961 using old dormitories and classrooms. The United States Government responded quickly to a request for capital aid and new classrooms and dormitories were completed by November 1962. One of the conditions of USAID had been that the KIA should establish a relationship with an American University. Accordingly, this was made with the Maxwell Graduate School of Citizenship and Public Service at Syracuse University. Only two United States personnel were directly involved in training. One, a training specialist, arrived three months later.

Training for the Administration Service (comprising the Provincial Administration and Central Ministries) was given priority by the Chief Secretary so that the most senior positions (Permanent Secretaries, Provincial Commissioners and most District Commissioners) could be occupied by Kenyan African Officers at Independence. In 1961, only 21 out of some 228 officers in the Provincial Administration and nine of ninety-three posts from Assistant Secretary to Permanent Secretary in the central Ministries in Nairobi, were occupied by African Officers. Up to Independence, of the 115 officers trained on the first six courses, the vast majority were non-graduates, mostly ex-schoolteachers and headmasters. The only exception was a 1963 course who were all recent graduates from Makerere University in Uganda. Otherwise, no course had more than three or four graduates. The non-graduates were not of lower intellect than the graduates. The lack of a degree mainly reflected the fact that entrance to university had been more difficult to obtain and scholarships many fewer prior to 1959. Also, the older boys in families were usually expected to obtain work as soon as they completed secondary education, so that their earnings could help towards payment of school fees for younger brothers and sisters. Despite the warnings of cynics about 'lowering of standards', when African Officers took over the most senior Administrative posts, hindsight has shown how creditably they performed during the early days of Internal Self-Government and Independence which, amongst many other changes, included national elections, Regional Government and constitutional change to single party government.

Initially, the direction of the KIA and its early development, was under the Acting Principal, Eric Gordon, a District Commissioner seconded from the Provincial Administration. He filled a difficult role with great skill, given that he had limited terms of reference for his task and that there were no job descriptions or specifications for the administrative posts in the central Ministries or Provincial Administration for which he was required to train African officers. He was assisted by two officers seconded from their District Officer posts (myself and Robert Chambers). In 1962, Gordon was succeeded by Peter McEntee (a former Senior District Commissioner) and he in turn by Alan Simmance (a former District Officer and Crown Counsel to the Kenya Government). In 1965, after a period as Deputy Principal, J.E. Kariuki became the first African Principal of he KIA He proved to be a most able head of the Institute, popular with staff and trainees, although he went to the Institute with no previous experience in the Public Service, having been a training officer with Shell.

The syllabus and ethos of the first two courses reflect Eric Gordon's own background and qualifications and were probably more appropriate than some contemporary critics thought. He had served in the Royal Navy, had degrees in geography and agricultural economics, and experience as an administrative officer up to District Commissioner level. He knew that Kenya's first African administrators would require confidence and self discipline to carry out their duties successfully, not only because of the many changes and uncertainties with which they would have to cope, but also because many people, local and expatriate, would be watching their performance, some of whom would be only too ready to criticise. This was the main reason for the khaki shirts, shorts and stockings, the early morning parade and the 'mess dinners.' For the visit to the East African Navy in Mombasa, sailing and rowing whalers and having sessions about authority and discipline and for the three-week course at the Outward Bound Mountain School at Loitokitok. The purpose of all these activities was to build an *esprit de corps*, pride in the Administrative Service and themselves, self-confidence and self-discipline, not, as many critics misguidedly thought, to toughen them up. It is interesting to note how, some forty years later, private companies and government departments in the industrialised countries send their managers on expensive outdoor management exercises for the very same reasons.

Lectures and visits under the heading of 'natural resources' reflected the assumption that, on completion of their courses, most officers would take up posts in the provinces, but report writing and English, finance and establishments and management were subjects which would be just as, if not more, important for those officers posted to central ministries. Some training in law was provided, since administrative officers were still required to pass a law examination before they could be confirmed in rank. Breadth to the syllabus was provided by studies in politics and government, economics and, to a lesser extent, sociology. On pre-Independence courses, these were given by the College of Social Studies at Kikuyu.

In the early days, the training was carried out mainly through the medium of lectures supplemented by fieldwork, but towards the end of 1962, two interesting and valuable innovations were introduced by Robert Chambers. As mentioned earlier, before 1963 administrative trainees were mainly non-graduate, but the number of graduates had been increasing slowly and, in early 1963, the first all-graduate intake arrived. The main need of the non-graduates (who had 4–13 years of experience) was to read and handle paperwork more quickly and to acquire thinking and decision-making skills at policy level. The main need of the graduates (who had 5–7 months' experience) was to learn more about Central Government procedures, minute and letter writing, and analysis and handling of files. Robert's response to these needs was to seek co-operation from officers in the Ministry of State for Constitutional Affairs and Provincial Administration to identify files which would be suitable as case-studies to meet the overlapping but different training needs. Two suitable files were located, their contents photocopied and then reproduced on stencils, including any hand written comments on the originals. These were then cyclostyled so that each trainee built up his own file. The names of the officers handling the files were rarely changed and, since many of them were very senior officers who were known to the trainees, this created added interest. These case studies provided material for individual exercises in memo-writing and decision-making from Assistant Secretary to Permanent Secretary levels and for group discussions on a whole range of administrative issues.

Permission to use these case studies by the Ministry of State continued when, after Independence, it became the Office of the President. The President himself, Jomo Kenyatta, took a strong personal interest in the training of his administrative officers. Whenever he came across them on safari, he would send the ever-present contingent of the KANU Youth Wing out of earshot so that he could speak frankly to the trainees. On one such occasion, he told them, 'Although I have the Kenya Police and the Special Branch, you are my eyes and ears. I trust and depend on you.'

A second initiative of Robert's was to introduce a District Development Project to the syllabus. This replaced the end-of-term projects in which syndicates of three to four trainees had gone into the field to study topics such as a water reticulation scheme or an artificial insemination programme. This had been followed by the writing of a report and plenary sessions, in which all the reports had been discussed. Although practical and useful, these exercises had usually been confined to single topics and had not required the trainees to think as rigorously as they would have to after taking up posts in the field.

Initially, the format used by Chambers was to divide the course into syndicates, which had to produce a Development Plan for the chosen District. The trainees role-played key staff of the district, and their plans had to include financial estimates which also specified grant and loan proportions and interest rates.

The project began with introductory lectures at the KIA about the selected district. The course was then flown over the district and other parts of Kenya in a Beverley aircraft used for training Kenya Air Force pilots and navigators. This helped to illustrate aspects of the natural resources syllabus and gave the trainees a bird's eye view of the potential and problems of the selected district.

This was followed by a two-week safari in the district. As much of the preparation as possible was delegated to the trainees. A course of some eighteen or nineteen trainees, two trainers and two cooks, needed a lorry and driver, two land-rovers, camping equipment, initial food supplies, maps, health and first aid planning and an imprest. On the safari the trainees met local farmers, politicians, civil servants, missionaries, teachers etc, and consulted local files and reports.

On return to the KIA, trainees had an opportunity to consult ministries and other authorities in the Nairobi area, before a final three and a half days for working out Development Plans and producing them in reports with estimates. There followed a short break for the staff to analyse and compare the reports, and then a day's plenary session to discuss the plans and what had been learned. Innumerable learning opportunities were presented at all stages of this project about knowledge and skill requirements for identifying development needs, planning solutions and implementing them. The project was intellectually and physically demanding and, therefore, it replicated almost all aspects of the Outward Bound mountain exercise of earlier courses and replaced it.

The generally smooth and efficient way in which Kenya was administered in the year before and the years immediately after Independence, was due in no small measure to the ability and dedication of the African administrative officers who shouldered responsibilities at senior levels at relatively short notice. The majority were trained at the KIA although there were others who served with distinction, notably Geoffrey Kariithi, the first African Secretary to the Cabinet and Head of the Civil Service, who also gave great support to the work of the Institute.

Last Post

ROGER HORRELL

Towards the end of my leave in 1962, I received a letter from the Secretariat telling me I was posted to Meru (good), but that it was imperative I return two weeks earlier than planned, ie. just before Christmas (not so good). When I reached Meru, the DC, David Shirreff, asked why on earth I had come back before Christmas. 'They said .....' I explained. But we never tried to find out who or why.

In contrast to Kwale, Meru contained some of the most impressive and successful agricultural development in the country. On the other hand, there were still three gangs in the forest, which refused to accept either that the Emergency was over or that independence was nigh without their efforts. The most notorious of the three gang leaders was Mwariama, who eventually emerged from the forest in late 1963, wild eyed, dreadlocked and odiferous. After being photographed clinging to an embarrassed Kenyatta, he was not heard of again. Before that, Odinga and Tom Mboya came to Meru for a political rally. Ben Gethi, the smartest police officer I have ever seen anywhere, was commander of the local force. Odinga and Mboya visited his office to discuss the security situation and said they had been in touch with the gangsters. I asked which of the three gangs they were talking to. 'All both,' replied Mboya, thus ensuring we were none the wiser.

Unlike Kwale and Kilifi, Meru had an enormous population. The final pre-Independence General Election in July 1963 involved logistical exertions of some magnitude for both the poll and the count. I believe the majority of the successful candidate, Jackson Angaine, was well over 60,000; but every vote was scrutinised with the same care as would be necessary in a marginal constituency. The large team started counting at 8am and finished after 6pm.

By now, it was necessary to think of a new career. I had arrived at the tail end of a Colonial era, which in Kenya spanned some seventy years; a period plagued by two World Wars, and the most severe depression. It is not for me to enumerate the manifest achievements of the Service. In a transition of miniature symbolism, I moved from a world of Tilley lamps, paraffin fridge and gramophone worked by batteries in Kinango to a Meru District which contained all the appurtenances of modern life, electricity, telephones, high quality medical and educational services, thriving tea and coffee plantations (owned by native co-operatives), herds of exotic cattle, and so on. In the long leave sandwiched between the two districts I had driven from Mombasa to Cape Town through Tanganyika, Northern, and Southern Rhodesia, showing my passport for the first time at Beit Bridge. There was not much tarmac on the route, but neither was there any suspicion of personal danger.

I have nothing but respect for the predecessors and contemporaries who left much, much more than a footprint in time. I am proud to have played a part, however small. And I am grateful to various mentors – District Commissioners, other colleagues, wise Senior Chief Julo and forward looking (though opinionated) Chief Johnson of the Duruma, and the countless good humoured, wonderfully rounded, characters one met in the bush. What a job! To think we were paid for it too.

10
Uhuru and After

Directing the Independence Ceremony — Arthur Horner
A Strong Wind of Change — George Hampson
An Incident at Isiolo — Peter Fullerton
A Price on my Head — John Golds
After Jamhuri and Uhuru — Michael Philip
The Army Mutiny — John Johnson
The Kenya Institute of Administration — Nick Scott
A Journey Back in Time — Henry Wright
A Mau Mau General to Tea — Jean Johnson

Introduction

Uhuru (Independence) for Kenya came swiftly after the Lancaster House Conference of 1960. Even in the mid 1950s it had seemed more remote. New European DOs were being selected by the Colonial Office every year up to 1960. The gradual approach to institution building and the recruitment of local officers was abandoned. The priorities had changed. The British Government was seeking a viable Government and an African leader to whom they could hand over power. An early retirement and compensation scheme was introduced and many European officers were leaving. Landless Africans, particularly in the overcrowded Kikuyu areas, were clamouring for land. Many European farmers felt threatened and looked for opportunities to realise their capital and move on.

The symbolism of Independence was important. A ceremony had to be organised and Arthur Horner sheds amusing light on the problems involved. George Hampson was District Commissioner of a settled area (ie. a European farming district) in the run-up to Independence. He describes the departure of farmers and the settlement of African smallholders on their farms; and he records the transformation of the city of Nairobi.

The territorial integrity of Kenya was at risk because of the Somali demand for secession. Trouble had been brewing since Somalia became independent in 1960, and John Golds recounts the risks which faced him in Wajir. Peter Fullerton gives a perceptive insight into Somali views in the period immediately before Kenya's Independence. Michael Philip stayed on and was in the thick of the dangerous conflict with the Somali *shifta* guerrillas. Another threat was posed by unrest in a part of the Kenya army. John Johnson describes how the Government dealt with it.

Meanwhile, training the new Administration was an urgent task. Nick Scott carries forward the story of the Kenya Institute of Administration which operates to this day.

Many administrators went back to visit Kenya and their old districts. There were great changes, many for the better, as Jean Johnson found. But in some places time had stood still. Henry Wright recounts a voyage of discovery thirty years later.

Directing the Independence Ceremony

AS RECOUNTED BY ARTHUR HORNER

A.W. Horner was Director in charge of the Kenya Independence celebrations. The design of the flag, the new national anthem and the ceremonial itself were all his responsibility. He answered to Tom Mboya who was Minister for Legal and Constitutional Affairs. He had been landed with the job when he was Permanent Secretary to Mboya. The Acting Governor, Eric Griffith-Jones, had called a meeting of Permanent Secretaries to discuss who would run the Independence ceremonies which were to take place some eight months hence. He looked enquiringly around the table but there were no takers. Griffith-Jones then looked at Horner and said, 'Actually, Arthur, the Africans have asked for you.'

Horner was wise enough to hesitate and asked for time to think about it but one of the other Permanent Secretaries said to him as they were leaving the meeting, 'Do you realise that this is an enormous compliment to you, Arthur?' Flattery got the future Kenya Government everywhere and he decided to do it. But 'It nearly drove me mad,' he told me with feeling. Later when it was all over and he had returned to England, he found it difficult to forget that Tom Mboya had been publicly rude to him on the day of the ceremony.

The main problem for Arthur Horner was that African regard for the finer points of formality was, at best, unreliable. The stands were built around the ceremonial arena and were marked off into areas for general guests and, of course, a special area for VIP's. Arthur had wanted the boys from the Technical College to be ushers in order to ensure that everyone was courteously guided to the correct seat, but Mboya vetoed this idea and said that he wanted KANU people to do it. Arthur conceded but he could

UHURU AND AFTER

not get any African to take it on. In the event, therefore, he had had to get a Captain from the British Army to do it. The day before the ceremony there was to be a meeting of the ushers at 2pm. They turned up at 3.15pm, many of them slightly tiddly from lunch, and said, 'We're not going to do this sort of European thing.' And on the day of Independence not one usher turned up in the VIP stand. Despite each guest having a numbered ticket, chaos ensued. People who were not supposed to be there, such as two Chinese with no English, settled themselves in the VIP seats.

This caused Mboya to turn on Horner and publicly swear at him, reducing Mrs Horner almost to tears. Arthur gave a spirited response and the Bishop of East Africa, the Rt. Reverend Leonard Beecher who was sitting nearby, intervened to try to defuse the situation. But in the event, to his everlasting gratitude, it was a large, powerful Kikuyu lady and a friend of Arthur's, who took charge in a cheerfully bossy way and sorted it all out to everybody's satisfaction.

Arthur's troubles were still not over. Unseasonally for mid-December, it poured with rain and many of the guests' cars became bogged down in mud on their way to the stands. Horner had sent the Public Works Department to the arena prior to the ceremony to patch the soft places but the Police had been told not to let anybody into the arena and so they stopped the PWD too. The quagmires therefore remained.

The Ugandan Prime Minister, Milton Obote had not actually been invited: the invitation had instead gone to the President of Uganda, who was the Kabaka. But word had reached Horner a few days beforehand that Obote had confiscated the Kabaka's Rolls Royce and had forbidden him from going. He planned to attend himself.

On his arrival in Nairobi Obote telephoned the Police and demanded an escort of despatch riders. They had not been briefed and had no idea that he had to be deposited at the back of the stands. They therefore duly escorted him into the arena with the intention of allowing him to alight at the foot of the VIP stand. When a black Rolls with a flag fluttering came into sight, Arthur said to the President, Jomo Kenyatta, 'Here come Prince Philip and the Governor.' And together they went down to greet them. But it was Obote's car. However, instead of reaching the foot of the stands it sank into the mud up to its axles. Mrs Obote, a delightful Mugandan lady, thought it terribly funny, but Obote's face was like a 'storm cloud'.

The crises, Arthur told me, were legion but nonetheless, at midnight on 12 December 1963, the Union Jack was lowered and, after Prince Philip's famous question, 'Are you sure you won't change your mind?' had been declined, the green flag with a shield and crossed spears signifying the nation of Kenya, was raised. The new National Anthem 'God Is Our Creation' was played.

Arthur also told me of the manner in which the National Anthem tune was chosen. Two tunes for the anthem were submitted to Jomo Kenyatta for consideration. One was written by a Kenya African studying music in Britain and it was on the lines of a traditional hymn tune. The other was a coastal Pokomo tune, which had been adapted by a European and his students at a music school at Ngong. When Kenyatta had listened to them both played by the Police band, he was hesitant. But someone said to him, 'Watch the *totos Mzee*.' And then the band played both tunes again. During the hymn tune the children stayed still but when the Pokomo tune was playing they began to dance. *Mzee* wisely settled on the latter. And so it was that small matters such as whether or not the children chanced to dance, helped to shape the new nations of Africa.

A Strong Wind of Change

GEORGE HAMPSON

From May 1960 to May 1963 I was DC, Thomsons Falls (now Nyahururu) in charge of Laikipia district (now Nyandarua). As a member of the committee appointed to review Administrative and Electoral Regions in the preparations for Independence, I proposed these Kikuyu names which, being appropriate in meaning, were accepted and gazetted. The district extended from the northern ranching area bordering Samburu through a central area of mixed farming including a sizeable Afrikaner population in the Ol Kalou Division, north of Naivasha. This was a period of intense political activity, culminating in Elections, the Lancaster House Conference and Internal Self-Government. The main thrust of government activity at all levels was the promotion of a multi-racial society with constitutional representation of minority groups, African, European and Asian. The Afrikaner farmers could not tolerate the prospect of an African government. They left their farms and trekked back to southern Africa. This released a large amount of land in the Ol Kalou area, which was augmented by the purchase of several large English-owned estates in the Wanjohi valley and Kipipiri to become one of the first re-settlement areas for landless Kikuyu. I had a team of Agricultural Officers, Resettlement and other specialist staff working on this for several months. We divided up the farms into units with a water supply, averaging about seven acres each. These were then allocated to selected Kikuyu on a freehold basis. The selections were made through the Rehabilitation pipeline with the help of local authorities and agricultural committees in the African Reserves. There were teething problems but on the whole the arrangements worked well and hundreds of Kikuyu families were settled with expectations of subsistence. At the same time we seriously doubted whether their traditional maize crops would succeed on land at that altitude. Livestock, particularly sheep, were more appropriate but the plots were too small for this and the pressing need was for mixed farming. This presented a long-term problem for the Agricultural Department and Settlement Officers.

My last appointment was as Officer-in-Charge (DC) Nairobi Extra-Provincial District in the transition period at Independence. I was, *ex officio*, a member of the City Council with direct responsibility for the surrounding African residential areas. The population of these areas was rapidly increasing and this produced serious social problems with implications for Law and Order. As the thousands of Mau Mau detainees had been released from the Detention and Rehabilitation centres, many had returned to Nairobi, in search of employment, rather than stay in the reserves. They were in effect detribalised. The Nairobi security committee of which I was chairman had much to deal with. There was some suspicion and resentment of the Kikuyu dominated Government among other tribes. Shortly after Independence unrest among some non-Kikuyu troops of the new Kenya Army stationed in Nairobi was quickly resolved with the ready co-operation of State House and some British Army help. Another factor contributing to unrest was the influence of the Marxist revolution in Zanzibar, which was disproportionately pervasive during the emotionally volatile period of Independence.

In my official capacity we played our part in the colourful Independence celebration. Thereafter we watched the rapid transformation of Nairobi into a cosmopolitan international city. Most remarkable was the large influx of diplomats and representatives of all kinds from many countries, and in particular from West Africa, China and the USSR. The Republic of China, for example, sought unsuccessfully to establish an Embassy with about 100 personnel. Generally expectations were high, undoubtedly too high, but there was much goodwill and confidence in the future. I retired and we returned to UK in May 1964

An Incident at Isiolo

PETER FULLERTON

As the countdown to Independence for Kenya quickened after the first Lancaster House conference in 1960, the future of the old Northern Frontier District (NFD) looked increasingly gloomy to those of us serving there. The population of Wajir, Garissa, Mandera, and Moyale districts was largely Somali. They were alarmed at the prospect of being handed over to an African Government, which they regarded as totally alien. The Somali word for such people was *Adon,* a term of contempt for an inferior race. They looked instead to Somalia, which they regarded as their homeland and their rightful destination after Independence.

At the DC's meeting in Isiolo in 1961, George Webb (Moyale), Bob Finnimore (Mandera), Tony Savage (Garissa), Mike Power (Isiolo) and I (Wajir) decided that it was time to confront the PC, Peter Walters, with the problem. We felt that we, and he, had a duty to make it clear to the Government at that stage that forcing the Somalis into independence within Kenya would be wrong and could only lead to bloodshed. We wanted it put on the record that we did not wish to be party to that policy. Events were to prove us right, but the demarche got short shrift from Peter Walters. The big picture of Kenya Independence, he told us, could not be dismantled. I doubt whether he ever transmitted to anyone in Nairobi the early warning we sounded.

There was another big picture which we felt was being totally ignored – Somali nationalism. In the 'Scramble for Africa', the Somali people had been divided and incorporated in five different colonies. In the north, British Somaliland had been made a Protectorate; in the east, the Italians had gained the 'Berbera Coast' and Mogadishu as a colony; the hinterland had remained part of the Ethiopian Empire, and was known as the Ogaden Province; the French had gained the port of Djibouti and a small territory around it to be known as French Somaliland; and the huge area between the Juba and the Tana rivers, which the Somalis had overrun in their long migration southwards, was incorporated into the colony and Protectorate of Kenya. In 1925, the whole of 'Jubaland' was given to the Italians as a reward for not gaining any of the German colonies after World War 1, and the Kenya border was moved southwards to where it is today.

After World War 2, a nationalist movement, the Somali Youth League, was formed in Mogadishu and Hargeisa for the foundation of Greater Somalia. This was to include all the five regions in which Somalis were living. The emblem of Greater Somalia, which later became the Somali flag, was a five-pointed star representing these regions. The movement was only partially successful. The British Government agreed that British Somaliland should join with Italian Somaliland, which was already on the road to Independence as a result of the defeat of the Italians in the war. Somalia duly gained Independence as a unified Republic in 1960. The Emperor of Ethiopia, restored to his throne after the war, adamantly refused to consider the secession of his Ogaden Province. The French too refused to allow Djibouti to join Somalia and offered instead a special status to the Somalis living in that territory.

The Somalis of the NFD watched all these events from afar. Almost all the 270,000 living there were semi-nomadic tribesmen. There were only four small townships with settled populations. At that time there were no Somali leaders in the NFD other than their chiefs, none of whom had had any formal education. Nor had they had much contact with any of the leaders of the nationalist movements in Somalia. The NFD Administration did its best to isolate the Somali tribesmen both from the politicians in Somalia and from the detribalised Somalis in Isiolo and Nairobi. This was not difficult given the strict movement control that was exercised under the Outlying Districts Ordinance, especially in the Somali districts; and the fact that there was no road traffic across the border between Somalia and the NFD.

It is curious to reflect now on how totally isolated the NFD was from the rest of Kenya. This was the policy maintained by successive 'Officers in Charge' and Provincial Commissioners – Vincent Glenday, Gerald Reece and Richard Turnbull. The policy was inherited from the Military Administration, which finally brought Law and Order to the area in the 1920s. Visitors of any kind were discouraged; traders were strictly licensed; and journalists were kept out. It is said that Turnbull was once asked by a newspaper reporter for a permit and retorted, 'There is nothing of any conceivable interest to the general public in the NFD; and if there was it would be confidential'. It was jokingly said by administrators that 'Everything in the NFD is generally prohibited unless it is specifically allowed'.

Independence Day in Somalia in 1960 was marked by jubilation in Wajir, Garissa and Mandera. I remember hosting a rather prim tea party for government staff in the *boma* to celebrate the event. But Independence for Somalia did not at that time destabilise the Administration or lead to any immediate political demands. Later that year, however, the accelerated timetable for Kenya Independence envisaged in the first Lancaster House Conference caused the Somalis in the NFD to realise with a shock that they were heading for 'Kikuyu rule'. Such a fate was simply not acceptable to them. The local chiefs, the *dubas,* civil servants, and Somali traders all began to make this plain to us. When Independence came to Kenya, they said, the Somali districts should be allowed to secede to Somalia.

It was hard not to agree with the justness of this cause. The Somalis were united by a common language, a common religion, and an oral tradition of being an Islamic people unique in Africa. They believed themselves to be (and indeed were) a different race from the Bantu and other tribes with whom they had come into contact in their long push southwards. They had, in fact, all the ingredients of nationhood on their side. They could also claim to have, thanks to the NFD Administration, a recognised geographical boundary with the rest of Kenya. The 'Somali line' had been imposed by Glenday in the 1930s. No tribal Somalis were allowed to live or graze south and west of this line. The line ran from the coast near Lamu, up the Tana River to Garissa, and thence along the Wajir/Isiolo District boundary to the

Ethiopian border near Moyale. It was rigorously enforced by DCs through the *dubas*, the NFD Tribal Police Force. The Somalis resented the line, since it had halted and reversed their migration and penetration southwards into Orma, Boran and Meru territory. But the line rapidly became the basis for secession and their territorial claim to join Somalia.

The mood of Somalis in the NFD towards the Kenya Government changed rapidly after 1960. There were no Local Councils or political representatives in Wajir at that time, but we did not need such bodies to tell us what was going on. Government staff began to talk quite openly about their contempt for Kenya politicians and their hope that HMG would allow the Somali districts to join Somalia. Farah Isaak, my interpreter, had been a sergeant in the KAR. He had seen a lot of Kenya, and war service in India and Burma. Like many Somalis who had been in the KAR he was proud of its record and displayed a shrewd loyalty to his later Government service. In return, he expected the Government to recognise that Somalis were different from other Kenyans. He simply could not understand how the British officers whom he had grown to know well and respected could be planning to betray and hand them over to a 'Kikuyu' government.

We got the same message from the *dubas*. They were 'the thin red line,' and we depended on them totally for the effective running of our districts. The loyalty of the *dubas*, and their success in implementing unpopular policies on grazing control and tax collection was legendary. They lost friends and made many enemies amongst their own people in carrying out our orders, particularly in impounding stock to pay Court fines and taxes. They were prepared to do this, not just because they were paid by the Government but because they could see that the regime run by DCs brought peace and harmony. That regime had seemed likely to them to last a long time. The thought of it disappearing quite soon and the prospect of having Kikuyu DCs was enough to test that loyalty. The *dubas* began to wonder whether we were on their side. As DOs we were closer to the *dubas* than to any other people in the district. We did long foot and camel safaris with them; we camped and ate with them; and we trained alongside them for the annual twenty-five mile forced march and shooting competition (the Reece Shield). They talked more freely to us than any other Somalis. It was painful to hear them say: 'Surely you won't let this happen to us, will you'.

That was the message we felt we had to convey to Peter Walters at the DCs meeting in Isiolo. I think he regarded it as either subversive, or thought that we were all suffering from 'Somaliitis'. This was the popular term for officers who had served too long in the NFD and saw everything from the Somali point of view. In fact as DCs we all sincerely believed that it would be wrong to include the Somali Districts in an independent Kenya because it would not be accepted by them and would lead to violence. We were right.

I have chosen to call this memoir: 'An incident at Isiolo.' It reminded me of 'The incident on the Curragh' in 1912. At that time the Government had instructed British regiments in Ireland to prepare to move in and disarm the Protestants in Ulster who were determined to resist the imposition of Home Rule. The British officers stationed on the river Curragh let it be known to their commanders that they would not obey the order. The order was withdrawn. The army thereafter referred to it as an incident and not a mutiny.

The 'Incident at Isiolo' achieved nothing at the time, but I am glad to think that we at least put down a marker. Later that year (1961) in the first Kenya General Election Ali Aden Lord was elected unopposed as MP for the Province on a secessionist ticket. He attended the second Lancaster House Conference in 1962 at which the Colonial Secretary, Reginald Maudling, was persuaded to agree to a Commission 'to enquire into the state of public opinion' in the NFD. More than a year later, the Commission reported that Somali opinion in the NFD was unanimous in favour of secession. Opinion in Nairobi dictated otherwise. In March 1963, Duncan Sandys made a statement that the NFD would remain part of Kenya. Somalia broke off diplomatic relations with Britain and all the Somali chiefs and headmen in Wajir resigned. The scene was set for violence. Later, two DOs, Neville Judge and Ken Arnold were assassinated, in two separate attacks, by *shifta*. John Golds, my successor at Wajir in 1961, continued for two turbulent years after Independence, quite literally to hold the fort, as it became once again the DC's residence. His experiences made my time in Wajir seem like a golden age.

A Price on My Head

JOHN GOLDS

I stayed in Wajir District for almost five years and what a wonderful and exciting experience it proved to be. During this time much of Moyale district was added to Wajir and later I often seemed to be responsible for Mandera district as well. One spent at least two weeks each month on safari, living under canvas, and I often walked 20 to 25 miles a day. However I preferred to do most of my travelling on a camel if possible. Here for the first time I became an active Magistrate (First Class) and whilst hearing my first criminal cases reflected that, although I had passed the required examinations, I wish they had included a little practical instruction on running a court room.

I remember in one of my first cases, robbery with violence, I found the accused guilty and sentenced him to two years in prison. He bent down and I thought how courteous, bowing to me on having heard his case so fairly. He took off his shoe and threw it at me. In another case where I had to use an interpreter, I read out the charge and asked if he pleaded 'guilty' or 'not guilty.' The interpreter and accused spoke to and fro without translation to me. I eventually said, 'What is going on, he only has to reply guilty or not guilty' The interpreter replied, 'Sir, I am only trying to save time. He said he was not guilty, but since we all know he is guilty why does he not save time for us all and be honest?'

Within two years Wajir openly became the centre of Somali Youth League (SYL) demands that the North Eastern Region should either remain under British control or be permitted to secede to eastern Somalia. Clearly a policy which might have been acceptable to the British government, but was certainly not acceptable to the new Government of Kenya. An Emergency was declared and my time in the North Eastern Region became one of great violence.

My first year was also one of record rainfall for the NFD (average annual rainfall for Wajir was 3", in one month alone we had 30"). Needless to say I was known as the wettest DC ever to serve in Wajir – I hope they were referring to the rain and the floods!

However, despite security being the prime concern, we managed to make many advances in improving the conditions and independence of the Muslim peoples of the area. I created the first District Council (ADC) in the north, legalised the sale of the fairly harmless drug, miraa, control of which was almost impossible, and taxed its import. With this income plus a cess on all exported livestock the Wajir ADC became wealthy and provided the funds to improve significantly the district education, health and the water supplies, including the protection of the incredible system of Wajir wells, alleged to have been dug by a mythical tribe of giants.

I learnt how to ride a camel with the *dubas rakub* section and even learnt to like camel milk and meat. As Commodore, I encouraged and expanded the off beat Royal Wajir Yacht Club. On ceremonial occasions one wore a Royal Navy cocked hat, epaulets stuck to one's shoulders, black bow tie, kikoi and little else! We particularly enjoyed telling our VIP guests that the club was having a 'Black Tie,' supper in their honour and watching their embarrassment arriving perfectly turned out to find their hosts, very strangely garbed. One guest was John Profumo, the Minister of Defence; and even today my photograph appears frequently in the strange uniform of the Commodore of the RWYC with John Profumo. An occasion often described by the world's press as one of his last happy moments before he was forced to resign from the British government.

Because of the Somali insurgency and Kenya's approaching Independence, which the Somalis wanted no part of, and because of the photogenic appeal of the district, the fort, the Beau Geste film and a Camel Corps, we got more than our fair share of world publicity during my period as DC. But one of the chief joys was that, with one exception, the whole of the Somali *dubas* in Wajir remained loyal to the end and they remained responsible for much of the security work in spite of the huge pressures on them by the Somalia Government and the SYL, to desert with their weapons. I had agreed that I would serve for not less than twelve months under the new Government, led by President Kenyatta, but first I asked for some of my large accumulation of leave. At the end of 1963, just before Independence, I went on a carefully pre-planned six months leave.

I first flew to Jordan at the invitation of Glubb Pasha and his famous Camel Corps. Thence to Stockholm, where, in the interval of a performance of a stirring opera, the manager of the Opera house appeared on the stage and asked if there was a John Golds in the audience. If so he was to come to his office. I went and was told that the DC acting for me, Neville Judge, a New Zealander, had been tragically murdered and that the new Kenya Government had asked me to return immediately. But there was a second message from the Colonial Office in London saying that I was not to return without first flying to London to report.

I flew to London to be told not to return to Kenya, as HMG would find the murder of yet another expatriate DC most embarrassing! I agreed that I might find it equally embarrassing; but, as I had promised both the Kenya Government and the Kenya Somalis I would return, I defied instructions and flew back to Kenya the following day, for another year of service in Wajir.

During that year I had a £500 price placed on my head by the Somalia Government as a reward to anyone who managed to kill me, I was rather offended by the smallness of the bounty! Twenty years later I met the Somali responsible for my death threat, driving a taxi in Atlanta, where he was attending a Police Command Course for overseas students. The USA was providing free tuition and accommodation but his Government had not paid him for some time and therefore to feed himself he had to drive a taxi between lessons. He kindly turned off the meter when he learnt who I was in return for any inconvenience he had caused me! But to return to Wajir, I was ambushed a number of times but well protected by my Somali *dubas*. However, many of the improvements we had worked hard to create were destroyed by the *shifta* terrorists.

In late 1964 I decided enough was enough and asked to retire. At the urging of Lord Howick (previously Sir Evelyn Baring), I joined the Commonwealth Development Corporation (CDC). So ended a wonderful ten years in which I remember particularly two great senior officers whom I served under, Sir Francis Loyd and Douglas Penwill; and two hugely supportive Governors, Lord Howick (who I then served under for a further ten years in the CDC) and Malcolm MacDonald who tried so hard to find a peaceful solution to the Somali crisis and was prepared to give me significant discretion in my negotiations with the Somalia Government.

After Jamhuri and Uhuru

MICHAEL PHILIP

December 1962 to December 1963 was the year of *Jamhuri*, Internal Self-Government, the first step to Uhuru. It was thought that there should be a complete change of nomenclature to make the new regime, so Provinces became Regions, PCs became Civil Secretaries, DCs became Regional Government Agents and DOs, Assistant Regional Government Agents. Never once during that year did any African ask to see 'Bwana ARGA'. We remained 'Bwana DO' or 'Bwana DC' or 'Bwana PC'. So obvious was this that after Independence the new Government reverted to the old titles.

I started the year of *Jamhuri* in Central Nyanza, living in Maseno, but running four divisions. This situation was brought about by the early retirement of many DOs in early compensation schemes, to enable the administration to recruit Africans to be trained 'in service' to eventually take over as DCs and PCs. We left Maseno on 19 March 1963 for long leave, which we had chosen to take at the coast rather than take three young children to Britain. While on leave I was dragooned into being a Returning Officer in Mombasa during that year's general election. I also learned that I was posted to Embu, which had become the regional HQ of the newly formed Eastern Region. I was to be Assistant Secretary, Admin., equivalent to the erstwhile PA to the PC, but also with duties connected to the Regional Assembly.

The *Jamhuri* re-shuffle had split the old Northern Province, taking the Boran districts of Isiolo and Marsabit into Eastern Region, leaving the Somali Districts to the North Eastern Region. We arrived in Embu on 27 August.

On 28 June, while I had been on leave at the coast, Daudi Dabasso Wabera the first non-white officer to be a DC in the NFD, was assassinated in Isiolo district by Somali terrorists, known as *shifta*. Killed also was the Boran senior chief Haji Galma Dida. This tragedy opened what became a war against the *shifta*.

David Worthy was immediately available and was sent to Isiolo to take over. When we arrived in Embu, I discovered that David was only to be temporarily in Isiolo. I asked the Civil Secretary if I could be posted there when Worthy left. This was agreed. There followed ten weeks in a very boring job in a boring *boma*. Then in November we were posted to Isiolo.

Some time before Internal Self-Government, the British Government had appointed a commission to consider the future of the Northern Province. They found and reported that a significant majority of the people there opted for secession to Somalia. They, being Hamitic and mostly Muslim, chose to be governed by Hamites and Muslims rather than Bantu and Christians. To them KANU, the majority party, meant Bantu and, as the Hamitic tribes had never been defeated by the Bantu in history, it was extremely difficult for them to accept Bantu supremacy through politics. The British Government, having received the Commission's findings, took the weak way out and declared it must be a matter for the 'newly sovereign Government of Kenya' to decide. Their not unexpected declaration was, 'we shall not give up one inch of our Sovereign Territory'.

I took over from David Worthy one month before the celebrations of full Independence on 12 December. The Boran and Somali in the District were in no mood to celebrate and Special Branch reported that the local *shifta* were planning to disrupt the celebrations. A Company of 11 Bn Kenya Rifles was sent from Nanyuki to help protect the celebrating Kikuyu and Meru from Isiolo Township. I held a Garden Reception on the last day of the Raj and at sundown we had a full-dress parade, the *dubas* in their flowing white ceremonial uniforms, and the DC in whites, sword, helmet and all. The occasion was very moving and there were tears in my eyes when the Sgt. Major handed me the flag. I still have that Union Jack. The show of force kept the *shifta* away and the celebrations went on all day at the airstrip. The Kenya Rifles Company Commander, an old friend called Tony Catchpole, and I, and from time to time, my wife and children, spent most of the day on top of the water tower, from whence we had a long view of any approach to the airstrip.

Before the murder of Wabera and the Senior Chief, the Boran were solidly behind secession. That is not to say they approved of terrorism. Many young Boran did become *shifta* and the threat of assassination and theft of stock kept the tribe's Elders from co-operating with the government. Despite the supposedly inviolate Somali line, west of which the Somali tribes were not allowed to encroach, Borana had gradually been infiltrated by Degodia, Aulihan and Abd Wak. Most Boran manyattas had a resident *Shegat*, a Somali who was allowed to live among them to teach the children the Koran. These *Shegats*, however, also taught the children to be Somali. Thus, in Isiolo District, the Northern Province Somali terrorists found sanctuary from their own area where there was a far greater concentration of security forces. My job, as I saw it, was to win over the Boran, not necessarily to change their political aspirations, but to turn them against using terrorist means to gain their political ends. The first step was to show them practically that we would deal with those that succoured the *shifta* as harshly as the *shifta* dealt with Loyalists.

The best instrument to this end, in my opinion, was the *dubas*. After the murder of Wabera, their DC, morale slumped. By smartening them up and working them very hard they soon regained their pride. The Kenya Police, because of their static duty commitments, escorts, court duties and guard duties, were never able to offer more than one or two constables for an operation. Usually we only took *dubas*, unless a Police General Service Unit or the Army were involved.

The meagre number of *dubas* were divided into Sections of ten. I chose the best ten to be the DC's Section and they were identified as the elite by wearing two leather bandoleers instead of one. With reluctance, I bought and issued khaki turbans to be used on patrol. I say with reluctance because *dubas* means Red Hat and their distinctive headgear was part of their *heshima*, their pride of service. The NCO in charge of the DC's section was Sgt Racho, a tough character with many tales of Isiolo *dubas*' victories against marauding Abd Wak or Degodia.

I hoped that continual raids on villages known to be militantly secessionist would keep the *shifta* out of the district. Long safaris among the Boran showed them that there was a Government with teeth. When, which was unhappily often, I had information of *manyattas* succouring the *shifta*, I quickly took in the men and seized ten per cent of their stock. When charged, if found guilty, the stock was sold to pay the fine. This was our way of showing that it was as onerous to support the *shifta* as it was dangerous to stand against them. After a General Service Unit platoon was ambushed, their vehicles burned and their weapons taken, we raided the *manyattas* in which the *shifta* had sheltered. They were gone with the weapons, but the helpers had their stock seized.

When we took stock, cattle and camels, we would run them from beyond Garba Tula to Isiolo. And I mean run. We did not want to let the *shifta* get ahead and prepare an ambush. Depending on the size of the operation there would be two, three or four sections of *dubas*. One section would run with the camels and scout ahead, while the other sections followed closely behind in a lorry and a land-rover. Every hour a section would be relieved. In this way the stock would run the seventy or eighty miles in as short a time as possible. Camels will put down milk as often as you milk them and the *dubas* would fill a mug on the run. Camel's milk kept us going until we arrived in Isiolo. I ran with my section and was consequently fitter than ever before. The *dubas* loved to be led.

On arrival home in Isiolo, Shirley, my long-suffering wife, while holding her nose, would dispose of my camel-stinking clothes, while I re-hydrated in a bath.

The area most visited on operations was the almost impenetrable area of 'wait a bit' acacia thorn around Skot on the Isiolo/Wajir/Garissa border. The biggest operation there involved a battalion of Kenya Rifles under Colonel Anderson, a great friend, and three sections of *dubas*. The Kenya Rifles were ambushed and lost three men. However we came up with the *shifta* and took their camels. We then had the greatest difficulty extracting ourselves from this thorny wilderness. Col. Anderson, in an aeroplane overhead, could see our route, but messages thrown out of the aeroplane kept falling into impenetrable bush.

Neville Judge spent a night with us on his way to Wajir to take over as DC. He left his VW Beetle, a proud possession, with us. Tragically he was shot and killed by *shifta* a short while later.

Although the *shifta* problem was always there, there was still a district to be run. The Court, both Criminal and Civil took up a lot of time. My case numbers in 1964 were over a thousand. Taxes still had to be collected. Stock sales had to be organized and protected. Stock theft and affrays, unconnected with the Emergency, still happened. There was one very serious incursion by Rendille, who stole hundreds of camels from the Boran in the far north of the district. This provoked a counter-raid and the Boran managed to recover their camels and took some from the Rendille as bonus. The Rendille massed and gave chase. By this time word had reached Isiolo and the *dubas* reached the area and intercepted the stock before battle commenced. The Rendille fled. The Boran stayed with the camels, and I held court on the spot. I hoped the Samburu DC would deal with his people.

Because the Isiolo Boran and Somali had boycotted local elections there was no elected County Council. The affairs of the Council were run by a Commission appointed by Nairobi. The Commission was the District Commissioner. For some years the Game Department had been pressing for an area south of the Uaso Nyiro River, but contiguous with the Samburu Game Park, to be declared a reserve. The project had always been blocked by the Council. As it was obvious that a Game Reserve would be a great asset to the District I, as the County Council, decreed it should be and duly set aside the land, which included the much-frequented Buffalo Springs. The reserve brings in a considerable revenue to the County Council.

Isiolo Bath Club with its swimming pool was a great social asset to the *boma*. Late one night a visiting Police Armourer was drinking beer at the Bar with other Kenya Police officers. He was playing with a grenade, removing and replacing the pin. In a moment of inattention he let the handle spring up, arming the grenade. Thinking to minimize the danger, he threw the grenade into the pool where it detonated on the bottom and caused huge cracks in the concrete sides. That was the end of swimming at the Bath Club for some time.

Eventually the Kenya Rifles became a permanent fixture in the north. Their supply convoys would stop in Isiolo on their way south and invariably dump bodies outside my office claiming that they had been ambushed and these had been killed by return fire. Invariably the *dubas* would identify the dead as innocent Boran who happened to be near the road. 'This is Guyo Diba: he has a hundred camels; he is not a *shifta*,' they would say. I opened dozens of Preliminary Inquiries, which I sent on to Nairobi, seldom endorsed as justifiable deaths.

For operations within Isiolo district, I insisted that there should be *dubas* present, who could identify innocent Boran before they were shot. To many of the Kenya Rifles, and indeed the Kenya Police, anything in a *shuka* was a *shifta*. While the DC was still chairman of the District Security Committee such rules could be enforced. Later things changed.

Eventually it was deemed embarrassing to the newly sovereign Government to have a white DC in the emergency area. More and more the Army was allowed *carte blanche* on operations and indiscriminately shot Somali and Boran. My successor, a Meru, was not interested in actively keeping the Boran neutral and alive. He relegated the *dubas* to static duties, mostly to guard his house!

I was posted briefly to Kisumu as Deputy Civil Secretary, Nyanza, but was very soon transferred to Nairobi as Under Secretary in the Ministry of Agriculture. It was my good luck that the Minister was Bruce McKenzie. He and Charles Njonjo, the Attorney General, were the *eminences grises* sensibly advising Jomo Kenyatta and later Daniel arap Moi, on policies that kept Kenya reasonably governed for many years. As well as having the portfolios of coffee, tea, wheat, maize, sisal and horticulture, I became McKenzie's PA preparing briefs for answers in parliament and accompanying him overseas on aid-seeking visits and negotiations to enter the International Coffee Organization to which I became Kenya's Permanent Delegate. I remained in the Ministry until I resigned in 1967.

The *shifta* war dragged on for many years and only ended when Somalia realized that, if it continued, the Kenya Army would kill every Somali in Kenya.

Formally, a treaty was concluded between Kenya and Somalia at Kinshasa in 1967. But *shifta* activity went on.

UHURU AND AFTER

The Army Mutiny

JOHN JOHNSON*

In January 1964 I was descending from Point Lenana on Mt Kenya. The mountain loomed large in our lives in Central Province. It was important to the history and culture of the Kikuyu people. It had been one of the last strongholds of Mau Mau. It dominated our horizons when it was clear; and it beckoned. I had been up on its moorland several times and this was my last chance before returning home.

My wife met me at the top of the Naro Moru track with the news that the Tanganyika Rifles had mutinied at Dar-es-Salaam and Tabora and British troops had been called in. By the time we got back to Thika, the Uganda Rifles at Jinja had arrested a government minister and refused to obey orders. The situation in Kenya was tense.

Soon afterwards there was trouble at Lanet Barracks, Nakuru with 11 Bn Kenya Rifles. The Government of Jomo Kenyatta did not hesitate to ask for help from the British troops who were still stationed in the country. The key targets – airport, TV and radio station and telephone exchange – were secured. The British CO of 3 Bn Kenya Rifles based in Langata, Nairobi, took the precaution of sending the keys of the armoury and ammunition stores out of the camp. Despite incitement from the mutineers at Lanet, 3 Bn remained loyal.

In Lanet a force of Kenya Police and Royal Horse Artillery in the infantry role exchanged shots with the mutineers. Then the RHA attacked the barracks and after a short battle, the mutineers surrendered. It was all over in a day and a half. The Kenyan troops had a grievance over pay. Politicians had promised increases when Uhuru came, but none were given. The trouble in Uganda was also dealt with by British troops. In Tanganyika the mutiny had been more widespread and President Nyerere could not initially be found. The Kenya Government had taken quick decisions, not shirking the embarrassment of pictures of British troops in action after Independence.

---

* With acknowledgement of the detailed information in the Newsletter of the King's African Rifles.

The Kenya Institute of Administration

NICK SCOTT

I joined the Kenya Institute of Administration in December 1964, a year after Independence. My DC from Homa Bay, Ezekiel Josiah, was by then a Civil Service Commissioner and was on the panel that appointed me to this post that led directly to my subsequent appointments in Papua New Guinea and Australia.

The KIA grew out of the old Community Development training centre, Jeanes School, with a huge expansion and upgrading of buildings during the period 1961–3, largely financed by USAID. To the best of my recollection there were departments of accounting, administration, community development, law and local government, with staff drawn from government departments and local government, and with an academic team from Syracuse University with specialists in economics, law and politics. There was usually also a Ford Foundation expert in residence, specialising in human relations and related themes.

The administration training group was set up chiefly to give new African District Officers a six-month course in the basics of their duties, ranging from letter and report writing to local development planning, law, the supervision of local courts, constitutional development and ethics. My own first assignment was as the administrator of a course for perhaps twenty-five newly recruited African diplomats, from all over sub-Saharan Africa, financed by the Carnegie Endowment for International Peace and run by a senior politics lecturer from the London School of Economics, lasting some eight weeks.

I then took over a course that had started rather experimentally a year or more before as a programme for senior officers, which had lapsed for lack of staff. Well before mid 1965, I had relaunched this as a series of senior management courses which I ran until my departure on retirement from Kenya service in mid 1969. This programme provided what was in reality a basic management course mainly for the new African District Commissioners and Provincial heads of departments, a six-week course running five times a year. Its content was guided, and to a degree provided, by members of a committee drawn from senior managers in the private sector, including notably the General Manager of Shell Kenya. Topics included such basics of management courses as communications skills, understanding motivation, decision making and delegation; much emphasis was put on syndicate discussion, particularly in handling elaborate administrative case studies left by my predecessors. Finally an important part of every course was an investigative project chosen by each syndicate of students themselves and perhaps involving a week of travel and interviewing, with the requirement to write up a report and present it to their peers and to the directing staff at the end of the course.

Not surprisingly just about all the forty-one District Commissioners came through the course in my time. I was fascinated, on visiting the Institute of Local Government Studies at Birmingham University in 1983, to find that President Moi had consigned his entire cadre of DCs to an extended and rigorous retraining program there, nearly fifteen years after I had left the KIA.

A small start was made with the recruitment of African officers into the Provincial Administration with the handful of African Assistant Administrative Officers in the early 1950s. Even if their numbers were too small to make much difference at the time, several of them did eventually find their way into senior positions in the Independence era. The great expansion of the Service during the Mau Mau Emergency brought large numbers of young Africans with intermediate or secondary education into the Service, initially as District Assistants or as junior staff in land consolidation and registration, but left them well placed for advancement just before or soon after Independence. Clerks with long service in the Provincial Administration had similar opportunities. But the greatest opportunities went to the graduates of the 'Mboya Airlift' as they returned from the USA in the first years of Independence. Only in the early 1960s were the first Africans being appointed as DCs. Besides long-serving members of the Provincial Administration some senior professional officers, such as Education Officers, found their way into this senior level of the department.

A Journey Back in Time

HENRY WRIGHT

My wife and I sailed by dhow from Lamu to Kipini (Tana River District) in April 1996. The sea was rough. As soon as we cruised into the estuary at Kipini, we felt a lot better. The dhow moored not far from the old DC's house. I could see the dramatic changes to the estuary due to major erosion. Local residents, Swahili and Arabs, visited the dhow out of curiosity as Europeans hardly ever visited Kipini, especially by *dhow*. We walked into Kipini eager to see if anything had changed since we last saw it in 1964.

I had lived and worked in Kipini in 1957 and 1958 and mature locals were trying to remember me. Some did, and one man, Mohammed, remembered a strange seven-day safari we did together on the Tana River. We introduced ourselves to some local dignitaries and had a look at the old DC's house and office. (The District HQ had been moved up river.) The office had collapsed and the DC's house looked every bit of its ninety years of age. The three graves of European Administrators and a wife who died there in the early 20th Century were covered in bush. We paid two of my old employees to clear the ground and clean them. The ghosts of Kipini still haunt the old *boma*.

I planned the next day's safari. We were to walk to the ruined city of Ungwana wa Mashaa via a track past the old DC's house, then to the beach and to the ruined cities of Shaka and Mwana. We had a large bottle of water and some fruit. This would have been an eight-hour safari.

It was very hot when we arrived in Ungwana. Some locals were drawing water from a well that had been dug at Ungwana more than 500 years ago. We walked amongst ruined houses and tombs that had been part of Ungwana for just as long. Fresh, steamy buffalo droppings were seen and we decided to walk towards the sea and estuary for relief. We walked around Ras Shaka and came to the city of Shaka which was eroding rapidly into the sea forty years ago. After high tide, I used to find shards of Ming china and pottery in the eroding cliff face. On this occasion the land had reclaimed itself a hundred and fifty meters and the city was covered by thick bush. We walked further towards Mwana

At the riverine village of Ozi there were ten canoes tied up to a stake. We had to clamber over them to reach the bank. There was a meeting that day of visiting local headmen who came down to meet us. When they realised I had been a DO forty years before in this area, they made us welcome. Ozi had changed little over forty years. The huts were the same design, mud walls, thatched roof and earth floors. The school was similar with simple home-made furniture. The maize fields looked healthy and there is always a good rice crop as the soil is fertile, being silted twice a year from the floods.

On return to Kipini we were befriended by an African named Orsman, who invited us to see the remains of the motor launch Pelican. This was the DC's boat which was used in the 1950s to go on safari to administer the local riverine tribe, the Wapokomo. Orsman took us to a mangrove swamp just outside Kipini and there in mud and water was the skeleton of the once magnificent motor launch. It was the Pelican, as we could recognise the name of the side, and just the rusted hull remained. I had memories of many happy safaris on board.

UHURU AND AFTER

A Mau Mau General to Tea

JEAN JOHNSON

My husband was appointed High Commissioner to Kenya in 1986, which had been our fervent hope as a final post in the Diplomatic Service.

I had first gone out to Embu, as a young bride, in 1956 to join John who was a District Officer. We lived in a bungalow set in a large garden, with distant views to Mt Kenya. We had no electricity; cooking was done in a smoky outside kitchen on a *kuni* stove, and we used pressure and aladdin lamps for lighting. Our milk was delivered each day from a farm at the top of the *boma* by a man with a churn perched on a bit of old sacking strapped to the back of his bicycle. If demand exceeded supply the deficit would be made up from the furrow which was fed by one of the rivers that flowed down from Mt Kenya. Boiling and straining were essential.

Later we moved to Kerugoya Division where there was a big vegetable garden to look after and then with great excitement, we bought a cow from one of the settler farms and supplied fresh milk to the *boma* – I had been brought up on a farm in Wales. Babies arrived. Our fair-haired children were a great fascination on public occasions such as sports days. The chiefs' wives and older women loved to pass them around from knee to knee. Our childrens' first play mates were the children of our domestic staff. Having a first baby without the support of a mother or health visitor could have been difficult but Barbara Wilks the DC's wife, who had three daughters, was a great support to me.

Life was never dull and I do not remember being lonely. All around Kenya there were gardens that had been expertly laid out and planted up by *boma* wives, often with the help of detainees from the local jail who were inside for non payment of *kodi*. A DO was always on call. Sitting one evening there was a shout from outside, '*Bwana, Bwana*, come quickly, *Bwana* Akers houseboy has fallen down the *choo*' – and he had too, on his way to deliver a message. Not a pleasant job getting him out. One day John was asked to plant a tree in the centre of Kerugoya *boma*. After the ceremony the elders told me that their folklore said that if the sapling died the man who had planted it would also die shortly afterwards. I watered and tended it and it thrived and grew into a fine specimen. However, many years later it was chopped down to make room for a new office block.

But it was time to move on again. All our belongings were piled onto the back of a lorry with our grinning cook Mureithi sitting in one of our armchairs on top, prepared for the long dusty journey to Kericho.

This brings me to our return to Kenya. This time with a container full of belongings to be moved into the High Commissioner's Residence in Muthaiga; a lovely house with a beautiful garden and a thatched *banda* at the bottom which had been built for bird watching by Malcolm MacDonald. We were warned that we would find that many changes had taken place since our colonial days. Old friends and ex-colleagues greeted us and it was wonderful to be back. Geoffrey Kariithi, now a Minister, who had been with us in Kerugoya, was one of our first guests, and he and Mary invited us to their coffee farm in Ruiru. We had lunch in Embu with Jeremiah Nyagah, also a Minister. Together we listened to a recording of Jomo Kenyatta's speech in 1963 to the white farmers in Nakuru. Everywhere we went in Central Province we saw development: new schools, coffee and tea plantations, farms, and smiling faces. However, it was disturbing to see the hundreds of eager, bright-eyed children going into school – where would they find employment later on? There had been a population explosion.

As John went round the country we were always shown much hospitality. DCs and PCs felt they were introducing an old colleague and we were proudly shown the boards in the DC's offices bearing the names of all the past DCs, European and African. We visited our old homes. The houses were well looked after but in the gardens several other houses had been built and in any spare space maize, potatoes and beans were growing. Whenever our children came out for a visit one of John's old TPs, Mbochi, from Kikuyu and Chiefs Munyutu and Reuben and their wives would invite us to their homes for a tea party. We in turn invited them to the Queen's Birthday Party at the residence and they would enjoy being at the same party as their Ministers, Ambassadors and all our other guests.

Sir Michael Blundell, our neighbour, now in his 80s became a dear friend. He would visit us most Saturdays for tea always carrying two baskets of home grown fruit and vegetables, one for our house staff, and one for us. He told us of a recent visit to his old farm near Nakuru which he had sold to Kenyans long ago. He found the pipes of his carefully laid irrigation scheme broken, his beautiful garden a maize and bean *shamba*; on the lush pastures where his prize winning cattle had grazed there were now native goats and sheep on poor grass. But, everywhere there was happiness, smiling faces and friendship. As he drove away he thought: well, that farm had supported himself, his wife and daughter Suzie – now it is the livelihood for over 100 people. He was content.

John found that young Kenyan journalists were interested in Mau Mau and the Emergency. They introduced him to (ex) General China. Towards the end of our time we invited him to tea at the residence. He arrived with his young wife. Unlike most of the other freedom fighters he was prosperous and was educating two of his daughters in America. He told us his own Mau Mau story in a delightful mixture of English, Swahili, and Kikuyu. Whoever would have thought in 1956 that the notorious General China would be taking tea in the High Commissioner's residence in 1990.

A Rap on the Wrist

VERONICA BELLERS

In 1940 South African Troops and battalions of the King's African Rifles were pouring into the Northern Frontier District on their way to take part in the Abyssinian Campaign. The area was on a war footing and more administrative officers were required. In October my father, Hal (C. H.) Williams, was transferred to Garissa from Narok. Because women were strongly discouraged from living in the NFD even in peacetime, he lived there alone, leaving my mother to stay where she could with her toddler son. Rented accommodation proved too expensive, staying with her aunt could only be temporary, and working as a nanny was not a very happy experience.

Once the main body of troops had left for the campaign, low morale began to sap his energy. He did not have enough to do, he was lonely and he was worried about money. In March 1941 he sent an official request for a transfer to 'The Hon. Chief Secretary, Nairobi. Thro' Officer-in-Charge, NFD'.

1. *I have the honour to ask that the question of my transfer from Garissa be considered by Government.*
2. *The facts are that in October 1940 I was stationed in Narok when I was notified of my transfer to Garissa. In common with the great majority of the Administration I had applied to be released for military service but had not applied for administrative service in the NFD and had no desire to leave Narok, involving as it did the keeping up of two separate establishments. However as I understood it was a special case and that my services were considered to be of use to the war effort at Garissa (which was then a war zone) the situation was accepted without complaint and I was only too happy to stay as long as those conditions applied.*
3. *I would now submit however that these conditions no longer apply and would ask that my transfer be arranged as soon as is convenient.*
    I have the honour to be
    Sir,
    Your obedient servant.

His request did not find favour. Hoskins, the Chief Secretary made him sweat for five weeks before sending this blistering reply on 26th April 1941.

A RAP ON THE WRIST

PERSONAL & CONFIDENTIAL
Dear Williams,
I have deliberately delayed answering your letter of 11th April for some time until I could have an opportunity of discussing it with Reece and also of making a cool and unbiased judgement on it ...

After five years of the most comfortable stations in the Colony you have been required to serve in the Northern Frontier District and you have been there six months and find yourself bored to death with no work to do. The work in the NFD and in other outlying stations – even in Narok – is what you make it. If you are content to wait for work to be forced on you there may be less than half an hour's work a day, but I cannot believe that in a district of the extent and population of the Garissa District there is not ample work, and surely a mass of arrears of work, to keep two men busy ...

As to the double establishment, your wife, has, I know, relations in Kenya, and my latest intelligence was that she was with you in Garissa.

You were certainly sent for a special purpose to Garissa but the war is not over, though its focus has altered ...

Had you put your back into the job at Garissa, even though you did not like it, I would have done my best to have met your wishes over your next station, but the best advice I can give you now is work. Look for work and make yourself enjoy work with the consolation that you are doing the job that you are required to do in wartime.
Yours sincerely, ...'

The letter gave him a tremendous jolt. By the time it arrived, Hoskins was correct about my mother's arrival. Without telling my father, or seeking permission from the Administration, she had packed the toddler and the ayah into the family Ford V8 and set off before the dawn from Thika. To my father's amazed delight, she drew up at his house just after lunch. The fan belt was in tatters and would have torn a few yards further on.

In July Hoskins wrote again:

Dear Harold,
Some weeks ago I wrote you a stinker ... You deserved it!

Gerald Reece is now in Nairobi ... [and] seems to be very pleased with the way you are doing the job and I want to thank you for the way you have got down to it ....

Good luck to you both, don't let your wife stay too long, as she hasn't quite got your robust frame.

My mother and father spent a happy year in Garissa. She was quite robust enough to survive and she was able to make life more comfortable for my father and others in the *boma*. She brought a dozen hens from Nairobi and made a vegetable garden, she nursed the sick and injured that arrived in the *boma* and helped my father on safari. She exploded the myth that women should not live in the NFD and thereafter they accompanied their husbands without government demur.

Valedictory

TEXT OF A LETTER FROM PAUL MBOYA MBE TO C. H. WILLIAMS CMG, OBE

2 November 1956
Dear Williams,
I have taken this opportunity for writing to you because I have received information that you are retiring during this month. Myself I think that you have not reached the retiring age. The news of your retirement is being known gradually in South Nyanza District, and the people who have heard of it are taken by surprise.

I greatly appreciate your being in Nyanza Province for a long time and I think you have spent most of your life in the Province. I will not forget the period when you were District Officer in South Nyanza and how you were cycling in the Karachuonyo location, teaching people how to grow fruits and how to put manure in the gardens. It was in 1934 and early in 1935 when you did so. You left the Province for a certain period, and later you joined it as the District Commissioner of Kakamega, North Nyanza, after which you were appointed the Provincial Commissioner of Nyanza.

Your being in Nyanza Province for seven years as the Provincial Commissioner, has brought immeasurable blessings to the inhabitants of the Province. You have been leading us peacefully, gently and happily. You have been always kind to the people of South Nyanza. The only example which I have learnt from you and also which pleased me is your seeking advice from African leader at the time of crisis. You prevented Mau Mau from entering the Province because you were calling people and talking to them together in order to find means of preventing it. Not only for Mau Mau that you did so, but also when the Province confronted with any serious trouble.

You have been organizing peacefully because you did not like force. I believe many people like myself will be surprised to hear that you have gone without bidding them good-bye, although this is due to shortage of time.

Through good leadership with which you have led our council, we have now improved conditions of the South Nyanza African Council because you very kindly considered and recommended our petitions which were submitted to you from time to time through our presidents. You have been doing the same with Central Government because you have had the African's welfare in your mind. I believe even the Europeans could state the same thing. We greatly miss you, as we do not know as yet whether we shall have another Provincial Commissioner of your type.

I pray God to be with you until you come back to Kenya in your farm where you are going to settle.

VALEDICTORY

Remember me to Mrs Williams and inform her that I hope to see you again when I shall have the opportunity of paying you a friendly visit at your farm.
                Yours sincerely
                Paul Mboya
                Secretary, South Nyanza District Council

Conclusion

JOHN JOHNSON

British rule was a pinprick in Kenya's history. It lasted for less than 70 years from 1895 when a Protectorate was declared over British East Africa until 1963. This book covers only the latter part of the story. It begins with a glimpse of the 1930s and 1940s; a time of austerity but also of comradeship, of long safaris in the bush and conviviality in the *boma*. But the tempo of administration changed radically after 1950; and this dominated the life and work described by the contributors. A detailed historical account is given in Charles Chenevix Trench's *Men Who Ruled Kenya*.

What was the balance sheet of British administration in Kenya in this period? What was achieved? What were the failures?

Most outstandingly, failure to prevent the Mau Mau rebellion, mainly a movement of protest centred on the Kikuyu, Embu and Meru peoples. It had its roots in the alienation of African land for European settlement early in the 20th century, the growth of a landless community and of social deprivation. The dangers of political upheaval were apparent soon after World War 2, particularly with the return of the African servicemen, but the government was slow to take action. The response after Baring's arrival in 1952 was effective and peace was restored; but not without hardship and bloodshed. Administration in the areas affected was brought closer to the people. Government priorities were focused on improving social conditions and generating prosperity. More money was made available from Britain. The Swynnerton Plan for African agriculture was the key. Land consolidation in Central Province, spreading quickly from Kiambu District, enhanced the impact. As a result Kenya now has some of the most successful small holding farming in sub-Saharan Africa.

The problem of land shortage was alleviated by making Crown land available for African resettlement. Several thousand landless people were given freehold title to land by 1963. A programme of purchase of European farmland for Africans continued the process.

Africanisation of the civil service was delayed for too long. The process is well documented in these pages. It was vital to catch up with political developments and train administrators quickly. Many of the Africans in the Provincial Administration moved into senior positions and ran the country smoothly at Independence and after. British administrators in the districts were replaced.

CONCLUSION

In common with other colonial powers, Britain failed to keep pace with the rise of nationalism in Africa. On the ground, administrators were often slow to interact with politicians and the growing Kenyan elite coming out of the universities. They worked more closely with the chiefs, headmen and district councillors whom they knew and trusted. Constitutional change came in the late 1950s, and African elected members assailed the dominance of the officials and European settler minority in the Legislature.

After the troubles of the 1950s there were grave doubts about Kenya's future. Ethnic rivalries threatened political ferment, but leadership remained strong and unity was forged. The success of Kenya's colonial administrators was reflected in the stability of the country in the immediate post-Independence period. Jomo Kenyatta adopted the existing system of administration and indeed strengthened it to make the PCs accountable personally to the President. This was a signal tribute to the work described in these pages.

The Administrators

Askwith, Tom A. Wife, Patricia
Born 1911 Served 1955–62
DO, Municipal African Affairs Officer, Nairobi, Commissioner of Community Development.
UN Adviser in Afghanistan; UK Adviser in Turkey; International Briefing Centre, Farnham.

Barlow, John E. Wife, Ann
Born 1933 Served 1957–64
DO Kisumu, Kakamega, Narok, Nandi, Acting DC Nakuru, Asst. Sec.Rift Valley Province.
Financial Services.

Barnett, Christopher J. A., QC Wife, Marlies
Born 1936 Served 1952–62
DO (KG), DA, DO Maseno (Central Nyanza)
Barrister; Queens Counsel; Circuit Judge.

Boyle, Ranald H. M., DSC Wife Norma
Born 1921 Served 1956–64 (after Sudan Political Service)
DO Central Nyanza, Baringo, Fort Hall, Mombasa, Meru, DC Nairobi.
FCO; merchant banking; Arab banking; consultancy.

Brown, Peter H. Wife, Ann
Born 1918 Served 1941–63
DO, DC Embu, Kilifi, Nandi, Nairobi, Senior DC, Acting Civil Secretary, Rift Valley Province.
Franks Commission; Sec. University of Oxford Medical School.

Butter, John H., CMG, OBE Wife, Joyce
Born 1916 Served 1950–65 (after Indian and Pakistan Civil Service)
Exchange Controller, Perm. Sec., Treasury (returned to post after Independence at request of PM Kenyatta).
Financial Adviser, Kenya Treasury; Dir. Gen. Finance Dept., Abu Dhabi.

Campbell, John D., CBE, CVO,MC+bar, Desp. Wife, Shirley
Born 1921 Served 1949–61 (after Popski's Private Army)
DO Kitui, Karatina, Kisii and Homa Bay; and including time with Kenya Regt., Game Dept. and commercial fishing.
FCO, HM Consul General Naples; Company Director.

THE ADMINISTRATORS

Cashmore, T. H. Richard (Dick)
Born 1928   Served 1953–62
DO Kilifi, Thika, Garissa, Isiolo, DC Wajir, DO Narok, Machakos, DC Mandera.
CRO/FCO Research Dept.; Pearce Commission and Electoral Observers, Rhodesia; Commonwealth Observers Group Group, Uganda.

Chenevix Trench, Charles P., MC   Wife, Mary
Born 1914   Served 1948–63 (after Indian service)
DO, DC Garissa, Moyale, Samburu, Senior DC.
Millfield School; author.

Christie-Miller, David G., Desp.   Wife, Joan
Born 1918   Served 1944–62 (after KAR and Sudan Defence Force)
DO Machakos, Kitui, Lamu, DC Moyale, Thika, Nakuru, Naivasha, Director Population Census.
Arthur Guinness & Son & Co (Brewers).

Coutts, Sir Walter F. (Wally), GCMG, MBE   Wife, Janet (Bones)
Born 1912   Served 1936–61 (except W. Indies 1949–55)
DC Fort Hall. Minister of Education, Chief Secretary.
Governor Uganda, Governor General Uganda.

Cowley, Kenneth M., CMG, OBE, Desp.
Born 1912   Served 1935–1962
DO Kakamega, West Suk, Rumuruti, DC Voi, Secretariat, PC Southern Province.
Secretary, Overseas Pensioners Association.

Crichton, Patrick   Wife, Barbara
Born 1920   Served 1947–65
DO Kisii, Turkana, Narok, Asst. Sec. Ministries of Local Govt. and Commerce and Industry. Director of Africanisation.
Guinness Overseas Ltd., Controller for Marquess of Bute.

Cusack, J. W. (Jake), CMG, OBE, Desp.
Born 1907   Served 1930–59 (except army service and
                                   Chief Secretary, Italian Somaliland)
Senior DC, Minister of Defence.

Dale, David K., CMG, Desp.   Wife, Hanna
Born 1927   Served 1960–64
DO, DC.
Admin.Officer, New Hebrides; Permanent Sec. & Deputy Governor, Seychelles; FCO, Governor Montserrat.

Dempster, Peter M.   Wife, Sheila
Born 1930   Served 1954–62 (after ASP, Kenya Police)
DO Narok, Meru, Embu. DC Marsabit.
Salmon Fishing Tourism (Ireland).

Derrick, Peter B.   Wife, Meg
Born 1920   Served 1944–62
DO, DC Embu, Kiambu, Senior DC.
FCO, HM Treasury.

Dobson, Robert L. A.   Wife, Kathleen
Born 1920 d.1958   Served 1952–58 (after army service in E. Africa)
DO Kakamega, Kilifi, DC Moyale, DO 1 Embu.

Edgar, Thomas L., MBE Desp. (2)   Wife, Florence
Born 1919   Served 1949–62 (after army service)
DO Kilifi/Malindi, Baringo, Nyeri, Kericho, Nanyuki. DC Kajiado.
Company Secretary; W. Pacific High Commission; Overseas Trade Sec.
Birmingham Chamber of Commerce.

Ellerton, Sir Geoffrey J., CMG, MBE, Desp.   Wife, Peggy
Born 1920   Served 1945–63
DO Turkana, Nyanza, Asst. Sec. Secretariat, Perm. Sec. Ministry of Internal Security and Defence, Perm. Sec. Ministry of Constitutional Affairs and Administration, Perm. Sec. PM's Office and Cabinet Sec.
Director, Ocean Steam Ship Co.; Chairman Local Govt. Boundary Commission for England.

Evans, David W. R.   Wife, Ann
Born 1933   Served 1957–61 (after national service in KAR)
DO Moyale, Elgon Nyanza, Kisii, West Suk, Meru.
EA Airways; Govt. of W. Australia; Dept. of Foreign Affairs & Trade, Australia.

Evans, Michael N., CMG   Wife, Mary
Born 1915   Served 1939–64
DO Kilifi, South Nyanza, Kericho, DC Nandi, African Courts Officer, Acting Commissioner, Local Govt. Department, Acting Director of Information, Perm. Sec., Min. of Health & Housing.
Vice Consul, British Consulate, Cape Town.

Forrester, David A.   Wife d., Fay
Born 1932   Served 1955–64
DO Fort Hall, Nandi, Central Nyanza, Nairobi, Min. of Local Govt., Min. of Lands.
Crown Law Dept., Govt. of Western Australia; Barrister, Perth.

THE ADMINISTRATORS

Fox, Eric D., Desp.   Wife, Jill
Born 1924   Served 1950–64
DO North Nyanza, Turkana, Taveta, Nairobi, Kiambu, Machakos, DC Baringo.
Min. Local Govt., Botswana; UK Family Planning Assoc.; NHS Hospital Secretary.

Fuller, Colin   Wife, Hazel
Born 1932   Served 1957–67
DO Kakamega, Elgeyo Marakwet, Machakos, Head of Dept., Kenya Institute of Administration.
Institute for Development Policy and Management, Univ. of Manchester.

Fullerton, Peter G. P. D.   Wife, Elizabeth
Born 1930   Served 1953–62
DO Kipini, Kakamega, Bungoma, Meru, DC Wajir, Elgeyo Marakwet.
FCO; Home Civil Service, Dept. of Energy.

Gardner, Charles A., MBE   Wife, Annette
Born 1933   Served 1956–62
DO Taita, Turkana, DO & DO1 Fort Hall.
George Williamson Kenya Ltd; Eastern Produce Kenya Ltd; Eastern African Assoc.

Gavaghan, Terence J. F., MBE   Wife, Nicole
Born 1922   Served 1943–63.
DO Kitui, Kisii, Kisumu, Mandera, Kakamega, Mombasa, Taita/Taveta, Nyeri, DC Samburu, Kiambu, i/c Rehabilitation, Min. of Local Govt., Treasury, Office of Chief Secretary, Under Sec. Governor's Office, Cabinet Office.
Pfizer International; Texaco Oil Exploration; UN Agencies; Voluntary Agencies; Academic Research, University of York.

Golds, John M., MBE, Desp.
Born 1927   Served 1953–63
DO Kiambu, Asst. Sec., DC Wajir.
Commonwealth Development Corporation, Company Director and Consultant.

Gordon, Eric D.   Wife, Audrey
Born 1925   Served 1951–62 (after Royal Navy)
Secretariat, DO West Pokot, Mombasa, Taveta, Embu, PA to PC Central Province, DO1 Central Nyanza, Acting Principal Kenya, Institute of Administration.
University of Southampton.

Gordon, Peter M., CMG, Desp.　　　　　　　　　Wife Marianne
　Born 1919　　　　　　　　　　　　　　　　Served 1946–63
　DO, Acting DC Isiolo, North & Central Nyanza, DC Mandera, Elgon Nyanza, Senior DC, Asst. Sec./ Under/Sec./ Perm. Sec. Min. of Agriculture.
　University of Exeter; Election monitoring, Zimbabwe & Uganda.

Hampson, George N., MBE, Desp.　　　　　　　　Wife, Mildred
　Born 1924　　　　　　Served 1948–64 (after British Mil. Admin, Ethiopia)
　DO Meru, Mukogodo, Nyeri, Taita & Taveta, Nakuru, Min of Defence, admin. Liaison Officer (Intelligence) Special Branch, DC Trans Nzoia, PA to PC Nyanza Province and Provincial African Courts Officer, DC Laikipia, DC Nairobi.
　Ministry of Defence.

Hardy, Noel G.　　　　　　　　　　　　　　　　Wife, Dawn
　Born 1923　　　　　　　　Served 1946–63 (after army service)
　DO, Officer i/c Mau Mau Investigation, DC Naivasha, Asst. Sec. Min. of African Affairs, DC Thika.
　UK Ministry of Defence.

Hector, Gordon M., CMG, CBE　　　　　　　　　Wife, Mary
　Born 1918　　　　　　　Served 1946–52 (after military service)
　DO Baringo, Elgeyo Marakwet, Nandi. DC Wajir, Secretariat, Secretary to Road Authority.
　Secretary to Govt. of Seychelles; Secretary to Govt. of Basutoland and Govt. Representative i/c External Affairs.

Hennings, Richard O., CMG　　　　　　　　　Wife, Constance
　Born 1911　　　　　　　　　　　　　　　　Served 1935–62
　DO, Secretariat, Perm. Sec. Min. of Agric., Deputy Chief Secretary, MLC.

Herdman, J. Mark A., CBE, LVO　　　　　　Wife, Elizabeth (Betsy)
　Born 1932　　　　　　　　　　　　　　　　Served 1955–64
　DO Meru, Kwale, Elgeyo Marakwet, Acting DC Lamu, Marsabit. DC West Pokot.
　FCO, Deputy Governor, Bermuda; Governor, British Virgin Islands.

Hodge, Donald L. V., OBE, Desp.　　　　　　　　Wife, Wendy
　Born 1924　　　　　　　　　　　　　　　　Served 1947–65
　DO, DC Thika, Nanyuki, Meru, Asst. Sec. Cabinet Office, Private Sec. to Governor & Governor General.
　EA Breweries; Bursar Bloxham School; Election Co-ordinator Rhodesia; Save the Children Fund.

THE ADMINISTRATORS

Horrell, Roger W., CMG, OBE
Born 1935   Served 1959–63 (after national service in Kenya)
DO Kilifi, Kwale, Meru.
FCO.

Hunt, R. Geoffrey   Wife, Victoria
Born 1927   Served 1951–63
DO South Nyanza, Isiolo, Narok, Acting DC Laikipia, Elgeyo Marakwet,
PA to PC Rift Valley, Special Branch HQ, DC Central Nyanza.
Ministry of Defence; Seconded to NATO Brussels.

Hunt, Kenneth J.A., MBE, TD   Wife, d
Born 1912   Served 1945–62 (after military service in KAR)
DO Kakamega, Kisumu, Dept. of Information, Nairobi and Mombasa.
FCO.

Jeary, Rod A.   Wives, Nancy d., Marion
Born 1927   Served 1951–62
DO Kisumu, Wajir, Nandi, Naivasha, Machakos, Narok, Kericho. DC Kilifi.
Banking, JP, Assessor, Race Relations Act.

Johnson, Sir John R., KCMG   Wife, Jean
Born 1930   Served 1955–64
DO Embu, Kericho, Kiambu. DC Thika.
CO/CRO/FCO, Under Sec. for Africa, British High Commissioner Zambia and Kenya; Teacher, University of Oxford; Chairman, Countryside Commission; Chairman, Chilterns Conservation Board.

Johnson, Peter L., Desp.   Wife, Daphne
Born 1926   Served 1951–63 (after Royal Navy)
DO Kwale, Embu, Naivasha, Elgon Nyanza, PA to PC Central Province, Acting DC Embu, Private Secretary Government House.
GKN plc; Manager of vineyard.

Johnston, Carruthers M., '**Monkey**', CMG, Desp.   Wife, Barbara
Born 1909   Served 1933–59
DO, DC, PC Rift Valley and Central Provinces, Special Commissioner for Kikuyu, Embu and Meru, Chief Native Commissioner, Minister.
GCHQ, Cheltenham.

Jones, Philip H., OBE   Wife, Veronica d
Born 1921   Served 1942–62 (after military service)
DO Elgeyo Marakwet, Nakuru, Baringo, North Nyanza. DC Samburu, Under Sec., Min. of Agriculture.
Confederation of British Industry.

279

Knowles, Oliver S., OBE, Desp.   Wife Elizabeth June (author)
Born 1920   Served 1948–69
DO Turkana, Malindi, Kiambu, South Nyanza, Secretariat, UK Treasury, Planning Directorate, Acting Perm. Sec. Treasury,
Inter Regional Adviser, on Economic Cooperation, UNCTAD.

Lambert, J. David   Wife, Pat
Born 1935   Served 1955–63 (after service in 3 KAR)
DA Naivasha, Samburu, DO Embu, Fort Hall, Turkana.
Head of Information Systems, Meyer International plc.

Liddle, Alan L. K.   Wife, Sue
Born 1934   Served 1957–62 (after service in 23 KAR)
DO Kilifi, Kitui, PA to PC Southern Province.
Gallaher Ltd.; Greenwood Oil Ltd., Wiltshier Group plc.; Consultant.

Lindsay, Ian D. St G.   Wife, Joy
Born 1931   Served 1959–63 (after Kenya Police 1952–59)
DO Nyeri, Nairobi Extra Provincial District.
Australian Red Cross; Royal Australian Air Force.

Lloyd, G. Peter, CMG, CBE, Desp.   Wife, Margaret
Born 1926   Served 1951–60 (after ADC to Governor, Kenya)
DO Nyeri, Mombasa, Lamu, Machakos, Asst. Sec., DO1 Fort Hall.
Colonial Office; Colonial Sec., Seychelles; Chief Sec., Fiji; Sec. for Security, Hong Kong; Deputy Governor, Bermuda; Governor, Cayman Islands.

Loyd, Sir Frank A., KCMG, OBE, Desp.   Wife, Monica
Born 1916   Served 1939–63
DO Embu, Garissa, North Nyanza, Private Sec. to Governor, DC Mandera, Moyale, West Suk, Nyeri, Fort Hall, Kiambu, PC Central & Nyanza Provinces, Acting Chief Commissioner; Perm. Sec. Governor's Office and Cabinet Sec.
HM Commissioner, Swaziland; Director, London House for Overseas Graduates.

Luce, The Rt Hon. Lord (Richard), GCVO.   Wife, Rose
Born 1936   Served 1960–63
DO Isiolo, Embu.
MP, Minister of State FCO, Minister for the Arts; Vice Chancellor, University of Buckingham; Governor and C-in-C, Gibraltar, Lord Chamberlain.

Lunn, Jeremy   Wife, Jane
Born 1934   Served 1957–62
DO Kwale, Narok, Kakamega, Marsabit, Machakos, Kisumu.
BP

Maciel, Mervyn A. B. Wife, Elsie
Born 1929 Served 1947–66
Secretariat, Voi, Turkana, Marsabit, DA South Nyanza, Min. of Agriculture.
Credit Controller; Office Manager; author.

Mackenzie, Kenneth W. S., CMG, CVO Wife, Kathleen
Born 1915 Served 1948–62 (after Colonial Service in Basutoland and Mauritius)
DO, Secretariat, UK Treasury, Perm. Sec. Treasury, Minister of Finance and MLC.
Colonial Office; UK Treasury; Dept. of Environment; Royal Institute of Public Administration.

McCartney, Fergus J. A. Wife, Angela
Born 1939 Served 1954–62 (after Kenya Regt.)
DO KG, DO Kiambu, Central Nyanza, DC Mandera, DO1 Kajiado.
Coffee farming; General Manager Ker & Downey Safaris Ltd.; Horticulture and Coffee farming.

McEntee, Peter D., CMG, OBE, Desp. Wife, Mary
Born 1920 Served 1946–63 (after KAR)
DO, DC, Senior DC, Principal Kenya Institute of Administration.
CRO/FCO: HM Consul-General, Karachi, Governor, Belize.

Merifield, Sir Anthony J., KCVO, CB Wife, Pamela
Born 1934 Served 1958–65
DO Kilifi, Taita, Isiolo, South Nyanza, PC's Office, Nyanza Province.
Home Civil Service: Dept. of Health and Social Security, N. Ireland Office, Cabinet Office retiring as Under Sec.; Ceremonial Officer, Cabinet Office.

Minter, Chris J. W. Wife, Lynda
Born 1933 Served 1957–62 (after 23 KAR)
DO South Nyanza, Moyale, West Pokot, Turkana.
Harveys of Bristol; BMRB; Survey Research Hongkong; Executive Surveys/China Research Services; Internat. consultancy; Readers Digest Assoc.

Mitchell, John K. Wife, Jane
Born 1930 Served 1952–63
DO Central Nyanza, Baringo, Mandera, Kericho, Nakuru, Nairobi., Treasury, Ministry of Commerce & Industry, DO Machakos.
Monopolies and Mergers Commission.

Newton, W. Carruthers C.   Wife, Minkie
Born 1930   Served 1954–64 (after The Nigeria Regt.)
Administrative Assistant, DO KG, DO Nakuru, Kiambu, Elgon Nyanza, DO1 Nyeri.
Estate Agent in South Africa.

Nicoll-Griffith, David   Wife, Eileen
Born 1929   Served 1952–62
DO Kericho, Marsabit, Kitui, Mombasa, Fort Hall.
Teaching French and German in Bermuda; Registrar, Bermuda College.

Nottingham, John C., Desp., Order of Grand Warrior (Kenya)   Wife, Joyce
Born 1928   Served 1953–62
DO Nyeri, Machakos, Nandi, North Nyanza, Nakuru.
Lecturer, Makerere University and College of Social Studies; Publisher.

O'Hagan, Desmond, CMG   Wife, Pamela
Born 1909   Served 1931–59
DO South Nyanza, North Nyanza, Garissa, DC Isiolo, Wajir, Machakos, Fort Hall, Native Courts Adviser, PC Central and Coast Provinces.
Chairman, Transport Licensing Authority, Tanganyika; Coffee farming.

Otter, Robin G., Desp.   Wife, Elizabeth
Born 1926   Served 1951–62
DO Kiambu, Marsabit Fort Hall, South Nyanza, DC Moyale, Taita, PA to PC Nyanza.
Partner in Moore, Brown & Dixon, Solicitors, Tewkesbury; Consultant.

Paul, Robin J. L., TD   Wife, Yvonne
Born 1937   Served 1961–64 (after Royal W. African Frontier Force)
DO Meru and Turkana.
BP.

Peet, F. A., (**Tony**) Desp.   Wife, June
Born 1922   Served 1949–62 (after E. African Engineers)
DO Kitui, Garissa, Taita, Fort Hall, African Affairs Officer, Mombasa, DC Fort Hall, Kiambu, Mombasa, SDC.
Partner in Solicitors' firm.

Philip, Michael C. S., MBE   Wife, Shirley
Born 1932   Served 1956–67
DO South Nyanza, Baringo, Nandi, Central Nyanza, Asst. Civil Secretary, Eastern Province, DC/RGA Isiolo, Deputy Civil Secretary, Nyanza Province, Ministry of Agriculture.
Private Company.

THE ADMINISTRATORS

Pratt, Gerald P. Wife Yvonne
Born 1931 Served 1955–62
DO Kilifi, Mombasa, Meru. Personal Asst. to PC Coast Province, Treasury.
Home Civil Service: Home Office and Cabinet Office.

Preston, Thomas D. Wife, Jennifer
Born 1932 Served 1954–63
DA Nyeri, Fort Hall, Taita, Turkana, Senior DA, Kajiado.
Harrison & Crossfield: Chairman MD Nairobi; Director London; Chairman and CEO, Australia.

Risley, Eric H. Wife, Bridget
Born 1914 Served 1953–63
(after KAR and Administration in Tanganyika)
DC Nanyuki, Baringo, Trans Nzoia, Kisumu, Thomson's Falls, Kilifi, West Suk, Kwale. Senior DC.
Executive Officer, Kenya Wildlife Soc.; Executive Officer, Coffee Board of Kenya; own safari business.

Ross, C. John M., Desp. Wife, Deidre
Born 1923 Served 1959–62 (after Colonial Service in Nigeria)
Ministry of Works, Ministry of Defence, Governor's Office, Prime Minister's Office.
New Zealand Foreign Service, Ambassador to Peru.

Ross, Iain C.
Born 1937 Served 1960–63
DO Marsabit, Garissa, Personal Asst. to Civil Secretary, NE Region, Acting DC Mandera.
National Parks Service Uganda; FCO.

Russell, B. John F., OBE
Born 1929 Served 1954–64 (after Kenya Regt.)
DOKG, DO West Pokot, Kilifi, Elgon Nyanza, Central Nyanza, Naivasha, Nyandarua.
Administrative Officer Western Pacific High Commission, Solomon Islands, Vanuatu.

Savage, A. (Tony) N., ISO Wife, Jane
Born 1929 Served 1954–64
DO Baringo, Kiambu, Narok, North Nyanza, DC Garissa, DO1 Nairobi, Asst. Sec., Acting Deputy Sec., Ministry of Local Government.
Commercial/Industrial work in E. Africa; Administrative Officer, Hong Kong; Chief Executive Officer, HK Industrial Estates Corporation.

Shirreff, A. David, MC, Desp.   Wife, Dione
Born 1919   Served 1945–63 (after KAR)
DO Machakos, Samburu, North Nyanza, Central Nyanza, DC West Suk, Kwale, Kisii, Meru, Senior DC.
Solicitor, Deputy District Judge.

Simmance, Alan J. F.   Wife, Diane
Born 1931   Served 1953–66
DO Kilifi, Fort Hall, Kiambu, Crown Counsel, Vice Principal and Principal, Kenya Institute of Administration.
Adviser, Cabinet Office, Zambia; UNHCR.

Stephens, Anthony W., CB, CMG.   Wife, Mytyl
Born 1930   Served 1954–63
DO Kilifi, Narok, North Nyanza, Personal Asst. to PC Southern Province, DC Taita.
Home Civil Service: Ministry of Defence, N. Ireland Office.

Swan, Sir Anthony, C.C. Bt., CMG, OBE, Desp.   Wife, Jean
Born 1913   Served 1935–62 (except for KAR)
DC Kiambu, PC Nyanza, Minister of Defence.

Symes-Thompson, R. (Dick), Desp.   Wife, Gillian (Jill)
Born 1923   Served 1946–64
DO Isiolo, Garissa, Kitui, Meru Elgeyo Marakwet, Nakuru, Kericho, Kiambu. Asst Sec., DC Embu, Taita, Naivasha, Nandi, Senior DC Kiambu.
Asst. Bursar and Bursar, Eton College.

Thompson, W. H. (Tommy), CMG, CBE, Desp.   Wife, Sheelagh
Born 1924   Served 1947–63
Civil Reabsorption Officer, DO (CD), DO Fort Hall, Elgon Nyanza, DC Tana River and Eldoret, African Courts Training Officer, Principal, Maseno Training Centre, African Courts Officer (Supreme Courts)
Colonial Sec. Acting Judge Supreme Court, Falkland Islands; Administrator British Virgin Islands; HM Commissioner, Anguilla; Governor Monserrat; Local Govt. UK.

Turnbull, Sir Richard G., GCMG, Kt. St John, Desp.   Wife, Beatrice
Born 1909   Served 1931–58
DO, Secretariat, PC Northern Frontier Province, Minister of Defence, Chief Secretary.
Governor Tanganyika, Governor General Tanzania, Chairman Kenya Land Board, High Commissioner for Aden and the Protectorate of South Arabia.

Usher, Elizabeth M., OBE Married name, Blair
Served 1947–61
Dept. of Lands and Survey, Asst. Sec. Treasury, Under Secretary Ministry of Agriculture.
Town Clerk, Beaminster.

Wainwright, Robin E., CMG, Desp. Wife, Bridget
Born 1913 Served 1935–63
DO Kilifi, Nairobi, Machakos, Nyeri, Laikipia, DC Kajiado, Embu, Kisumu, Secretariat, PC Rift Valley Province, Chief Commissioner.
FCO: Administrator, Turks and Caicos Islands.

Waller, H. de W. 'Pat', Desp. (twice) Wife, Elizabeth
Born 1923 Served 1948–63
DO Meru, Kitui, Nyeri, Malindi, DC Moyale, Nakuru, Narok, South Nyanza.
FCO; Director Salmon and Trout Association.

Walker, P. Hugh, MBE Wife, Anne
Born 1931 Served 1953–64 (after Somali Scouts)
DO Narok, Fort Hall, Kiambu, DC Mandera (twice) Asst. Sec. Min. of Defence.
Assistant Adviser, Aden; BBC Somali Services; Hong Kong Government.

Wasilewski, Michael Z. Wife, Bridget
Born 1930 Served 1957–62
DO Kwale, Isiolo, Turkana, Kisii, Narok, Machakos.
Home Civil Service: Department of Trade and Industry.

Watts, Tom A., MBE Wife, Molly
Born 1920 Served 1941–74
DO Kitui, Meru, Turkana, North and Central Nyanza, DC and Senior DC Marsabit, Mombasa, Kisumu, Kakamega, Machakos, Nairobi, Min. of Agriculture, African Courts Officer and Admin. Sec., Judicial Dept.
Bursar Ashford School.

Williams, C. Harold (Hal), CMG, OBE Wife, Joy
Born 1908 Served 1931–56
DO Kiambu, Meru, Mandera, Kisii, Kisumu, Kwale, DC Garissa, Narok, North Nyanza, PC Nyanza Province.
Farmer and Teacher.

Williams, John A.
Born 1933 Served 1957–62 (after 23 KAR)
DO ElgonNyanza, Isiolo, Thomson's Falls, Nandi, Special Camps, Machakos.
Director, International Affairs, Institute of Chartered Accountants; Australian Defence Department.

Wilks, H. Charles F., OBE Wife, Barbara
Born 1916 Served 1946–63
DO Meru, Fort Hall, Kericho, DC West Suk, SDC, Asst. Sec., Secondment to Colonial Office, DC Embu, Central Nyanza, Acting PC Nyanza Province.
General Manager, Ker and Downey Safaris; Administrative Secretary, Tea Research Institute of E. Africa.

Willis, Ian B. Wife, Diana
Born 1925 Served 1955–64
DA Machakos, Elgeyo-Marakwet, Kakamega, Kisii, Samburu.
Schweppes; Self-employed (own trading company).

Williamson, Robin J. Wife, Rachel
Born 1937 Served 1961–65
DO Turkana.
Kenya Agricultural Department; Teachers' Service Commission in Nandi and Nakuru; Schoolmaster, Hurstpierpoint College.

Wilson, F. Richard (Dick), CMG, OBE, Desp. Wife, Dorothy
Born 1920 Served 1947–63
DO Kitui, Kiambu, Malindi, DC Kwale, Kitale, West Suk, Embu, Intelligence Adviser to Governor, Private Sec. to Governor, PC Central Province.
Commonwealth Development Corporation: Regional Controller, Southern Africa, Controller of Administration.

Windley, Sir Edward, KCMG, KCVO, Desp.
Born 1909 Served 1933–57
PC Central, Chief Native Commissioner/Min. of African Affairs.
Governor, The Gambia.

Winser, Robert S. Wife, Anne
Born 1921 Served 1943–63
DO Central Nyanza, Embu, Mombasa, Kisii, Secretariat, Municipal African Affairs Officer Mombasa, DC and Senior DC Garissa, Thika, Elgon Nyanza, Nakuru, Civil Sec. NE Region.
BSI.

***

Editorial note: This is not a complete list of colonial administrators in Kenya. It is confined primarily to those who responded to the questionnaire.

Chronology

1895	Proclamation of British East African Protectorate.
1896–1901	Building of Uganda Railway.
1902	Transfer of eastern part of Uganda (most of later Nyanza and Rift Valley Provinces) to BEAP.
1914–18	1st World War: British Imperial forces eventually defeat Germans in East Africa.
1920	BEAP becomes Kenya Colony and Protectorate (to distinguish it from ex-German East Africa, now Tanganyika).
1923	Colonial Office White Paper ('Devonshire Declaration') states paramountcy of the interests of 'the interests of the African natives' in Kenya.
1924	Jubaland, eastern part of NFD, handed over to Italian Somaliland.
1926	Rest of Turkana tranferred from Uganda to Kenya.
1930	World depression: serious impact on Kenya's economy and finances.
1935–6	Italy invades and occupies Abyssinia (Ethiopia).
1939–45	2nd World War. British Imperial forces defend Kenya and free Somaliland, Ethiopia and Madagascar. East Africans forces participate in North African and Burma campaigns.
1944	Sir Philip Mitchell, Governor.
1946	Jomo Kenyatta returns from Europe and becomes President of Kenya African Union (KAU).
1948	Census: Kenya African population 5.25 million + 30,000 Europeans, 125,000 Asians/others.
1952	Sir Evelyn Baring (later Lord Howick), Governor. Declaration of State of Emergency. Kenyatta arrested.
1953	Kenyatta tried, convicted and sentenced to 7 years imprisonment. KAU banned. Kabaka of Buganda deported.
1954	Lyttelton Constitution. 1st African Minister appointed.
1955	East African Royal Commission report on economic, land/agricultural, industrial and social issues. Swynnerton Plan for African agriculture. Kabaka returns.
1956	End of Emergency military operations. Sudan independent. Suez invasion.
1957	1st African elections for Leg. Co. (8 seats: limited franchise). Ghana independent.

1958	Oginga Odinga praises Kenyatta and Mau Mau in Leg. Co. debate.
1959	Deaths of detainees at Hola Camp. Sir Patrick Renison, Governor
1960	1st Lancaster House constitutional conference. 3 elected Africans join Council of Ministers. KANU and KADU parties formed. Ministry of African Affairs abolished. Harold Macmillan's 'Wind of Change' speech in Cape Town. 16 African states become independent, including Somalia and (ex-Belgian) Congo. Congo civil war: refugees enter Kenya. Part of 'White Highlands' opened to Africans.
1961	KANU wins elections but refuses office before Kenyatta's release. KADU minority government. Kenyatta freed from restriction: subsequently enters Leg. Co. Drought and famine, followed by floods. Tanganyika independent.
1962	Malcolm MacDonald, Governor (Governor General on Independence). Coalition Government: Kenyatta and Ngala Ministers of State. 2nd Lancaster House conference: 'Majimbo' policy agreed. Census: Kenya African population 8.37 million + 56,000 Europeans, 215,000 Asians/others. Uganda independent.
1963	KANU wins 1st universal suffrage elections on a common roll. Kenyatta Prime Minister. Shifta war with Somalia begins, with killing of African DC. KENYA INDEPENDENT.
1964	Kenya becomes a Republic, with Kenyatta as President (MacDonald British High Commissioner). Zanzibar revolution. Small-scale army mutinies put down in Kenya, Tanganyika, Uganda. Regional powers abolished: KADU disbands and joins Government.
1978	Jomo Kenyatta dies and is succeeded as President by Daniel arap Moi.

Glossary 1

ADC	African District Council
ALDEV	African Land Development
CDO	Community Development Officer
Chief	locational head
Desp.	Mentioned in Despatches
DO1	Deputy to DC
DRO	District Revenue Officer
District	administrative area
Division	part of district
FANY	Forces Auxiliary Nursing Yeomanry
goat-bag	funds not accounted for
GSU	General Service Unit (paramilitary police)
Headman	sub-locational head
KADU	Kenya Africa Democratic Union
KANU	Kenya Africa National Union
KAR	King's African Rifles
KAU	Kenya African Union
KEM	Kikuyu, Embu, Meru
KG	Kikuyu Guard
EG	Embu Guard
MG	Meru Guard
KPR	Kenya Police Reserve
Leg Co	Legislative Council
Location	Chief's administrative area
Mau Mau	militant nationalist movement
MLC	Member of Legislative Council
NFD	Northern Frontier District
Province	regional administrative area
Pseudo gang	turncoat group used to hunt Mau Mau
RM	Resident Magistrate
Reserve	African land
Secretariat	Government HQ in Nairobi
Settled areas	European settlement
Tribal Police	administrative police
(White) Highlands	land set aside for European settlement

Glossary 2

Language notes: All words are Kiswahili except where shown:
Kam. = Kikamba
Kik. = Kikuyu
Maa = Maasai
Afr. = S African origin
Ind. = S Asian origin.
Ahm. = Amharic

akili	intelligence
askari	soldier, policeman
asubuhi	morning
balozi	governor, consul
banda	open-walled building
baraza	public meeting, reception
bibi	woman, wife
boma	enclosure = government office
bundu	'bush' country (coll.)
bwana (pl = ma-)	Mr, Sir, husband
bwana mkubwa	DC
bwana mdogo	DO
choo	lavatory
dafu (pl = ma-)	coconut
dak bungalow	rest house (Ind.)
dawa	medicine
debe	tin container
dhow	arab sailing vessel
dini	religion, faith
doum	variety of palm tree
dubas	red turban (Som.) = Tribal Police in NFD
dudu	insect
duka	shop
effendi	Sir (military)
eupe	white
fitina	intrigue, discord
fundi	skilled worker
gari	wheeled vehicle (Ind.)
godown	workshop, factory (Ind.)

GLOSSARY 2

habari	news, information
harambee!	work together!
heshima	respect, prestige, honour
jamhuri	republic
jilaal	dry season (Som.)
kadhi	judge
kanzu	man's gown
karai	metal basin
karani	clerk
kazi	work
kiama	court, group (Kik.)
kiama kia muingi (KKM)	group of many (Kik.), c/f Mau Mau
kibuyu	gourd
kikoi	men's skirt
kitete	mongoose
kodi	tax
kuni	firewood
laibon	seer (Maa)
laioni	youths (Maa)
liwali	chief
lugga	watercourse (Ind.)
mabati	corrugated iron
mahindi	maize
majimbo	regions/ regionalism
makuti	palm leaf roofing
malaya	prostitute
manyatta	house, village (Maa)
mbari	land-owning group (Kik.)
mchele	rice
memsahib	Mrs, wife (Ind.)
moran	warrior (Maa)
mpishi	cook
mtoto/toto	child
mudir	head man
mungu	God
mweithia	self-help (Kam.)
mzee (pl. wazee)	elder
ndizi	bananas
ngoma	dance
nyoka	snake
nzige	locust
ole	son of (Maa)
panga	matchet

pombe	African beer
rakub	riding camel (Som.)
safari	journey
shamba	farm, plot
sharia	(muslim) law
shauri (pl = ma-)	advice, consultation
shenzi	uncouth, uncivilized
shifta	bandits, irregular forces (Amh.)
shuka	piece of cloth
sime/simi	short sword
sindano	needle, injection
sufuria	metal cooking pot
tamaam	ready, on parade (Arab)
tamasha	show, spectacle
tarboosh	tasselled red hat
tembo	palm wine
uhuru	freedom, independence
vlei	damp hollow (Afr.)
wananchi	citizens
watu (sing. = mtu)	people

Bibliography

BOOKS BY COLONIAL SERVICE OFFICERS AND FAMILIES

Askwith, Tom	*From Mau Mau to Harambee*	Cambridge African Monographs 1995
Askwith, Tom	*Getting My Knees Brown*	publ. T Askwith 1996
Butter, J.	*Uncivil Servant*	1989
Carson, J. B.	*Sun, Sand and Safari*	Robert Hale 1957
Chenevix-Trench, C.	*The Desert's Dusty Face*	Blackwood 1964
Chenevix-Trench, C.	*Men who Ruled Kenya*	Radcliffe 1993
Gavaghan, Terence	*Of Lions and Dung Beetles*	Arthur H Stockwell 1999
Goldsmith, Anne	*Gentle Warrior*	Editor and Publisher 2001
Hennings, R.O.	*African Morning*	Chatto & Windus 1951
Maciel, Mervyn	*Bwana Karani*	Merlin Books 1985
Nottingham, John and Rosberg, Carl	*The Myth of Mau Mau*	Praeger/Pall Mall 1966
Russell, John	*Kenya, beyond the Marich Pass*	Radcliffe, 1994
Reece, Alys	*To My Wife Fifty Camels*	Harvill 1963
Seaton, H	*Lion in the Morning*	1963
Watkins, Elizabeth	*Jomo's Jailor*	Britwell Books 1996

SELECTED BOOKS ON KENYA

Blundell, Sir Michael	*So Rough a Wind*	Weidenfield 1964
Blundell, Sir Michael	*A Love Affair with the Sun*	Kenway, Nairobi 1994
Brown, Monty	*Where Giants Trod*	Quiller Press 1989
Bennett, George and Rosberg, Carl	*The Kenyatta Election*	OUP 1961
Huxley, Elspeth	*A New Earth*	Chatto and Windus, 1960
Huxley, Elspeth	*Nine Faces of Kenya*	Collins Harvill, 1990
Kanogo, Tabitha	*Squatters and the Roots of Mau Mau*	Currey, 1987
Kariuki, J. M.	*Mau Mau Detainee*	OUP 1963
Kyle, Keith	*The Politics of the Independence of Kenya*	Macmillan 1999
Throup, David	*Economic and Social Origins of Mau Mau*	Currey, 1987

Index of Names

Note: Page numbers in **bold print** refer to authors of chapters.

Adamson, George 106
Adie, Jack 75
Al Amin bin Said, Sheikh 43
Al-Amin bin Said El-Mandhry, Sheikh 46
Ali Aden Lord 253
Ali bin Namaan, Chief 43
Alleyne, Ted **52**
Amin, Sergeant Idi 194
Anderson, Colonel 259
Anderson, Farnsworth 80
Anderson, Alistair **121**
Arap Moi, President Daniel 231, 260, 263
Arere Anenta 59
Arnold, Ken 253
Atkins, Charles 13
Avuaguto, Flora 146
Awori, W.W.W. 144

Back, Peter 124, 176
Balfour, Johnny 64
Baring, Sir Evelyn 68, 70, 78, 85, 94–5, 143, 162, 171
Barnett, Christopher **201**
Baron, Donald 75
Bearcroft, Punch 112
Beecher, Bishop Leonard 247
Bellers, Veronica (Williams) **115, 268**
Benson, Jack 199
Berning, John 198
Blundell, Sir Michael 83, 85, 96, 218, 232, 266

Boreham, Temple 117
Brayne-Nicholls, Dick 151
Bromley, John 186
Brooke-Anderson, Colonel 4
Brothers, Peter 13
Brown, Donald 79
Brown, George 10, 129
Burton, John 88
Butter, John 78
Buttery, Duncan 79, 201
Byrne, Sir Joseph 2

Cade Bobby 138
Campbell, John 121, 201
Candler, Jimmy 195, 197
Caradon, Lord 98
Cashmore, Dick **117, 182**
Catchpole, Tony 257
Cavendish-Bentinck, Sir Ferdinand 73, 82, 86, 96
Chambers, Robert 240, 241
Chaundy, George 104
Chenevix Trench, Charles 272
China, General (Waruhiu Itote) 266
Clay, Don 213
Cohen, Sir Andrew 70
Colchester, Tom 88, 237
Cooke, S.V. 83
Coutts, Sir Walter **224**, 9, 83, 218, 331
Cowley, Kenneth 203
Crawford, Sir Frederick 203

INDEX OF NAMES

Crichton, Patrick **12, 235**, 177, 234
Cumber, John 89
Cusack, Jake 75
Cuthbert, Ray 231

Davies, Eric 74, 86
De Souza, Marcus 124
Delamere, Lord 20
Dempster, Peter **62, 63, 167**
Denton, Christopher 25
Derrick, Peter 47, 62
Deverell, John 129, 189
Deverell, Sir Colville 74

Ellerton, Sir Geoffrey **79, 85,** 69, 76, 88, 93
Evans, David **132, 185**

Fent, Father Ferdy 118
Finnimore, Bob 250
Fletcher, Mike 24
Fouche, Leon 138
Fox, Eric **47**
Fuller, Colin **239**
Fullerton, Peter **249,** 169

Galma Dida, Haji, Senior Chief 256
Gardner, John 46, 189
Garland, Tommy 88
Gavaghan, Terry 89, 230
Gichuru, James 93
Golds, John **137, 253**
Goodbody, Frank 211
Gordon, Eric **55,** 235, 240
Gordon, Peter **73, 109, 133, 141,** 13, 128, 145
Grant, Hugh 184
Griffith-Jones, Sir Eric 81, 89, 96–7, 246
Grogan, Col. Ewart 47, 83

H.M. The Queen Mother 118

H.R.H. Prince Philip 247
H.R.H. Princess Margaret 146
Haddon-Cave, Philip 79, 232
Hall, Dennis 8, 27,
Hampson, George **14, 248**
Hardy, Noel 19, 204
Harris, Ted 61
Hartwell, Charles 74, 75, 176
Hector, Gordon 75
Heywood, Claude 24
Hinde, General 198
Hinga, Chief 21
Hodge, Donald 43, 92
Holford Walker, Fionn 221
Homan, Derek 34
Hook, Raymond 17
Hope-Jones, Arthur 74, 80
Horne, Justice 80
Horner, Arthur **246**
Horrell, Roger **54, 171, 200, 243**
Hosking, John (Willie) 268
Hosking, Roger 62
Howard, Henry 96
Howard, John 10
Hughes, Pat 17, 176
Hume, Andrew 78
Hunter, J.A. 11
Hunter, Kenneth 225

Irvine, Dr Clive 199

Jeremiah Jimmy 45
Johnson, Lady (Jean) **265**
Johnson, Peter **16, 96, 196, 218,** 19, 69, 204
Johnson, Sir John **140, 214, 261, 272**
Johnson-Hill, Gerry 27
Johnston, 'Monkey' 34, 55
Jones, Philip **48**
Josiah, Ezekiel 226, 262
Josiah, Sam 226
Judge, Neville 130, 253, 255, 259

295

Kago, General 195
Kariithi, Geoffrey 73, 102, 140, 218, 226, 228, 243, 266
Kariuki, J.E. 240
Kariuki, Bishop Obadiah 65
Karyu, Chief David 46
Kelly, Paul 128, 151, 171, 187–8
Kenyatta, President Jomo 9, 17, 77, 82, 85, 89–94, 96, 100, 219, 221, 223, 238, 242, 273
Kenyatta, Peter 223
Kiereini, Jeremiah 227
Kihori, Jerome 21
Kimani, Dan 62
Kittermaster, Sir Harold 5
Knowles, Oliver **39, 176,** 79
Kolbe, Ludwig 140

Lake, Dick 234, 235
Lambert, David **19, 119, 203**
Lawrence, Arthur 13
Lennox Boyd, Alan 71, 87
Leslie, Jock 143
Lewis, Taxi 71
Liddle, Alan **24, 158**
Lloyd, Peter 67
Lobo, Caesar 231
Loke, Christine 99
Lokori, Chief 56, 57
Loyd, Sir Frank 9, 62, 89, 91–2, 98, 137, 145, 255
Luce, Sir Richard 29, 64
Lunn, Jeremy **133,** 24
Luyt, Sir Richard 236

MacDonald, Malcolm 68, 77, 91–3, 98–101, 256
Maciel, Mervyn **110,** 104
Mackenzie, Kenneth **78, 82,** 69
Mackley, Geoff 17, 201
Macleod, Iain 71, 90, 96–8
Maconochie-Welwood 96
Marsh, Nigel 23

Masindet, Philip 117, 185
Masoud Mohamed Muhashamy, Sheikh 45
Matheson, W.A.C. 234
Matthews, Victor 74
Maudling, Sir Reginald 90, 96–7, 253
Mbiu Koinange, Senior Chief 112
Mboya, Tom 5, 82, 89–90, 97, 223, 234, 236, 243
Mboya, Paul 13, 270
McCartney, Fergus **198**
McEntee, Peter 235, 240
McKenzie, Bruce 83, 97, 260
McWilliam, Sir Michael 79
Meinertzhagen, Richard 172
Merifield, Sir Anthony **220**
Mills, Roger 37
Minter, Chris **21,** 24
Mitchell, Sir Philip 68, 74
Montgomery, Harold 2
Moyne, Lord 6
Mungai Njeroge 219
Munyutu, Chief 266
Musa Nyandusi, Senior Chief 59
Musyoka Mboti, Chief Henry 161
Mwenese, Matthew 227

Naftali Temu 223
Ndegwa, Duncan 79, 93, 237
Nderi, Senior Chief 21
Ndoo, Senior Chief Kasina 161
Neil, Tom 234
Newton, Carr 24
Ngala, Ronald 46, 89–91, 96–7, 100
Ngeleyo, Chief 179
Nicoll-Griffith, David **65, 107,** 45, 47
Njage, Chief Ephantus 62
Njiri Karanja, Senior Chief 196
Njonjo, Charles 260

INDEX OF NAMES

Njoroge Michuki, John 229
North, Myles 11, 47, 176
Nyachae, Simeon 60
Nyaga, Chief Kathuru 161
Nyagah, Jeremiah 266
Nyandika Maioro 59

O'Hagan, Desmond **2**
Obote, President Milton 247
Oginga Odinga, Vice President 82, 97, 227, 230, 236–7, 243
Okwirry, Isaac 218
Ole Lemeke, Francis 226
Ole Pasha, Chief Simeon 202
Ole Sangale, Chief 182
Ole Tameno, J. 231
Ombito, Washington 225
Osborne, Anna **155**
Osborne, Paul 4
Otter, Bob 135, 136, 229
Ouko, Robert 24, 78

Parker, Ian 171
Paul, Robin **192,** 29
Peacock, Roger 201
Pedraza, Jim 76
Peet, June **117**
Peet, Tony **151**
Penwill, Douglas 137, 139, 255
Petrie, Edward 78
Philip, Michael **38, 256**
Plant, Gordon 167
Poole, Peter 88
Potter, Henry 74, 85
Powell, Tom 100
Power, Michael **41,** 39, 250
Pratt, Gerald **45, 79**
Profumo, John 254
Pryor, Gerry 128, 187

Rankine, John 73, 74
Rany, Dr. 42
Rashid Ali al Riyamy, Sheikh 45

Ratzburg, Frank 139
Reece, Sir Gerald **132,** 251
Renison, Sir Patrick 68, 89–91, 96–8, 162
Reuben, Chief 266
Rickets, Peter 232
Risley, Eric **178,** 171
Robinson, Hugh 5
Rodwell, Edward 5
Ross, John **87, 89,** 69
Rowlands, Johnny **146,** 123

Sagini, Laurence 223
Salter, Clive 96
Sandys, Sir Duncan 90, 92, 98, 100, 253
Savage, Tony 250
Scott, Nick **225, 262,** 218
Sheldrick, David 172
Shirreff, David **10, 180**
Simmance, Alan 234, 240
Simpson, Sandy 178, 180, 201
Skinner, Tom 232, 237
Skipper, Gordon 43, 60
Slade, Sir Humphrey 82–3
Slater, David 138
Slater, Sam 180
Stephens, Tony **228,** 226
Swann, Sir Anthony 76, 88, 99
Sweatman, Eric 201
Sykes, Pop 27

Taita arap Towett 225
Tannahill, Ginty 75
Tatham Warter, Digby 20
Tennent, John 62
Thompson, Michael 31
Thompson, Tommy **8, 122, 145, 194, 205,** 103, 142
Thornley, Colin 74
Thorp, John 10
Thuku, Harry 21
Trestrail, John 198

Turnbull, Sir Richard **148**, 2, 71, 83, 134, 252

Usher, Elizabeth (Blair) 79

Vasey, Sir Ernest 78, 84, 86

Wabera, Daudi 130, 256
Wainwright, Robin **114**, 97, 204
Walker, Hugh **18, 76, 164,** 69
Waller, H. (Pat) de Warrenne **34**
Walters, Peter 250
Wasilewski, Michael **36, 187**
Watts, Tom **6, 104, 105, 152, 154, 178,** 103
Wavell, Major 16
Weaving, L.A. 75
Webb, George 76, 250
Webster, John 75

Whitcher, Paul 19
Whitehouse, Leslie 104, 111, 176
Whyatt, John 74, 75, 85
Wild, Windy 29, 108, 112
Wilkinson, Roger 115
Wilks, Charles **69,** 201
Williams, Harold **23,** 58, 142, 268, 270
Williams, John **120, 127, 210,** 24
Williamson, Robin **28, 190**
Willis, Ian **129**
Wilson Paul, Chief Judah 47
Wilson, Dick **94, 101,** 55, 69
Winser, Bobby 13
Winter, Dudley 189
Worthy, David 257
Wright, Henry **126, 169, 172, 263,** 103, 124
Wyn Harris, P. 73, 176

Index of Bomas (Districts)

Bungoma (Elgon Nyanza) 128, 141–5, 227

Dol Dol (Nanyuki) 15, 16

Embu 8, 62, 114, 140, 196, 200, 211, 214, 265

Fort Hall 9, 21, 65, 117, 194

Garissa 148

Hola (Tana River) 122, 205
Homa Bay (South Nyanza) 23

Isiolo 4, 15, 33, 34–6, 120, 128, 187, 257

Kabarnet (Baringo) 38, 48, 60, 179
Kajiado 201
Kakamega (North Nyanza) 2, 48–51, 115, 141
Kapenguria (West Suk/Pokot) 55–8, 70
Kapsabet (Nandi) 11, 60–1, 128
Kericho 23
Kiambu 121, 137, 218
Kilifi 25–8, 52–3, 171
Kipini (Tana River) 122, 126, 172
Kisii (South Nyanza) 2, 13, 22, 58–9, 133, 222, 270
Kisumu (Central Nyanza) 23, 256

Kitale (Trans Nzoia) 29, 113
Kitui 7, 151, 159
Kwale 16–17, 36–8

Lodwar (Turkana) 29–31, 104–5, 111, 152, 176, 178, 190, 192
Lokitaung (Turkana) 177

Machakos 10
Malindi (Kilifi) 39, 156
Mandera 109, 164
Maralal (Samburu) 48, 155, 182, 259
Marsabit 63, 105–8, 112, 154–5, 167–8
Meru 14, 33, 198, 243
Mombasa 5, 41–5, 45–7
Moyale 135, 185

Nairobi 249
Naivasha 19, 119, 203
Narok 18, 117, 133, 182
Nanyuki 146
Northern Frontier (NFD) 4–5, 132, 148, 164–6, 249, 256, 268
Nyeri 21

Taveta (Taita) 47
Thomson's Falls (Laikipia) 248

Voi (Taita) 16, 37, 47

Wajir 130, 148, 169–70, 249, 253

KENYA 1960:
Provincial and District Boundaries

ETHIOPIA

Mandera

Moyale

VINCE

Y A

Wajir

SOMALIA

NORTHERN FRONTIER
DISTRICT

Isiolo

Garissa

River Tana

Kitui

Tana River

Lamu

VINCE

akos

COAST PROVINCE

Taita

Kilifi

Indian
Ocean

MOMBASA

Kwale